THE ORIGINS
AND NATURE
OF LANGUAGE

Advances in Semiotics

Thomas A. Sebeok, General Editor

THE ORIGINS

BY GIORGIO FANO

AND NATURE

Translated by Susan Petrilli

OF LANGUAGE

Indiana
University
Press

BLOOMINGTON & INDIANAPOLIS

Originally published as *Origini e natura del linguaggio*
by Einaudi Editore.

la parte prima copyright © 1962 Giulio Einaudi
editore s.p.a., Torino
la parte seconda copyright © 1973 Giulio Einaudi
editore s.p.a., Torino
II presente volume è stato curato da
Anna e Guido Fano

The paper used in this publication meets the minimum requirements of
American National Standard for Information Sciences—Permanence of
Paper for Printed Library Materials, ANSI Z39.48-1984.

Manufactured in the United States of America

Library of Congress Cataloging-in-Publication Data
Fano, Giorgio.
  [Origini e natura del linguaggio. English]
  The origins and nature of language / by Giorgio Fano ; translated
by Susan Petrilli.
    p.   cm. — (Advances in semiotics)
  Translation of: Origini e natura dei linguaggio.
  Includes bibliographical references and index.
  ISBN 0-253-32121-2 (cloth)
  1. Language and languages—Origin. I. Title. II. Series.
P116.F3613   1992
  401—dc20   90-23963

1 2 3 4 5 95 94 93 92

To the dear companion of my life,
Annetta Curiel,
remembering the ancient words:
Proverbs XXXI, 10-28.

CONTENTS

BOOK ONE: PART ONE
INQUIRY INTO THE ORIGIN OF LANGUAGE

Introduction   3

General Doubts Concerning Theories of the Origins of Language—Real and Assumed Difficulties with the Problem—Confusion between Historical and Psychological Considerations—Confusion between Philosophical and Empirical Considerations—Theological Sophistry—Inadequacy of Results So Far Attained—Positivism and Doubts Concerning Broad Conceptual Syntheses—A Scientific Solution Does Not Seem Impossible in the Light of Today's Knowledge.

1. How the Origin of Language May Be Explained by Studying the Origin and Evolution of Writing Systems   10

Pictography and Mnemotechny   10

Real Object Messages—Painting and Pictography—Concrete, Symbolic, Ideographic, and Phonetic Signs—Transition from Pictography to Ideography—Progressive Prevalence of Analysis over Synthesis.

Mnemonic Signs   20

Antiquity of Mnemonic Signs—Knot Writing Systems—Message Sticks—Unfruitfulness of Mnemotechnic Signs—Compromise between Mnemotechny and Pictography.

Contents

Contents   IX

Justification—Requirements of the Semantic Criterion and of the Logical Criterion Are Different—Precedents of the Semantics of Neopositivism—The Semantics of Tarski—Scientific and Philosophical Interest in Rectifying Methodological Errors.

Convergence of European Neopositivism and American Pragmatism—A Scientific Definition of the Sign—Positivist Denial of Self-Consciousness—Academic Creation of New Sciences—Trained Dogs and the Classifications of Signs—Transition from the Irrational Philosophies to Science—The Pseudo-Mathematical Apparatus Used by These Authors—Carnap's Hairsplitting.

Historical Background of Croce's Theory: Herder—Individuality of Linguistic Expression Asserted by Herder—Spirituality of Language in Humboldt—But Spirituality, Essential to Every Human Production, Cannot Be Considered as a Characteristic Feature—Humboldt Denies the Distinction between the Origin and Subsequent Development of Language—Universalistic Claims Favor Innatistic and Theological Solutions—Antinomy between Individuality and Universality of Language—Mystic Conclusion—Denial of the Problem of Language Origin in Steinthal—Myth Explains the Essence in Terms of Temporal Origin, Abstract Idealism Confuses the Question of the Origin with That of the Essence—Complexity and Organic Unity of Croce's Conception—Identification of Representation, Expression, and Language—Uselessness of Lexical Studies—Unique Individuality of the Word—Negation of Unity in Language—A Universal Language Cannot Be Created—Grammatical Rules and Phonetic Laws Are Devoid of Scientific Value—Technique Is of No Importance in Artistic Creation—As It Is a Spiritual Category Language Does Not Have a Temporal Origin—Contradiction in Croce's Concept of Category—The Individuality of Intuition Contradicts Its Communicability—And Renders It Inexpressible and Not Intuitable—Pure Universality and Pure Individuality Are Abstract Elements in Concrete Experience—Croce's Denial of Mathematics and the Natural Sciences—The Empirical Nature of Concepts Cannot Be Eliminated—The Inadequacy of Translations Derives from the Diversity of Linguistic Conventions—And from the Different Musical Expressiveness of Words—Refusal to Recognize Technique Derives from the Lacking Analysis of Intuition—And from the Presumed Insuperable Individuality of Expression—Merits of Croce's Aesthetics.

APPENDIX

Plato's Work Has Reached Us Deformed by Later Interpolations and Revisions.

Translator's Introduction

Iconicity and the Origin of Language:
C. S. Peirce and G. Fano

The first partial edition of *Origini e natura del linguaggio* appeared in 1962 under the title *Saggio sulle origini del linguaggio* (Essay on the origins of language). The 1973 edition, which we are now presenting for the first time in English translation, is an amplification with respect to the first because of its twofold character, concentrating upon two main topics: not only that of the origins but also of the nature or essence of language.

Of the two books making up the 1973 edition, the second, in our opinion, is the more interesting and topical. It works in the perspective of a general linguistic and semiotic framework, thus enabling us to overlook certain excessive and unfruitful efforts of analysis made by the author in the first book on language origin.

In truth, Giorgio Fano himself declares his diffidence toward glottogonic theories and criticizes certain interpretations of an empirical-inductive, psychological, and theological nature. He points out the difficulty if not the absolute impossibility, given the current lack of adequate scientific data, of formulating a definitive scientific solution to the problem of language origin. The gestural-mimetic theory that Fano is inclined to support, and according to which human language was originally a mimetic language accompanied by emotional cries, is certainly not new. We find it taken up in relatively recent times by a rather rash author such as the Russian linguist Ja. Marr, renowned for the superficiality of his reckless linguistic theories, and at the opposite extreme by another Russian author, Mikhail Bakhtin, whose fame today is becoming more and more widespread in the United States as well as throughout Europe, thanks to his noteworthy contribution to the study of language, signs, and literary genres with particular reference to the novel (see Bakhtin-Vološinov 1929b[1]: 93–113, and the highly informative monograph on Bakhtin by Clark-Holquist 1984).

The problem of language origin should not be undervalued, especially if viewed as an attempt at avoiding those orientations that theorize upon the gap dividing human language from animal communication. Such orientations lose sight of the essential semiotic continuity that somehow links animal communication within the unity of our biosphere to human communication (as

---

[1]Similarly to the other books by V. Vološinov, this one too was written in such close collaboration with M. Bakhtin as to be attributed to the latter.

Thomas A. Sebeok's zoosemiotics has shown). Focusing upon such succession from the point of view of the continuity of communication from animal sign systems to the human, Sebeok, citing Gregory Bateson, points to the "complex forms of art, music, ballet and the like, and, even in everyday life the intricacies of human kinesic communication, facial expression and vocal intonation" as the perfected forms of the nonverbal aptitudes and organs in animals. At the same time, however, we must not consider animal languages and human languages as being homologous especially in the direction of anthropomorphic interpretations. As Sebeok has clearly stated, verbal language is a species-specific feature of *Homo sapiens* so that "man alone has the competence to communicate by *both* nonverbal *and* verbal means, often inseparably interwoven" (see Sebeok 1986: 12–13).

Like all those theories supporting the thesis of the gestural-mimetic origin of language, Giorgio Fano's glottogonic theory can hardly be confuted given its nonscientific character. At the same time, however, it must also be pointed out that Fano's hypotheses are distant from those conceptions which, because of the lack of trustworthy scientific documentation, cause even the most convincing theories to assume the character of hypothetical speculation or of science fictional experimentation—the reference is especially to those theories which claim to explain the origins of language by giving their unquestioning support to the "talking" dogs, horses, monkeys, and dolphins that have "argued" their way through the relevant literature of the past century. One of the most efficacious and scientifically informed contributions to the demolishing of such science fictional theories has come from the same Thomas A. Sebeok who has rigorously stated that:

> Attempts to seek the "origin of language" in the communication system of any ancestral species are based on a fallacious miscalculation. Thus the naive efforts of a handful of psychologists, who tried to justify the public toll required to instill what they misguidedly believe to be language-like propensities in a few enslaved primates by claiming that they are thereby about to uncover the roots of language, are bleakly self-delusive. The unschooled public, enthusiastically whipped on by an irresponsible but sizeable segment of the media—whether cynical or simply sharing its readership's credulity—has been bamboozled into believing that man's unique verbal code is in an evolutionary continuum with the multifold and diversiform nonverbal codes of the extinct hominoids, presumed to be still embodied in the extant great apes. (Sebeok 1986: 12)[2]

The problem of the origin of human verbal language has remained unsolved and in reality is of relatively little interest given the impossibility of furnishing scientifically valid and exhaustive documentary materials upon which to base an investigation. Bakhtin-Vološinov abandon the issue altogether. Certainly more interesting are those theories that apply such cate-

---

[2]For further criticism of such anthropomorphic interpretations I will limit myself to citing also Sebeok 1979.

gories as human work to the study of the evolution of language. As is well-known, such an approach was followed, for example, by Engels who described hominization as the process of reproduction through the social environment and identified work as a necessary condition of anthropogenesis. In Engel's estimation, human work and language are the two main conditioning factors in determining the process of hominization (see Engels 1896). In Italy, with the aid of a doubtlessly far more updated and refined conceptual apparatus, Ferruccio Rossi-Landi proceeded in the same direction (his book *Il Linguaggio come lavoro e come mercato* [Eng. trans. *Language as Work and Trade 1983*] appeared in 1968, six years after the first edition of Fano's book), further developing the categories of work, trade, and social reproduction, which provide him with fertile results in his research into hominization and the production and nature of language. On the other hand, Rossi-Landi does not fail to warn us against the danger of all those theories that, while rightly emphasizing the importance of human work and of the social environment, end by leaving aside the slow and continuous work of nature in the genesis of the biological structure of organisms immersed in a complex network of relations with the environment (for all these aspects see Rossi-Landi 1968; 1972; 1985).

That which should not pass unnoticed in Fano's work is the wealth of detail and "evidence" called upon in the attempt at demonstrating his thesis. We believe that such documentation is of central interest, independently of whether it contributes or not as hard proof to the scientific validation of the glottogonic theory he is inclined to support. This is what we meant when we stated at the beginning of this introduction that the second book, that which inquires into the nature and essence of language, plays a primary role in the economy of the work as a whole and manages to lead the first book.

For numerous reasons—including the way in which the argumentation is conducted, the attention given to the various types of signs and of writing systems, and above all, the fact that Fano is distant from phonocentric conceptions[3]—the first book of this work (which is intended to support the thesis of the priority of mimetic language with respect to verbal language) ends by acquiring value in itself as the integration and completion of the second book. On proposing a historical excursus into the development of language, this first part in fact contributes not so much (as the author has intended) to explaining the genesis of language as to evidencing its nature. This nature may be identified, as Charles Sanders Peirce has demonstrated, in the predominance (as well as antecedence from the viewpoint of formation and development—which leads to the possibility of utilizing Fano's analyses to the advantage of the thesis of the mimetic origin of language) of iconicity in verbal language, and in signs in general with respect to indexicality and symbolicity. We are now obviously making use of the terminology of Peirce

---

[3]See J. Derrida's criticism of phonocentrism in *L'écriture et la différence*, Editions du Seuil and also J. Kristeva's interview with J. Derrida, "Sémiologie et grammatologie,' in *Essays in Semiotics*, Mouton: The Hague, Paris, 1971.

who distinguishes in all signs an iconic component, an indexical component, and a symbolic component. Briefly, the presumed antecedence of the mimetic as well as of the gestural aspects of communication with respect to the verbal aspects reconfirms the clear stance taken by Fano against phonocentrism. It would appear, therefore, that it is not the acoustic factor but rather the visual factor which has genetic and structural priority in verbal language. This antecedence of the visual and its extensibility (as occurs in the extensibility of the use of the verb "to see"; "see to it yourself," "see what I mean," etc.) tells of the importance of the role of the image (the visual image and the mental image, but also the *acoustic* image [Saussure]) in the verbal sign as well as in nonverbal signs. We do not know very much about the genesis of verbal language in the process of hominization, but we are certainly able to state that in the ontogenetic genesis of language, that is to say, in language acquisition on behalf of each individual infant, the iconic component is of fundamental importance. One of the limits of Noam Chomsky's transformational grammar, as well as of the behavioristic theories he criticizes, possibly lies in the fact that the iconic factor was not sufficiently taken into consideration.

We believe that all of Fano's work, reread today in the light of Peirce's semiotics—with particular reference, as we have just mentioned, to his classification of signs into icons, indices, and symbols—acquires noteworthy theoretical and documentary value. Fano makes direct references to Peirce (whose influence upon both American and international philosophical-semiotical scholarship did not escape him) in a chapter dedicated to criticism of Peirce's identification of logic with semiotics (Fano says "semantics," but, as we will see, what he really means is "semiotics"). This is a criticism we object to, for, as we are well aware today, thanks also to the contribution of such scholars as Max Fisch in America, as well as the already mentioned Thomas A. Sebeok (see, for example, Max Fisch 1986; and Sebeok 1976; 1979; 1981; 1986), and of such scholars as the previously mentioned Rossi-Landi, Augusto Ponzio, Massimo Bonfantini and Umberto Eco in Italy (see respectively, for example, Rossi-Landi 1953; 1975; 1985; Ponzio 1985a, 1985c; Bonfantini 1980, 1987; and Eco 1984), Peirce actually develops his logic as well as his pragmatic philosophy within the context of his science of signs.

Fano makes a distinction between "logic" and "semantics" and therefore between "thought" and "word," "concept" and "symbol," "representation" and "expressive signs." His particular use of this terminology may today appear rather odd to us and needs clarification. In fact, Fano himself says, for example, that by word or language he intends any system of expressive signs, verbal and nonverbal. These as such are the objects of study in semantics, while linguistics is a branch of the latter, so that semantics may be viewed as equivalent to semiotics and therefore includes linguistics. According to Fano, semantics concerns the expressive instruments of logical representation.

For a critical interpretation of the identification between semantics and semiotics, we refer the reader to Rossi-Landi's 1972 (now 1979²) book which, moving in the direction indicated by Peirce and Morris, distinguishes between semantics and semiotics, considering semantics one of the three aspects of semiotics, the other two aspects being syntax and pragmatics. As to the critique of the Peircean identification of semantics (in reality semiotics) with logic, Fano obviously did not bear in mind the necessary connection between sign and interpretant, and therefore between semiosis and interpretation, and furthermore between semiosis and inference, and consequently between semiotics and logic. This is a limitation in Fano's work, but it must also be remembered in his favor that he was one of the first scholars in Italy to have recognized the importance of Peirce and of semiotics as a science. In Italy, with the exception of a few sporadic pioneer manifestations, these things were only just beginning to attract interest in the early 1960s.

Fano, therefore, did not realize that signs, especially verbal signs, are not only instruments but also the material out of which our thoughts and conscious life (together with the unconscious) are made (see Peirce on the relation between man, thought and sign in *Collected Papers (CP)* 5.264–317). The deferral from one interpretant to the next in an infinite chain (unlimited semiosis) causes us to think and signify not only by using signs but also by "elaborating and transforming" sign material. In Italy these concepts were clearly expressed by Rossi-Landi in his 1968 book.

Thus, while Fano makes a distinction between that which is intended by *thought* and that which is intended by *sign*, Peirce goes so far as to unite them in the coined expression *thought-sign*, with the aim of underlining that thought is in fact sign reality, made of both verbal and nonverbal signs. He contends that

> . . . there is no element whatever of man's consciousness which has not something corresponding to it in the word; and the reason is obvious. It is that the word or sign which man uses *is* the man himself. For, as the fact that every thought is a sign, taken in conjunction with the fact that life is a train of thought, proves that man is a sign; so, that every thought is an *external* sign, proves that man is an external sign. That is to say, the man and the external sign are identical, in the same sense in which the words *homo* and *man* are identical. Thus my language is the sum total of myself; for the man is the thought. (*CP* 5.314)

According to Peirce's definition, logic is a general theory of representation, a theory of the conditions of validity which enable the sign to relate to the world veridically. The relation is triadic in the sense that it involves reference of the sign to its object via the interpretant:

> Now a sign has, as such, three references: first, it is a sign *to* some thought which interprets it; second, it is a sign *for* some object to which in that thought it is equivalent; third, it is a sign, *in* some respect or quality which brings it into connection with its object. (*CP* 5.283)

Or in the more famous formulation: "a sign, or *representamen*, is something which stands to somebody for something in some respect or capacity." Furthermore, the relation itself of the sign to its object is triadic: in other words, it is connected to the above-mentioned division of the sign into the three main classes of icon, index, and symbol. In icons the relation of the sign to its object is based on resemblance and the putative sharing of qualities: this sign is characterized by its relative autonomy with respect to the object, that is, by its "firstness." It includes not only the more obvious cases of "realistic" images such as paintings, pictographs, but also things such as algebraic formulas, graphs, and diagrams. Indices are related to their objects on the basis of contiguity: that is, they signify through a necessary connection with their objects. Symbols, on the other hand, are not directly connected to their objects but are arbitrary signs that signify on the basis of a rule-governed code. With his concept of "degeneracy" (taken from the language of mathematics), Peirce specifies that no one sign is purely an icon, index, or symbol, but rather all three modes are present contemporarily in varying degrees with the prevalence of one mode over the other two depending upon the type of semiosis in action. In other words, in the semantic relation of the sign to its object via the interpretant, a predominant role is carried out either by convention (symbolicity), contiguity (indexicality), or resemblance (iconicity).

We believe that Fano's criticism of Peirce's identification of logic and semantics has its roots in his implicit adherence to the Saussurean model of sign which privileges the conventional or arbitrary character of signs, thus focusing upon the symbol (as intended by Peirce) while losing sight of the iconic and indexical components of sign systems, as well as of the role of the intepretant-sign in the process of semiosis. However, Fano does overcome this limitation through his insistence upon the iconic component of signification even if he does so with the aim of supporting his thesis of the gestural origin of language. It is for this reason that I began my introduction with the statement that if we leave aside the underlying thesis on the origin of language, this work gains in interest for the thesis it proposes on the nature of language. Though the conventional character of language is obvious, at the same time, however, even verbal language has in its very make-up a strong iconic component. Fano puts this into evidence through his parallel investigation into the history of the development of writing systems, showing the gradual transition from high levels of iconicity—as exemplified by the pictographic and mnemotechnic scripts of primitive man, or in a more stylized form, by the ideographs of ancient Chinese scripts or of Egyptian hieroglyphs—through to the alphabetical scripts where conventionality (symbolicity) prevails, even if, at both extremes, recourse to a conventional code guarantees and regulates the transmission of information. By analogy Fano identifies the same kind of development in spoken language by pointing to the iconic quality of such expressive expedients as the use of metaphor, interjections, and onomatopoeia. Furthermore, Fano's research is avantgarde, from the point of view of semiotics, with respect to his acute analysis

of the syntactic structure of mimetic language in terms of the prevalence of
the pictographic element, or icon, over the conventional element, or symbol.

Peirce himself mentions the nonlogical iconic nature of primitive writing
and, like Fano, hypothesizes upon the gradual transition in language from
the predominance of iconicity as incorporated by mimicry to the predominance of conventionality as manifested by auditory signs and in which, however, the iconic component is not excluded but rather proves necessary for
comprehension:

> That icons of the algebraic kind, though usually very simple ones, exist in all
> ordinary grammatical propositions is one of the philosophic truths that the
> Boolean logic brings to light. In all primitive writing, such as the Egyptian
> hieroglyphs, there are icons of a nonlogical kind, the ideographs. In the
> earliest form of speech, there probably was a large element of mimicry. But
> in all languages known, such representations have been replaced by conven-
> tional auditory signs. These, however, are such that they can only be explained
> by icons. But in the syntax of every language there are logical icons of the
> kind that are aided by conventional rules. (*CP* 2.280)

Moreover, man's capacity for discovering new truths, that is, his propensity towards invention and creativity, is also attributed to the role of the
icon as "firstness" in the inferential process. And while symbols serve to call
something to mind through the kind of mental association that is governed
by convention, the meaning of these symbols is still communicated and even
founded upon the iconic relation connecting the interpretant-signs of a se-
miotical chain:

> The only way of directly communicating an idea is by means of an icon; and
> every indirect method of communicating an idea must depend for its estab-
> lishment upon the use of an icon. Hence, every assertion must contain an
> icon or set of icons or else must contain signs whose meaning is only explicable
> by icons. (*CP* 2.278)

In the case of verbal language, the discovery of new truths or novel ideas is
often characterized by the use of the expedients of figurative speech and
metaphor developed upon the basis of analogy between different fields of
experience. Analogic association, whose process we may describe as syn-
thetical-iconic, consists in establishing relations of resemblance between
things which would appear to be completely unrelated, thus favoring man's
powers of innovation and creativity.

In his analysis of the nature or essence of language, Fano too focuses
upon creativity in man, underlining the importance of memory, as a glottogonic category also, in the transformation of sensible impressions into what
he calls "aesthetic images":

> That light in us, that cathartic liberation we experience when we succeed in
> contemplating that which is happening inside us, derives from the evocative
> act of memory. An act which gathers the multiplicity of our impressions and
> emotions within the unity of its synthesis. Memory makes aesthetic contem-

plation possible by operating the first *synopsis* of the uncoordinated elements
of the senses: this is symbolized well in that Greek myth which names Mnemosyne the mother of the Muses.

Memory is considered as a constitutive component of cognition; that is, its
function is not limited to the mere reproduction and preservation of representations but is involved in the actual formation of such representations.
Fano draws an analogy between scientific synthesis and aesthetic synthesis
where we may interpret "synthesis" as the iconic capacity (as against
"analysis," also in the Kantian sense of the symbolic mode) of relating a
multiplicity of experiences, conceptual and sensory, into a harmonious whole
through and by virtue of the act of memory.

Fano, like Peirce, perceives that the creative aspect of aesthetic expression
(as manifested, for example, in dance, music, painting, literature), as well as
of the sciences, is largely the effect of iconicity.

In book two, entitled "On the Nature or Essence of Language: Principles
for a General Linguistics," it is important that Fano takes a critical stance
with respect to the concepts of "aesthetics" and "semantics" as elaborated
by Croce and Vossler:

> Croce denied technique all importance in the process of creation because, in
> the light of his concept of intuitive individuality, he would not accept that
> two images could be compared to each other, or that one image could be
> considered more encompassing and more profound than the other. In reality,
> however, the artist continually compares his images and expressions and passes
> from vaguely outlined representations to more elaborate ones. Technique and
> creation interact so that the artist, after having conceived something, fixes it
> on paper or on canvas, which helps him to see better and to pass from a
> poorer and more imperfect representation to another that satisfies him more.

This passage highlights Fano's intuitive awareness of the "aesthetic" (we
may read "iconic") component of any form of expression identifiable not
only in the more obvious forms of both verbal and nonverbal creative activity,
but more than this, as a constitutive part of verbal language and sign systems
at large. In fact, in proposing a general theory of expressive signs in which
he distinguishes between pictographic (that is, iconic) signs and mnemotechnic (that is, conventional) signs, Fano demonstrates how linguistic (that is,
verbal) signs share in the characteristics of both and shows the difficulty of
making them enter into any one class to the exclusion of another. For confirmation of this description of the essential nature of verbal signs, he points
to the lack of a rigid distinction between nonverbal artistic expression and
verbal communication in the early phases of linguistic development as exemplified by the language of primitive man.

Another noteworthy aspect of Fano's research lies in the fact that he
turns his attention to Charles Morris's semiotic behaviorism, thus anticipating
theoretical interests which have only just recently occupied a central position
among the concerns of Italian semioticians. Nor does Fano fail to mention

the monograph on Morris by Rossi-Landi which appeared in Italy as early as 1953, but which was destined to pass unnoticed until its reprinting in 1975. Furthermore, Fano's criticism of abstract idealism is also of interest, analogous as it is to the critical stances elaborated by Bakhtin-Vološinov in the 1929 book *Marxism and the Philosophy of Language*.

In conclusion, it is worth repeating that what we find most remarkable in Fano's investigation into the origin and nature of language is his awareness of the iconic dimension of verbal communication, so that more than a historical survey of the genesis of language, this book is of value as a contribution to the structural analysis of language itself.

I wish to thank Augusto Ponzio (Director of the Institute of Philosophy of Language, Bari University) for having patiently read the entire manuscript of this translation. I have had the benefit of his specialized advice in dealing with problems arising from the difficulty of transposing a work such as this from the language of one cultural system to that of another. His assistance in solving specific terminological questions has been invaluable. Many thanks as well to Thomas A. Sebeok for having suggested this project.

THE TRANSLATOR

Bibliography

Bakhtin, Mikhail, and Valentin N. Vološinov
1929a   "Cto takoe jazyk?," *Literaturnaya Učeba, 2*; Eng. trans. by N. Owen, "What is Language?" in *Russian Poetics in Translation*, vol. 10, *Bakhtin School Papers*, ed. by A. Shuckman, pp. 93–113, Oxford: RPT Publications.
1929b   *Marksizm i filosofija jazyka: Osnovnye problemy sociologiceskogo metoda v nauke o jazyke*, Leningrad: Proboj 1929, 1930²; reprint in the Hague: Mouton, 1972; Eng. trans. by L. Matejka and I. R. Titunik, *Marxism and the Philosophy of Language*, New York: Seminar Press, 1973.
Bonfantini, Massimo A.
1980   (intro., trans., & ed. by), Charles Sanders Peirce *Semiotica*, Turin: Einaudi.
1987   *La semiosi e l'abduzione*, Milan: Bompiani.
Clark, Katerina, and Michael Holquist
1984   *Mikhail Bakhtin*, Cambridge, Mass.: Harvard University Press.
Deledalle, Gérard
1979   *Théorie et pratique du signe*, Paris: Payot.
1987   *Charles S. Peirce, phénoménologue et sémioticien*, Amsterdam/Philadelphia: John Benjamins; Eng. trans. & intro. by S. Petrilli, *Charles S. Peirce: An Intellectual Biography*, Amsterdam/Philadelphia: John Benjamins, forthcoming.

Derrida, Jacques
1967   *L'écriture et la différence*, Paris: Editions du Seuil.

Eco, Umberto
1984   *Semiotica e filosofia del linguaggio*, Turin: Einaudi; Eng. trans. *Semiotics and the Philosophy of Language*, Bloomington: Indiana University Press, 1984.

Engels, Friedrich
1896   *Dialektik der Natur*, B. XX in *Werke*, Berlin: Dietz.

Fano, Giorgio
1962   *Saggio sulle origini del linguaggio*, Turin: Einaudi.
1973   *Origini e natura del linguaggio*, Turin: Einaudi.

Fisch, Max H.
1986   (ed. by K. L. Ketner and C. J. W. Kloesel), *Peirce, Semeiotic, and Pragmatism*, Bloomington: Indiana University Press.

Fisch, Max H., Kenneth L. Ketner, and Christian J. W. Kloesel
1979   "The New Tools of Peirce Scholarship, with Particular Reference to Semiotic," *Peirce Studies*, 1, pp. 1–17.

Ketner, Kenneth L., and Christian J. W. Kloesel
1975   "The Semiotic of Charles Sanders Peirce and the First Dictionary of Semiotics," *Semiotica*, 13: 4, pp. 395–414.

Kloesel, Christian J. W.
1979   "Charles Peirce and the Secret of the Harvard O.K.," *New England Quarterly*, 52, pp. 55–67.
1983a   "Peirce's Early Theory of Signs (1863–1885): The First Barrier," *American Journal of Semiotics*, 2: 1–2, pp. 109–19.
1983b   "Bibliography of Charles Peirce 1976 through 1981," in *The Relevance of Charles Peirce*, ed. by E. Freeman, La Salle, Ill.: Monist Library of Philosophy, 1983.

Kristeva, Julia
1971   (interview with J. Derrida) "Sémiologie et grammatologie,' in *Essays in Semiotics*, Paris and The Hague: Mouton.

Mininni, Giuseppe
1982   *Psicosemiotica*, Bari: Adriatica.
1988   *Discorso in analisi*, Bari: Adriatica.

Morris, Charles
1938   *Foundations of the Theory of Signs*, in *International Encyclopedia of Unified Science*, 1:2, Chicago: University of Chicago Press.
1946   *Signs, Language and Behavior*, Englewood Cliffs: Prentice-Hall.
1964   *Signification and Significance: A Study of the Relations of Signs and Values*, Cambridge, Mass.: MIT Press.

Peirce, Charles Sanders
1931–1958   *Collected Papers*, Cambridge, Mass.: The Belknap Press of Harvard University Press.

Petrilli, Susan
1986   "On the Materiality of Signs," *Semiotica*, 662: 3/4, pp. 223–245.
1987   "Sign and Meaning in Victoria Lady Welby and Mikhail Bakhtin: A Confrontation," in *Essays on Significs*, ed. by H. W. Schmitz, Amsterdam: John Benjamins, 1987.
1988a   "Il contributo di F. Rossi-Landi al pensiero di C. Morris," *Per Ferruccio Rossi-Landi, Il Protagora* (ed. by S. Petrilli).
1988b   "Introduzione," in C. Morris, *Segni e valori: scritti de semiotica, etica ed estetica*, It. trans. and ed. by S. Petrilli, Bari: Adriatica.
1988c   *Significs semiotica e significazione*, Bari: Adriatica.
1989   "La critica del linguaggio in Giovanni Vailati e Victoria Welby," in *Scritti su Vailaii*, ed. by M. Quaranta, Bologna: Forni.

1990a "On the Semiotics of Interpretation: Introduction" in G. Deledalle, *Charles S. Peirce: An Intellectual Biography*, Eng. trans. by S. Petrilli, Amsterdam: John Benjamins.

1990b "Introduction," in A. Ponzio, *Man as a Sign: Studies in the Philosophy of Language*, Eng. trans. and ed. by S. Petrilli, The Hague: Mouton.

1990c "Introduzione," in T. A. Sebeok, *Penso di essere un verbo*, It. trans. and ed. by S. Petrilli, Palermo: Sellerio.

Ponzio, Augusto

1984a "Notes on Semiotics and Marxism," *Kodikas/Code*, 1/2, pp. 131–39.

1984b "Dialogue and Alterity in Bakhtin," *Revue roumaine de linguistique/Cahiers de linguistique théorique et appliquée*, n. 2, pp. 159–73.

1984c "Semiotics between Peirce and Bakhtin," *Recherches Semiotiques/Semiotic Research*, 4: 3/4, pp. 273–302.

1985a A bilingual text in collaboration with M. A. Bonfantini and G. Mininni, *Per parlare dei segni/Talking About Signs*, Eng. trans. by S. Petrilli, Bari: Adriatica.

1985b "The Symbol, Alterity, and Abduction," *Semiotica, 56:* 3/4, pp. 261–77.

1985c Filosofia del linguaggio, Bari: Adriatica.

1986 "Economics," in *Encyclopedic Dictionary of Semiotics*, ed. by T. A. Sebeok, Berlin, New York, Amsterdam: Mouton, De Gruyter.

1988 *Rossi-Landi e la filosofia del linguaggio*, Bari: Adriatica.

1990 *Man as a Sign: Studies in the Philosophy of Language*, intro., Eng. trans., and ed. by S. Petrilli, The Hague: Mouton.

Rossi-Landi, Feruccio

1953 *Charles Morris*, Milan: Bocca.

1968 *Il linguaggio come lavoro e come mercato*, Milan: Bompiani; Eng. trans. by M. Adams et al., *Language as Work and Trade*, South Hadley, Mass.: Bergin and Garvey, 1983.

1972 *Semiotica e ideologia*, Milan: Bompiani, 2d ed. 1979.

1975 *Charles Morris e la semiotica novecentesca*, Milan: Feltrinelli-Bocca (2d ed. of Rossi-Landi 1953).

1985 *Metodica filosofica e scienza dei segni*, Milan: Bompiani.

Sebeok, Thomas A.

1971 (ed. by) *Writings on the General Theory of Signs*, The Hague: Mouton.

1976 *Contributions to the Doctrine of Signs*, Bloomington: Indiana University Press.

1979 *The Sign and Its Masters*, Texas: The University of Texas Press.

1981 *The Play of Musement*, Bloomington: Indiana University Press.

1986 *I Think I Am a Verb*, New York and London: Plenum Press.

Introduction by Luigi Heilmann

In the opening lines of his *Introduction* to this volume, Giorgio Fano reminds us of the solemn warning given by the Société linguistique of Paris which, in 1886, excluded all papers on the origin of language as well as on the problem of artificial languages. The glottogonic issue is inconceivable from the viewpoint of a historical-reconstructive methodology. The latter, in fact, starts from the data of historical languages and proceeds by means of comparisons towards hypothetical models interpreting prehistoric stages. Even if we subsequently compare such reconstructed models (e.g., Indo-European and the Hamitic-Semitic language), we always arrive at more or less valid and complex models of completely formed hypothetical languages, while the true original nucleus of the phenomenon itself remains unexamined.

An inquiry (synchronic or diachronic) into "languages" may furnish a few interpretative cues, but, paradoxically, it does not solve the problem of the origin of language. The latter draws on problems and methods from other disciplines, from psychology to semiotics and zoosemiotics, within the complex framework of the communicative process. We are therefore dealing with (to use a word currently in fashion) an exquisitely "inter-disciplinary" issue. Through a diligent critical examination of the numerous solutions proposed—from antiquity to the present day—and through the objective evaluation of the contributions of the single disciplines, Giorgio Fano has put forward a theory of his own, the product of an intimate doctrinal and emblematic conviction expressed in the *Foreword* to the first edition of this book.

His *Saggio sulle origini del linguaggio* (Essay on the origins of language) met with success. But, in my opinion, this is not the only fact that justifies a new edition. The most recent approach to linguistic studies within the framework of a typological investigation, linked to research on linguistic universals, deep structures, and the social conditioning of language, has created a favorable atmosphere for the revival of this ancient problem and for the hypothesis of the gestural and mimetic origin of language formulated by the author. On the other hand, developments in semiotics in the most diverse fields, taking place before our very eyes, are throwing more and more light on communication processes.

Also of great interest are the unpublished pages added to this new edition, which do not alter its original equilibrium and intimate doctrinal coherence. On reading it today in the form re-presented to the public, this book fully reconfirms its scientific validity and importance as a stimulating contribution to the progress of research.

BOLOGNA 1973.

Note on the Edition

This new edition of the work on the origin of language is here presented in the complete form originally intended by the author, ten years after his death. The final, necessary revision of the formerly unpublished theoretical part is therefore lacking. The careful reader will perhaps find a few formal imperfections and repetitions of what has already been expounded in the previously published part which the author would certainly have remedied had he had the time to do so. Moreover, a large number of notes (accompanied by an ample bibliography), which the author intended to use in a second edition, have been recovered quite recently. Unfortunately, it has not been possible to use this material owing to the risk of introducing arbitrary changes in the work's style and scientific orientation.

Preface

The author of this essay is not a glottologist, but a scholar of historical dialectics. In his essay *Teosofia orientale e filosofia greca* (Oriental Theosophy and Greek Philosophy) (Florence 1949), he attempted to show that the logical and organic development of our civilization cannot be understood if we do not acknowledge that Greek thought is naturally related, by antithesis and development, to oriental thought; which, in its turn, is closely connected to the magical, mystical, and dogmatic mentality of primitive man.

At this point the author asked himself: what are the fundamental achievements of these three stages in the evolution of man? To Greek thought we owe the perfection of aesthetic contemplation and the foundations of logic and mathematics, to the oriental mentality the foundations of the religious spirit. And to primitive man? To him we owe, if nothing else, the conquest of what most clearly distinguishes man from animals, that is to say, language.

He felt the need therefore to clarify to himself and to his readers the problem of the origin of language: and so this book was born.

BOOK ONE

PART ONE

Inquiry into the
Origin of Language

Introduction

General Doubts Concerning Theories of the Origins of Language—Real and Assumed Difficulties with the Problem—Confusion between Historical and Psychological Considerations—Confusion between Philosophical and Empirical Considerations—Theological Sophistry—Inadequacy of Results So Far Attained—Positivism and Doubts Concerning Broad Conceptual Syntheses—A Scientific Solution Does Not Seem Impossible in the Light of Today's Knowledge.

As far back as 1886 the Société de linguistique of Paris included this solemn warning among the opening articles of its statute: "la Société n'admet aucune communication concernant, soit l'origine du langage, soit la création d'une langue universelle," meaning by this that the learned members of the Society had no intention of wasting their time with eccentric problems and unfounded arguments.

Before dealing with the issue ourselves, it may prove useful to examine the main reasons for the general discredit into which it has fallen.[1] Such reasons may be summarized as follows:

It must be acknowledged that the problem presents, or seemed to present to nineteenth century scholars, some almost unsurmountable difficulties.

Even if we do not want to go so far as to identify thought with words as Humboldt did (or language with intuition as did Croce), it is clear that without the use of words, mankind would not have been able to attain high levels of intellectual development. Unlike some, we would not maintain that it is impossible to get the slightest idea of what is heavy without the word "heavy" or of the color red without the word "red," but there is no doubt that if we did not have a word or any other external sign to signify such general and abstract notions as "equality," "revenge," "belief," "hope," etc., those concepts would either not exist or they would retain a totally imprecise and confused form.[2]

But on the other hand, language may be considered as a very elaborate system of phonetic signs established with the aim of recalling and expressing an undefined multiplicity of images and concepts, a system whose establishment requires intuitive and intellective capacities that are already highly developed.[3]

But if elevated intellectual faculties are necessary for the creation of a semiological system like language, and if it is impossible to reach a high level of intellectual development without the use of language, how will we ever escape from this vicious circle?

Indeed this seems to be one of those brain-teasers that popular philosophy has symbolized with the question of whether it was the chicken or the egg which came first; a question that invites us to bow down before mystery and to acknowledge that first of all there was God, who created animals, human beings, language, and all that exists.

Rousseau also remarked: "Si les hommes ont eu besoin de la parole pour apprendre à penser, ils ont eu bien plus besoin encore de savoir penser pour trouver l'art de la parole"; and the difficulty seemed so arduous to him that he was induced to believe in direct superhuman intervention given "l'impossibilité presque démontrée que les langues aient pu naître et s'établir par des moyens purement humains."[4]

The solution to the problem also does not appear to be easy because it concerns events that took place in the obscurity of prehistory, a period about which it will never be possible to have any direct documentation.[5] What is even more perplexing is the fact that we are not dealing with purely physical events, like geological conformations or planetary motions, but with facts concerning human psychology, which hardly seem reducible to the uniformity of natural laws. Moreover, we are dealing with the psychology of living beings very remote from us, who mark the transition from animality to humanity and with whom it is almost impossible for us to identify.[6]

The problems of linguistics may be considered from a historical-philological point of view (when we ask which words or grammatical forms were used by a given people in a given era); from a psychological-naturalistic point of view (when we describe the characteristics of specific languages or try to classify them and formulate certain general laws that emerge as the languages evolve); or from a philosophical point of view (when we attempt to define the place and value of language among the fundamental activities of the human spirit, and its relationship to problems of logic and aesthetics).[7]

The problem of language origin obviously cannot be considered as a historical-philological problem, for the institution of language is not an action that may be singled out and described in minute detail in relation to how, by whom, and in what period it was accomplished. This problem, like that concerning the origin of man, is a naturalistic problem and should be treated with the methods proper to the naturalistic sciences.

It is a fact that on reading the pages of many authors who proclaim the vanity of all theories on the origin of language, one has the impression that (in accordance with the habits appropriate to their philological studies) they imagine that if such a theory is to be true it should be based on indisputable documents, direct evidence, and even on archival research; and since in our case none of this is possible, they have concluded that the problem is insoluble.

Indeed these authors lack methodological clarity as to the procedure, requirements, and judgment criteria necessary in naturalistic research; if this were not so, they would have been convinced that no naturalistic theory could be saved if judged according to the aforementioned criterion: neither the theories of biological evolution, nor the Kant-Laplace theory, and not even Copernican theory. In naturalistic inquiry, where exact documentation of a historical-philological type is never possible, the hypothetical element is not pathological but rather constitutive. And it is not necessarily the case that such sciences should be of less value simply because they do not propose to understand events in their historical individuality, but rather within the framework of a general scheme.

The Greeks, who valued general notions more than specific ones, attributed greater dignity to the sciences than to history. Modern historians, who work from the opposite prejudice, are inclined to think more highly of history than of the science of nature; but every discipline has its own dignity, provided it is adequate for the task.

The philosophical and empirical points of view are distinct but cannot be separated from each other: if the two aspects are kept distinct they throw light upon and explain each other; if they are confused, we fall prey to the worst philosophisms.

We will explain what is meant with a few renowned examples. According to Herder (in his *Abhandlung über den Ursprung der Sprache*), just as a plucked cord reverberates, in the same way the animal reacts to impressions that strike it. In man this natural reaction becomes consciousness (*Besonnenheit*) and language. Proceeding in the same direction, Humboldt asserts that language belongs to the very essence of the human spirit. Words—he says—are necessary in order to reach truth and are not merely an exterior means for the representation of the truths that we already know.[8] Man talks just as the nightingale sings, he naturally joins sound and thought.

Without words, neither thought nor objects could ever present themselves to the soul. Language is an essential activity of the spirit. It is something immediately human and becomes totally inexplicable if considered as a construction of the intellect.[9]

Humboldt has the philosophical merit of having considered language, and in general the human spirit, not as a product but as production (not, he says, as *érgon* but as *energeia*), thus highlighting its creative spontaneity.

But as to the empirical problem that interests us here (concerning how, in a given period of human or pre-human evolution, that complex system of phonetic elements through which human beings communicate and which contributed so much to lifting them out of animal obtuseness, arose), Humboldt's reply has brought more confusion than clarity.

Croce improved on Humboldt's conception by defining language, in Vico's wake, not as thought but as the expressive and imaginative moment essential to thought.

Croce's suggestion, if correctly understood, could be helpful in solving the problem. It reduces the difficulty in understanding how primitive men, exuberant in senses and fantasy but poor in concepts, could have been capable of laying the foundations of language.

But as it was misunderstood (first by its own author, and later as applied by Vossler), Croce's theory became merely philosophical and led to the denial of all legitimacy to the empirical problem of the origin of language.

In fact, to the question of how language arose, Croce's theory replies that language is expression-intuition, that is, it is the faculty man has of expressing his representations to himself and to others, and that it does not make sense to ask when this faculty arose, because it is an eternal category, and no man or living being is conceivable without it.

This is a signal example of that philosophical mystification which seems to solve specific problems by submerging them in the Absolute. By this standard, historical and scientific problems could all be solved very quickly with a *fin de non recevoir*. If someone, for example, were to ask how the iron and steel industry, based on extensive mechanical installations and on the concentration of capital, arose, he would receive the answer that industry is nothing but a practical activity, and that it does not make sense to ask oneself when and how it arose, since no man or living being is conceivable without it.[10] This could also be a good reply for anyone aiming to throw discredit upon philosophy.

From philosophical to theological sophistry, the step is short. Hamann, for example, seems to waver between the two. "Language", he says, "was not invented by man. The inventive and reasoning faculties already presuppose the use of language and without it they are just as inconceivable as is arithmetic without numbers." The same can be said of Renan when he asks himself: "Si on accorde à l'animal l'originalité du cri, pourquoi refuser à l'homme l'originalité de la parole? Il serait absurde de regarder comme une découverte l'application de l'oeil à la vision ou de l'oreille à l'audition: il ne l'est guère moins d'appeler invention l'emploi de la parole comme moyen expressif."[11]

So then, instead of inquiring into the origins, one should be satisfied with the fact that man speaks because he is gifted with a faculty of speech which is as essential to him as are breathing and his other vital functions.

Not only do Renan and Hamann evade the scientific problem too hastily, but they also confuse the idealistic conception of an *a priori* category which creates language with the Cartesian and Augustinian conception of innate ideas and divine illumination. Many authors even today share this confusion, so that they are condemned to be torn between a naive theological conception and an equally naive and even clumsier naturalistic and materialistic conception.

The difficulty in finding a rational explanation persuades thinkers again and again to resign themselves to the *ignava ratio* of theological explanations.

We will certainly not deny that there is something divine in the creation of language, that is to say, that it reveals a spirituality not definable in naturalistic terms alone; but on this point Plato had already remarked in his *Cratylus* that to get oneself out of difficulty by resorting to an exterior supernatural intervention is a far too convenient way of resolving scientific problems.

Not even the Fathers of the Church admitted that the Creator bestowed a completely developed language upon man; thus delivering to Adam, so to speak, a pocket dictionary and a small grammar of the Hebrew language. In defense of a sentence by Basil, for example, Saint Gregory affirmed that just as God gave man the faculty of building houses, even though the actual houses were built by men, in the same way he gave us the faculty of creating language, though the invention of the word is human.[12]

So theological sophistry has nothing to do with faith, but, under the cover of faith, it hides our lack of competence and our idleness.

As already noted by Whitney,[13] no other linguistic problem has in the past been more frequently and more extensively treated than this one, and no other with less profit. The most disparate authors—theologians, philosophers, historians, naturalists, psychologists—have thoroughly expounded their opinions and hypotheses, but what has been lacking as a rule is research of a scientific character, such as to favor the gradual formulation of less inadequate solutions.

What scientific value does an opinion like Lessing's have when he states that language must have been communicated to man by creatures of a superior order, for otherwise it would have taken several centuries for language to develop, and divine goodness could not have deprived us of that benefit for such a long time?[14] Or what value does an opinion like Grimm's have when he states that men and women were created as adults and that the first man was never a child but the first child had a father, because the plant does not presuppose the seed, but the seed does presuppose the plant?[15]

Comparing Plato's *Cratylus* to these nineteenth century writings one really has the impression that in the intervening twenty-two centuries, far from there being progress, there has been regression in relation to the problem concerning us, and one soon realizes how research of this kind has fallen into discredit.

To all this we can add that in the second half of the nineteenth century the triumph of the positivist method in natural disciplines and of the philological method in historical disciplines made scholars increasingly diffident toward problems too general in nature and toward broad syntheses which, by attempting to encompass too much, sometimes ended up by groping about in a void. The password was to keep to the facts; a number of general theories, which had been the boast of comparative philology at the time of the various Bopps and Grimms—such as the theory of phonetic mutations, or that of the origin of grammatical desinences formed from the fusion of independent words, or again that of the classification of languages according to certain evolutionary stages (isolating, agglutinative, and inflecting)—were now considered with difference which, though sometimes able to foster seriousness in scholarship, more often than not impeded progress.

The norm of scientific progress should in fact consist of a *stirb und werde*, of a dying and rebirth of doctrines, so that as they advance each subsequent broader conception preserves whatever was vital in the preceding ones. Thus, for example, the biologists who succeeded Darwin found they had to rectify many aspects of his theory of evolution, but this was no justification for their return to naive pre-Darwinian conceptions.

The great philological syntheses which we have mentioned were rarely ever reexamined in the light of new arguments and completed or modified from a more comprehensive point of view. The new generation of scholars willingly kept away from them, with an attitude that seems to reveal indolence more than wisdom.

In all fields fruitful reactions to the philologists' work have not been lacking, but while the broader syntheses in the physical-mathematical sciences were being made, the philologists, in the field of glottology, thought they could separate facts from concepts, thus threatening to reduce their whole science to an infertile mass of inert material.

At the end of the nineteenth century and the beginning of the twentieth, an important revival of idealism took place in philosophy. But the beneficial influence that this new form of idealism could have brought, proclaiming the need to reconcile the concreteness of facts with the universality of concepts, was diminished and hindered by the scientific incompetence of some of its most important representatives, and by general recourse to an impoverished epistemology of the sciences.[16]

As we have said, studies on the origin of language today seem to have been completely abandoned and declared off-limits. At most, the problem is considered to be insoluble. At the very least, an evasive attitude is taken toward it. Philosophers will say that they cannot concern themselves with the problem of language origin because it falls within the competence of historians, historians will send it on to the psychologists and naturalists, and the latter will put it back into the hands of the philosophers. Just like all good officials in the Italian bureaucracy everyone hastens to declare that it is not his problem, thus sending the tiresome case to another office.

For our part, however, we believe that even difficult problems should be faced, and that, as Curtius says, it is better to commit an error in a bold attempt than to indulge ourselves in idleness and forego meditation and study.[17]

Even when we bear in mind the difficulties that the problem presents, we do not believe that excessive pessimism is still justified today. For a study to be conclusive, we need a vast, thorough, and reliable collection of materials on the one hand, and systematic, rational coordination able to systematize the ascertained facts into a synoptic theory, on the other. While in the golden age of glottology, when minds were more inclined toward bold syntheses, the knowledge of positive facts was still scarce and imperfect, in the last fifty years the assiduous efforts of historians, ethnologists, and psycholinguists have put an extremely vast collection of observations and facts at our disposal. This makes it legitimate to claim that, in the light of present-day knowledge, a scientific solution to our problem is no longer impossible.

Indeed, from a certain point of view, the solution may not only appear possible but even easy. The problem of language origin is a typical example of the kind of problem that the popular spirit has symbolized with the anecdote of Columbus's egg. The kind of problem that, as soon as we hear it formulated, makes us want to object: "No one in the whole world will ever be able to answer this"; and as soon as we get the reply, we feel like saying: "Big deal. I knew that already!"

This apparent lack of complexity has also been detrimental to the scientific treatment of the subject. As we shall see, intelligent and sometimes brilliant authors who have in some way advanced the solution that we believe is the correct one (that is, the thesis of the pictographic and mimetic origin of language) have not been lacking; but then these authors have not supported their theses with sufficient proof, often stopping at the mere formulation of the solution, in the belief that it is immediately and intuitively obvious. For this reason their doctrines generally have not persuaded anyone but their own authors, and the experts have continued to consider the problem unsolved.

In conclusion, the current state of glottogonic research may be described as follows: on the one hand, we have a great amount of documentary material with no clear conceptual orientation, and on the other, a few brilliant insights without reliable documentation. In our opinion, a carefully evaluated selection of the most significant facts with the precise and rational systematization of such facts is so far lacking: it is just this failure that we have attempted to remedy with our own research which we will now submit to judgment by the experts.

1. How the Origin of Language May Be Explained by Studying the Origin and Evolution of Writing Systems

Pictography and Mnemotechny

Real Object Messages—Painting and Pictography—
Concrete, Symbolic, Ideographic, and Phonetic
Signs—Transition from Pictography to Ideography—
Progressive Prevalence of Analysis over Synthesis.

As I have observed elsewhere,[1] the question "what is" a given historical institution is illegitimate and creates confusion. It is pointless, for example, to discuss whether the State or matrimony are juridical or moral institutions, for the simple reason that every historical institution can be considered just as well from one point of view as from the other.

Therefore we will not ask what language is, whether it is a logical construction, an artistic creation, or a system of conventional signs, but rather: whether we can throw more light on problems concerning the essence and origin of language by considering it from a logical, expressive, or semiological point of view.

As we will attempt to show in the second part of this work, the age-old problems concerning language become clearer when we consider it, firstly, as a semiological system and, secondly, as an aesthetic creation and a classification of concepts.

Language is certainly the most important system of expressive signs created by humanity; but it is not the only one. After language, the most important means of communication between men is writing which also has (particularly in the initial stages of its development) both semiological and aesthetic value.

Documents of the origins and initial stages of human languages are impossible to have since languages were only known to us from the moment they were preserved by phonetic scripts. At that stage they had already gone through a very long period of development and did not preserve greater signs of their origins than those found in the language we are continuously creating.

However, we possess a great quantity of documentary material concerning writing systems which enables us to follow their evolution from their pre-historic beginnings up to their most recent forms. Ancient grammarians had already dwelt upon this comparison between writing and language in the belief that it could throw some light on the essence of language itself.[2]

Studies in the history of writing soon reveal that this means of communication did not develop at random, but rather it obeyed analogous laws founded in the very nature of the human spirit, even in its evolution among peoples who had not been in any form of contact with others.[3]

The idea of examining the laws regulating the evolution of writing systems, of comparing these laws to those regulating other semiological systems, and of thus laying the foundation for a *general theory of semantics,* in which problems concerning the origin and evolution of language may be considered as special cases, is beginning to impose itself.

Something like this idea is already to be found in Saussure's *Cours de linguistique générale,* but at the time of its publication it was neither accepted nor developed to any extent by his disciples.

In the pages that follow we will attempt to pursue and systematically develop this idea. Should it be necessary to recall many generally known facts, we are convinced that the reader will excuse us on considering that we are not examining the history of writing for its own sake, but as a means of obtaining some clues about the undocumentable origin of human language.

Going back to prehistoric times, we find indications of two different types of writing systems: the *pictographic* and the *mnemotechnic.*

Those writing systems in which the directly expressive elements predominate are called pictographic, e.g., the drawing of a lion or of a tree signifies these concepts, so that anyone familiar with them can immediately comprehend the corresponding signs without the need of special training.

In contrast, signs which aim at recalling a meaning different from their immediate impression are called mnemotechnic. For example, if I make a knot in my handkerchief—as is customarily done (perhaps a remnant of a very ancient knot writing system)—to remind myself that a book must be returned to me, the knot in itself certainly does not resemble the book, but it can remind me of it.

Mnemotechnic signs can be of very different kinds: a pile of stones, a flag, the ringing of bells, etc. The slap dealt to Benvenuto Cellini by his father to impress upon his memory the day he thought he had seen a salamander wriggle in the fire in some way also belongs to this type of sign. The general characteristic of these mnemotechnic signs is that they cannot be understood by anyone who is not familiar with the associations established between the sign and its meaning.

We will begin by examining those writing systems that started with a predominance of the directly perceptive element. As the first stage in this direction we may consider the process of signifying through *real objects*, such as the oar planted by Ulysses on Elpenor's grave[4] to remind passers-by of the dead man's profession; or the signs that certain craftsmen display (a key, a bowl) to indicate the kind of work they do.

A real object message is that which, according to Herodotus,[5] Darius received from a Scythian king whom he had called upon to surrender. The message consisted of a bird, a mouse, a frog, and arrows, which the wise Gobryas interpreted as follows: "If you do not flee toward the sky like birds, if you do not hide like mice under the earth or like frogs in the water, oh Persians, you will be killed by our arrows."

Similar kinds of messages are still very much in use among primitive peoples. For example, to declare war, the Lutsu people of Eastern Tibet, who possess no other form of writing, have the custom of sending off a stick with numerous notches carved into it and a feather tied to it, a piece of charred wood, and a fish. The notches mean that they have thousands of combatants at their disposal, the feather indicates the rapidity of their assault, the fish threatens to drown the enemies, and the charcoal threatens to set their dwelling places on fire.[6]

The most highly developed stage reached by writing systems through real objects seems to be that of the Yoruba,[7] who for their communications use shells to which they sometimes attach a phonetic meaning. For example, six shells mean the number six which is pronounced "efa," but because the word efa also means attracted (from the verb "fa," to attract), a string with six shells sent to a girl means "I feel attracted to you" and corresponds to a marriage proposal. Eight shells mean the number eight which is pronounced "ejo," and because this word also means to agree, if the girl sends a string with eight shells back to her suitor, this means that she returns his sentiment.[8]

Owing to its complicated nature, it was not possible for real object writing to spread and develop any further. It was therefore an important step forward when the object was substituted with its graphic representation. One of the first incentives for designing objects was certainly the belief in the magic power thought to be inherent in certain representations. The use of amulets was very widespread and is still preserved among our own peoples (e.g., a horseshoe, the cuckold hand gesture, etc.). Magic power was attributed as much to the amulet itself as to its graphic representation.

Totemistic conceptions, that is, the belief that a given animal is the founder of the tribe or is in some way mysteriously related to it, also contributed to spreading primitive man's need to draw animals and use them as emblems. Thus we arrive at pictography proper.

Pictography is distinct from painting to the extent that the latter interests us as the expression of individual sentiment, while pictography is a technical means for communicating facts or concepts. In painting, as in works of art in general, form and content, that is, sign and meaning, tend to coincide, and—strictly speaking—there cannot be more than one way of expressing the same image, because all modifications of the sign would falsify the expression.

In pictography, on the other hand, the design is distinct from its meaning, so that different signs may serve to transmit the same message. If we wish to express pictographically that five armed men have surrounded a house, what should emerge from the design is that there were five men and that they were armed, but a great many details (expressions, lights, etc.) essential to a painting will be of no consequence and accordingly may vary without damaging communication. Vice versa, the clarity and univocal precision of communication essential to pictography, does not have the same importance in a work of art, in which it is no great fault if its obscure expressive power gives rise to rather different interpretations.

At the dawn of civilization a clear distinction between painting and pictography did not exist, just as there was a general lack of distinction between objective reality and imagination, between conceptual vision and poetic vision.

Weule tells us that during his stay in German East Africa he induced several natives—servants, soldiers, carriers, etc.—to make some drawings; and he observes that for these primitive artists drawing is always both objective pictography and fantastic representation.

Of the drawings he describes, he reports of one, by a native from the southern shores of Victoria Nyansa, picturing seven animal shapes on one side and squared stripes on the other (fig. 1). When asked what the animals on the left were, the negro replied: "Monkeys." "And the drawing to the right?" "A field." "Does the drawing represent monkeys invading a cultivated field?" "Yes, certainly," the negro explained, "that is *my* field, the field I owned three years ago, and those are the monkeys that invaded and devastated it the day my friend Mambo was married."

The same author reports various other examples of drawings which we would tend to consider as attempts at making small paintings and which instead were considered by their creators as faithful pictographic recordings by their authors.[9]

Rock paintings and engravings at least partly pictographic in character already existed in the Paleolithic age,[10] although it is almost impossible to

Figure 1

determine whether we are dealing with magic charms, drawings made for fun or for aesthetic gratification, or actual pictographic communications.

Figure 2 reproduces a prehistoric drawing found in 1911 in the grotto of Pasiego in Spain. The signs at the top left seem to represent grottoes or their entrances; the big footprints to the right mean "to go" or "to come." The other signs probably had a propitiatory or deprecatory meaning.

Figure 3 reproduces a rock pictography by Australian Aborigines.[11] The white designs at the top, possibly obtained by pressing their hands, dipped in paint, on the rocks, could be the result of a random distribution in a child's game, though the distribution and direction could also be meaningful. The two opposed hands (A), the figures of the radiant sun (B), and of the totem (C) are certainly magic and pictographic in character. The figure of a man with his arms raised and curved (D) recalls a common sign in hieroglyphic writing used to signify "joy." From the point of view of style both these Australian drawings and certain African rock paintings and engravings resemble prehistoric pictographies.

When dealing with prehistoric drawings, obviously our interpretations can only be based on conjectures. Nonetheless, ethnologists have supplied

Figure 2

Figure 3

us with numerous primitive drawings whose meaning has in fact been established.

Figure 4 represents pictographic drawings on a panel abandoned by a lost Indian hunter.[12] Sign A represents a canoe; B imitates a gesture with outstretched hands meaning "nothing"; C imitates the gesture of a person bringing food to his mouth and means "to eat"; the same figure C indicates, with the other hand, the direction of the tent. Figure D represents the tent. We may therefore translate the message as follows: "I've come this far with my *canoe,* I have *nothing* to *put in my mouth.* I'm *down there* in my *tent.*"

Figure 5 reproduces a pictographic letter by a Mandan Indian to a fur trader.[13]

To the right we see a bison, an otter, and a *Mustela canadensis;* to the left a shotgun, a beaver, and immediately after, thirty dashes. There is a cross between the two groups of objects. This is a sign that reminds us of the gesture of crossing the index fingers to signify barter.

The meaning of the letter is accordingly the following: "I offer you the skins of a bison, an otter, and a weasel in exchange for a shotgun and thirty beaver furs."[14]

Pictographic annotations and communications are such a natural media that even today there exist illiterate people who "invent" them for their own use. For example, Weule and other authors mention the picture writing of

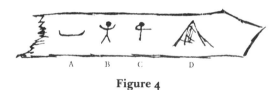

Figure 4

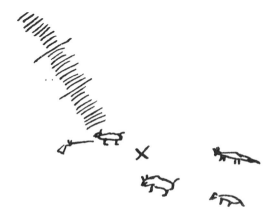

Figure 5

a messenger from East Friesland, who would make drawings in his little book as a reminder of his errands: a bottle, to remember to buy some wine; small circles meaning "rice"; an envelope to remember to deliver a letter, etc.[15]

Even more famous is the case of a London vagabond who had drawn up a topographic map for himself with pictographic annotations and conventional signs useful to his trade ("Beware of the dog!" "Good tips," "Dangerous," and the like).[16]

Figure 6 represents a feat of the Egyptian king Na'rmer, founder of the temple of Hierakonpolis (toward the middle of the fourth millennium B.C.). It is one of Egypt's most ancient graphic documents.

The text has been deciphered as follows: King Na'r [represented by the falcon A] conquered a great city [the oval figure B] leading six thousand men [the number six thousand is signified by the six lotus leaves D each of which (being extremely numerous in Egyptian swamps) signified the number one thousand] into captivity [this concept is represented by the cord C joining the enemy's mouth to the falcon's claw]. The defeated city was called Wa and was located by the seaside [this is made obvious by the harpoon E whose name sounded like the syllable "wa" and by the sign F representing the waves of the sea and acting as a determinative to signify "marine"].[17]

Figure 6

King Na'r's document seems to mark the transition from simple pictography—still a primitive phase—to ideographic writing. The stages in this development can be schematized as follows: 1) concrete pictographic signs; 2) symbolic signs; 3) conventional or agreed upon ideographic signs; 4) graphic signs with phonetic value.

We call those signs that directly represent the shape of the signified object, as in the cuneiform ideograms of the archaic era (fig. 7), concrete signs.

We call those signs that derive from a graphic metaphor, that is, that represent a given object with the purpose of calling to mind through spontaneous association a related meaning, symbolic pictographic signs.

Conventional or agreed upon signs, on the other hand, are those signs where a connection between the sign and its meaning is not perceived spontaneously so that the association is arbitrary.

The reason for the use of symbolic signs, like that of tropes in general, is both psychological and practical. When people say: "God weighs merits and faults justly"; "The entire theatre applauded"; "I drank a whole bottle," they are not aware of using synecdoches or metonymies, but indeed use such turns of phrases because they correspond to the very nature of human expression and intuition, and because, as Vico would say, these phrases derive from the poverty of the distinguishing intellect and from the exuberance of expressive passion. Nonetheless, that poverty serves to enrich our means of expression, as we may see precisely in the evolution of writing systems.

It was easy to express a man, a stick, a flower, a bird, etc., pictographically, but when it was a question of expressing abstract concepts, such as "to rule," "to guide," "to find," "many," etc., it became necessary to resort to tropes. So then, a man with a stick signified a person with the right to punish and to command, and therefore the figure of the stick alone signified, in Egypt, "to rule" or "to guide"; the lotus flower which grew in great numbers meant "many" or "a thousand"; the Ibis pictured as finding a grain of corn signified "to find," etc. Similar graphic tropes are common among all peoples just as metaphors are common in all languages in the world.

When, subsequently, use of the pictographic sign became widespread, it underwent abbreviations and stylizations due to the practical need for simplification, to the taste for decoration, and to the material used, the influence of which is particularly evident in cuneiform scripts and in Chinese writing. In this way, the original significance of the pictographic sign became unrecognizable as the purely conventional function gradually dominated.

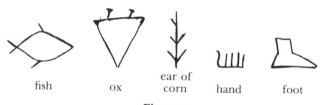

fish   ox   ear of corn   hand   foot

Figure 7

It is a fact that drawings and doodles that seem to have been partly ornamental and pictographic and partly symbolic, magic, and conventional can be traced back as far as prehistoric times. For example, it would seem that the famous swastika or uncinate cross had a triple meaning: as a purely ornamental design, as a symbolic representation of the wind rose, and as a magic sign expressing a power spreading out into the four parts of the world.

The plates reproduced in figure 8 show us one of the numerous examples of this gradual evolution of graphic signs.

If we consider the most recent signs alone it would be difficult or impossible to understand why the sign ◁̄ means sun, the sign ↪ⸯ̄ bird, the sign ⊣⫶ house, etc. Whereas if we go back to the most ancient signs the relation between the sign and its meaning is obvious.

The same kind of development can be observed in the writing systems of very ancient civilizations such as those belonging to primitive and semisavage peoples. Of the latter we will mention the ideograms (the so-called *Nsibidi*) of the Ekoi of Nigeria, some of which are outstanding for the clarity of their stylization and ingenuity of their symbolism.

In Figure 9 sign A means road traffic (the strokes in the middle represent the footprints of passersby); sign B signifies money (given that copper bars bent into the shape of a semicircle were used as currency); C means matrimonial discord (the line in the middle divides husband and wife who turn

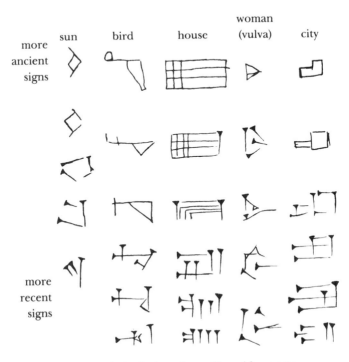

Figure 8. Evolution of cuneiform ideograms

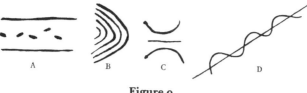

Figure 9

their backs to each other); D means discordant evidence (the straight line symbolizes truth, while the curved line symbolizes falsehood). Here too we see how some of these signs, which become increasingly more simplified with use, lose their pictographic-symbolic meaning in time and become purely conventional.

It must not be concluded that during such evolution the less developed signs were only to be encountered in the most archaic period, while the more developed signs arose *ex novo* only in more recent times; rather (as commonly occurs in the case of gradual development) the more evolved characters, which initially were hardly noticeable, gradually tended to predominate over the others until they completely replaced them.

That the more developed signs were already to be found in their early forms in the most archaic period is made obvious, for example, by the tablet of King Na'r where the pictographic character still predominates, but where we already find conventional signs (like the lotus flower to signify "a thousand"), and even a phonetic sign (the shape of a harpoon for the syllable "wa").

Together with the evolution just outlined, we may observe a progressive prevalence of analysis over synthesis, so that from the overall representation of a whole discourse we pass on to signs that break it down into propositions, words, syllables, and single letters.

Primitive pictography is a global expression in which it is not possible to distinguish individual signs analytically. What is expressed is a discourse which has not yet been articulated into words and sentences, and certain traditional signs are not yet present. Rather, the sign is created each time it is used at one and the same time with the image, as in an artistic creation. Only later do we find signs that represent whole propositions, and finally stylized ideograms that signify a well-defined concept. Most often a word from phonetic language corresponds to a conceptual ideogram, and subsequently it may be further analyzed into its syllabic and alphabetic components.

Even these analytic deconstructions, which seem extremely natural to us, turn out to be difficult for the unschooled intellect. This is made evident by the difficulty that illiterate adults encounter in persuading themselves, for example, that the syllable "scri" is to be written with the letters *s c r i*. Only after many centuries have people reached an understanding of the usefulness of this kind of analysis that has presented almost unbelievable difficulties and inhibitions.[18] In a certain sense we might say that even today because of historical, sentimental, and aesthetic obstacles, civilized populations have not yet achieved a rational alphabetical breakdown of their phonemes: the forty-four elementary sounds of the English language, for example, are expressed not with forty-four but with more than five hundred letters and combinations of letters.

We will not dwell for long on the transition from ideographic to phonetic writing, which is of little interest for our purpose. As we know, it occurs everywhere with the "rebus" method in which the names of the pictured objects represent words or parts of words made of sounds that are the same or similar.[19]

Mnemonic Signs

Antiquity of Mnemonic Signs—Knot Writing Systems—Message Sticks—Unfruitfulness of Mnemotechnic Signs—Compromise between Mnemotechny and Pictography.

We will discuss Chinese writing further on: it deserves to be considered separately both because it is the most perfect system of ideographic signs ever to have been developed, and because, according to certain authors, it did not evolve in the way we have described so far. That is to say, it did not begin with pictographic signs but rather with primitive mnemotechnic signs. But because the mnemotechnic origin of Chinese ideograms has not been demonstrated, we will first examine a few writing systems or semi-writing systems that doubtlessly do have such an origin.

As we have seen, so-called mnemotechnic signs do not refer to a given representation directly, but recall it through conventional association. The conventional element is a constituent part of mnemotechnic signs and is present from the very beginning, while in the signs we have so far examined such an element was, if anything, the unconscious result of gradual development.

The habit of resorting to mnemonic signs corresponds to a natural need in human psychology and can be traced back to most ancient times. Anyone ready to accept biblical chronology could say that the first to use a mnemonic sign was God Himself, when He created the rainbow to remind Himself and mankind of their pact and of His promise to never flood the Earth again.[1]

Again in the Bible, after the waters of the Jordan had opened up so that Israel could pass, Joshua ordered the Jews to raise a monument on that spot by piling up stones so that their sons would be induced to ask: "What do these stones mean?" and their fathers would answer them by narrating the memorable fact.[2]

The very ancient custom of piling up stones as monuments or of raising monoliths was practiced especially on top of graves and was almost a stylization of the pile of earth that remained visible once the body was buried. It was from this practice that the pyramids and obelisks were later to derive. The menhirs, dolmens, and cromlechs of the neolithic age have a similar explanation.

Geometric engravings (small circles, triangles, small crosses, etc.) which, as far as we know, served as distinguishing marks, are present on certain prehistoric monuments. Similar signs, more clearly recognizable as emblems, arms, or ownership brands are found on the terra-cotta vases of Neqade's royal tomb, attributed to Mêne, as well as on Delphic and Mycenaean vases. Seals, engraved with coarse distinguishing marks, have also reached us from as far back as the ancient Minoan period.

Mnemotechnic signs, which are based on an association arbitrarily established each time they are used, can only be interpreted on the basis of direct evidence. Consequently, documents from prehistoric antiquity cannot be deciphered. On the other hand, we are able to give a more or less perfect interpretation to the numerous semiological systems of this kind that ethnologists have observed among primitive peoples closer to us in time.

One of the most complex pre-graphic mnemotechnic systems is so-called knot writing, used by a variety of populations.[3] Knots have had a magical meaning from most ancient times, so that it probably became the custom to use them as amulets and subsequently as a means of expression.[4]

A great many small cords marked out by several knots were joined to a larger cord. The knots closest to the main cord referred to the most important objects, for example, if referring to men, they indicated the elders.

The most famous knot scripts were the Peruvian Quippus. As far as we know, they were used especially for statistical purposes. Garcilaso de la Vega observed that the Peruvians used them to record the number of soldiers, but not the content of a message.[5] Symbolic meanings were sometimes added to the mnemotechnic element, for example, by attaching small pieces of wood or tiny colored stones to the knots, and even the variation in color of the small cords had a symbolic meaning. Red indicated soldiers; yellow, gold; white, silver; and green, grain.

The Quippus have been preserved to this very day on the island of Puna and in Ecuador, but there, too, they only serve for registration and calculation purposes.

Another very widespread mnemotechnic medium of expression is the "message stick."[6] It is made of a small cylindric shaped stick or rectangular rod with notches cut into it. The notches are generally all the same and have a purely mnemonic function. They are carved into the stick in front of the messenger so as to impress upon him the number and succession of communications. Small sticks are also used as a way of authenticating the message itself.

Such sticks are used as heraldic and totemistic emblems by the Maoris of

New Zealand: each incision recalls the name of an ancestor. A greater distance between one notch and the next signifies extinction of the male lineage. The elders of the tribe teach the younger members their family genealogies by referring to these small rods.[7]

Here, too, symbolic or pictographic elements are often added to the purely mnemotechnic element. Figure 10 pictures two of these sticks, belonging to the tribe of Tongaranka of New South Wales.

The information that the messenger was to convey was the following: "The sender, his two brothers and another two elders invite the receiver to send his son to them for the initiation of the young, and they inform him that another two youths who are to be initiated are already on the spot."

We may imagine the procedure taking place more or less in the following way: the sender makes the messenger approach, he picks up the first small stick and says: "You will take this stick to so and so [on saying this he cuts out sign A] and you will tell him that his son and another two youths must be initiated [on saying this he cuts out signs B-C-D; he then shows him the other small stick]. Tell him again that it is *me* who is sending him this message, that I am here together with my *two* brothers [and he cuts out the signs E-F-G]; and that with us there are another *two* elders [and he cuts the notches H-I]." The messenger will then have to repeat the message to impress it upon his mind, and he will do so in front of the sender, pointing to the relative notch as he proceeds.

Message sticks were perfected by varying the signs according to the category of the objects signified, for example, a given sign was used for men, another for women, and yet another for guests, etc.[8]

Due to the great variety in the signs employed, some of the small message boards represent something between a mnemotechnic and an ideographic means of expression.

Figure 11 reproduces a small board belonging to the Boijni tribe from the

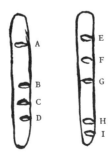

Figure 10

(A represents the receiver, B-C-D represent the son of the receiver and the two youths to be initiated; the signs E-F-G represent the sender and his two brothers; H-I the two elders.)

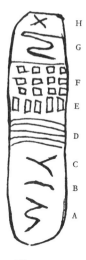

Figure 11

(A signifies a sand hill; B, a stream filled with silt; C, another hill; D, the region near Marion Downs; E, a plain; F, a village near Boulia; G, Hamilton river; H, the meeting-place.)

Boulia district in Queensland. It is an invitation to a meeting, and the single incisions indicate the various localities to be crossed in order to reach the assembly place.[9]

Progress in the evolution of these mnemotechnic media stops, however, at a certain point. It seems that neither ancient peoples nor contemporary primitive populations ever succeeded in using them for the transmission of more complex messages without first passing through the pictographic stage. Mnemotechnic signs have proven to be incapable of evolving into a proper writing system. They represent a sterile branch in the history of semiological systems.[10]

On the other hand, there are certain documents from primitive civilizations which present an interesting compromise between mnemotechnic and pictographic systems. For example, so-called Kekinowins are a kind of prewriting system used by priests and witch doctors of the North American Ogibway tribe from the Thousand Lakes area. Kekinowins consist of a series of figures, each of which calls to mind a line from a magic chant. We will transcribe a strophe from one of these chants (in which the concepts are not always clear):

1. What I offered you is made of flames.
2. The tree rises as it grows.
3. I cover the ground with my length (prostrating myself?).
4. Inside me is the force of a bear.

5. It emanates a magic force from its mouth.
6. Here, this is the sparrow hawk.
7. It is me who is sending you my word.[11]

In order to remember these lines the witch doctor makes use of the seven symbols reproduced in figure 12.

It is as though we were to design a mirror for "speculum justitiae," a vase for "vas spirituale," a rose for "rosa mystica," a tower for "turris eburnea," etc., in an effort to remember the invocations made during our litanies to the Blessed Virgin. This comparison should not seem irreverent, for in fact the Church itself, when addressing primitive peoples, resorts to similar mnemonic devices as is shown by the reproduction of the Credo in figure 13.[12]

To draw a vase, a bear, or a sparrow hawk as a way of referring to the relative concepts is pure pictography; but to draw them in order to remember certain verses is a mnemotechnic procedure; this is why we stated that we are dealing with a mixture of the two systems.[13]

Similar means of expression are used by a variety of populations: for example, the Ewe of Togo use them to remember lines from proverbs.

Figure 14 represents a needle and a ball of thread next to a loom with a cloth and signifies "The big cloth is made with the little needle," that is, important results can be obtained with modest devices.

While pure pictography, not yet properly distinguished from pictorial representation, represents a complete discourse, and ideological or hieroglyphic scripts represent single concepts, the Kekinowin and analogous means of expression represent phrases (Meinhof, in fact, calls them Satzschriften [phraseographiae][14]).

At times symbolic signs are so stylized that they seem to be conventional signs, as we may see in figure 15 which represents a charm in bamboo used by the Semang in the Malaysian peninsula.[15]

The blocks of stripes and dots symbolize clouds, the small oval circles drops of rain. For believers, showing or carrying an amulet in a procession is the same as raising an invocation to Heaven: "Clouds, clouds, hasten, carried by the wind! Clouds, clouds, melt into many drops and make the harvest fertile!"

The most complex example of mixed communication made of pictography, of symbolic, and of mnemotechnic signs is perhaps a love letter by a Jucagira, reproduced in figure 16.

1.   2.   3.   4.   5.   6.   7.

Figure 12

Figure 13

Figure 14

The Jucagiri are a people living between the Jana and Anadyr rivers in the Arctic regions. The letter is addressed to a Russian and should read as follows: "You are leaving. You love a Russian woman who puts obstacles on your path toward me. You will have children and you will take delight in them. But I will be sad forever and I will think about you even if another man loves me."[16]

We have dwelt for some time upon these attempts that do not yet form

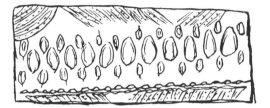

Figure 15

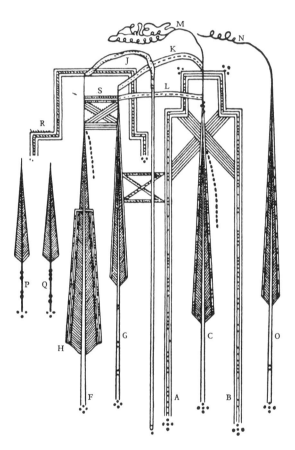

Figure 16

writing systems, but that are almost a *tatonnement* in the direction that may have given rise to writing. In fact, it is important to establish whether or not there are proven examples showing that purely mnemotechnic signs, unaided by pictographic elements, have evolved to the point of forming a complex and efficient semiological system. The answer is negative.

Chinese Writing

Fu-hi's Trigrams and Hexagrams—The Pictographic
Element Was Also Decisive in Chinese Writing—
Other Semantic Systems.

According to an ancient tradition, supported by certain Western scholars, Chinese writing developed from an earlier system of mnemotechnic signs similar to the Quippus or to notched rods or sticks. In Conrady's opinion, even the form and vertical layout of Chinese signs remind us of the ancient sticks. This hypothesis is strengthened not only by the shape of the signs but also by the fact that the ideogram signifying book, "ts'e," in its most ancient form depicts a bunch of small sticks.[1]

Signs that are definitely mnemotechnic in character form the ancient canonical *Book of Changes (I Ching).*

It contains sixty-four so-called hexagrams, i.e., signs made of six lines, each of which may either be composed of a long segment or of two shorter ones, as seen in figure 17.

According to tradition, hexagrams are a combination of eight trigrams ("pa-kwa") invented by Emperor Fu-Hi (2852–2738 B.C.).

What strikes us about these trigrams and hexagrams is their abstract and conventional form, completely devoid of pictographic elements. The fact that all possible mathematical combinations of two elementary signs in six lines were used for semiological ends in such an ancient epoch is proof of the precociously rationalistic character of that population. [2] With the exception of certain numerical signs, it will not be until very recent times that signs forming an equally schematic and abstract system, such as those of the Morse Code, will make their appearance.

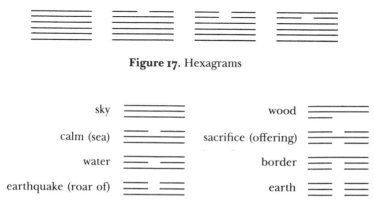

Figure 17. Hexagrams

sky	☰		wood	
calm (sea)			sacrifice (offering)	
water			border	
earthquake (roar of)			earth	

Figure 18. Trigrams

Though a single sign may have several meanings (e.g., water, rain, river, liquid, lunar, etc.), the hexagrams used in the *I Ching* are far too few in number to write a book as we understand it. Therefore, they probably only served as mnemotechnic signs, like the Kekinowin figures of the American Indians and the *Sutras* of primitive Indian literature.[3] If this hypothesis is correct the ancient *I Ching* presupposed that the reader was already familiar with its contents through practice and oral tradition, so that the hexagrams only served as cues for individual paragraphs. Thus, it is only natural that nowadays the *I Ching* should be incomprehensible without the aid of commentaries that specify and complete the meaning of each sign.

In spite of a promising beginning, and although the mentality of the people as well as the language itself were singularly favorable to the creation of abstract schemes, mnemotechnic signs in China (just as in all other parts of the world) have revealed their incapacity to evolve beyond a certain point without aid from the pictographic element.

That the latter was decisive emerges from a comparison between the most recent forms, in which decorative stylization confers a schematic and conventional appearance to signs, and the most ancient forms, in which the pictographic element clearly emerges.

For example, the ideographic sign reproduced in figure 19 means "feng," that is, "consignment or investiture of a fief." Now then, we must remember that the act of investiture of a fief, and perhaps the transfer of all landed estates, was accomplished in ancient times by handing over a lump of earth with a small *plant* to the new owner. From this mute and concrete language (as Vico would say) came the sign that is preserved in ancient writing and that portrays a lump of earth with a small plant (figure 20). The sign in figure 19 is obviously no more than a subsequent stylization.

The following table (figure 21) presents other examples of such progressive stylizations in which the function of conventional signs is conferred upon signs that were originally pictographic.

Sign A_1 represents two hands held back to back and curved in opposite directions and probably alludes to a similar imitative gesture. (That the sign represents a hand is evident from another ideogram with the same meaning.)

Sign B_1 represents two hands held out in a friendly manner, D_1 pictures two hands raised above the head: these are probably the graphic translation of greeting and submission respectively; F_1 represents the celestial vault with raindrops falling from it; G_1 represents the moon and therefore means eve-

Figure 19 & 20

newer sign   older sign

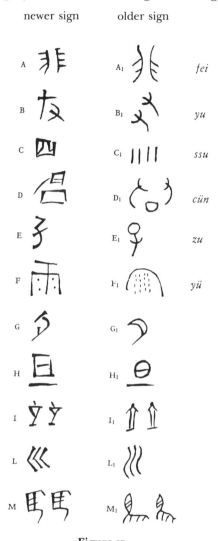

Figure 21

ning; H_1 represents the sun and was thus to signify "early morning" or generally "early."

We have already seen that even in the small primitive message sticks and boards, mnemotechnic signs are replaced by pictographic signs in the case of more complex communications. The same thing must have happened in Chinese writing.

In addition to writing we could examine other semiological systems such as the codes of maritime signals and road signs; but such systems are of little interest to us since most of the signs forming them were produced only re-

	100
	1000
	10 000
	100 000
	1 000 000

Figure 22

cently and did not arise from spontaneous use. At any rate, the pictographic element often works its way into these signs as well, as is obvious, for example, in the road signs signifying dangerous curve, level-crossing, school, etc.

Given their antiquity and the fact that they are more widespread, numeration signs are far more interesting. As these signs are rational in character, it is only natural that the abstract and conventional element should have more weight in them than in writing. However, here too the beginning is marked by pictographic expression.

In most primitive societies numeration consists of the simple repetition of the ideogram of the object that is to be numbered. In order to indicate ten men, ten identical figures are drawn, and for five horses, five horse shapes. Later the object is replaced with dots or with vertical or horizontal lines.

The ideographic origin is evident in Egyptian, in cuneiform, and in Chinese numeration systems. As we can see in figure 22, the Egyptian signs for one hundred, one thousand, ten thousand, one hundred thousand, and a million are pictographic. Each symbol was repeated as many times as was required according to the number to be indicated: three lotus flowers meant 3000; a frog, 100,000; four frogs, 400,000, etc.

In Roman numerals the first four signs represent fingers. As observed by Mommsen, the V is a stylization of the hand, and the X a reduplication of V.

In privileging the value of numbers arranged in a certain logical order, that is, in choosing a decimal, quinary, or vigesimal system, the influence of finger counting (i.e., of a system of directly expressive imitative signs) is almost always present.[4]

Conclusions from the Study of Writing Systems

Historians and ethnologists have collected a great quantity of documents and data in relation to the widespread development of writing systems everywhere: such material confirms the general concepts we have so far mentioned and which may be summed up in the following points:

1. As early as most ancient times, writing systems and prewriting systems developed from two different types of signs: precisely, either from pictographic (directly expressive) signs or from purely mnemotechnic signs.

2. Mnemotechnic signs by themselves did not develop into a more complex semiological system; all those writing systems that have reached a more complex stage through natural evolution have passed through a stage in which the pictographic element was dominant.

3. In all these writing systems, the pictographic element, evident and predominant at the beginning, gradually became less evident until the sign ended by assuming a purely conventional function. Conventional value is not established by "cold" logic from the very outset but is the result of slow and spontaneous development.

4. In the evolution of graphic systems, analysis progressively predominates over synthesis. From primitive pictography, which represents whole discourses, we progress to signs that increasingly deconstruct discourse into its constituent parts.

Let us now look into the question of whether these principles may also offer useful indications concerning the evolution of human (spoken) language.

2. The Pictographic Elements of Language

Interjections and Onomatopoeia

Immediate Comprehensibility and Spontaneity of such Expressions—Onomatopoeic Expressions Invented by Children—Objections to Their Glottogonic Value—They Mark the Boundary between Animal Sensitivity and Expression.

We have already seen that one of the main difficulties in relation to the problem of the origin of language is posed by the intertwining of language and thought. The institution of a system of expressive signs such as language seems to presuppose considerable intellectual development, and intellectual development does not seem to be possible without the use of language. This is the reason why certain thinkers hold that it is not possible to understand the birth of language without acknowledging direct divine intervention; and this is also the reason why so many modern scholars, having lost hope of finding a reasonable way out, have resigned themselves to an agnostic attitude: "ignoramus et ignorabimus."

Now then, we believe that the history of writing can help to free us from this *logo diallelo*. Doubtlessly, if a semiological system can only be established as the result of a premeditated decision, in other words, if human beings had to first agree and formally establish that a certain thing was to be called "bread," and something else "water," then, absurdly, we would have to admit that human beings already knew how to speak before language ever existed. But the history of writing has repeatedly shown that the conventional value of signs does not need to be established by "cold" logic from the very beginning (on the contrary, conventionality is normally the result of slow evolution), and that originally signs were no more than the direct representation of the object signified.

In the case of writing systems, the thesis of the conventional origin could in theory appear to be acceptable, for the signs of writing systems appeared when mankind already had another means of communication at its disposal. But in the case of language such a hypothesis is inconceivable. How was it possible for primitive man (who did not have any other more intuitive means of expression at his disposal) to agree on attributing a given conventional meaning to this or that phoneme?

As the first result of our inquiry we may now formulate the following proposition:

The pictographic element of human language, that is, the directly expressive element, initially predominated; the conventional value of single phonemes is the gradual result of subsequent development.

We are able to easily ascertain that in the evolution of language the conventional element progressively dominates, just as in writing systems. Early scholars of comparative philology had already noticed, for example, that the prefixes, suffixes, and desinences of cases and verbal forms were originally independent little words with a precise meaning, which only as time passed acquired the function of pure grammatical convention.[1]

The same thing emerges from most etymologies. For example, the word "money" has the value of a pure convention for a modern Englishman, just as the word "moneta" has for an Italian, whereas for the citizens of ancient Rome this word was more directly evocative, for it recalled the mint building located near the temple of "Juno moneta." Similar examples are very common. With prolonged use many words and phrases lose their original expressive resonance which, however, is sometimes subsequently recovered through etymological research.

Most interesting is the obvious analogy between the factors that intervene to modify graphic signs so as to gradually accentuate their conventional value, and the factors that intervene in the modification of words.

As we have already seen, the former include: influence of the material used, simplifications and abbreviations determined by use, aesthetic and decorative requirements, and the convenience of using easily distinguishable signs. In the evolution of natural languages, the anatomical conformation of the vocal organs and the physiological peculiarities of the single races from which the phonetic laws derive, correspond to the influence of the material used in writing systems. The well-known contractions dictated by the "law of minimum effort" and the transition from isolating formations to agglutinative and inflected ones, correspond to simplifications and abbreviations. And, lastly, the same aesthetic requirements (euphony) as well as the need for clarity and differentiation exert their influence on spoken language also. The tendency observed in the evolution of writing and that which is still operating in the evolution of language is therefore the same. This enables us to formulate what, in our opinion, should be the fundamental question posed by general linguistics: *"What are the pictographic elements of human language?"*

We must now ascertain whether it is possible to single out the pictographic elements and then use them as the basis for the formulation of a reasonable hypothesis on the origin of language.

As early as Plato's *Cratylus,* that is, from the first piece of systematic writing on this subject, and many times after, it occurred to scholars that language could have originated from the onomatopoeic imitation of natural sounds. This is understandable: even though the problem of language origin has never been clearly articulated, it was instinctively felt that, in order to give a natural explanation of its beginnings, language must be viewed as deriving from a directly expressive or pictographic means of communication, which was to be searched for where it was most obvious. Let us now examine whether and to what degree we may clarify the issue in question by following this line of inquiry.

Interjections and onomatopoeic expressions have all the characteristics that distinguish primitive pictography from conventional writing systems, that is, immediate and universal comprehensibility, creative spontaneity, and the globality of an expression not yet articulated into different parts of discourse.

An Italian child imitates the barking of a dog with "bu-bu!," the English with "bow-wow!," the German with "wau-wau!," the French with "oua-oua!," the Dutch with "waf-waf!," the Japanese with "wan-wan!." But despite the different alphabetical composition, we do not need a dictionary to understand them.

The diversity in composition corresponds to the different ways in which the same image may be stylized in pictographic ideograms (e.g., hieroglyphic signs). Not only does this depend on the will of whoever created the stylized sign in question, but also on the material used and the general style dominating in that given system. In phonemes, the physiological conformation of the vocal organs corresponds to the material used in pictographic ideograms. Phonetic style, that is, the relation between a new sound and the *corpus* of traditionally used sounds, corresponds to graphic style.

As with writing, in spoken language too the passage from immediate pictography to conventional signs is gradual. The result is that at a certain stage, we have a mixture of pictographic, and therefore universally comprehensible, lexical elements and more stylized elements which can only be understood by whoever belongs to the linguistic community in question. It must be kept in mind, however, that alphabetic transcription only roughly conveys the actual sound, which, when heard, is more easily comprehensible than its transcription.

On this point a comparison between elements that are familiar to us and those of linguistic families distant from our own may prove to be instructive. Here is a list of onomatopoeic expressions used in Japanese baby language: "do-do," horse; "mo-mo," cow; "wan-wan," dog; "nya-nya," cat; "ziu-ziu," mouse; "ka-ka," crow; "kokko," chicken; "po-po," dove; "bun-bun," bee; "sin-sian" or "gon-gon," bell; "zirin-zirin," door bell; "don-don," drum; "gara-gara," cart; "goro-goro," thunder; "kon-kon," cough; "fu-fu," fire (from the vocal mimicry of blowing to light it or put it out); "uma-uma," to eat (analogous to "yum-yum"); etc.[2]

In the list that follows[3] some Chinese and Manchu expressions are compared to our own.

Natural sounds	Chinese	Manchu
cock	Kiao-kiao	Gior-gior
wind	Kao-kao	Kor-kor
wind and rain	Siao-siao	Cior-cior
baggage wagons	Lin-lin	Kungur-kungur
mating dogs	Ling-ling	Kalang-kalang
chains	Ziang-ziang	Kiling-kiling
drums	Kon-kon	Tung-tung
bells	Tsiang-tsiang	Kiling-kiling

The physiological peculiarities of individual peoples are felt more in interjections—the stylization of sounds spontaneously emitted in emotional outbursts. The fact that they are stylized makes such sounds less comprehensible to anyone not belonging to the linguistic community in question, as we may see from the following Chinese interjections: "hu-fu," surprise; "tsai!," admiration and approval; "i!," breathlessness; "tsie!," vocative particle; "a'i!," disdain; "u'-hu!," pain; "scin," "i! ah!," really; "pu-sin!," alas; "nga!," stop![4]

As far as creative spontaneity is concerned, we must observe that the field of interjections and onomatopoeia is the only one in which totally new expressions (that is, which are preceding roots) emerge rather frequently. This is true for common language, and especially the language of infants, as well as for literary language. We all remember the cry of Sophocles' Philoctetes: ἀτταταῖ ... παπαῖ παπαῖ, ἀπαππαπαῖ παπαῖ, παπαῖ παπαῖ παπαῖ ... παππαπαππαπαῖ, etc.[5]

On this point, Jespersen's observations concerning onomatopoeic expressions invented by children are interesting.[6] A two- to three-year-old child spontaneously called a crow "vak-vak"; a two-year-old child called soda water "ft"; watches and trains were designated with the expression "ghinghiri"; and the act of smoking or perhaps the cigar with "poh."

A child of one year and nine months used the sound "boom!" to signify the noise of a falling object, and later also for a small slap or a spanking. Next the child would use that expression for anything causing her pain, such as soap stinging her eyes: this is a good example of linguistic signs that lose their directly expressive meaning and, in short, acquire a value that seems purely conventional. If we were not familiar with its "philological precedents," that is, with the history of the expression, it would be difficult indeed to see a natural connection between the phoneme "boom!" and the stinging of one's eyes.

Another child of one year and eight months used the same word "boom!" to designate a dish that had fallen, then for a broken dish even if he did not see it fall, and later for any broken object at all, for example, a torn garment or a missing button. In these examples we almost seem to be witnessing the birth of primal roots.[7]

In regard to the globality and semantic polyvalency of such expressions, it will suffice to recall the number of different meanings that can be signified by "oh!," "ah!," "ahi!," and "hem, hem!"; such polyvalency is also maintained by actual words when used as interjections.

A significant example of the latter is found in certain modulated cries used by pedlars, in which only a vague intonation and sing-song, but no single words, can be identified.

However, it has been affirmed that the birth of language cannot be explained through interjections and onomatopoeia, for natural sounds are congenitally incapable of evolving into words and, in fact, a wide gulf separates them from the spoken word. Language, says M. Müller, commences where interjections end. There is as much difference between a word like "to laugh" and the sound "ha! ha! ha!," between an expression like "I'm suffering" and the cry "ouch!," as there is between the involuntary loud noise of a sneeze and the verb "to sneeze". Sneezing, coughing, and, in general, all other involuntary convulsions accompanied by sounds have as much right to be called words and parts of discourse as the neighing of a horse or the barking of a dog.[8] A number of other linguists are of the same opinion: interjections—says Benfey—may be considered as the negation of language, for they are used when someone does not know how to or cannot express himself in words.[9] And Bühler, pointing to the inability of these expressions to evolve and become proper words, speaks of a "syntactic bolt" closing the doors of language to interjectional and onomatopoeic expressions.[10]

It is necessary here to distinguish between a question of fact and a question of theory. The former asks whether, in the languages we know, interjections and onomatopoeia are able to and have in fact given rise to real words; whereas the latter concerns the conceptual diversity between natural sounds and words. Confusion between these two problems has rendered difficult and obscure a question that in itself is anything but arduous.

As to the facts, there is no doubt that in all known languages imitative sounds have effectively given rise to words and we may cite as many examples as we wish; the Latin "ululare," "jubilare," "ejulare," the Italian "bisbigliare," "gargarismo," "abbaiare" (from *baubari*), the German "achzen," "paffen," "plumpsen," etc.

The passage of natural sounds into the grammar of a linguistic system is not rare in the languages of civilized peoples; in primitive languages it is extremely common. For instance, in the Runasimi or *keshua* language of Peru it is the custom to form verbs by adding the verb "nig," which means "to say," to an interjectional expression. It is as though, in English, we were to use the expression "uff-say" for to be fed up with, "ouch-say" for to moan, "poo-say" for to despise, "oh-say" for to marvel at something, etc.[11]

In order to show that natural sounds only exerted a small influence on the formation of language, certain glottologists have observed that, in general, languages tenaciously resist any forms that are not compatible with the syntax of the language in question, as well as any excesses in the formation of neologisms. The spirit of a language tends to progressively eliminate any imitative elements: e.g., the Latin "querquedula" loses its onomatopoeic reference in the French "sarcelle," just as "pipio" loses its onomatopoeic reference in the Italian "piccione" and the French "pigeon."

In our opinion, these observations are quite correct, however they demonstrate that primitive language was much richer in natural sounds than the languages spoken by modern peoples. This corresponds perfectly to the predominance of the pictographic element in more ancient times and its subsequent gradual elimination, which is so evident in the evolution of writing systems. In primitive languages imitative sounds abound, but synonyms also abound, often rather surprisingly.[12] This cumbersome wealth of expression is gradually eliminated and in the selection, as a rule, the less onomatopoeic sounds are preserved. As in the case of excessive gesticulation, the abundance of sounds is considered by many as primitive and coarse.

We said that it pays to distinguish between the facts just examined and the theoretical problem of the conceptual difference between natural sounds and language. We will analyze this problem in greater detail later on. For the moment, it will suffice to remark that in so far as natural sounds such as coughing or yawning are purely physiological manifestations, they are certainly *toto coelo* different from the spirituality of language. No one would say that a child affected by whooping cough formulates interjections. The physiological manifestation in itself must be distinguished from its expressive stylization. A yawn provoked by sleepiness is a physical reaction, but when a yawn is imitated to signify boredom, reference is made to that same physiological manifestation for expressive purposes. Therefore, interjections and onomatopoeic sounds mark the separation from sensation intended in the animal sense and the passage to the contemplation and expression of experienced sensation. Consequently, those who see a starting point for language in natural sounds are just as correct as those who stress the distance between these two manifestations. The same can be said in general of the relation between feeling (understood as a sensual and emotional impression) and artistic contemplation: anyone who stops at feeling will not reach art, but art must begin from feeling. Art is *Aufhebung*, that is, the negation, preservation, and elevation of feeling.

From what we have said about natural sounds, it would appear that they are doubtlessly among the pictographic elements that contribute to the formation of language; but, as all linguists now agree, those sounds on their own are totally insufficient to account for the birth of language.

The words that can be traced back to such sounds are only a small minority. Playthings, says M. Müller, and not the agents of language. If the principle of an onomatopoeic origin of language were true, it should be particularly evident in the names of animals, however, this does not emerge on analyzing the names of the chicken, duck, sparrow, pigeon, cat, dog, etc., in the various languages. Indeed, if these names sometimes seem imitative, on analyzing the root the onomatopoeia often proves to be a subsequent addition and not a characteristic of the root itself.[13] For example, the German word "Rabe" (crow), Anglo-Saxon "hrafn," High German "hraban," Sanscrit "karava," and Latin "corvus" would each seem to derive from an onomatopoeia, while in reality they derive from the roots "ka" and "rava" which together mean "make a raucous cry."[14] Even the word "monotonous," in which the same vowel is repeated four times, could seem onomatopoeic, whereas it is obviously a conceptual combination of two words. In the same way, the English "thunder," the German "Donner," and the Latin "tonitru" could seem to be imitative in origin, but in fact they come from the root "tan" (to extend) from which derive the Greek "tonos," the French "tendre," the Latin "tener" and "tenuis" (extended and thin).[15]

Given that onomatopoeia and interjections, as we have so far examined them, cannot provide us with an adequate foundation for the formulation of a glottogonic theory, we will now extend their reach so as to include, if possible, all the pictographic elements of language.

Abstract Language and Concrete Language

Not All the Phonemes of Spoken Language Can Be Expressed Alphabetically—Necessity of Extending the Concepts of Onomatopoeia and Interjection—Rhythmic Cries that Accompany Work—Symbolic Onomatopoeia—Oral Mimicry—Reduplications—Intonations, Rhythm, and Inflections—Word and Song—Inadequacy of Onomatopoeic Theories.

We must attempt to understand the concrete nature of language. Real language is what is actually spoken, as has been stated many times from Humboldt onwards. However, the extent to which the words of the language listed in dictionaries and studied by the linguists are an abstraction is commonly ignored.

A shrill cry, or a cry filled with passion, an ironic little cough, eye-rolling, amorous or threatening airs, etc., are all manifestations of concrete language. These are taken into due account by the stage actor, but because of its very nature written language necessarily neglects them.

Alphabetic signs are no more than an abstraction and stylization of the sounds we actually pronounce. It is immediately obvious that the graphic signs of alphabets impose a certain uniformity upon pronounced sounds that modifies and impoverishes them. This is particularly evident when considering popular speech.

Modern phonetic research has shown that in the development of languages there is an increasing tendency toward simplifying alphabetic sounds. This reduces the muscular effort necessary for their pronunciation and renders the single sounds more uniform and more clearly distinguishable.

In our literary languages, for example, suction and clicking sounds *(Sauglaute* and *Schnalzlaute),* produced by breathing in air, are no longer used, while sounds pronounced by breathing outwards have been preferred. In our spoken languages, however, we sometimes use sounds that cannot be transcribed by the letters of the alphabet.[1]

If we sum up the letters of all languages we have roughly seventy alphabetic sounds, including the aspirates, the nasals, the sibilants, etc. But the line of demarcation between articulate and inarticulate sounds is obviously anything but distinct: sounds that seem easy and natural to a given population are strange and unreproducible for another. For example, the French nasal sounds, the English *th,* the Greek *theta,* the intermediate vowels between the *a* and *o* of English, etc., may not seem perfectly articulate sounds to the Italian ear.

There are peoples such as the Mohawks who do not know how to pronounce the labial consonants *p, b, m, f, v*; others who do not pronounce the letters *l, f, s, r, z*. Of the overall seventy sounds, any one population uses only a small number: Hindustani has forty-eight consonants, Hebrew twenty-three, Greek seventeen, Finnish eleven, and certain Australian languages only eight.[2]

On the other hand, vocalizations and sing-songs that figure in no alphabet whatsoever abound in dialectal and common speech. Furthermore, certain nuances in tone, rhythm, and inflection can be distinguished by the ear, even if the intellect is not able to define their specific characteristics. We may distinguish between people who speak with a certain dialectal accent, just as we distinguish a familiar voice from a thousand others, without being aware of the peculiarities upon which our identification is based.[3] Thus, if we wish to form an idea of all the directly expressive elements in concrete language, we must greatly extend the traditional concepts of onomatopoeia and of interjections.

According to certain authors the rhythmic chants with which people often accompany their work, such as those used by sailors, dockers, stonebreakers, and the like, exerted a notable influence on the formation of language. These chants are mostly made of aspirate sounds because man experiences a certain relief on breathing deeply and rhythmically when his chest is oppressed by strong muscular effort. They are also a sign for fellow workers to exert their energy together and not to waste it in individual efforts. Bühler dealt with this phenomenon at length in his essay *Arbeit und Rhythmus.*[4]

As early as Plato's *Cratylus* it was observed that not only direct onomatopoeia but also figurative or symbolic onomatopoeia exist. Taking up the same concept Grimm held that all alphabetical sounds had their own natural expressive value,[5] C. de Goeie observes that in the linguistic families of the Caribbean islands of South America this natural relation between alphabetical sounds and meaning is of fundamental importance.[6] Similar observations have been made by various other ethnologists and linguists and particularly by Westermann in his essay on the languages of West Sudan. There seems to be a physiological reason for this: on examining the vocal apparatus with x-rays, it appears that greater muscular effort is required for the pronunciation of certain letters, such as *i* or *o*, than for others.

However, in the light of our current knowledge about the subject, we do not believe it possible to establish (other than very tentatively) such detailed correlations.

We doubtlessly have figurative onomatopoeia in language that renders acoustically impressions that are non-acoustic. What is sweet to the palate is signified with a sweet sound, what is harsh with a harsh sound and so on. The Italian expression "ghirigoro" is certainly not onomatopoeic because of any direct resemblance to the whimsical twisting and winding of curved lines, but rather the association is of a symbolic nature. The same is true of the expression "zig-zag," in which the fast shift from the *i* to the *a* symbolizes a change in direction. Similarly we say "brrrr it's cold!," not because "brrrr!" imitates a sound but because its wavering sound recalls the trembling of the body.[7]

In Paget's view certain groups of letters have analogous symbolic value not only among Indo-European languages but also among languages of very distant families, such as Sumerian, Chinese, Bantu, and the Semitic languages. In such cases linguistic coincidences are not thought to derive from a common origin but from a symbolism with a physiological basis.[8]

Analogous concepts derived from the Stoics were expressed with admirable precision by Saint Augustine:

> Donec perveniatur eo ut res cum sono verbi aliqua similitudine concinat, et cum dicimus aeris tinnitum, equorum hinnitum, ovium belatum, tubarum clangorem, stridorem catenarum (percipis enim haec verba ita sonare ut ipsae res quae his verbis significantur). Sed quia sunt res quae non sonant, in his simitudinem tactus valere, ut si leniter vel aspere sensum tangunt, lenitas vel asperitas literarum ut tangit auditum sic eis nomina peperit: ut ipsun lene cum dicimus leniter sonat, quis item asperitatem non et ipso nomine asperum judicet. Lene est auribus cum dicimus voluptas, asperum cum dicimus crux. Ita res ipsae adficiunt, ut verba sentiuntur. Haec quasi cunabula verborum esse crediderunt, ubi sensus rerum cum sonorum sensu concordarent. Hinc ab ipsarum inter se rerum similitudinem processisse licentiam nominandi; ut cum verbi causa crux propterea dicta sit, quod ipsius verbi asperitas cum doloris quem crux efficit asperitate concordat, crura tamen non propter asperitatem doloris, sed, quod longitudine atque duritia inter membra cetera sint ligno similiora sic appellata sint.[9]

As we all know, as early as the Homeric era onomatopoeic effects have been frequently used by poets who are the continual creators and renewers of language; but it is interesting to note that while the more conscious and less spontaneous artists willingly turn to the direct imitation of natural sounds ("Pour qui sont ces serpents qui sifflent sur vos têtes?," or "Und hohl and höhler hört man's heulen"), in artists of more immediate inspiration indirect or symbolic onomatopoeia prevail, expressing a feeling rather than a sound.

Bally and A. Sechehaye, Saussure's editors, have already observed that while Saussure always speaks of "images acoustiques," every word bears the representation of the muscular impressions necessary for its articulation. In his book on *The Expression of the Emotions,* Darwin had already observed that man's mouth moves unconsciously together with his hands. This is perfectly visible in children when they are learning to write, but it may also be observed in many other circumstances.

Maurice Grammont, possibly the most diligent scholar in the field of phonetics, says:

> Il y a des mots espressifs dans lesquels certains phonèmes prennent leur valeur dans les mouvements de physionomie que nécessite leur prononciation. Cette sorte de grimace qu'ils nous obligent à faire se confond parfois avec des jeux de physionomie muets dont la signification nous est connue par ailleurs, et cette signification se reporte par une traduction sur le phonème, qui a engendré ce mouvement du visage, si bien que nous pouvons interpréter ce son aussi aisément et aussi sûrement qu'un geste fait avec la main.[10]

German psychologists call the sounds that derive from the instinctive mimicry of the mouth "Lautgebärden"; these too may be considered to be onomatopoeia in a broad sense.

For example, the syllables "am-am" signifying to eat belong to this group because they imitate the gesture and movement of the mouth rather than the sound. It is from this oral gesture that the syllables "mum," "ham," and "am" derive, which (as Darwin had already observed) are commonly used in many languages to indicate food and the mouth. Similarly, the sounds "le-le-le" and "mu-lu" often recur to signify the tongue, and the sounds "puh-puh" to signify to blow.[11]

The stems of the words mother and father also probably derive from phonetic mimicry, and, as has often been observed, they are common to many languages of the most different families. For the concept of father the sounds "pa," "ap," "ta," "at," "ba," "fa" predominate, for mother the sounds "ma," "am, "na," "an."[12] In the case of the latter an association with the concept of eating may come into play, but the main reason for the universal diffusion of such interpretations is probably to be searched for in the fact that the sounds "ap-ap," "am-am," "at-at," etc., belong to the very first instinctive babblings of children, which are then emotionally interpreted by relatives and nurses.

A particular linguistic formation that broadly belongs to onomatopoeia are reduplications, in which an attempt is made to give pictographic expression to the length and rhythmic variation of natural sounds. Dogs do not go "bow," but "bow-wow!"; the wind does not go "o," but "ooooh!"; the clock does not go "tic," but "tic-toc," etc.

In this way not only are the impressions of duration expressed but also those of intensity and quantity. That this corresponds to the spirit of language is also obvious from such expressions as "a long, long time ago," "big big," "quickly quickly," and the like.[13]

The lengthening of vowels also lends words an emphatic accent expressing intensity and quantity: "a hu-u-u-ge fortune," "Sno-o-o-w everywhere,"
etc.

Like all pictographic elements, reduplications and sound lengthenings
also are of greater importance in the languages of the more primitive peoples, in which they are often used to form plurals. In the Mexican language,
for example, "siwatl" (woman) becomes "siwaa" in the plural; "teotl" (God)
becomes "teteooo"; in the language of the Mpongwe of West Africa "tyo"
means to jump, "tyo-tyo" to skip; "saza" to think, "saza-saza" to think and
rethink about something; in that of the Fijis "kaci" means to call, "kaci-kaci"
to call several times; "kere" to beg, "kere-kere" to go begging; etc.[14] In the
Southern dialect of the Guarani language the suffix of the present perfect
tense "yma" is pronounced more or less slowly according to whether we are
dealing with a past that is more or less remote. On this point Humboldt
rightly observed: such a way of signifying almost transcends linguistic use and
borders on mimicry.[15]

Not only do such elements abound in primitive language but also in children's language, in fondling, and in erotic childishness (Lolotte, Fifine, Jou-
Jou, etc.).

The various intonations and accentuations of the voice are of great expressive importance. As observed by Sievers,[16] we must distinguish, however,
between the universal characteristics of certain sentiments and the characteristics that predominate in given national languages.

In Germanic and Anglo-Saxon languages, a descending rhythm (trochaic
and dactylic) predominates while in Romance languages an ascending rhythm
(iambic and anapestic) predominates. In modern French, rhythmic accentuation is far less developed than in Italian, while tonal modulation is more developed. On the basis of these differences in rhythm and tone and with the
characteristic features of alphabetical pronunciation, we are able to recognize the foreigner who speaks our language.

In most current European languages (Italian, French, Spanish, English,
German) difference in tonality (high or low) only serves to give an emotional
coloring to the sentence; in others, such as ancient Greek and Sanskrit, or
Lithuanian and Serbian among the modern languages, almost every word has
its own tone. In such languages two words that are otherwise identical may
have different lexical meanings which are determined by the tone.[17]

In Chinese and Siamese one and the same syllable may have four different meanings depending on the tone with which it is pronounced or practically sung.[18]

As already mentioned, however, there exists a universal language of feeling which finds expression through the rhythm and inflections of the voice, a
language which seems to be intimately connected to our physiology. If we
watch the performance of a play in a language very distant from our own, we
are at times able to follow the action thanks precisely to such inflections.

The language of a man in a rage becomes a song, said Carlyle. Scholars of phonetics have worked hard at rendering with accents and musical annotations, and at recording with special instruments, the variations that the voice undergoes while prey to the various passions. In our opinion, it is a question of nuances which the art of the poet and of the actor is able to express, but which are hardly quantifiable by scientists. What counts is that the words of a single sentence do in fact change meaning according to the intonation with which they are pronounced. For example, the sentence: "He spoke to the Emperor" may be uttered as the simple admission of an objective fact, as a warning, as an eager inquiry, as an ironic question, and so forth. For a correct understanding, such pictographic elements may be just as important as the lexical elements.

It is a fact that variations in tone and inflection are of far greater importance in the most primitive[19] and the most ancient languages (or in the most ancient forms of any language). This also proves that the pictographic character predominated in the earliest forms of language.

The greater musicality of primitive languages noted by travellers and ethnologists has caused certain authors to believe that song preceded speech. On observing the analogy between the song of birds and certain modulated trills ("yodels") of the Tyrolese inhabitants of the Alps, Jaeger remarks that, when sexually excited, both animal and man give out groans and calls that become a song of attraction and of invitation to the individual of the other sex.[20] That this must have been an important starting point for language is also shown by the simultaneous development of the vocal and sexual organs.

Birds sing and emit their calls only after they have reached sexual maturity, and the human voice also changes in tone at puberty.

However, we do not have sufficient evidence to assert that human beings sang first and spoke later. The fact that children first develop the capacity to emit articulated sounds and to repeat the words they hear in their own way and only much later develop a musical sense favors the opposite thesis. It seems likely that, originally, there was the same lack of distinction between word and song as there was between painting and early pictographic writing systems.

If we extend the concepts of onomatopoeia and interjection to include the rhythmic chants with which man accompanies his work, figurative and symbolic onomatopoeia, sounds deriving from oral mimicry, reduplications, and finally anything that may be directly expressive in vocal emissions, that is, intensity, rhythm and tonal modulation, what we have is a truly remarkable system of pictographic elements in human language. All these elements predominate in the languages of primitive peoples and doubtlessly must have been important in the formation of early linguistic roots.

Nonetheless, if we ask ourselves whether it is possible to base a scientifically founded hypothesis on the origin of language on such data, we cannot answer in the affirmative.

If we are convinced that language (like all other semiological systems which arose spontaneously through collective cooperation) must have gone through a pictographic stage, we will also have to admit that, in that initial stage, directly expressive devices must have satisfied the most common necessities of communication for a long period of time, constituting the basis for the incipient intuitive and logical faculties of man, faculties indispensable to subsequent spiritual development. Now, it is a fact that phonetic imitation, understood also in an extremely broad sense, cannot on its own serve even the most elementary necessities of social life.

It is not difficult to find actors who are very skillful in imitating not only animal sounds but also a number of such noises as those produced by the rain, the wind, trains, etc., and the sounds characteristically produced by the various types of artisans. But if, as an experiment, we invite one of these actors to convey one of Aesop's fables or some other very simple tale or newsworthy event solely through the imitation of sounds, we will soon discover its inadequacy.[21]

It is a fact that from Plato's time through to the contemporary era several attempts have been made to explain language origin on the basis of interjections and onomatopoeia (explanations that Max Müller satirized, calling them the "ahi-ahi!" and "bow-wow!" theories), though all serious and competent scholars have recognized their insufficiency.

If it were not possible to single out some other more effective pictographic element which, together with physiological and imitative utterances, may have satisfied the initial need for communication, we would have to conclude that, in the light of present knowledge, the problem of language origin cannot be adequately solved, and that those scholars who are dissatisfied with vague suppositions and declare the problem unsolvable are right.

But this is not the way things are. Man possesses, and has always possessed, a very efficient means of direct expression through which even the most complex communications may be transmitted, without any aid from convention. We are alluding to mimetic language which has been mentioned here and there in the preceding pages, and to which our inquiry will now turn.

3. Mimetic Language

Origins and Characteristics

The Two Origins of Mimetic Language—Mimetic Tropes—Spontaneity of Mimetic Pictography—Its Universal Comprehensibility.

Mimetic expression is so closely related to language that a single sentence may completely change its meaning according to the mimicry accompanying it: a declaration of love accompanied by a farcical gesture becomes a joke.

Owing to its immediately expressive character, mimicry is universally comprehensible and does not call for specific instruction: "Say *rascal!* to a dog, to a child who does not know how to speak, or to a foreigner, accompany the word with a benevolent smile and all three will interpret it as an expression of friendliness. Say *dearest!* instead with a threatening gesture and they will consider it an insult."[1]

Mimetic expression has two sources: the instinctive physiological reaction of a conscious subject, and the indication or imitation of external objects or movements; in phonetic expression, interjections correspond to the former, onomatopoeia to the latter.

At times it is easy to recognize the biological function of certain imitative reactions, e.g., sighing, fist-clenching, teeth-grinding, screwing up one's eyes to see better, gasping for breath, etc.; at other times the biological motivation escapes us. Nevertheless when we see those manifestations, we usually understand the feeling which has provoked them and can then use them as a *sign* of that feeling.

The expressive capacity of mimicry is increased and strengthened by association with analogous feelings. For example: we raise our upper lip and wrinkle our nose not only to defend ourselves from a bad smell, but also to express disgust or contempt.[2] Different flavors, sweet, bitter, sour, etc., seem to act on specific areas of the palate and tongue, consequently provoking particular expressions of the mouth and face. The mimicry of these physical sensations are then also reflected when mimicking feelings. Just as we are able to speak of a sweet hope, a bitter decision, a sour character, we are also able to observe the same associations in the field of mimicry.

Each of us will easily recall examples of mimetic metaphors. For example, that of the peoples of the Upper Nile, reported by Petterick, who would rub their bellies when they saw trinkets that appeared very desirable to them, or that of certain Australians, observed by Leichhardt, who would open and close their mouths as though savoring something good whenever they saw handsome racehorses.

The variety and shades of feeling that can be conveyed through facial expressions and body postures has often been commented on.[3]

The extent to which the imitative gesture is natural is highlighted by the fact that anyone of us may fail to remember the name of something and signify it with a gesture. For certain concepts mimetic expression comes more naturally to us than speech. If, for example, you ask a certain number of people to explain exactly what a "spiral staircase" is, nine out of ten will probably outline an ascending spiral with their finger while searching for the right words.

As specialists have observed, an atavistic tendency to create and use mimetic signs seems to emerge clearly among deaf-mutes. The latter are able to use the first sign system that happens to be offered to them with surprising quickness, and when they do not find it readily available, they create it spontaneously.[4]

Vuillemey tells the story of a rather spoiled eight-year-old deaf-mute living in a family without previous experience in dealing with other deaf-mutes. Once, on being scolded by his mother, this eight-year-old child flew into a rage, grabbed a stick, and simulated going into a battle. Using the stick as though it were a gun, he leaned it against his cheek, aimed, and pretended to shoot. Finally, he made the gesture of being hit, threw himself to the ground and remained there still and stiff for some time.

A teacher with experience in dealing with deaf-mutes interpreted the meaning of this little scene as follows: "Since they treat me badly at home, I want to become a soldier, fight in a battle and get killed."[5] Whoever recalls primitive picture-writing, which is something between the aesthetic representation of a sentiment and the communication of a fact, will recognize in that scene all the characteristics of mimetic pictography.

Mime shows were very fashionable among the ancients, who appreciated their universal comprehensibility. Macrobius narrates that the mime Roscius challenged Cicero as to who could express himself best, whether he through mime or Cicero through speech. Lucian, in his treatise on dance recalls an Oriental king who, after seeing the performances of a pantomimist at Nero's court, asked for the pantomimist as a gift in order to use him as an interpreter in his dealings with Asiatic countries with which he could not trade because of language barriers. Similarly, in his *Institutiones oratoriae*, Quintilian calls mimicry "omnium hominum communis sermo."[6]

It is a fact that, owing to the predominance of pictographic elements over conventional elements, mimetic language is more immediately comprehensible than spoken language with respect to writing. The deaf-mutes of various countries generally understand each other after a very short time even though some of the signs they use are different.[7] They have often proven to be capable of understanding even the mimicry of certain primitive peoples.[8]

Concluding Hypothesis

Human Language Must Have Originally Been a Mimetic Language Accompanied by Emotional Cries.

We have already stated that pictographic elements must have originally predominated in human language, and that the conventional value of single words can only be the result of gradual development. Consequently we asked ourselves the following question: "What are the pictographic elements of language?"

We then traced these elements in emotional and imitative calls, intonation patterns, rhythm, inflections of the voice, etc., but we were forced to acknowledge that, on their own, such phonetic expressions were inadequate for even the most basic necessities of communication. Nonetheless, we have just seen that with mimicry man possesses a very effective way of intuitively expressing his feelings and representations, and which may sufficiently cater for all the needs of a primitive human society.

We may therefore set forth the following concluding hypothesis for the first part of our work: "Human language was originally immediately intuitive in character and, therefore, it must have been mimetic language accompanied by emotional and imitative calls."

We saw that in the evolution of writing, and generally of all expressive sign systems which have arisen naturally, two periods may be identified: an initial period in which the pictographic element predominates and another in which the conventional element eventually predominates. Now then, if we examine phonetic language, and especially literary language (even that preserved in the most ancient literary monuments such as the Veda, the Bible, and Homeric poems), we will discover that the initial evolutionary stage is almost completely lacking. If, however, we consider mimetic language, we will be obliged to observe the opposite, that is, that it seems to have stopped at the first stage, the stage in which the immediate element predominates.

In our opinion, the most plausible explanation of these two facts is obtained by accepting the hypothesis that primitive language was an indistinct union of gestures and sounds (both arising from the same source, i.e., from physiological automatism and imitative instinct), and that initially mimetic expression prevailed accompanied by a few spontaneous shouts (*clamor concomitans*), though subsequently phonetic expression prevailed, by then stylized into conventional forms, with gesture as an accompaniment. This would allow us to identify the two degrees of development that characterize all spontaneous semiological systems in the evolution of human spoken language as well.

It is now a matter of seeing whether the facts confirm our hypothesis in order to see if it is scientifically founded: that is, is it a theory which, though it cannot be verified on an experimental basis, is able to organize and explain fairly well all linguistic and semantic phenomena so far known.

Infant Language

Languages Invented by Children—The Child's Attention Falls on Visual Signs Earlier Than Auditive Signs—Gestures Are More Comprehensible Than Words.

The crucial experiment or instance for the explanation of the birth of language might be, according to a legend reported by Herodotus, the one done by Psammeticus, king of Pittus, who entrusted two newborn babies to a shepherd with an order to keep them away from all human contact, to take care not to pronounce a single word in their presence, and then to report the first word they pronounced.[1]

If a similar experiment could be conducted, it would certainly give us a few clues as to the larger or smaller presence of mimetic or phonetic elements in a language arising outside of all tradition. However, this experiment could only involve children born in our own times and whose physiology and brain development is, therefore, already hereditarily predisposed. Consequently, it would not provide absolute proof of the passage which took place in the obscurity of prehistory from *homo alalus* to *homo loquens*.

In any case, what counts most in scientific observation are not the facts in themselves, independent of the observer (about which no one could ever tell us anything), but the facts as they are observed by someone. If by chance a philologist should find himself in the position of observing children who have grown up on an island isolated from the rest of the world, and who have spontaneously created a language of mimicking gestures, accompanied by a few semi-articulate cries, and if the observer should take as his starting point the presupposition (shared by many philologists) that only phonetic language exists, he could then report that those children emitted emotional cries but did not know how to speak. Let it not be said that we are talking about an unintelligent observer, for something similar actually happened to Jespersen, a highly competent glottologist.

He describes the case of a young girl, born at the beginning of the last century on a farm in northern Iceland, who spoke to her twin brother in a language incomprehensible to others. Her brother died and her relatives tried in vain to teach her Icelandic. In order to make themselves understood, they had to learn the new language which was based on unrecognizably modified Icelandic words. The word sounds and grammatical constructions were completely different from Icelandic.

"The vocabulary was so poor," says Jespersen, "that the girl had to continually complete her sentences with hand gestures and facial expression, so that it was difficult to converse with her in the dark."[2]

The author, who did in fact make the problem of the origin of language the specific object of his study, did not realize what a precious clue could have been obtained by examining more closely this spontaneous substitution of spoken language with mimetic language.[3]

In 1903 Jespersen was again able to study personally another interesting case. It concerned twins who, having lived in isolation with an old deaf woman, spoke a language which they had invented. Here, too, the author examines words and sentences and fails to take the mimetic element into account. That mimetic expression played its part in this case, as well, can perhaps be inferred from the fact that the syntax of the sentences quoted by Jespersen has nothing in common with Danish syntax, while, on the contrary, it is surprisingly similar to the syntax of mimetic language.[4]

Since we are not able to repeat the experiment by Psammeticus, we will have to limit ourselves to searching for enlightenment in the daily language of children living around us, basing our observations on the well-known principle that there is usually some correspondence between the evolution of the species and that of the individual.

Mallery rightly observed that the desires and impressions of the child in his first and second year of life are expressed in very few words, but with a great variety of gestures and facial mimicry. The child's gestures are an intelligent medium of communication long before he speaks, even though everyone around him tries to teach him words and no one instructs him in gestures. From the time that he begins "risu cognoscere matrem" and for a long time after becoming familiar with words, the child consults the gestures and mimicking expressions of his parents and nurse, as though he were trying to translate and explain the words he does not yet know with the aid of a language which is more natural to him.[5]

Herder, also, stated that: "Children—like savage peoples, children of nature—are natural mimes, they imitate all that is related to them with the maximum vivacity, and with mimicry, dances, games, tricks, and discourse they reveal their peculiar mentality".[6]

In *Ideen zur Geschichte der Menschheit*, he had also remarked that "there is in man, and even in the monkey, a strange imitative instinct which does not seem to be the consequence of rational reflection, but the immediate testimony of an organic inclination."[7]

Already in the early months of life the child, who does not yet have a sense of distance, moves his hands even toward distant objects or stretches out his arms to be lifted up. His imitation of other people's gestures is at first purely mechanical, like that of certain little monkeys, but his understanding of mimetic expressions is extremely precocious. He instinctively makes facial expressions analogous to those of the person speaking to him and thus perceives, through physiological inclination, feelings of anger, fear, pain, joy, etc.[8]

It has often been observed that in all languages infant language abounds in labials and dentals (ma-ma, da-da, poo-poo, etc.), that is, in those articulate sounds that derive from the most obviously visible movements. Children who are born blind, thus lacking this visual aid, start talking later than the others.[9] This fact also shows that the child's attention is more easily fixed on the expressive signs which strike one's sight more than on those which strike the hearing.

The language of children, not only in the first years of life but also much later, is full of immediately expressive elements; it is interspersed with incredible interjections and onomatopoeia, with gesticulations and very lively movements of the whole body. For this reason the comic strip pictography ingeniously invented by Walt Disney exerts on children the attraction of an art akin to their own primitive psychology.

Passing on to a sadder field of observation we might remark that the alienated and the degenerate, who through an atavistic reversion sometimes reflect the conditions of prehuman life, not only abound in gesticulation but understand gestures and obey them even when they are incapable of understanding words; and furthermore, that semi-idiot children, who are incapable of learning more than the initial rudiments of language, understand gestures and use them better than words.[10] But let us leave such questions, which go beyond our own competence, to the specialists.

Mimicry among the Ancients

Gesticulation among the Common People Is a Residue of More Lively Ancient Gesticulation—In Greek Theater the More We Go Back in Time the More Mimicry Prevails Over Words—In Magic Practices Gestures Are Used as an Archaic Language.

Mimicry among the ancients was studied in detail by Andrea De Iorio and more recently by Karl Sittl.[1] Many gestures still common today among the people of Southern Italy were already in use among the ancient Romans. Their gesticulating was more vivacious than that of modern Europeans as emerges from their interest in pantomime and from the value, documented by Quintilian, attributed to gesticulation in their discourses.[2] In Wundt's opinion gestures used today by the lower classes are only residues of the more vivacious accompaniment of phonetic language characterizing ancient speech.[3]

As Condillac had already observed, in many episodes of the Bible, spoken language and "action language" merge into a single expression.

For example, in order to convince the kings of Judah and Israel that the hour had come to attack and conquer Syria, the prophet Zedeki'ah applied horns of iron to his forehead and armed in this way appeared before the throne, saying: "Thus says the Lord, 'With these you shall push the Syrians until they are destroyed' " (I Kings 22:11).

In Jeremiah 13:1 ff. we find a similar form of expression:

> Thus said the Lord to me, "Go and buy a linen waistcloth, and put it on your loins [. . .] go to the Euphra'tes, and hide it there in a cleft of the rock" [. . .]. And after many days the Lord said to me, "Arise, go to the Euphra'tes, and take from there the waistcloth which I commanded you to hide there." Then I went to the Euphra'tes, and dug, and I took the waistcloth from the place where I had hidden it. And behold, the waistcloth was spoiled; it was good for nothing.
>
> Then the word of the Lord came to me: "Thus says the Lord: Even so I will spoil the pride of Judah and the great pride of Jerusalem. This evil people, who refuse to hear My words, who stubbornly follow their own heart and have gone after other gods to serve them and worship them, shall be like this waistcloth, which is good for nothing. For as the waistcloth clings to the loins of a man, so I made the whole house of Israel and the whole house of Judah cling to Me, says the Lord, that they might be for Me a people, a name, a praise, and a glory, but they would not listen."

Again: The prophet Ezekiel takes a clay brick and impresses on it the map of Jerusalem with its walls and its counterforts, he designs enemy camps with battering rams around the city, he places an iron plate like a wall around the city, and he wanders about the streets calling out: "This is a sign for the house of Israel" (Ezekiel 4:1 ff).

The same Ezekiel then lies down on his left side and loads weights upon himself which symbolize the iniquity of Israel. Then he turns on to his right side loading other weights upon himself which symbolize the iniquity of Judah. And facing the clay brick on which he had drawn the city of Jerusalem, with his arms outstretched, he cries: "And, behold, I will put cords upon you, so that you cannot turn from one side to the other, till you have completed the days of your siege." He then takes some dark flour made of barley, lentils, and vetch, he bakes some bread with it in the ashes and covers it in cow dung. He remains lying down for many days nourishing himself with that bread and prophesying in a great loud voice: "Son of man, behold, I will break the staff of bread in Jerusalem; they shall eat bread by weight and with fearfulness; and they shall drink water by measure and in dismay."

Then he shaves his head and his beard and weighs the hair on a scale, dividing it into three parts. A third he burns in the fire in the midst of the city, a third he strikes with the sword and spreads throughout the city and a third part he scatters to the wind, prophesying against Jerusalem: "A third part of you shall die of pestilence and be consumed with famine in the midst of you; a third part shall fall by the sword round about you; and a third part I will scatter to all the winds and will unsheathe the sword after them."

In chapter 12 Ezekiel attracts the attention of the people by preparing for himself an exile's baggage; he carries all his furniture out of his house and, in the evening, in front of all the citizens, he digs a hole in the walls of the house and goes out through it onto the road. He then lifts his baggage upon his shoulders and covers his face, so that he may not see anything more. When the citizens ask him: "What are you doing?" he replies: "I am a sign for you: as I have done, so shall it be done to them; they shall go into exile, into captivity. And the prince who is among them shall lift his baggage upon his shoulder in the dark, and shall go forth; he shall dig through the wall and go out through it; he shall cover his face, that he may not see the land with his eyes."

Elsewhere Jeremiah gets himself an earthen flask and together with some of the elders of the people and some of the senior priests he goes out to the gates of the city proclaiming: "Hear the word of the Lord, O kings of Judah and inhabitants of Jerusalem. Thus says the Lord of hosts, the God of Israel, Behold, . . ." And in front of the crowd which has gathered around him, he throws the vessel against the stones, saying: "Thus says the Lord of hosts: So will I break this people and this city, as one breaks a potter's vessel, so that it can never be mended" (Jeremiah 19:1–14).

In chapter 28, Jeremiah wears yokes on his neck and the false prophet Hanani'ah throws himself upon him and breaks them. Some time after, the Lord inspires Jeremiah to say the following to Hanani'ah: "Thus says the Lord: You have broken wooden bars, but I will make in their place bars of iron. For thus says the Lord of hosts, the God of Israel: I have put upon the neck of all these nations an iron yoke of servitude to Nebuchadnez'zar king of Babylon, and they shall serve him, for I have given to him even the beasts of the field" (Jeremiah 28:13–14).

In chapter 51, verses 59–64, the ambassador Serai'ah goes to Babylon, on instructions from Jeremiah, taking with him a parchment manuscript with the description of the defeat and destruction of that kingdom. After having read it, he is instructed to bind it to a stone and throw it into the midst of the Euphra'tes, saying: "Thus shall Babylon sink, to rise no more, because of the evil that I am bringing upon her."

The same may be said of the gestures used among certain Oriental peoples, tenacious preservers of ancient customs. In Arabian schools, for example, gestures were studied as an integral part of discourse, and the philologist Al-Gáhiz (869 A.D.) dealt with mimetic language as one of the four principle ways of expressing thought.[4] The Arabs say "to gesticulate" with the expression "to speak with one's fingers" just as the Greeks used to say χερσί λαλεῖν and the Latins boasted of their "loquacissimae manus" and of the "linguosi digiti" of their pantomimists.[5] Finally, the fact that the Latin "dicere" and "digitus" like the Greek δείκνυμι have the same root might also be significant.[6]

In classical drama the word prevails over gesture, in the most ancient mime plays dialogue and mimetic action balance each other, but in primitive religious plays, from which Greek theater originated, mimetic action prevails by far over the word. If the evolution of language corresponds to that of stage performances this would be confirmation of our hypothesis.[7]

Further confirmation comes from the epithet "winged" (πτερόεντα) that Homer gives to words which, according to D'Ovidio, continue to evoke the impression made on ancient man who was struck by the fact that the voice, unlike gesture, is not accompanied by any great effort or movement, but reaches its destination by simply travelling through the air.[8]

Dance, which is related to gesture as song is to the word, also has a sacred origin. It was thought that the movements of imitative magic would favor an abundant harvest, hunting, and victory over the enemy. These magic dances may be defined as a kind of prayer and invocation without words.

Even in the more advanced religions, which have a history of evolution of thousands of years behind them, the "action language" of the liturgy is at least as important as oral prayer. However, in magical practices which go back to the dawn of civilization, and in those still in use today among primitive peoples, the imitative element prevails over the spoken formula.

In initiation practices the neophyte is sometimes obliged to express himself solely through gestures, and we might say that, just as in the rites of present-day religions we very often turn to an archaic language, in the magical practices of primitive man mimetic expression is used as though it were the archaic language of the human species.[9]

Importance of Primitive Mimicry Confirmed by the Most Ancient Graphic Signs

Ancient Chinese Ideograms Are Often Reproductions of Expressive Gestures—The Same Is True of Egyptian Hieroglyphs—Not to Mention the Writing of Certain Primitive Peoples—Influence of Gestures in Primitive Numbering Systems.

A few precious clues concerning the gesticulation used by our forefathers are offered by the history of writing. Historians and ethnologists agree that references to an antecedent mimetic language are continually to be found in hieroglyphs and in pictographic designs. They have collected an impressive quantity of data concerning such very different peoples and countries as

China, Syria, Egypt, the Eskimos, and the natives of Oceania, African peoples and the Indians of North America. Given that in most cases the hypothesis of reciprocal influence may be excluded, we must ask ourselves what the common cause was behind such a general phenomenon.

In one of his dissertations written in French,[1] the Chinese philologist Tciang-Tceng-Ming divides the primitive history of Chinese writing into four periods. He maintains that the first three periods derive wholly from the language of gestures, and that the major part of the most ancient morphograms are not direct reproductions of natural objects, but schematic reproductions of descriptive manual gestures. Indeed, many of those signs are not comprehensible if we do not keep in mind that ideally they need to be completed with a movement, for they do not refer to a static gesture but to a movement of the fingers or the hand.[2]

The sign ∕ , for example, means to advance or to retreat. At first glance we cannot see why a simple little stroke should have this meaning, but it is self-explanatory when we consider that it represents a finger which in mimetic language is moved in a given direction to indicate a forward movement and in the opposite direction to indicate retreat.

The signs ⁄ ➘ or ⁍ ⁋ , which mean to divide, are clear if we remember that they refer to the gesture of a finger as it cuts through the air moving first to the left and then to the right. The sign Γ , which means to pull, is the reproduction of a gesture made by hooking the index finger and moving it as though pulling an object towards oneself.[3] The Ⓒ , which is pronounced "hwee" and means to return, recalls a spiral moving from right to left outlined in the air with the finger, a gesture that still today means to go back on one's steps. The sign ∂Ɛ which is pronounced "fei" means "backwards" and refers to a gesture made by curving the hands and placing them back to back. The sign ⅄Ⴤ which means "yu," i.e., friend and friendship, represents two hands held out amicably. The sign ꜞoꜞ means "cün" (prince) and is the graphic stylization of a gesture of submission and greeting, made by raising one's two hands above one's head.[4]

Furthermore, we could quote certain archaic ideograms designating animals which, more than the animal itself, seem to picture a man imitating a given animal. Similar observations may be made in reference to Egyptian hieroglyphs. We will limit ourselves to remembering the sign ɤ̣ meaning to invoke and to call, ɤ̓ which means high and to exult, ⅍ meaning me (a hand is used to point to one's own chest), ȹ meaning to eat, to drink, to talk, and to think. (Note that it would be difficult to find a common origin for those four words in a spoken language, while in mimetic language the gesture is the same for the first three concepts, and for the fourth, to think, the gesture must have been only slightly different, that is, with the hand going to the forehead, instead of to the mouth). The sign ⌣ʋ means to give, and ⳡ', which reproduces the gesture of someone pretending to carry a heavy load with raised hands, signifies a big quantity.[5] Information collected by the ethnologists enable us to make similar observations about primitive peoples. The Sioux and Ojibways Indians, studied by Tomkins, not only have a very well-developed gestural language, but also a hieroglyphic writing system which often reproduces those same gestures.

Let us consider the following examples:

Figure 23 means to come and reproduces a "calling back" gesture which we too use; figure 24 means hunger and reproduces a gesture made by hitting oneself on the stomach with the hand side-on (an analogous gesture, obtained by hitting one's hand on the hip, is also used in Italy). Figure 25, which means peace, symbolizes two hands drawing near as in greeting or in making a pact.

To signify "day" in mimetic language the Indians trace out a semicircle with the thumb and index joined so as to form a small circle (this represents the route followed by the sun) and to signify the concept graphically the ideogram in figure 26 is used. The sign $\times$ of figure 27 means barter or commerce and corresponds to a gesture with the same meaning made by making a cross with the two forefingers.[6] Figure 28 means "under" and reproduces the gesture made by quickly bringing the back of one hand under the palm of the other.

The correspondence between graphic signs and mimetic language is still more evident among the Eskimos, whose pictographs are often composed of human figures that mime the concepts to be communicated.[7] Even without further examples, it would seem possible to conclude that the frequent reference of primitive graphic signs to mimetic language (of which there are also traces in prehistoric petroglyphs) could reasonably lead us to the conclusion that at the dawn of civilization gestural language was widespread and perhaps equal in importance or even more important than phonetic language. This is also confirmed by primitive numbering systems. That it was common to signify numbers with the fingers is made evident, among other things, by the diffusion of the decimal, quinary, and vigesimal systems. The quinary system is based on the fingers of a hand and the vigesimal system on both the fingers and toes.[8]

In various primitive languages numbers are designated with the names of those parts of the human or animal body referred to by the mimetic language: for example, "eyes" means two, "hand" stands for five, "ostrich foot" means four, etc. Even the sign V, common to the Romans, Sabellians, and Etruscans is the graphic imitation of a gesture made with the open hand.

Primitive numerical mimicry was continued and systematically developed in the *system of finger counting,* already known to the Egyptians, Hebrews, and Persians and preserved for us by medieval writers.[9] With this system it was possible to signify even the highest numbers by bending the joints appropriately.

A few numbers not commonly used among certain primitive peoples (e.g., the Bacairi, the Abiponi, the Tasmanians, etc.) do not have a corre-

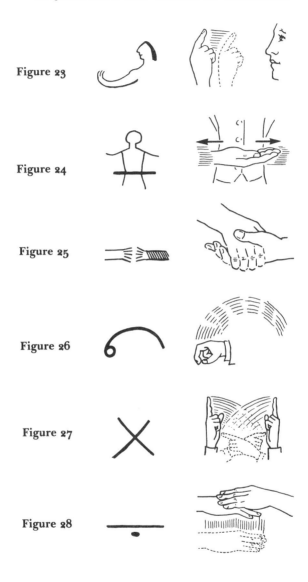

Figure 23

Figure 24

Figure 25

Figure 26

Figure 27

Figure 28

sponding name but are indicated with gestures. This would appear to be a survival of an earlier mimetic language.[10] Some ethnologists (such as M. Müller) speak of tribes completely devoid of words to indicate numbers, but Wundt rightly observes that we cannot easily acknowledge the absolute lack of numbers in a language, however primitive, and that probably in the tribes in question numbers were indicated with gestures: a hypothesis confirmed by subsequent research. This is yet another example of the erroneous conclusions formulated as a result of disregarding mimetic language.

Gestures in the Language
of Ancient Egyptians

Owing to the Great Number of Synonyms and
Homonyms, Hieroglyphs Could Not Be Deciphered
without Explanatory Figures that Accompany
Them—In the Same Way Spoken Language Would
Have Been Unintelligible without Its Completion
with Gestures—It Seems that Ancient Chinese Was
Also a Mixture of Mimicry and Phonetics.

According to Carl Abel,[1] documents concerning Egyptian language and writing prove that the language used by the Egyptians, at the beginning of their civilization, was not purely phonetic, but rather a mixture of which the mimetic element was a necessary component.

He observes that the study of Egyptian is particularly fruitful, for it is possible to follow its evolution from the most ancient documents, which go back to about four thousand years before Christ, to the documents of Coptic literature[2] which reach 1000 A.D. It would seem that the inherent rationality of all expressive sign systems requires a one-to-one correspondence between sign and meaning; in other words, there should never be a sign with multiple meanings nor multiple signs for the same meaning. But it is only natural that anything in the process of development should overcome an initial period full of imperfections; and languages were initially extremely imperfect semiological systems. In particular the archaic Egyptian language, in Abel's opinion, is so full of homonyms and synonyms that it seems unintelligible. For example, about thirty different words (almost all of which were used in the same epoch and in the same region) signify "to cut," and the word "net' " can mean: green, plant, container, a kind of stone, sacrificial flat bread, water for the eyes, to offend, etc., and because such semantic polyvalency occurs for almost all concepts, we immediately wonder how the Egyptians ever managed to understand each other in a similar language.

Indeed, hieroglyphic writing systems would have been unintelligible to their users, and indecipherable for us, without the running commentary provided by the explanatory figures used by the Egyptians to accompany their phonetic signs.

Every word in hieroglyphic texts (except certain grammatical terms which were comprehensible in themselves) was first written phonetically and then illustrated with a determinative sign, that is, with a small figure that specifies the meaning of the word, by indicating the conceptual class to which the designated object belongs. For example, "tebh" means grain, but it may also signify utensil, to pray, to close, an offer, useful, container, etc. A small plant drawn next to it indicates that, from its many meanings, the one indicating a vegetable is to be chosen. "Ap-t" signifies fish, but because the same word also means bread, vase, measure of grain, stick, part of a ship, garland, etc., a small drawing of an animal is added to indicate the class to which that concept belongs.

Moreover, the Egyptian language is rich in small words capable of signifying two opposite concepts, such as: with/without, always/never, strong/weak, ascend/descend, everybody/nobody, scream/keep silent, big/small, long/narrow, old/young, light/dark, hot/cold, etc.

Many examples of these strange antithetical homonyms are to be found in Chinese, Arabic, and other languages. The Italian word "mai-sempre" (never-always) (to signify always), the English "without," and the East Prussian word "mitohne" (for without) are perhaps the remains of an ancient custom.

In these cases, and in Egyptian writing, meaning is specified by the addition of a small determinative figure. For example, the phonetic sign ⟨glyph⟩ (pronounced "qen") signifies both "strong" and "weak." For the first meaning it is followed by the figure of a man standing up straight and holding a stick ⟨glyph⟩; for the second by a man reclining on the ground with lowered arms ⟨glyph⟩.

It is interesting to note that in the language of the Copts, used thousands of years later, most of the homonyms disappeared. Of the synonyms, some were eliminated and others were preserved to indicate the various signifying nuances of a single concept. In this way the semiological rationality of language came to prevail over the primitive lack of distinctions.

It is clear, says the author, that if the language spoken by the ancient Egyptians had had the more or less univocal form of the languages of today's civilized populations, the continual use of those small, explanatory figures would not have been necessary. In fact, they are neither a simple decorative embellishment, nor an archaic habit preserved out of respect for tradition, but rather they represent a necessary completion for comprehension of the text.

At this stage the following question arises: given the semiological imprecision of their phonetic language, how did the ancient Egyptians manage to understand each other? How was comprehension possible if the same word meant strength and weakness, high and low, to scream and to keep silence, etc.? The author identifies the solution in the fact that words were constantly accompanied by traditional gestures. Indeed, it would seem that the little explanatory figures used in writing were no more than a sort of graphic transcription of those gestures. The ancient language of the Egyptians was probably an indissoluble union of gesture and word, and this might be considered as a characteristic compromise between previous mimetic language and subsequent phonetic language.

Abel's considerations are persuasive both because they seem to be reasonable themselves, and because they fit in well with a set of arguments and observations (which we are now in the course of expounding) that confirm the same thesis examined from different points of view. But we lack the competence to be able to give an expert opinion on the subject.

In any case we must complete these observations concerning Egyptian language and writing by comparing them to analogous episodes occurring in other countries and especially in China. In the Chinese language, as in languages of the monosyllabic type in general, we find a very high number of homonyms;[3] in Chinese writing, just as in Egyptian writing, classificatory determinative signs are currently used, without which the written language would be incomprehensible.

Because a direct influence between the two civilizations can be reasonably excluded, the obvious analogy between the development of the two countries' semiological systems strongly suggests a common natural cause. That this cause was, as Abel believes, the mystic, phonetic-mimetic character of the languages in question seems to be confirmed for China by the observations of the Chinese philologist Tciang-Tceng-Ming reported above.

Moreover, it would be interesting to compare these ancient languages which we believe were mimetic-phonetic with one accessible to our observation, that is, to the language of the semi-educated deaf-mutes, who generally communicate through a mixture of gestures and words. Indeed, deaf-mutes often use the same term for antithetical meanings, a phenomenon that Abel found occurring in the Egyptian language, in the Arabic language, etc. For example, one of these deaf-mutes would say: "The police obeys that . . . ," "The director obeys you to give me chocolate," and would accompany the sentence with command mimicry.[4] Another would use the word hot to signify both hot and cold, accompanying the word with the gesture of blowing on his fingertips; but for "hot" he would blow strongly, as though to cool off something that was scorching hot, and for "cold" he would breathe on them lightly as though he were warming his fingers with his breath. A similar lack of distinction could be mentioned for backwards and forewards, today and tomorrow, over and under, etc.

Homonymy among opposite concepts is not only determined, as one might think, by confusion between concepts, but also by the characteristic globality of all pictographic expressions. Opposites are indeed terms belonging to the same relation, and picture writing almost always conveys an overall meaning without separating it into its component parts. The meaning of both "to ascend" and "to descend" is conveyed by drawing a ladder. This characteristic globality and lack of analysis will also be confirmed by a more detailed study of the syntactic construction of mimetic language.

The Syntactic Characteristics
of Mimetic Language

Prevalence of the Pictographic Element over the
Conventional Element—Fluidity and Looseness of
Signs—Globality of Expression—Prevalence of Lexi-
con over Grammar—Lack of Distinction between
Noun and Verb—Lack of Distinction between
Noun, Adjective, and Adverb—Ambiguity and Poly-
valency—Importance of Word Arrangement—Lack
of Distinction between Interrogative Particles—Ab-
sence of the Passive Form—Absence of Subordinate
Clauses—Frequency of Reduplications—Formation
of Comparatives and Superlatives—Past and Future
Expressed through Adverbs—Specification through
Circumlocutions.

Glottologists have frequently observed that immigrant peoples sometimes
preserve the syntax of their native language for many generations, even after
they become accustomed to using the language of their new country. Syntax,
which is more closely connected to a given *forma mentis,* is far more tenacious
than lexicon.

Now, it is a fact that mimetic language has certain syntactic characteristics which reflect a particular mentality, and which are the same all over the
world. If the thesis we support has any truth in it, that is, if mimetic-
onomatopoeic language is the mother tongue of the human race, it may be
possible to find traces of such syntactic characteristics in the languages of the
ancients as well as among present-day primitive civilizations known for the tenacity with which they have preserved their traditions throughout the centuries.

As we have not discovered any specialized text in which the forms peculiar to mimetic language are specifically presented and studied, we must be
content with a few observations gathered by various authors, especially those
observations concerning deaf-mutes. The most instructive ones are those
made in relation to the spoken language of semi-educated deaf-mutes, in
which the *forma mentis* and, therefore, the construction of mimetic language
is initially maintained. We will now enumerate the main characteristics of the
latter:

The most important feature of mimetic language from which almost all
the others derive, is the absolute predominance of the pictographic element
over the conventional element. This is a natural feature of all primitive semiological systems, whether we are dealing with graphic or phonetic-mimetic
signs.

This leads to the fluidity and looseness of mimetic signs, which are not
fixed once and for all, but may be invented as they are needed. For example,

to signify "horse" one person will make the gesture of pulling the reins, another will open his legs wide and curve them, a third will place two right-hand fingers on the saddle of the left-hand index finger, and others will concentrate on still other aspects of the animal's body or movements.

For the same reason signs invented in certain circumstances can end up being unintelligible in others. For instance, a deaf-mute from the Paris Institute said: "He came to visit us gymnastic evening," where the word "gymnastic" stood for "Saturday," the day when there was a gym lesson which the students indicated by imitating the exercises.

In a painting, expression has its own synthetic unity so that it would be artificial to separate the parts and use them for a different painting. As we have seen, in picture writing analysis of such unity begins to emerge and conventional signs already start making their appearance. In hieroglyphic writing systems the process of analysis continues, discourse is articulated into its parts, and the conventionality of signs imposes itself more and more.

Mimetic language is predominantly pictographic and synthetic, but here too the same process of analysis is increasingly accentuated.

In the language of semi-educated deaf-mutes, just as in children's speech, words which signify a whole sentence are common. The word "more" accompanied by a particular facial expression, can signify: "I've eaten everything," "there's no more left," "I'm sorry," and "I'd like to have some more." Or: "I'm full," "that's enough for me," and "I don't want any more!"[1]

"Hand" can signify: "Please help me by giving me your hand," or "I've hurt my hand, medicate it for me," etc.

In every semiological system we may distinguish between the *content*, that is, signs as such, and the *form,* which concerns the rules according to which signs may be modified so as to acquire new meanings, and rules that unite these signs systematically.

In the most primitive systems content alone prevails. For example, primitive numeration consisted of a simple juxtaposition of tallies, while the Roman and so-called Arabic numbering systems became more and more systematic.

In mimetic language regularity is scarce, just as what the Chinese call "empty words" (a, of, that, among) are rare and mostly implied.

Discourse is often reduced to a mere juxtaposition of concepts.[2]

The same gesture often indicates both the object and the action referring to that object, for example, horse-riding, water-drinking, pen-writing, cow-milking, etc. So that on learning to speak, the inexperienced deaf-mute might say: "Go get a sitting," "Give me a cutting," etc.

Distinctions emerge subsequently. For example, to signify "scissors" the index and middle fingers are moved, and for "cutting" the same gesture is used while moving the hand forward as though cutting a piece of material.[3]

It is usually the action that is imitated to signify the object and not vice versa. This has led certain glottologists to believe that in primitive languages verbs were used before nouns.[4]

In mimetic language colors are signified by indicating a part of one's own body, or an object of the desired color. Expressions such as: "cloth smoke" (for grey), "horse tooth" (for white), "dress crow" (for black), etc. are therefore common in the speech of deaf-mutes. Generally, to distinguish between nouns, adjectives, and adverbs is not easy.

In the work of deaf-mutes expressions like the following are found: "Mommy is very kindly." "The car is early." "The airplane is more speed than the car." "The soldier is courage," etc.

To be and to have are often implied and sometimes confused. For example, "child [is] naughty," "cat [is] black," "Miss Anna [is] young," "I [have] books," "you [have a lot of] money," "dog [is] eat bone," etc. The Italian verb "fare" is sometimes used as a general auxiliary, similarly to the English "do." For example, "tu fare coltello qui" (you do the knife here) for "cut here," or: "locomotiva fa fumare" (locomotive does to smoke).

In the light of such lack of distinctions, it is not surprising that mimetic expression is often ambiguous and confusing. However, ambiguity is determined more by verbal translation than by actual mimetic language.

Mimetic expression is polylogic, like a painting that may be variously interpreted according to the sentiment with which it is considered.

The deaf-mutes observed by Pellet used a complex gesture to signify "it's not true," "it's an error," and the like. On transposing the same mode in spoken language, they would say, for example, "John is a liar, he said 7 by 9 is 56." Or, on mixing various colors without obtaining the desired shade, "These liar colors." Similarly, a small packet which, because it contained lead weighed more than expected, was called "liar packet."[5]

In speech, deaf-mutes may confuse the content with the container. For example: "garage is in automobile," "barn in the hay," and the like. Confusion is probably due to the fact that the most important word is usually put first, so that "garage inside" or "garage in" means "inside the garage."

In languages which, similarly to Latin, have reached a high level of grammatical development, word arrangement is not of decisive importance to the meaning of the sentence. For example, in the line "lurida terribiles miscent aconita novercae" the work order could be changed in as many as a hundred and twenty different ways, while the meaning would remain more or less the same.[6] On the contrary, in mimetic language, which has a very low level of grammatical development, word arrangement is of the greatest importance, for the distinction between nominative, accusative, etc., is based more than anything else on word order. As a rule the concrete precedes the abstract, and therefore, for example, numerals come after the noun, so that we will say "boy two" and not "two boy." As a rule the adjective and the verb are placed after the noun and the adverb follows the verb.[7] But our grammatical classifications are inadequate for mimetic language which is based on a syntax that is more emotional than conceptual.

Interrogative sentences usually begin with a question gesture, which usually consists of a hand held out with the palm open, a gesture which roughly means "tell me whether . . . ," or "tell me how," or "when," etc.

In the speech of deaf-mutes the same interrogative particle may signify: who? which? how? why? when? how much? etc.

To say "Who was that Indian I saw with you today?" we would say "Who Indian I see, with you, this day?" But also "Who day we leave?" for "On what day will we leave?"[8]

The passive forms of verbs are usually avoided so as not to confuse the subject and the object. They are often understood backwards. In a class of deaf-mutes, the following sentence was read: "Henry IV was murdered by the insane Ravaillac." One of the students asked: "Why did Henry IV murder that madman?" The sentence: "During the age of terror Marshal Ney was shot, nine thousand people were imprisoned" is interpreted as: "Marshal Ney had nine thousand people shot, who were in prison." The sentence: "The child is much loved by his parents," is repeated like this: "Parents child loves much."

This is a very widespread and tenacious characteristic. For example, the sentence: "Napoleon, after having conquered Austria, which was then a great Empire, turned his troops against Russia, to avoid being attacked from the back," is rendered with: "Austria first great Empire. Napoleon conquers her. He thinks: Russia also great Empire beat back me. Then he beats Russia."

We have already seen, in relation to onomatopoeia, that pictographic language makes use of reduplications to accentuate intensity and quantity and, therefore, to signify the plural of nouns and the frequentative forms of verbs. The same can be said of mimetic language in which the gesture meaning man, food, money, repeated several times means many men, much food, much money; and the gesture of walking or studying, on being repeated means to walk for a long time or to study intensely. On the other hand, analogous forms are preserved even in our own languages in such expressions as "he walked and walked but didn't get anywhere," "If at first you don't succeed, try, try, try again," and the like.

In mimetic language the comparative and the superlative are sometimes formed with the word "first" or also with "one." To say "I'm as big as you are," one of Vuillemey's students said, "you, I, same big." And to say "I'm bigger than you" she said "I, first big." "The strongest boy of all" is conveyed with "boy one (or first) strong."

The lack of differentiation between one and first derives from the habit of signifying these concepts by raising the thumb. Therefore, the expression "one fruit?" could be used to ask whether the fruit should be served first.

Time specifications are limited to the present, past, and future, which are commonly formed with the addition of the adverbs today, yesterday, tomorrow. However, the past is sometimes indicated by adding the word "before," and the future, by adding the word "after." For example, "I 5th January am before twelve years old," for "last January 5th I was twelve years old"; or "We Christmas after presents many" for "next Christmas we will receive many presents."

Spatial tropes are frequently used for temporal indications. For example, here for now, back or behind for before and the like.

Given the difficulty involved in expressing abstract concepts mimetically, several particulars are often enumerated to signify the general concept. For example, "he is happy and content" will be expressed with "he dance, laugh, jump." "That man is studious" could be conveyed with "man books, man write, man teach," etc.

Syntactic Characteristics of Ancient and Primitive Languages

Fluidity of Primitive Languages—Pictographic Immediacy—Globality and Conciseness—Lack of Grammatical Distinctions—Correspondence between Mimetic Syntax and the Syntax of Primitive Languages.

Almost all the characteristics so far listed, without claiming that they are complete, are to be found in ancient languages as well as in present-day primitive languages.

In relation to the fluidity or looseness of mimetic signs (which is one of their most significant traits), that such a characteristic should emerge is only natural when aesthetics prevails over semantics, that is, when immediate expression prevails over conventional signs. The painter who in his paintings expresses an individual sentiment is certainly freer in his choice of expressive devices than a clerk transmitting the signs of the Morse code.

In spoken languages we find neither the mechanical rigidity of artificial conventions nor the limitless freedom of immediate expressions. Imagine the linguistic extravagance of a writer if he deliberately decided to call water "Ba," bread "Be," wine "Bi," etc., choosing alphabetical combinations haphazardly, or according to his own personal criterion. Languages evolve like all living things, but lexical and grammatical conventions prove to be extremely tenacious. In today's languages new combinations of preexistent words or roots, initials obtained from abbreviations, and the like are common: but, as has often been observed, in the course of hundreds and thousands of years, new alphabetical combinations have hardly ever occurred which were not natural and unconscious modifications of preexistent phonemes. Words used today are formed from the same roots which came forth from the mouth of our forefathers in prehistoric eras.

The conservative spirit is more tenacious at the popular level of society than among the more cultured classes (antiquated forms are common, for example, in the Tuscan countryside and forms recalling Latin are common in the Abruzzi mountains), so that we would expect to find less fluidity in the languages of non-civilized peoples than in our own, especially because such peoples are attached to tradition and reluctant to deviate from it.

On the contrary, the exact opposite is true. The languages spoken by certain primitive populations in America, Polynesia, central Asia and Africa flourish—as M. Müller had already observed—and in a state of continuous combustion and effervescence.

According to the missionary Gabriele Ragard, rarely among the Hurons does one find two villages that speak the same language; the lexicon and forms change so rapidly that often a language becomes unintelligible to anyone who has been absent from the village for a few years. It is only in the less savage tribes that a more stable language is used for speeches during gatherings and for religious and juridical rituals.[1]

These observations have often found confirmation. Jespersen was struck by the fact that in Oregon, a region not much bigger than France and inhabited by a very scarce native population, there are at least thirty different language families; and that in Brazil, the indigenous population speaks a surprising variety of languages, though it is homogeneous at the level of somatic features.[2]

In Loango, writes Pechül, everyone handles language in his own way, or rather, the language which comes out of each person's mouth is different, depending on the circumstances and his frame of mind. This way of using language is (I could not myself find a better comparison) just as loose and spontaneous as the sounds emitted by birds.[3]

Glottologists have wondered about the cause of this linguistic phenomenon which contrasts so strangely with all we know about modern languages and those of classical antiquity. In the study we have already quoted, Jespersen remarks that he is mainly dealing with peoples whose subsistence is based on hunting, which means that children are sometimes easily left behind by the rest of the tribe. And because in those climates isolated children are able to survive more easily than elsewhere, the author advances the hypothesis that the exuberance of new words and forms is caused by the glottogonic instinct of children who have grown up in isolation.[4] It seems that this hypothesis has not been tested and, in our opinion, it is not persuasive. But it does carry the following truth: creative exuberance is probably not caused by the hypothetical abandoned individual child, but in general by the childlike spirit of such peoples.

From all reports we learn that the language of these peoples abounds in interjections, onomatopoeia, and gesticulation, a language which comes rather close to the immediacy of pictographic expression.

Members of the Ewe tribe, says Westermann, use a language extraordinarily suited to conveying immediate impressions through sounds. They have an irresistible tendency to imitate anything they hear, see, and generally perceive; and to describe these things through one or more sounds. These sounds are certainly not onomatopoeic in our sense, but rather they are *vocal gestures,*[5] that is, sounds accompanying sensations of well being, satiety, disgust, pain, etc. These sounds refer firstly to body movements, but subsequently they are associated with representations of specific smells, tastes, and tactile impressions.[6]

In the above-mentioned report, Pechül states that among the natives of Loango, words are not rigid and fixed once and for all, but rather they are *vocal gestures,* which delineate and design the action or object in question in the same way that hand gestures do.

In the Rongo language, says Junod, use of interjective and descriptive sounds varies greatly from one individual to another. They sometimes decorate and fill out discourses to the point of rendering them unintelligible for anyone who does not belong to the same circle of acquaintances; but many of the sounds spontaneously invented subsequently become proper words and are incorporated into the common language.[7]

The language of these peoples is something almost halfway between direct aesthetic expression and indirect expression through conventional signs. Therefore, complicated hypotheses are unnecessary to explain that great creative freedom which is part of the very nature of all pictographic expressions.

As to correspondences concerning the other characteristics listed, we will limit ourselves to just a few examples.

The globality and concise nature of the language spoken by the Indians of North America are brilliantly highlighted by Mallery. He maintains that as the words of an Indian language are part of a synthetic discourse not yet analytically differentiated, from this point of view they are strictly analogous to the gestures forming the elements of mimetic language. Examination of the latter is precious for a comparative study of the words comprising the former. One kind of language clarifies the other and neither one can be studied without knowledge of the other.[8]

Perhaps the most characteristic example of the tendency toward synthesis is that offered by Eskimo language: almost every word corresponds to six or seven words in any European language, and sentences with a very complex meaning may be expressed with a single word.[9] In regard to the characteristic lack of distinctions between nouns, verbs, and adjectives, etc., we will remember that in the opinion of certain authors there was a stage in which grammatical distinctions had not yet been established in the development of languages of the most archaic Indo-European family and perhaps of all languages.

The lack of distinctions is obvious in the Egyptian and Chinese languages. In Egyptian, according to Bunsen, there is no formal distinction between noun, verb, and adjective; for example, "an'h" may signify life, to live, living, vivacious.[10]

In ancient Chinese, and in monosyllabic languages generally, grammatical distinctions are reduced to a minimum and emerge mainly from the syntactical position of words.[11]

The same may be said of many primitive languages.[12] There is a correspondence between the use of auxiliary verbs and time indications made in the language of primitive men and usage in mimetic language.[13]

The same is true of reduplications forming plurals, intensives, and frequentatives[14] in the various languages, and especially of individualizing constructions.

Often there are no general terms such as tree, fish, bird, but only specific terms referring to each variety.[15] For verbs, too, general terms are often lacking while terms indicating the varied nuances abound.[16]

We could easily continue adding examples to illustrate the correspondence between the syntax of ancient languages and that of current primitive languages, but a more detailed examination is best left to the experts.[17]

Nonetheless, even the layman will notice the correspondence if he compares the speech of deaf-mutes with a few primitive songs or stories; for example, the following story, reported by M. Müller, tells of how a white man first gives the Bushman native a friendly welcome, offers him gifts, and consequently succeeds in getting the negro to work for him; and of how he then takes advantage of the situation by mistreating the native to the point that the poor man can take no more and escapes, while the white man goes in search of another native Bushman with whom the same story is repeated: "Negro here runs toward white man. White man give tobacco him smoke. He fill bag tobacco. White man give meat. Negro eat meat. Go there happy. Graze white sheep. White man beat negro. Negro scream pain. He escape. White man run. Here another negro graze sheep."[18]

At times the influence of mimetic language is certain; at other times, however, the correspondence could derive from the analogy between two mentalities which prefer simple and immediate constructions. But this, too, is valuable for our purposes, for it shows that the most simple and primitive mentality has a natural preference for immediate forms typical of pictographic expression.

Mimicry in Primitive Man

In Certain Primitive Languages Gesture Is a Necessary Element for Comprehension—Certain Primitive Mimetic Languages in Given Circumstances Fulfill All Communicative Needs—The Gestural *Lingua Franca* Used in North America—For Primitive Man Thought and Gestures Are Naturally Related Just as Thought and Words Are for Us—The Mimetic Languages of Primitive Man Originate from a Prephonetic Expressive Habit.

We have mentioned the mimetic expressions of primitive peoples here and there but it will now be appropriate to return more specifically to the subject. If what we have said up to now is correct, the importance of mimetic expression among such peoples (whose level of development is close to our very distant forefathers) should still be much greater than it is, for example, among the inhabitants of southern Italy. In the case of the latter, gesture mostly integrates and accentuates spoken languages, while among primitive tribes it is what remains of a true pictographic language which originally sufficed in itself. Let us see what the documents and evidence we have at our disposal say on the matter.

Already in the second half of the nineteenth century missionaries and travelers reported that in certain tribes gesture seemed to be a necessary complement to the word. Monboddo relates that according to Father Greenhill the language of certain tribes to the east of Cape Palmas, in Africa, is not intelligible in the dark, because it depends on gestures to be understood; according to Mrs. Pfeiffer, the Puris only have one word which means "day," and which may signify "today," "tomorrow," and "yesterday" depending on whether, in pronouncing it, the finger is pointed upward (today), backward (yesterday), or forward (tomorrow). Glottologists did not usually take such anecdotes seriously, for it seemed rather too odd to them that there should exist men who speak with their hands.[1]

Subsequent studies have confirmed and completed this information: there is no doubt that in some languages gesture is a necessary component for the comprehension of words. In English New Guinea the natives indicate all numbers with a name together with a gesture, and sometimes the same word means different numbers according to the gesture accompanying it, for example, "anho" means ten if pronounced while touching the left side of the neck, and fourteen if the right side is touched.[2]

According to W. Macgregor, in the Papuan language the word "doro" means two, three, four when pronounced while touching the ring finger, middle finger, and index finger of the right hand, and nineteen, twenty, twenty-one when the same fingers of the left hand are touched.[3] Among the

Bantu-speaking peoples of South Africa demonstrative pronouns acquire meaning from the gesture accompanying them,[4] and among the natives of West Africa the temporal and modal specifications of the verb are indicated by gestures. Among the Coroados of Brazil gestures are often indispensable in determining the meaning of words. For example, to say "I'll go into the forest," or "I want to go into the forest," the native says "forest," or "go forest," and sticks out both his lips with a movement meaning "I'm hungry."[5] Among the Zuni also—according to the testimony of such a scrupulous observer as Cushing—verbal forms are specified through given movements of the hands. Among the Halkomelen of British Columbia at least a third of word and sentence meanings relate closely to gesture, and cannot be understood without gesture.[6]

But for many peoples mimetic language is something more than a complementary element necessary to spoken language; it is a completely autonomous language, able to fulfill all communication needs without the help of words.

In certain regions of Africa and Australia a period of silence varying from a few months to a year is imposed upon widows for religious reasons, and during that time they talk to each other in mimetic language. As Spencer and Gillen relate, gatherings of women can be seen where, although remaining in absolute silence, they entertain each other and make animated conversation by means of gestures.[7]

In an official report it is stated that these widows speak a sort of deaf-mute language, and that it is perfectly understood by the men as much as by the women.[8] The Aborigines of Port Lincoln also use a number of signs without any voice emission. These signs are particularly useful when hunting.[9]

Finally, mimetic language is universally used by the Indians of North America. It is a proper language with its own lexicon, forms, and syntax. It would be possible—says one explorer—to write a bulky grammar of this language. Its wealth can be judged from the fact that the Indians of two different tribes, neither of which understands a single word of the phonetic language of the other, can easily spend half a day talking and chattering, telling each other all kinds of little stories through movements of their fingers, heads, and feet.[10] Thanks to the studies of G. Mallery, W. E. Roth, W. Tomkins, and F. H. Cushing,[11] these mimetic languages are now vastly documented, including not only an impressive quantity of careful observations and registrations, but also two special dictionaries.

If we now ask why these aphonetic languages ever arose, the usual reply is that their development was stimulated by communication needs among populations speaking different languages. But in the first place, it is not true that mimetic language serves this end alone. It is also often used among individuals of the same tribe who speak the same dialect. Furthermore, we would still have to ask ourselves why a simplified phonetic language was not used, even a rather messy one, being similar to the "lingua franca" of the past, and to the numerous Creole languages still in use today, to broken English, etc. Since mimetic languages are used among the aborigines of countries which are very distant from each other, such as America, Africa, and Australia, we will have to acknowledge that their widespread presence has a common psychological cause, one that is inherent in the level of development and mentality of those peoples. This is confirmed by a series of brilliant observations made by Cushing. Just as our thinking is closely connected to phonetic language, so that it would be impossible to elaborate a complex piece of reasoning without in some way formulating it in interior discourse (for which reason certain philosophers have stated that if the word is lacking, so is thought lacking[12]), in the same way a natural relationship exists between thought and gestures in primitive societies, to the extent that Cushing thought it right to speak of "manual concepts."[13]

The progress of civilization, he says, has come about through the reciprocal action of hand over spirit and spirit over hand. To relive the mentality of the aborigines we must rediscover in ourselves the movements of their hands from which—and we are going back as early as prehistoric times—their thinking is inseparable.[14]

De Iorio and Sittl have shown how many of the gestures used by southern Italians were already in use in Augustus's time, though some of our gestures probably go back to the very distant past. For example, our affirmation and negation gestures, made by moving the head downward or from right to left, probably go back to the time when man was still very close to animal life. In fact the downward movement of the head reminds us of the way an animal throws itself on its food and seizes it with its mouth, and the right to left movement may be observed in young monkeys (as well as in our children) when they refuse food they do not desire. Such atavistic memories naturally are far more common in the gestures of primitive men, and both Mallery and other ethnologists have shown that they are depicted in ancient pictographs, and even in certain prehistoric caves.

By relating these considerations to those of our previous chapters, we believe it is possible to conclude that the language used today by our primitive peoples (so intimately connected to the whole of their *forma mentis*), far from being recent, goes back to very remote times and is probably the residue of an instinctive prephonetic expressive habit.[15]

According to some authors, there are also anatomical and physiological reasons which would lead us to support the thesis of the prevalence of mimetic language over the phonetic. A study in the medical review "The Larynx," of 1928, for example, reports that the formation of the human larynx was probably such in prehistoric times that the very complex, delicate, and precise modulations which characterize today's languages would be inconceivable.

(Cf. also the paper delivered at the last congress on phonetics in Amsterdam, "The Evolution of the Larynx and the Voice in Animals" and the essay by M. N. Negus, "The Mechanism of the Larynx," London, 1929.)

Mimetic Languages Created
by Uneducated Deaf-Mutes

The Way Deaf-Mutes Express Themselves Makes It
Possible to Study Semantic Systems Which Have
Arisen outside Our Linguistic Tradition—Some Examples of How New Semantic Conventions Arise
among Deaf-Mutes—An Atavistic Glottogonic Instinct Comes to Life Again in the Mimetic Languages Created by Deaf-Mutes.

Would children raised outside all linguistic tradition be capable of creating a
language by themselves? And what characteristics would such a spontaneous
way of expressing oneself have?

The experiments attributed to Psammeticus and the interest with which
glottologists and language psychologists have studied infant languages reveal
the importance attached to these questions by both the ancients and modern
man. Now, it is a fact that, as a consequence of their infirmity, deaf-mute
children are cut off from all our linguistic traditions, and yet they still manage to communicate with each other by means of a more or less rudimentary
system. Thus, in working toward a theory of the origin of language, it would
have been interesting to study the language of deaf-mutes with patience and
method, especially in those very common cases where there are several deaf-
mute brothers and sisters in the same family. But the prejudice that phonetic
expression is an essential feature of every language, even today, diverts major language theorists from this fruitful field of semantic expression.[1]

For my part, though without the preparation, aptitude, and opportuni-
ties which a convincing study would require, I wished to get at least some
idea of the issue by visiting a few institutes and by observing in particular the
way deaf-mutes who had not yet been educated express themselves.

It should be remembered that in all European institutes the oral teaching
method now prevails and that everything possible is done to ostracize mimetic expression;[2] nevertheless, despite all prohibitions, students use it,
spontaneously, and going against the rules create among themselves real mimetic languages, perfectly suited to their needs.

What strikes us most is the naturalness and simplicity with which these
languages are formed, and the remarkable ease with which newcomers, after
a short time, manage to understand and use them.

It is common knowledge that, on being moved to an environment where
a different language is spoken, all children intuitively learn the new language
with great ease (at the beginning, they too are considerably helped by mimetic expression), but still greater is the speed with which deaf-mutes of different origin manage to comprehend each other. This is only to be expected
given the notably pictographic character of their language.

On average, deaf-mutes are far less quick and intelligent than normal children. Therefore, we may admire not only the ease and speed with which they manage to establish among themselves a system of expressive signs, but also the subtlety and force revealed in their choice of the most characteristic gestures.

If you ask a normal man how he would convey a given concept mimetically and then compare his gesture with that used by deaf-mutes, the former will almost always be more general, dull, and artificial, and the second more plastic and spontaneous. In other words, in most cases the former will be the result of cold excogitation, while a spark of creative ingeniousness will shine through the second.[3]

For example, I asked two friends what they would do to signify an "egg." One outlined an oval figure in the air with his index finger, and the other tried to form the same shape by joining his thumb and forefinger into a small circle: rather generic gestures which could signify a quantity of other things. On the other hand, for the same meaning I saw certain deaf-mutes use the far more characteristic gesture with which the housewife, when making the dough, holds the egg between the fingers of her two hands and with a quick movement opens the shell and lets the content fall into the flour.

If we were to attempt to express mimetically the concept "to forget," we would soon find ourselves in difficulty. The deaf-mutes from the Cagliari Institute expressed this concept by passing the palm of the hand over the forehead and then shaking it, which conveys well the idea of something which has been wiped out or which has "left the mind."

Most gestures arise casually from some observation which impresses itself upon the deaf-mute's mind. I will give a few examples: one of the boys played with a small mirror and amused himself by reflecting it into the eyes of his companions. From then on the word "mirror" was signified by holding the hand flat in a vertical position with the fingers united and the palm facing outwards while moving the wrist quickly with short rotations, thus giving the idea of a mirror reflecting the light. Later this same gesture became a conventional sign to signify glass, and not only a sheet of glass, which may also reflect light, but any glass object whatsoever.

On another occasion the children were playing outside while the crescent of the moon shone in the sky. One of them pointed to the moon and then placed his open hand sideways along his nose to signify that the moon looked like half of a human face. From then on that gesture was used to signify the moon in general.

These same children signified the word "to look about inquisitively," "to be curious," and the like, by turning up the nose and sniffing here and there as though looking for something. Later the gesture was stylized by simply pointing the index at the nose.

The "top of the class" or "class-leader" was signified by holding out the thumb and keeping the other fingers closed. The same gesture was then used to signify the head, director, president, etc.

The children had observed an old man dozing with his chin resting on his two closed fists. This gesture (simplified by resting the chin on one fist only) came to signify grandfather and old. Subsequently it was used for anything old (for a dress or pair of shoes), and because old things are less clean than the new (or, perhaps, because the old man observed originally did not look very clean), the same gesture was also used to mean dirty.

The fact that a certain sign language gradually develops spontaneously in all communities of deaf-mute children is not, in itself, proof that normal children too, if segregated from the rest of the world, would create a mimetic language. It is clear that normal children would have the possibility of using gestural signs or phonetic signs equally, while the latter are unavailable to deaf-mutes.

But if we consider that all signs created by deaf-mutes originally have a directly expressive value (that is, they are indicative, affective, or imitative gestures) and acquire a conventional value only later, and that the directly expressive phonemes are relatively few and certainly insufficient for communication needs, it will not seem too bold to hold that even a language created spontaneously by normal children would probably be a gestural language, even if accompanied by affective and imitative cries.

From the few observations I was able to make on the deaf-mutes, I received the impression that their wonderful creative ease and expressive wealth can only be explained in terms of the revival of a latent atavistic glottogonic instinct. The fact remains that their languages offer us an ideal opportunity to observe how a semantic system may spontaneously arise and flourish under our very noses, and there is no doubt that, should the experts decide to study such languages systematically, their observations and experiences would shed new light on the most difficult problems faced by language psychology.

4. Observations on the Psychology of Anthropoid Apes with a Particular View to Their Expressive Capacity

Preliminary Observations

Scarceness of Information Most Relevant to Our Purpose—Vagueness of the Concepts of "Expression" and "Language"—Distinction between Physiological Manifestations and Meaningful Expressions.

The birth of language coincides with the transition from animal life to human life. In the preceding pages we considered the psychology and characteristic features of the language and mode of expression of primitive man (i.e., of the human families least distant from animality). We will now consider the expressive capacities of anthropoid apes (i.e., of those animal species closest to humanity) trusting that, in this way, we will be able to form some idea of the psychological environment in which the earliest language arose.

Valuable studies on animal psychology are not lacking, but even the best offer little information that might be useful to our argument. The problems which naturalists have dwelt on at most length concern the capacity of animals to reason and to act intentionally. The big problem has always seemed to be that of establishing whether a rational soul (as it was called in Thomist-Aristotelian terminology) may also be attributed to animals and, in particular, whether the actions carried out by animals may all be explained in terms of instinctive automatism or whether there are some actions which testify to the ability of taking individual initiative and consciously directing it toward the accomplishment of a purpose.

No doubt the problem is important and the observations collected on the subject are both interesting and decisive, but this does not justify our forgetting the fact that there exist intermediate capacities or activities, such as emotivity, memory, and imagination, that stand between purely animal sensitivity and rational intellectualism. If these intermediate links are ignored, the chain appears discontinuous and the transition from one stage of development to another remains obscure and confused. In particular, when we ask ourselves whether there is something similar to language in animals, and what the expressive possibilities of animals generally are, it must be borne in mind (something that, as a rule, naturalists forget) that the emotional, mnemonic, intuitive, and imaginative faculties are more important in linguistic production than are the purely logical faculties.

Various other factors have made studies into the psychology of anthropoid apes less fruitful than they would have otherwise been: first of all we are dealing with animals which have reached a remarkable level of psychological complexity and which present considerable diversity from one individual to the next. The naturalist, as such, will usually give most prominence to the characteristics present in all representatives of a given species, leaving aside what can only be observed in exceptional cases; on the contrary, as far as we are concerned, it is often the very individual characteristics that present the major interest, especially when they are more marked.

One reason why progress in the natural sciences was slow and insecure in past centuries was the superficiality with which even the most fanciful information was accepted. It was really only after 1700 that a greater critical sense was to become widespread, thanks to the much maligned Enlightenment. A significant example of such superficiality is reported by Locke. Prince Maurice d'Orange told him that a Brazilian parrot, which had been brought into the room where he was with some of the dignitaries of the Dutch court, asked him, screaming: "What's this assembly of white men?" and when it was asked, on pointing at the prince, who he was, the parrot answered: "One or the other of the generals." Again the prince asked him: "Where do you come from?" and the parrot: "From Marinnon." "Who do you belong to?" "To a Portuguese." "What is your occupation?" "I watch over the chickens."

Locke limited himself to asking what language the parrot had spoken, so as not to offend the prince. The latter answered: "In Brazilian." "And you understand Brazilian?"

The prince answered that he did not and added that the parrot's words had been translated for him by a Brazilian. Locke then expressed his suspicion that there was some trick on the part of this Brazilian (*Treatise*, II, ch. 27).

A precise definition of what is to be intended by "expression" and "language" is necessary in order to explain our problem through observation and experiment. However, in almost all naturalists these concepts are rather uncertain and changeable. For example: "language" is commonly used to designate uniquely phonetic language thus completely ignoring mimetic language, without realizing that the exterior character of phoneticity is not at all an essential part of this psychological manifestation, that is, language. In fact what distinguishes man from animals is not his ability (or his greater ability) in pronouncing articulate sounds, but rather his spiritual capacity for the use of a system of conventional expressive signs (phonetic or not, it does not matter) which enable him to express himself to himself, to fix his representations, and to communicate them to his fellowmen. Otherwise we would have to say that a trained parrot possesses a language and that a writer without a tongue does not.

The same uncertainty and confusion surrounds the concept of "expressive manifestations." After Darwin's fundamental essay on "The Expression of the Emotions in Man and Animals," naturalists have often dwelt on this subject and have rightly related it to problems concerning the language of animals.

But the term "expressive manifestations" is almost always employed ambiguously for those instinctive physiological reactions which are the sign or symptom of given emotions, as much as for the expressions of language. As though a yawn or retching may be placed on the same level as a line written by a poet expressing boredom and disgust: "Taedet animam meam vitae meae!" We do not deny that there may be some connection between physiological manifestations and meaningful expressions. Indeed, we too believe that there is a natural connection between these two. But there also exists an essential divergence, and we deplore the fact that naturalists have not attempted to clarify the relation between the two concepts.

The difference is this: physiological manifestations are produced by organic processes in what could be called a mechanical fashion, they are instinctive in character and devoid of conscious intentionality. On the contrary, expressions of the linguistic or aesthetic type require contemplation of one's state of mind and signs suited to recalling it to the memory and communicating it to others.

It so happens that in its initial pictographic stage, language uses these physiological manifestations spontaneously as expressive signs. But to achieve this the mechanical-physiological stage and pure sensuality must be overcome, thus making possible that detachment necessary for contemplation and evocation.

To return to the example above, retching is a physical reaction of the organism, which indeed no one would call spiritual, but if the man in the street refers to that physiological motion mimetically to signify "that turns my stomach," it would then become a mimetic expression, essentially similar to linguistic expression. The instinctive motion is a manifestation of animal life, the expressive act marks the transition from purely animal life to human or prehuman life.

Precisely because physiological motion is always the starting point and medium of the expressive act, it is often difficult or even impossible to distinguish one from the other and clearly decide whether we have pure physiology or whether it is the beginning of a more spiritual form of expression. The crying and screams of a newborn baby are a physiological manifestation, but after a few months it will not always be easy to determine whether we are dealing with "real" tears or an expressive device used by the screamer in order to be picked up and cradled.

It is not difficult, at times, to follow the gradual transformation of an instinctive manifestation as it slowly becomes a real expression: the baby who moves his lips in search of the nipple to suck his mother's breast accomplishes a physiological act, but when he rubs his lips on her face as a display of affection (something which young monkeys also do occasionally), we already have the beginnings of an expressive act which becomes more explicit in the kiss until it loses its initial physiological character altogether in the act of "throwing a kiss" to signify: "I love you."

The naturalist who makes observations and undertakes experiments on the expressive capacities of animals, but then lacks all criteria for establishing whether the physiological or the expressive element prevails in individual cases, runs the risk of incoherence. For the moment the following criterion may be helpful: when a given manifestation is hereditary and is invariably present in all individuals of the same species, this is a sign that the physiological element prevails in that species and we may exclude the possible existence of expression: physiology belongs to the species, expression to the individual. On applying this criterion to the example mentioned above, it is easy to see how prevalence of the expressive goes hand in hand with prevalence of individuality. The movement of the lips while feeding is purely instinctive and hereditary at the same time and varies only slightly from individual to individual; but expressive signs are already present in the affective display of the kiss with noteworthy differences at the individual and national levels,[1] and finally when we make the gesture of throwing a kiss with the fingers, we well and truly have a mimetic language where this gesture takes on a multiplicity of individual meanings thus expressing passionate love or burlesque irony, depending on the circumstances.

Studies on our subject have been mostly unsatisfactory as they generally follow no order or criteria and lack in that information which, in our opinion, would have been most appropriate in the understanding of the transition from animality to humanity. Given such a state of affairs, we must now concentrate on this topic more than would have been otherwise necessary.

Importance of Memory in the Spiritualization of Animal Life

Feelings and Affections, Worked upon by Memory, Become Images—Memory as a Glottogonic Category—Experiments on the Memory of Anthropoids—Animal Memory is Less Broad and Selective and More Mechanical Than Human Memory.

In animals the senses are more acute and the impulses more robust than in man. As regards finality, the coordination of instincts may often be amazing (as was observed many times especially in relation to insects) while the impulses of certain animals (and, at times, those of man) are in certain cases so violent as to annul biological finality.[1]

A certain emotional spiritualization of the immediate impulses may be noted in higher animals. Living alongside man has certainly had an influence on domestic animals, such as dogs and horses, but such spiritualization has also come about spontaneously in anthropoid apes, away from all human influence.

As emerges from a number of episodes, some of which we will discuss, monkeys are not only capable of those impressions and impulses which are closely related to their physiological needs, such as hunger, sexual excitement, fear, drowsiness, etc., but also of a number of more complex feelings and emotions, such as likes and dislikes, pity, fidelity, jealousy, revenge, gratitude, emulation, envy, pride, humility, guilt feelings, vanity, cunning, sense of humor, etc.

The factor most felt in sensations and instincts is the need of immediate physiological satisfaction and certainly not that of contemplation and expression. When it is a question of feelings, on the other hand, physiological urgency diminishes and the need to express and communicate increases. When feelings and sentiments are then taken in and elaborated by the memory, they are transformed into images and representations, and pass from the obscurity of a subconscious psychic process to the light of expression.

Indeed, this is one of the reasons why it would be interesting for us to establish to what extent animals, and especially anthropoid apes, are endowed with memory and therefore with the possibility of spiritualizing their emotional life. But there is yet another reason still more intimately connected to the problem of the creation of language. Not only is language a creation of images and expressions, it is essentially the institution of a system of conventional signs with the aim of recalling given representations to the memory. What matters most in the learning and use of a language is that the associations established between a sign and its meaning be remembered. In order to know a language it is not important to examine whether those associations are more or less logical or more or less aesthetic. What does matter is that we *remember* what they are, for example, that the motion of the head from right to left signifies "no," or that the expression "tlacatecuhtli hueytlatoani" in Mexican means "supreme master." Even grammatical forms, which establish strict relationships between signs, have essentially the same semiological function. Indeed, it may well be stated that memory has the same importance in language as imagination in art, or deductive logic in mathematics.

We do not have the fortune of possessing works that are wholly satisfying on the memory of animals. In fact, observations and experiments by different authors often arrive at different conclusions. This happens because for studies in psychology, it is always difficult to take into consideration all the elements that come into play, and because the mnemonic capacities of single individuals within the same species are anything but uniform.

Hunter and Köhler are among those naturalists who have studied the subject with most attention. By offering appropriate rewards, Hunter accustomed various animals, and together with them a two-year-old child, to move toward a compartment where a colored electric light bulb had been switched on not long before. The experiment confirmed that memory of the impressions generally lasts longer in the more intelligent animals. In other words, the stimulus no longer present but retained by memory ceases to be effective after a longer period of time. Representation of the turned on light preserved its effectiveness for ten seconds in the mouse, twenty-five seconds in the worker raccoon, five minutes in the dog, and twenty-five in the child.[2]

According to Köhler's experiments remembered images retain their efficacy much longer in chimpanzees. He chose a sandy surface of four hundred square metres and in the monkey's presence buried some unscented fruit in a given spot. He then carefully flattened the sand. In a series of experiments, on being let free after progressively longer periods of time, the chimpanzee headed for the right point, without hesitation. This topographic memory proved to be effective up to sixteen hours later.[3]

Hunter's and Köhler's experiments obviously cannot be placed on the same level because, in the former, animals were being accustomed to associate the taste of a fruit with the light of an electric light bulb, an association which is too distant from those to which the animals are accustomed in their natural surroundings, whereas the latter experiment required less artificial associations.

Kleuver[4] set up a series of experiments with young Javanese monkeys and a lemur and was able to ascertain that certain associations were remembered even after 368 days.

Tinklepaugh[5] carried out experiments with two chimpanzees and two macaques: for example, the animal was presented with two covered and identical containers. A reward was placed inside one of these. The chimpanzee, which was taken away for a certain period of time and then brought before the containers again, would initially forget what its task was after a day's interval but, after five or six experiments, memory became more tenacious and the accuracy of its reaction increased. The correct choice was obtained in the end, even after a whole week.

On one occasion, after putting a banana in one of the two containers in the chimpanzee's presence, the experimenter substituted the banana with a carrot while the animal was being taken away. On being called back, the monkey went straight to the right container, put the carrot in its mouth, and was about to return to its place. But suddenly it stopped, took the carrot (which was less to its taste than the banana) out of its mouth, examined it perplexed, returned to the container, turned it upside down and looked all around as though looking for something, made a gesture of impatience by hitting the floor; finally it gave up, sat down on its stool, and ate the carrot.

It seems obvious to me that in this case not only did the chimpanzee remember the previous situation, but it also in some way reasoned about it. At a certain point it seems to have said to itself: "There should have been a banana in the container, how come I now taste a different flavor?" The chimpanzee took it out of its mouth and looked at it to verify it. There's no doubt, it's a carrot! But then where did the banana get to? It turned the container upside down, looked for it, did not find it, became impatient, and at last adapted itself to the circumstances.[6]

Other notable examples of memory in animals are to be found in some of the "little scenes" which we will report later on, but as we have said, a more complete study on the topic is so far lacking.

As a general rule we may observe that animal memory is more mechanical and—so to speak—more photographic than our own. It is less selective, concentrates more on particulars, and grasps a more restricted field. Human memory is able to take in a high variety of impressions and feelings in a single image, animal memory prefers to dwell on rather isolated impressions. If we call the quantity of impressions received in a single representation "intensity," we may state that the intensity of animal memory is inversely proportionate to its duration, that is, that the more complex representations are those which last the least.

Among the various difficulties in forming an idea of the inner life of animals and in establishing to what extent they are capable of more complex representations there is also the fact that our own images are prevalently visual and auditory, while in animals olfactory images usually prevail. The sense of smell, which has a far greater practical utility for animals than it has for us, is often so developed as to allow perception not only of very distant smells, but also of smells that remain in the environment a long time after the relative object has been removed, even when the object itself seems to us to be completely devoid of smell. When we say, for example, that the dog remembered a given person or given surroundings, what it remembers is perhaps above all an olfactory impression, which is most closely associated with its feelings and which influences its likes and dislikes. This is the reason why Buffon, in his considerations on the nature of animals, rightly stated that for animals the sense of smell is "a universal organ of the sentiments."

It has been observed on several occasions that the memory of animals is more ephemeral and discontinuous than our own. This depends, however, more on the weakness of memory as such, and on the difficulty experienced by animals in keeping their attention fixed on the same object for a long time, so that they often divert their attention from the purpose they mean to accomplish and leave what they are doing unfinished.

A monkey, for example, tried to grab a fruit which was outside its arm's reach. It became aware of a rod hanging from the ceiling and thought the fruit could be reached with that. But the rod also was too high so the monkey pushed a box under it, jumped onto the box, and managed to take hold of the rod. But when the monkey had the rod in its hands it considered it perplexedly and did not know what to do with it because in the meanwhile the monkey had forgotten about the fruit.

After a while, the monkey would sometimes suddenly remember, thus brusquely turn around and run to accomplish the action it had interrupted. From certain observations it would seem that the actions and comprehension of monkeys proceed in momentary flashes and lack in continuity, but there are other facts which on the contrary testify to a remarkable constancy and continuity in action and memory. Perhaps what we should say is that animals oscillate between pure immediacy and pure continuity, just as they oscillate between the blind and disordered violence of single impulses and the age-old placid changelessness of habit.

Aesthetic Memory and Imitation

The Difference of Opinion Concerning the Imitative Ability of Monkeys Stems from a Misunderstanding—Their Lively Sense of Mimicry and Liking for It Emerges from All Research—But It Is Prelogical Imitation—Imitative Ability as a Pre-Aesthetic Moment—Monkey-like Imitation as a Necessary Precedent to Mimetic Language.

It is a generally known and easily ascertained fact that monkeys have a special tendency and gift for imitating the actions, gestures, and expressions of others, so much so that in almost all languages the word signifying "to ape" means both to imitate and to mimic. To say that Capocchio was a good imitator, Dante says that he was "by nature a good monkey."

Therefore it may seem strange that most naturalists should have concluded on the basis of their experiments that these animals are lacking in imitative ability. Watson and Thorndike[1] are among the most firm supporters of this negative thesis, but also according to Shepherd Warden, Jackson, and Yerkes, etc., the imitative ability of monkeys is far inferior to that of children.

On the contrary, other authors, Hornaday, Kohts, and especially Kinnaman[2] acknowledge that these animals have a remarkable liking and capacity for imitation.

Discussions among the supporters of these two opposite views are not lacking, but the difference of opinion is based on a misunderstanding arising from the use of the term "imitation" in two different senses. Supporters of the negative view understand imitation in a pedagogic sense, to mean the ability to acquire technical skills and to increase one's own experience by observing the behavior of someone already expert in a given operation.

Watson, for instance, observed a monkey which lived in the company of another more adult monkey, whose movements it imitated. He concluded that the younger monkey learned to open a locked door or to perform other such actions, not through observing and imitating the movements of its companion, but through the usual methods of random attempts, from which those movements which did not prove to be useful were gradually eliminated.

Shepherd placed a fruit inside a glass tube and trained a monkey to introduce and push a small rod into the tube so as to get hold of the fruit. In numerous experiments, another monkey, though seeing its companion accomplish that same operation several times, did not succeed in imitating it. Warden and Jackson conducted 354 tests with fifteen monkeys, always considering imitation in the sense we have called pedagogic. In 24.6 per cent of the cases the result was totally negative, in 46.3 per cent of the cases a modest capacity of learning through imitation was confirmed.

Those, however, who speak of a remarkable imitative capacity in monkeys understand imitation in the so-called aesthetic sense (as we shall see, pre-aesthetic would be a better term); that is to say, as pure play, for the simple fun of repeating or of mimicking. This sort of imitation may be observed either in acts devoid of a useful purpose, or in acts which have such an immediate purpose as not to present any difficulty in understanding.

Mrs. Kohts has emphasized the tendency of chimpanzees to imitate the movements of their keepers. Her chimpanzees perform the act of cleaning the floors with a broom or of scrubbing them with a cloth; they use the comb in the same way they saw the keeper's wife use it, they put a tooth brush in their mouth as though to clean their teeth, they cover their head with a hat and make greeting gestures, pretend to smoke, to light cigarettes, etc. The author notes expressly that these acts are imitated "with little attention" or, rather, by paying attention to mimetic imitation and not to the practical effect.

The same thing emerges from many other experiments. Wolfe, for example, had shown a chimpanzee an automatic machine which with the introduction of a token would make a fruit fall into a cup. After having observed the thing several times the chimpanzee imitated the movements of its trainer in part, putting the token, however, not in the slot of the automatic machine, but in the cup where the food had appeared, after which it would stretch out its hand waiting for the fruit.[3] Episodes of this kind may help us to form an idea of how belief in magical influences arises among the primitives. If he is not able to account for the single causes which produced the desired effect, what remains in primitive man is the simple impression of a mysterious relation between a volitive impulse, a given gesture, and satisfaction of the desire.

The young monkey Joni, observed by Kohts, amused itself by knocking nails into the wall with a hammer, as it had seen a workman do; and though never succeeding in driving them in, because it only imitated the action partially, it persisted at the same game for a long time. On one occasion, after having seen a padlock being opened with keys, the young monkey also learned to open it, and very pleased with itself it immediately tried to fit all the keys into all the keyholes, without considering their size. Furthermore, the same monkey willingly imitated its master at the piano keyboard or at the table with a pencil in its hand pretending to write. Sometimes the monkey would scribble and smile, pushing out its tongue and lips, and accompanying its movements with a rhythmic motion of the lips. It very much enjoyed using ink, and if it did not have a pen, it would stick its finger in the ink-pot and scribble with that.

Similar observations were made by Hornaday and a number of other scholars. Not only chimpanzees but also monkeys belonging to various other species have a pronounced liking for mimicry. They pretend to read the newspaper, type, sew, hold a skein or roll wool into a ball, straighten out the beds, etc., and they easily learn to sit at table, eat with a fork and a spoon, drink from a glass, pour milk from a jug into a glass, use or pretend to use toothpicks, put on and take off clothes, and the like. What we are more interested in noting is that monkeys display great mimetic skill in all these actions. And in most cases they are completely lacking in the slightest comprehension of the practical purpose guiding the movements they are performing.

The imitative skill of monkeys is of the same kind as the ability to imitate sounds typical in certain bird species, for example, the hedge-sparrow (*Sylvia modularis*), various shrike species, the American mockingbird (*Mimus polyglottus*), and especially the parrot. As with monkey-like imitation, parrot-like imitation is "pure" and "pre-logical," or destitute, as far as this is possible, of conceptual comprehension.

Those naturalists who denied that monkeys are endowed with a notable imitative capacity were not simply unaware of what everybody knows, that is, that monkeys have a fancy for mimicking. Their position was based on the tacit conviction that imitation without conceptual comprehension could not have any value.

On the contrary, pure imitation plays an essential part in questions concerning language and art, and to deny such value bacause of an intellectualistic bias would be just as theoretically wrong as denying value to artistic imagination because it does not solve mathematical problems.

To give a suitable definition of pre-logical imitation is of some importance, in our opinion, not only from the epistemological point of view, but also from the psychological and naturalistic points of view.

Let us illustrate the characteristics of such imitation with some examples. Some actors have the amazing ability to imitate and copy the voices and sounds of all species, indeed one might say that as a rule there is not a skillful actor who does not know more or less how to catch and imitate the characteristic inflections of different voices. (I remember the great actor Ermete Novelli, who certainly was not an imitator, but who, while conversing, would often hint at some characteristic inflection or gesture of the people he was speaking about, so much so that it was as though we could see them in front of us.)

Now, we ask ourselves, what relation is there between this imitative capacity and that of the artist? We may answer as follows: the imitative capacity is a necessary but not sufficient element in art. The good actor must subtly distinguish, and know how to re-evoke, voice inflections and body movements, but photographic imitation alone will not suffice. That personal touch, that power of synthesis and creative originality peculiar to art are also necessary.

Let us look at some other examples: Some draughtsmen know how to reproduce a drawing or a real object with admirable precision and, all the same, are and remain mediocre artists; but, on the other hand, it would be impossible to find a good draughtsman or painter completely lacking in this ability, at least for those impressions that most interest him.[4]

The same thing can be said about music. Descriptive tricks and virtuosities are certainly contrary to the nature of this art, though the imitative and mnemonic capacities go to form what is called the "musical ear." A good ear is by no means the same thing as sharpness of hearing (it is possible to have excellent hearing but a very bad musical ear or vice versa) nor is it equal to good taste, for some people are able to remember and reproduce a motif with great ease but cannot distinguish for themselves what is good music.

Even in this case we will have to say that the musical ear is a necessary but not sufficient condition of artistic taste and creation. Sharpness of hearing refers to sounds as sensations, of the ear to sounds as images, where by "image" we intend representation of sounds in the absence of the stimulus, that is, sensations as they are remembered. Whoever has the best musical memory has the best ear. We have believed it appropriate to attempt an explanation of concepts regarding aesthetic imitation, because, as we have already seen, an inadequate and ambiguous conception of imitation has often been the cause of a mistaken evaluation of the facts.

Returning now to the imitative capacity of monkeys, we may conclude that it is a necessary precedent and almost a preparation for mimetic language. Just as, before knowing how to speak, the child stammers and amuses himself by mechanically repeating certain syllables thus preparing himself for future language, similarly, in the evolution of the species, the mimetic tendency of monkeys was a preparation for the mimetic language of primitive man.

Imitation naturally presupposes perception, because one cannot imitate what has not been perceived. From various experiments conducted by Kohts, Tellier, and Köhler, it emerges that monkeys have sharper and more exact visual perceptions than hearing. Joni the chimpanzee, for example, discerned thirteen plane geometrical figures (circle, oval, dodecagon, decagon, hexagon, octagon, pentagon, square, rectangle, rhombus, trapezium, circular sector, and semicircle), in addition to various forms of triangles, rectangles, etc.; and ten solid figures (sphere, cylinder, cone, and various pyramids and prisms). It should be noted that in monkeys the eyes are placed forward and are closer to each other tl an in other animals, so that the visual field is narrower and sight becomes binocular stereoscopic and permits a more exact evaluation of forms and distances.[5]

Imagination and Aesthetic Sense

Hallucinations, Erotic Images, Dreams—Disinterested Curiosity—The Liking for Adorning Oneself—Comic Sense, Pretense, and Tricks—Intellectual Capacity.

It was commonly held by zoologists of the past that animals were capable of feeling but not of contemplating their own sensations or of forming images and representations. How poorly founded such an opinion was has already emerged from what we have said about memory and imitation. Now we would like to dwell more specifically on the imaginative faculties and on the aesthetic sense of animals.

It is a fact that in certain abnormal states which, however, are not rare, animal imagination generally goes as far as to become hallucinatory. A cow, for example, may start fleeing as though from an imaginary dog, put itself into a defensive position, flee and turn around to look at the presumed pursuer, and lower its forehead to attack it in its turn.[1] Moreover, when in heat, cows are commonly tormented by erotic images and act out the sexual act with such evidence as to simulate the position of the male.

From various indications it emerges that animals sometimes relive a life of their own, made of images, in their dreams. The representative memory and imagination of horses seems to be particularly lively. Through their imagination they amplify the real object and transform it into a terrifying phantasm, so that, according to an old Italian saying (recalled also by Bretagnier) "fantasia da cavallo" means a strong and lively imagination.

That birds are not devoid of a certain aesthetic sense seems to be revealed by the dances and singing competitions performed by the males in courtship rites.

As far as monkeys are concerned, they often give proof of uninvolved curiosity which may perhaps be considered an initial sign of an inclination toward contemplation. They may spend a long time looking at, sniffing, and tasting whatever they happen to get their hands on. Brehm remembers a chimpanzee from the Berlin zoo which, whenever it was brought into a room with windows facing the outside, would rush to the window sill and amuse itself greatly as it watched the bustle on the road. Not even when offered its favorite foods would it be induced to abandon its place of observation. A phenomenon, observes the compiler, which would not have occurred with any other animal. The same young monkey would show its joy by hopping on one foot and then on the other, and sometimes it performed wild dances accompanied by cries of jubilation and hand clapping.[2]

All monkeys display an intense delight in shiny, transparent, and brightly colored objects (especially red, blue, yellow, and white ones). They like to collect small, round, soft and smooth objects, pieces of glass, nails, small stones, little sticks, and above all colored rags. They adorn themselves with the strangest objects, putting around their neck such things as a rag, leafy fronds, a chain, a cord. They strut and pose walking backwards and forwards and sometimes rhythmically stamping their feet.

Köhler observed a young monkey which "for decoration" held an empty tin between its teeth and another one which carried a stone on its back. They looked proud of their decorations and their companions would observe them with vivid interest.

The same author speaks of a chimpanzee which, on having found a bucket of lime, dipped its hand in it and brought it to its mouth to taste the flavor. After spitting out the repulsive drink, it realized that white traces remained on the black hairs of its hand. It then amused itself by dyeing its extremities with lime and later its body and all surrounding objects. Very soon the other monkeys imitated it and amused themselves with that game for some time.

Max Schmidt tells us about certain orangutans from the Frankfurt zoo which had fun draping themselves in big sheets of colored paper. Mostly they would hold two opposite corners tightly under the chin so that the head was covered by what looked like a hood. One of them, on receiving a grey blanket to cover its bed with, went to rummage through the wardrobe and, finding a vividly colored blanket which was under the others, took it and covered itself as though it were a cloak. Gua, the chimpanzee, raised by Mr. and Mrs. Kellog, showed a childlike taste for decorative scribbles, and, for example, would blow on the window pane and then doodle with its finger on the steamed surface.[3]

Confirmation that monkeys do not lack in a certain rudimentary imagination and capacity to amuse themselves by playing with images is to be found in their taste, however coarse, for comicality and practical jokes. Max Schmidt talks about a young monkey which delighted in pulling the beards of its trainers. Given that the latter were on their guard, the monkey would first make slow, delicate, caressing movements, and then take advantage of a moment of distraction to fulfil its aim; or it would hold a toy out to them or a piece of bread, and when they had come close enough he would grab them quickly by the beard pulling it in a friendly fashion. When the trick succeeded it would express its joy through an expression of the face and by clapping its hands.[4] Köhler describes certain chimpanzees which ate bread by a chicken coop and soon realized that the chickens would run up to the net to peck at the crumbs. One of the young monkeys put its hand with bread in it through the net and quickly drew it back when the chicken was about to peck at the bread. All the monkeys amused themselves with this game, and sometimes, when the chicken came running, they would prick it with a piece of wire which they had ready in their hand. Another thing which also happened was that the two monkeys would arrange to amuse themselves together with this game: one would lure the chicken with the bread and the other would prick it, thus displaying a malicious pleasure common not only to monkeys.

Only one chimpanzee showed a better nature by not drawing its hand back and taking pleasure in watching the chickens as they ate its bread. The relish for playing tricks was often noted by the experimenters who had trained some monkeys to pile up cases and climb on top of them. When one of the companions was on top in a rather unstable position, very often another young monkey would pass behind the monkey on the cases and gladly push it over. The young monkey would then quickly flee and, together with the others, take delight in its companion's misadventure.[5]

A rather anthropomorphic psychology would seem to emerge from the following case, narrated, after all, by as reliable an author as Thompson. A monkey was attached to a bamboo framework with a sliding ring. Two crows would wait for the moment when the monkey was distant from its food in order to steal it. Each time this happened, the monkey would express its disappointment and anger with an expressive piece of mimicry, but the two thieves were not at all bothered by this. Once, while the crows were taking hold of its food, the monkey pretended it felt ill, closed its eyes, and let its head fall; but while doing this it very slowly drew nearer. One of the crows, which had been deceived, did not move away, and with a leap the monkey was on top of it, grabbed it, held it tight between its knees, and took revenge by very calmly pulling out all its feathers thus leaving the crow bare and ridiculous.[6]

In his book on the origin of man, Darwin too recalls an episode of monkeyish revenge, witnessed by the zoologist A. Smith. At the Cape of Good Hope an official delighted in making fun of a baboon by playing little tricks on it. One Sunday, while the official was drawing near in his full-dress uniform, the monkey took some earth, mixed it with water, made a ball and threw it at him, covering him in mud. From that day onward the baboon would assume an air of triumph every time he saw the official. We believe that these episodes highlight sufficiently well that capacity of representing one's own mood to oneself, and of taking pleasure in certain images, which is an essential psychological premise to all language.

As already mentioned naturalists have stopped to carefully examine whether, and to what extent, anthropoid apes are capable of proper reasoning, and data collected on the matter are not lacking.

We have used the following obvious criteria in choosing and evaluating such data: (1) avoid superficially anthropomorphic interpretations by constantly asking ourselves whether an action which would seem to reveal a clear degree of intelligence and purposeful intent, was not, on the contrary, accomplished by instinct, that is, without awareness of the purpose to be attained. It should also be remembered that animals often reach a useful goal not through a rationally prearranged action, but through a series of random attempts, carried out blindly, and from which those attempts that do not produce useful results are gradually eliminated; (2) avoid the opposite fault, namely, that of finding the easy way out in all cases with the dogmatic assertion that the given result was not obtained as a consequence of reasoning, but through mere instinct; (3) in order to avoid arbitrary conclusions in the former sense and in the latter adhere to the principle that instinct belongs to the species and is hereditary, while intentional actions and reasoning belong to the individual. When an action is always accomplished in the same manner by all individuals of a given species, even when they have grown up in different environments, this is a sign that the instinctive element predominates; all the more so if the action continues to be accomplished mechanically even when, because of particular circumstances, it proves to be contrary to the purpose to be reached. On the other hand, those actions which are modified individually each time they are used in order to adapt them to the actual circumstances may be considered as not being devoid of conscious rationality. Doubts, moments of embarrassment, and perplexity before solving a problem are indications of reasoning, while instinct usually goes straight to its goal.

From the many facts at our disposal we will mention a few among the most significant.

1st experiment.[7] The chimpanzee is in a room two meters high. A fruit is hanging from the ceiling. In the room there are two crates next to each other, some poles, and some sticks. The monkey first tries to make the fruit fall with the help of a short pole, then with a longer one, which being too heavy oscillates in its hands. It becomes infuriated, throws away the pole, and bangs the wall with its fists. Fatigued, it then sits on one of the two crates, looks all around, and rather perplexedly scratches its head. It stares at the nearby crate, seizes it and pushes it toward the fruit, it takes hold of a stick, climbs onto the crate, and takes the fruit.

2nd experiment. The next day the same monkey is put back into the room where there are two crates, a light table, and no pole. The monkey pushes the crate under the fruit, makes a rough estimate of the distance, realizes that it is too big, turns to the other crate, draws it near and clumsily tries to place it on top of the first one. It does not succeed and flies into a rage. Once it has calmed down a bit, it becomes aware of the table, which is rather lighter than the crate. It seizes it and pushes it toward the crate but, given that it acts too hastily, the table falls upside down, and, discouraged, the monkey abandons the enterprise.

3rd experiment. There is only a small rung-ladder in the room. The monkey moves it under the fruit. Awkwardly, without leaning it against the wall, it attempts to climb up the ladder and does not succeed. The experimenter approaches the monkey to encourage it. The monkey takes advantage of this and pulls him by the hand right under the fruit. It rapidly jumps onto his shoulders and takes hold of the reward.

It has been observed by the Kellogs and others that a coordinated action, which requires the shifting of various objects, is performed more easily when the objects can be taken in with a single glance, otherwise, while looking at one of the objects, the monkey ends up by forgetting the others and is distracted from its goal. However, chimpanzees are clearly capable of remembering topographic representations even when they can no longer see the objects. In one case a monkey not seeing a crate or ladder it might use, ran down the corridor into another room, which was more than eight meters away, to get a rung-ladder which it had noticed there some time before.

4th experiment. In order to reach the fruit hanging up high the chimpanzee finds a crate, open at the top and with three big rocks inside. It looks inside, becomes aware of the rocks, takes out one first and then a second. Without taking out the third it pushes the crate under the fruit with a great effort and reaches it.

By repeating the experiment a couple of times, the monkey learns to remove all three rocks immediately and then to shift the crate to the desired position. On another occasion the experiment was altered by putting sand into the crate instead of rocks. The monkey partly emptied it and then moved it.

5th experiment. Köhler carried out various experiments with some rods and sticks. Sometimes he would put sticks at the chimpanzee's disposal which were all too short to use for reaching the fruit. In these cases, a quick look was usually enough for the animal to form an idea of the inadequacy of the sticks.

One day, not being able to reach the fruit with either of the two sticks, the young monkey held these tightly in its hand with the two extremities united so that in its eyes they produced the image of a longer stick. The attempt of course failed, but it gave the experimenter the idea of using rods with holes in them so that they could be inserted into each other. The first time the two rods were perhaps joined by chance, but afterwards the young monkey became accustomed to the new maneuver and took pleasure in joining the various rods so as to obtain a longer pole.

6th experiment. One of the monkeys already accustomed to using the sticks to draw the fruit near is in a ten meter long cage with a banana outside the cage, at a distance where it cannot be reached with the arm only. Not having a rod at its disposal, the monkey searches anxiously here and there. Its eyes fall on a kind of box made of strips of wood at the other end of the cage. It stares at it for a long time, approaches it, tears off a strip, runs to the other end of the cage, and with the help of the strip takes possession of the fruit. The experimenter (Köhler) observes that while the monkey was moving its eyes around in search of a useful tool, it had the obvious expression of someone with "a problem to solve" on its face.

On another occasion the monkey had at its disposal a piece of wire bent into a ring, and on realizing that the ring was too short, straightened out a part of it with its hands and teeth so as to lengthen the wire and reach the fruit.

However, for numerous actions accomplished by monkeys, it is not easy to distinguish how much should be attributed to mechanical training and how much to the initiative and intelligence of the animal. For example, a chimpanzee from the Vienna zoo called Maja (which the people there had baptized "Mr. Mayer"), on hearing from the keeper the words "it's cold, light the heater," would immediately go to the heater, open the door, fetch some paper and straw from a corner of the room, put everything into the heater, and spread out the paper with its hands so that the air could circulate. The chimpanzee would arrange some pieces of wood on top, fetch some matches, light them skillfully and cautiously, and set fire to the paper. Before moving away it would make sure the fire had lit properly and immediately after it would close the door and go off. All this would take place without intervention by the keeper.[8]

We will leave aside other examples, given that not only the few typical experiments just reported, but also almost all the episodes we have so far described to illustrate memory, imagination, etc. (just as those we will mention further on), all reveal a certain degree of intellectual capacity.

Mimetic Expression and Phonetic Expression

Examples of Mimetic Displays—Indicating Gestures—Signs of Intentional Communication—Experiments on the Mimetic Capacity of Monkeys Are Lacking, While Those (Providing No Results) on Their Phonetic Capacity Abound.

On the basis of the episodes so far described and of what has been said above regarding imitation, it seems to us that anthropomorphic monkeys are endowed with all the psychological premises necessary to the birth of mimetic language, while being almost devoid of the necessary requirements for the birth of phonetic language.

The mental conditions of these animals are not difficult to follow and interpret, for they find spontaneous expression not only in the almost grotesque vivacity of facial expressions, but often in real, little imitative scenes. In most cases such scenes remain at the level of immediate physiological manifestations, but here and there a few more explicit and intentional communicative symbols already begin to appear.

Let us look at some examples.

The structural unit of monkeys living in society is that of a family composed of a male and several females. The male, called the "overlord" by English scholars, terrorizes the females and does not allow them to be approached by other males. The young "bachelor" monkeys recognize the overlord's supremacy, at least temporarily, and usually do not dare touch food until it has had its fill. If one of them makes the smallest act of resistance or insubordination, the overlord comes upon it, seizes it, and holds it tightly with its hands and symbolically imitates a position similar to that of the male during the sexual act, as though to say "I'm the 'overlord' and you're the female weakling!" Vice versa, when the young monkey does not feel up to facing a struggle with the overlord but wishes to display its submission, it symbolically imitates the position of abandon proper to the female.

On rare occasions a female may be stronger than all the males of its group and may usurp supremacy. In such cases the female dominates the males as much as the other females, and to symbolize its power it simulates the movements typical of the male.

The act of picking off fleas, which mothers usually practice on their little ones, sometimes assumes a symbolic meaning of affection and protection. Maslow speaks of an overlord that had invited one of the subordinate young monkeys to pick off its fleas. However the bachelor did not dare accomplish that act on its dominator which signified protection and in a certain sense supremacy. To make it understand that it was momentarily foregoing its prerogative, the overlord then imitated the position of the female. Persuaded by this act of submission the bachelor began at once to pick off the fleas.[1]

It seems to me that a sort of embryonic mimetic dialogue is evident in this episode.

Regarding sexual relations, Zuckerman describes the following "exquisitely feminine" episode. The overlord turned around because something attracted its attention. One of its females took advantage of this to offer itself to a bachelor that happened to be close by, and the latter very soon met its wishes. The overlord suddenly turned around again and became aware of the betrayal. The female freed itself of its accomplice, ran screaming toward the overlord and offered itself, while at the same time threatening its "seducer" with expressions of disgust and threatening gestures almost as though to say: "I didn't want to, that rascal raped me!"[2]

Females are usually dominated and even terrorized, but cases of more affectionate relationships are not lacking. Fr. Specht, who paints animals, speaks of a chimpanzee from the Stuttgart zoo that had been separated from its companion during a long voyage. As soon as they found each other again the two of them remained silent for a few moments, then they threw themselves into each other's arms and kissed each other repeatedly. The female ran to get its blanket, spread it out on the ground, sat on it and, using gestures, invited the male to sit down and make itself comfortable. During the meal they sat next to each other eating from their own dishes. The female took the male's glass with delicacy, drank a sip from it, and gave it back to him.[3]

While raising their offspring mothers make themselves understood by means of gestures. As soon as the little one is able to stand up, its mother puts it next to objects which it may seize with its hands and shows the objects to it. She accompanies the little one close to the iron bars of the cage and then slowly draws away to a corner, leaving it in a standing up position. After a while the infant monkey learns to climb up the iron bars but does not know how to come down again, is afraid and begins to whimper until its mother goes to fetch it. Its mother teaches it to walk on four legs first and then on two. She holds it by the hand and with threats and caresses induces it to walk standing up. Sometimes, while in a squatting position, the mother calls the young monkey both vocally and through gestures, and waits for it with outstretched hands.[4]

Experiments with orangutans could prove to be particularly interesting. As they are almost completely mute, they have no other means of displaying their impressions and emotions than through mimicry. A hunter reports that when he held out his hand to some wounded orangutans, they squeezed it delicately, giving him the clear sensation of a friendly and conciliatory shake of the hand. Another hunter speaks of a little one that expressed both its satisfaction and dissatisfaction with the funniest grimaces. When he showed it a palatable morsel it licked its lips, made some craving movements with its mouth and lightly rolled its eyes with an air of ecstasy.[5]

An orangutan observed by Max Schmidt enjoyed playing with children. To make friends it would offer them gifts, a stick, a cape, or the like. When the orangutan was planning some prank, a sly little mocking grin would appear on its face. When it was afraid, it would protrude its bottom lip or both lips.

Once a mirror was placed against the walls of the cage. At first the orangutan moved away from the mirror showing diffidence and fear, then it went back, looked at its image with anger, tried to throw its cape and some food remains at the image, and as a sign of its contempt spat on it. After some time it began to become accustomed to the image and tried to induce it to play. The orangutan fetched a piece of white paper, which seemed particularly beautiful to it, and held the paper out toward the mirror waving it back and forth, just as we would do to attract a child's attention.[6]

Joni, the chimpanzee raised by Mrs. Kohts, would also get angry on seeing its own image, would strike the mirror, and when the mirror was taken away, would shake its fists threateningly. The threatening gesture made by shaking the fists and sometimes by striking oneself on the chest is generally quite common.

Not only are embraces and kisses a common way of displaying likes and affection, but so are hand shakes or the placing of an arm on the shoulder of the loved one or companion. According to Teuber (who together with Köhler spent a long time in the experimental camp of Teneriffa) young monkeys are in the habit of pushing pieces of chewed fruit into the mouth of their loved companion as a sign of love.[7]

Köhler describes the following little scene: one night, while it was raining heavily, the scientist's attention was attracted by the plaintive cries of two young monkeys that were not able to return to their cage, as the key was broken and the keeper was not able to open the door. Köhler forced the lock, opened the door, and stood aside so that the two animals could enter the dry cage. However, though soaking wet and trembling from the cold, they did not enter immediately, but showed their gratitude by embracing him, one at the level of the chest, the other at the knees. Only after having thanked him in this way did they enter and lie down on the warm straw.[8]

It is common knowledge that the gesture of embracing the knees as a sign of affection by a person of lower rank with respect to his superior is a tradition among various populations.

The educational effectiveness of kindness even toward animals is made evident by the following episode. Dr. Martini was to operate on a chimpanzee seriously ill with an abscess on the throat. Four men held it still, but it struggled and pushed them away. Then the doctor, who had a good relationship with the animal, made the male nurses leave and tried to persuade it with caresses and affectionate words. Not only did the young monkey allow the abscess to be examined without rebelling, but it even brought the doctor's hand to the sore, looking at him imploringly. A keeper took it into his lap and the young monkey spontaneously curved its head backwards so as to facilitate the surgical operation. The intervention was accomplished without the animal having at all moved or screamed. Once it was finished, it sighed as though it had been freed and displayed an expression of joy on its face while with its own hands it seized the doctor's and the keeper's hands, squeezing them affectionately.[9]

Certain forms of greetings among monkeys recall human greetings. On meeting after some time, the chimpanzees observed by von Oertzen would greet each other by rising on their back legs, embracing each other and joyfully screaming. Köhler observed a chimpanzee which, to greet a person who was friendly to it, would hold its hand in a curved position, with the back toward its friend and the nails on the inside so as not to offend in any way. The gesture is equal to a peace offering, similar to the Roman greeting, in which the hand is displayed unarmed.

Johann von Fischer observed some monkeys belonging to the *Rhesus* species in the Frankfurt zoo. They would welcome their fellow creatures by amicably turning their posteriors toward them, which, as we know, are brightly colored; and in this connection Darwin observed that certain displays of friendship among primitive man, such as rubbing noses or massaging each other's bellies, may seem equally odd.

Extremely common are indicating gestures which are sometimes very close to language or actually its equivalent. For example, Sultano the chimpanzee, who had learned to climb onto its trainers' shoulders (Köhler) to reach a fruit hanging from the ceiling, on becoming aware of the fruit when the trainer was at a distance, would run to him, grab him by the hand and pull him, making him understand its wish that it should be accompanied to the desired place.

Once, one of the keepers stopped under the banana hanging from the ceiling, and when Sultano jumped onto his shoulders the keeper played him the trick of crouching so that the young monkey could not reach the fruit. Sultano climbed down again, seized the keeper by the bottom of his trousers and, panting, tried to make him understand its need of getting up high. It seems obvious to me that in this case, the monkey had a clear intuition of what it wanted to reach and tried to communicate this to the keeper. Early mimetic language probably arose from communications of this kind.

An indicating gesture was also that made by the little female monkey Gua, raised by the Kelloggs. When sitting in its arm chair and wanting to be taken out and held, it would whimper with outstretched arms and as soon as it was contented would emit a characteristic sigh of relief. Monkeys may often be observed as they invite a companion to help them in some task. Crawford speaks of a chimpanzee that endeavored in vain to drag a heavy crate under the fruit hanging from the ceiling. It looked around perplexedly, perceived its companion at a distance, ran to it and through very vivacious mimicry tried to make the companion understand that it wished to be helped. The other at first did not understand and thought these gestures were made for fun and also began to gesticulate and play about. But the former insisted, pushed and pulled its companion toward the crate until it understood, followed, and joined in with the work.[10]

As observed by many trainers, the extent to which mimetic language is inborn in animals can also be seen from the fact that when a monkey which has already been trained is present at the training of another monkey, the former becomes impatient to show how the task should be accomplished and to help and correct its companion. It cheers while following all the actions of the other, accompanies every movement with similar movements of its own body, shows satisfaction at the right action and disappointment at the wrong one.[11] We saw above, in Wolfe's experiment, that after having put the token in the slot machine, the monkey would stretch out its hand and wait for the fruit. This gesture, which is similar to and sometimes completely identical to the human gesture of holding out one's hand to beg, has been observed several times by Nissen, Crawford, and others. For example, Crawford noticed that when he gave food to a monkey and left another without, the one left without food would stretch out its hands, waving them up and down while whimpering and pounding its feet to attract its companion's attention. And the latter not only understood but also often shared its food. I myself saw a little monkey at the Rome zoo which, on seeing a child eat bread, stretched out its left hand holding it in a slightly concave position, and with the index finger of the right hand lightly tapped on it, as though to say, "Here, put it here!"

Such expressions are not surprising, even if, from a spiritual point of view, they are equivalent to a linguistic expression. If we were to discover that animals use, without human intervention, phonetic expressions that correspond to the gesture just described, an enormous fuss would be made about it. But mimetic expressions do not seem so astonishing because everyone more or less knows that language, like all spontaneous semiological systems, must have gone through two stages of development: the first centered on directly expressive signs, the second on conventional signs; and that consequently it is only natural that signs of the first, more than of the second, should be found in anthropoid apes.

According to Mrs. Kohts the young monkey Joni not only expressed its desires through gestures but also tended to create a symbolism through them which enabled a reciprocal understanding. For example, when the monkey was hungry or thirsty it would begin to press its lips on Mrs. Kohts' hand and suck one of her fingers; if it moderately desired something, it would hold out its hand, but to signify a more intense desire it would hold out both hands. The refusal to eat was expressed by shaking the head and turning the other way, etc. If Mrs. Kohts had posed herself our problem, she probably would have noticed that these gestures were at first simple instinctive manifestations, but subsequently they were used intentionally for the purpose of communication.

I was forced to scrape together this scanty information about the mimetic capacity of monkeys from diverse authors, for there are no studies that I know of which treat the subject specifically. Indeed, even this scarce information is not usually given to us as data concerning mimetic expression (which in itself is hardly considered worthy of attention), but as observations casually made to illustrate the emotional and intellectual inclinations of these animals.

By contrast there are several studies, some of which have been compiled with incredible patience and accuracy, on the phonetic capacities of anthropoid apes. The best still remain those by Mr. and Mrs. Kellog and by Mrs. Kohts. The Kellogs listed four types of sounds emitted by the chimpanzee Gua:

(1) an aggressive bark similar to a dog's, which was the normal reaction toward strangers;
(2) a lower and often aphonic bark expressing satisfaction;
(3) a scream which recalled the high notes of a soprano and expressed fear or pain;
(4) the cry "uuh-uuh uuh uuh-uuh uuh uuh!" given out in all tones expressing uncertainty, worry, alarm, grief, or fear.

As time went by the meaning of these calls changed. Subdued barking became the symbol of approval, and the sound "uuh uuh uuh uuh!" ended up signifying general disapproval. These meanings, however, were acquired under the influence of the trainer.

All attempts at trying to make the monkey Gua pronounce the word "papa" failed. It limited itself to merely imitating the movements of the lips. The capacity of attributing a meaning to words also proved to be rather scarce, even if greater than the capacity of pronouncing them.

A series of special experiments were carried out by Yerkes and by Mrs. Learned.[12] The authors recorded (in the experimental station of the Canary Islands) four types of cries:

(1) those connected with waiting for food;
(2) those let out during meals;
(3) those used in the presence of man;
(4) those used in the presence of other monkeys.

The cries are numerous and not easily catalogued because the same sounds do not always correspond to the same impressions.

Yerkes then made a series of very patient attempts over a period of eight months, at teaching a chimpanzee to articulate the most simple syllables. The result was negative. The young monkey succeeded in moving its lips and imitating the mimicry of its trainer, but it did not produce any sounds. The author concludes: "My experiments lead me to believe that anthropomorphic monkeys have something to say, but do not possess the capacity of using sounds with which to express themselves: all sounds produced by them are manifestations belonging to the species and not individual expressions."[13] Furness also did his best and every day for six months he tried to teach an orangutan to pronounce the syllables "pà, pà." He would stand in front of a mirror so that the young monkey could observe both the movements of its teacher's lips as well as its own. After six months the orangutan succeeded in repeating the syllables "pà, pà." Later it became accustomed to considering that sound as symbolizing its trainer to the point that it would answer the question: "Where's pàpà?" by pointing to its trainer with its hand and amicably hitting him on the shoulder. Applied to a chimpanzee the same method gave inferior results. After five years' teaching the chimpanzee pronounced the syllables "mà, mà" very badly.

L. Boutan studied a young gibbon from birth up to its fifth year and recorded fourteen different affective sounds. But the gibbon did not prove capable of imitating natural sounds, nor of giving an individual impression to its own calls, and yet the author entitles his study *Le pseudo-langage.*[14]

Other authors have actually tried to compile dictionaries of monkey languages (R. L. Garner, *Die Sprache der Affen*, London 1905) and Schwidetzky entitles one of his studies *Lemurisch, Gibbonisch, Ureuropäisch,* and another *Pongonisch, Urdinarisch, Indogermanisch* as though we might speak of "monkey" languages just as we speak of Indo-European languages; but the content of his essays does not correspond to the label.

These authors did not take into account the fact, several times confirmed through observation, that the center of phonetic language (Broca's area) is absent in monkeys. They would seem to share the common conviction of an immediate transition between anthropoid apes as we know them and such human speakers as those of current primitive populations. It would seem that none of them considered the hypothesis of the existence of an intermediate link between the two stages of development. In our opinion, however, this intermediary stage probably lasted tens of thousands of years, a far longer period than that which has elapsed from the dawn of civilization to modern times, and, furthermore, we believe that it was in this period that early mimetic-pictographic language arose and developed.

Experiments carried out meticulously by naturalists on the capacity of monkeys to invent and use an expressive medium somewhat similar to language have not produced any positive results because they are founded on the preconceived notion that the only possible language is phonetic language. As we said, the premises which could have favored the birth of phonetic language are absent in monkeys, while the premises for the development of a language accompanied by emotional cries abound. Had naturalists devoted a tenth part of the time and trouble employed in the study of the phonetic capacity of monkeys instead to the study of their mimetic capacity, their results would have been far more fruitful. Especially deplorable is the fact that no researcher has so far carried out (with the help of an expert in the gestures used by deaf-mutes and by primitive men) any experiments that aim at discovering to what extent anthropoid apes may be trained to understand and use a mimetic language suited to their *forma mentis*. By selecting the most skillful individuals, such experiments, if carried out methodically, would certainly prove to be far more instructive and perhaps even decisive.[15]

Summing-Up and Concluding Remarks

An Attempt at Exemplifying the Glottogonic Process—Reciprocal Action between Linguistic and Social Development.

The hypothesis we have put forth and examined in the first part of our work is the following: unlike currently spoken languages, initially, human language was not a system of conventional phonetic signs. On the contrary, it was a directly expressive language, and precisely a mimetic-pictographic language accompanied by affective and imitative cries. In our opinion, this hypothesis cannot be accepted or refused in accordance with individual preferences, but rather it is the only scientifically plausible hypothesis at our disposal in the light of present knowledge.

Summing up, we may list the reasons that have led to our conviction as follows:

Considering that, after language, the most important means of communication among men is writing, and that, while we do not possess any documents on the initial stages of languages, we do indeed possess a vast quantity of material on the evolution of writing systems, we examined the development of the latter with a view to throwing some light on the laws which may have exercised their influence on the birth and development of phonetic language as well.

To this end, of particular interest are ideographic and hieroglyphic writing systems and not those involving phonetic references such as alphabetic and syllabic writing, etc. In fact, the former do not aim at calling to mind the words but rather the direct concepts of a given language. This occurs, for example, in Chinese writing, whose texts may prove to be comprehensible even to someone unfamiliar with that language. Such writing systems may well and truly be likened to a literary language, in which graphic rather than phonetic signs are used, more than to alphabetical writing.

In the development of writing systems among different peoples, we are able to detect uniform characteristics which may be considered to be the expression of laws founded on the psychological nature of man.

The most important of these characteristics are:

(a) All writing systems which emerged spontaneously and which have reached a high level of development were originally directly expressive and pictographic in character.

(b) In all writing systems this characteristic gradually diminishes in the course of evolution, and ultimately the conventional character prevails.

(c) The conventional character of the initial period does not derive from a premeditated convention but is the result of various factors which alter the initial pictographic character rendering it unrecognizable.

(d) These factors are: abbreviations and schematizations caused by the practical need for simplification and clarity, taste for decoration, and influence of the material used.

On examining the evolution of historical languages we find that analogous tendencies emerge. The progressive predominance of the conventional element may be observed not only in those words which gradually lost their onomatopoeic character ("pipio" becomes "piccione" [pigeon] and the like), but also in most of the words used in modern spoken languages (since almost all of them have lost a part of their original evocative resonance for whoever uses them without knowing their etymological history). The factors concurring in this accentuation of the conventional character of languages are much the same as those we observed in the history of writing; the anatomical formation of the vocal cords and the physiological peculiarities of the different races (from which derive the well-known laws of "phonetic changes") correspond to the influence of the material used, contractions due to the "law of minimal effort," and the transition from isolating formations to agglutinative and inflective ones corresponds to the simplifications and abbreviations. Finally, analogous aesthetic exigencies (euphony) as well as the need for clarity and distinction also exert their influence on language.

From all this we were able to infer that, similarly to writing, phonetic language originally must also have been pictographic and directly expressive in character. Thus it would appear that the ancient problem, debated by the Greek thinkers, whether language is "physei" or "nomo," in other words, whether the connection between sign and meaning is natural or arbitrary, may be solved by stating that in the beginning the expressive sign was "natural," but that during the course of evolution it was gradually transformed into something purely conventional.

That this is the way things are also emerges from the simple consideration that certain living beings, still close to the animal state, which would give out a cry of anguish in the face of danger, subsequently became accustomed to associating that cry with the idea of danger, though such conventional signs would never have been established intentionally. Just as it would not be conceivable for a child to come to an agreement with his mother concerning the use of conventional signs before knowing how to speak, it is understandable that he might begin whimpering once he somehow realizes that his mother will pick him up when she hears him.

Therefore, in order to solve the glottogonic problem, we must ask ourselves: "Which are the directly expressive elements still operating in human language that may reasonably be considered as having been of fundamental importance at the very birth of language?"

By examining not only interjections and onomatopoeia but also all expressive phonetic elements, we have identified a considerable set of pictographic elements which have doubtlessly been important in the institution of language. Nevertheless, similarly to most of the researchers preceding us, we have also had to acknowledge that phonetic imitation, even in the broad sense, is not able to serve even the most elementary communicative needs on its own. In fact, even today, a person who finds himself among people with whom he cannot communicate on the basis of a common language will certainly not succeed in making himself understood by imitating natural sounds, but rather will resort to the use of mimetic language.

The hypothesis that the language of gestures and of mimetic expression has had a decisive influence on the institution of language seems to find support in the following considerations and data:

(a) Children understand mimetic expression and use it spontaneously even before knowing how to speak; furthermore, certain languages invented by children who have grown up in isolation are so rich in mimetic expression that they are unintelligible in the dark.

(b) Gesticulation was far more important in the spoken language of the ancients than it is now in the language spoken by modern man.
Pantomimes and mime plays were extremely widespread in antiquity, and mimetic expression prevailed both in dancing and sacred performances as well in magic exorcisms which go back to the beginnings of civilization.

(c) The influence exercised by gestures on writing and on primitive pictographic designs. The fact that the most ancient hieroglyphs and morphograms quite often are not direct reproductions of real objects, but rather schematic reproductions of manual gestures, seems to suggest the existence of a previous language in which the mimetic sign had not yet been completely substituted by the phonetic sign.

(d) Since almost all words in the ancient Egyptian language have a multitude of different meanings, the question arises as to the possibility of understanding each other in such a language; and given that hieroglyphic texts are only comprehensible because every word is accompanied by little explanatory figures, we will have to concede, with Abel, that words in ancient Egyptian acquired a univocal meaning only because they were constantly accompanied by appropriate gestures. Indeed it would seem that the small explanatory hieroglyphic figures are no more than the graphic transcription of those gestures. Analogous considerations can possibly be made in relation to ancient Chinese as well.

(e) When a group of people adopt a language which is different from their own, their families usually preserve some of the syntactic forms proper to the previous language, even after many generations. The fact that the syntax of primitive languages resembles the syntax of mimetic language (as it may be observed for example in the language of semi-educated deaf-mutes) could be interpreted as indicating the existence of a previous gestural language.

(f) In various primitive languages, including those currently in use, gesture is so important that many words only acquire a univocal meaning from the gesture accompanying them (e.g., depending on the specifying gesture, the same word may mean "today," "yesterday," "tomorrow").

(g) The mimetic language of certain primitive peoples is so elaborate that it is able to serve all communication and conversation needs in given occasions. Such a language is in use among widows, in certain regions of Africa and Australia, who are obliged to observe a period of silence. A well-developed gestural "lingua franca," vastly documented by ethnologists, is used among other indigenous peoples of North and South America, Africa, and Australia.

(h) That these primitive languages not merely practical expedients which arose at some later stage, but the residues of an original prehistorical language, would seem to emerge from the brilliant observations made by Cushing, Roth, and other ethnologists. Cushing (who for years lived among the Zuñi tribes, adopting their customs and identifying himself with their *forma mentis*) observed that just as our way of thinking is influenced by the way we express ourselves in discursive language (so that, for example, there is a correspondence between the Aristotelian "categories" and the grammatical parts of discourse), in the same way the psychological formation of concepts in primitive man is clearly influenced by the way they express themselves in gestures, that is, by a natural language whose beginnings go back to the time when man's forefathers were still very close to animal life.

(i) Finally, on examining the psychology and expressive capacity of anthropoid monkeys we found that all the premises which could have favored the birth of phonetic language were lacking, while the premises for the birth and development of pictographic language abounded and indeed we were able to identify certain characteristic gestures which are something more than simple instinctive manifestations of the species, and to some extent already have the character of individual expression developed for the purpose of communication.

There is an obvious gap between the mimetic and phonetic expressions of anthropoid apes and the most primitive human languages. This is only natural, for as fossil residues testify, various species of Pithecanthropi and Paleanthropi, now extinct, existed between monkeys and mankind. In other words, monkeys existed which were more developed than those existent today and men who were less developed than our primitive man, but of the expressive abilities of those extinct families we have no direct record.[1]

The conquest of language, like all important human conquests, took place through several progressive stages: we believe the most important transition from a spiritual point of view, that is, the transition from restricted animal sensuality to primitive pictographic expression, was the first accomplishment. The beginnings of this transition can already be noted in the life of animals, in particular, among anthropoid apes. At a later stage the fluidity of pictographic expression must have become more and more clearly defined and stylized into a given number of conventional mimetic signs, accompanied by interjectional and onomatopoeic expressions. Finally we passed from a prevalently mimetic language to a prevalently phonetic language. Such transitions are not to be understood as distinct separations, but rather as the flowing together and interplay of different characteristics of which some gradually prevail over others.

If we were then to turn to history to discover exactly how these transitions in fact took place, we would also have to appeal to the imagination for help ("fortuna che ci avezza," as Manzoni would say). However, on the basis of the information and considerations we have expounded, we may attempt to formulate a probable hypothesis of our own.

As we have seen in the preceding pages, the young monkey whimpers and stretches out its arms to express its desire to be picked up. It acts out the act of feeding, or sucks its keeper's finger in order to obtain its milk ration; it nestles close to the person it loves and embraces and kisses him/her to express its affection. On the other hand, love for its playmate is displayed by taking food out of its own mouth and putting it into the other's mouth; when begging, the young monkey holds out a curved hand and sometimes points to its empty palm, hitting it with the finger; in order to win a person's friendship, the monkey hits him gently on the shoulder or grabs his hand and squeezes it; when it wants someone to go with it, the monkey grasps its companion by the hand or by the arm and persuasively pulls him toward the desired place; to express perplexity or embarrassment, the monkey pulls a pensive face and scratches its head; it stamps its feet with impatience or dissatisfaction and jumps or shuffles about clapping its hands for joy and happiness; to display anger or a threatening intention, the monkey waves its fist, beats its chest, or stretches out its curved hands showing its nails. On the contrary, as a sign of reconciliation or of greeting, the monkey holds up and displays the unarmed back of its hands; to show its contempt and disgust it spits on its adversary; to refuse food it turns its head to the right and to the left, and to express general refusal it turns aside with the whole of its body. The overlord, and at times some other member of the family group imitating the former, asserts its right to supremacy by imitating the sexual position of the male while the female position becomes the symbol of submission, and the act of picking out fleas, the symbol of maternal protection, etc.

These are mostly gestures in which it is not easy to determine the extent to which we are dealing with simple instinctive reactions or, on the contrary, with the expression of a more or less conscious and personal communicative intention. We may legitimately believe that, in one or more particularly gifted families of anthropoid apes, a greater abundance and variety of such manifestations developed in conjunction with a more conscious need for communication and a more accentuated tendency toward imitating the gestures and attitudes of others. Therefore, it would seem that in such families the capacity of understanding one another gradually increased. To move the mouth as though chewing or to protrude the lips could signify hunger or, more generally, appetite and desire; to hold the hand curved in front of the mouth and the relevant motion of the tongue: to drink, liquid, thirst; to rub the belly or to lick the lips: longing and gratification; a subdued groan and the rolling of the eyes: voluptuousness and pleasure; to bend down, lower the head, embrace the knees: respect toward one's superior; a triumphant attitude of command: the father; the gesture of suckling or of rocking to sleep: the mother; to indicate a short distance from the ground: small, young, baby; to wave the hands while summoning with the voice: the family, brothers and sisters, the clan; an aggressive bark: the enemy, danger, fighting; to cough, to pant looking tired: sick, old, dying; stiff hands and staring eyes: death; screams and jumping while waving the arms: victory; to curve the head downwards or to design a semicircle with the hands: grotto, refuge; the gesture of climbing: tree, nest; an acute trill: help, a call, an invitation to assemble; etc.

In order to clarify the purpose and bearing of these examples we must however observe: (1) that to avoid overindulging in invented particulars and owing to the impossiblity of giving alphabetic expression to screams, barks, moans, whimpering, etc., we did not always take note of the sounds which probably accompanied most gestures either as a natural affective reaction, or as the result of the very effort of making oneself understood, or of the need to attract attention; (2) that in the initial phase of freer creativity there must have been a great many similar gestures to signify different things, and very different ways of signifying the same thing. The enormous abundance of homonyms and the synonyms among the most ancient ideograms is, in our opinion, the residue of a similar period of free expressive creativity; (3) while in our examples we dwelt upon a certain number of fixed and restricted gestures, given the "global" nature of pictographic expression, at most a general form of mimetic representation, though not yet articulated, probably preceded the fixing of individual gestures. For example, if one of the bachelor sons who had gone off with his father on an expedition returned alone, and the others anxiously asked for an explanation, rather than simply make a gesture to signify "he's dead," the bachelor could reply by reconstructing through mimicry the scene of the ambush, surprise, struggle, his father's death, and his own escape; (4) according to the nature of mimetic language

the same gesture could acquire an unlimited number of analogous and derived meanings by being partially modified, or accompanied, by different positions and expressions. This still happens today with many gestures used by
the man in the street. An angry threatening gesture made by showing the
fists and clenching the teeth is one thing and that made by smiling and moving the hand as though to give a spanking is quite another. A caressing buffet
on the cheek is one thing, the hieratical gesture of a priest in the act of bene-
diction is another; a small blow on the belly or a slap on the hips expressing
merriment and cunning complicity is yet another. This polymorphic flexibil-
ity characteristic of the gesture probably gave rise in far more remote times
to the brilliant and fruitful idea, or better still usage, of forming an unlimited
variety of words through the modification and combination of a limited number of roots.

Had a family of primates developed such an expressive capacity as that
exemplified above, the advantage would have certainly been great for their
common defense against foes and bad weather, for the procuring of food
and the raising of offspring, and in general for the growth and consolidation
of family and social life.

The most efficient social system could not then have failed to produce, in
its turn, a richer and more complex affective life and therefore greater need
and increased capacity of expression. Affective, intuitive, expressive, intellectual, and organizational capacities must have influenced each other recipro-
cally, so that the development of one capacity favored the development of all
the others.

By moving in this direction it was possible to gradually develop a proper
mimetic-pictographic-onomatopoeic language, in which expressive signs
were to become more and more stylized into conventional forms.

As shown by the mimetic languages spontaneously created by deaf-mutes
and primitive man, such a form of expression succeeded in satisfying all social needs.[2] It constituted a necessary foundation for the further development of intellectual faculties prior to the rise of phonetic language, which
was both far less direct and far more complex and abstract.

5. Transition from Mimetic to Phonetic Language

Union of Mimetic and Phonetic Expression—Practical Advantages of Voice over Gesture.

Original pictographic language was probably never purely mimetic and completely devoid of phonetic elements, as indeed certain authors have maintained. It is no doubt true that calls and emotional cries are far more limited than gestures in their capacity of immediate meaningful expression—nevertheless they are just as spontaneous. In fact, in anthropoid apes, just as in most animals, gestures and mimicry are almost always accompanied by corresponding vocal expressions.

Even human hand gestures signifying threat, hatred, contempt, and love are combined with corresponding expressions of the face and mouth, so that there is an instinctive union between the words we pronounce and the mimetic expression accompanying them. Indeed it is not easy to pronounce words with a loving meaning and inflection, while accompanying them with an angry and disdainful mimetic expression, or vice versa.

According to an observation already made by Darwin in his essay on *The Expression of the Emotions* and taken up again in more recent times by Paget, our various muscular movements are coordinated and especially those of the hand and mouth, so that, for example, children learning to write feel the need to move their mouth and tongue. Movements of the mouth naturally affect voice emission: the muscular effort involved in lifting a weight is spontaneously translated into sounds rendered alphabetically with hard bilabial fricatives ("auhff!").[1]

In other physiological manifestations, which may sometimes acquire expressive functions, such as heavy breathing, coughing, sneezing, yawning, etc., the phonetic and the mimetic element form a "seamless" whole, so to speak.[2] If man's first language was a mimetic-pictographic language, accompanied by affective cries, and if both expressive manifestations became familiar, it is only natural that one of the two by itself should have recalled the other through association and at times even sufficed in itself to signify the desired concept. In certain cases it may have proven more convenient to use the mimetic sign only (e.g., while hunting) and in others the phonetic sign only (e.g., in the dark). If the concept "snake" was signified with a winding movement of the arm accompanied with a hissing sound, subsequently it could have been signified either mimetically or phonetically: this is true of a multitude of concepts such as "hunting," "enemy," "toil," "tempest," etc.

Once minds got used to such associations between gesture and voice, the medium which in practice presented the greatest advantages must have prevailed.

Whitney rightly remarked that the connection between the mental apparatus and the muscles which produce audible sounds is not greater with respect to the muscles producing visible movements, and that, therefore, human beings could have used mimetic signs as much as phonetic signs to communicate their thoughts. But, he adds, the practical advantages of use of the voice over gestures are numerous and evident. In the first place it is economical, for we engage a mechanism (mouth, tongue, and larynx) which can hardly be used for anything else, and those indispensible instruments which are our hands are left free for other purposes. The voice is more easily perceptible, so that slight differences can be impressed upon the senses at a distance at which movements become indistinct; words are not hidden by objects that get in the way and they leave the speaker's eyes and hands free for other activities; they can be distinguished in the dark as much as in the light and can attract and hold the attention of one person or many as no other means can.

Thus it seems that early phonetic signs (in a sense, the early roots of future languages) arose either as spontaneous affective and imitative sounds or as phonemes closely connected to mimetic expression. However, attempts made by various researchers to identify the "natural" origin of the roots in today's spoken languages seem naive and not very conclusive.

It will suffice to think of how certain expressions are formed in the language of children to convince ourselves of the difficulties, and in most cases of the uselessness, of such inquiries. Let us remember the case of the child who after having used the expression "boom!" to signify the noise of a fallen object and subsequently of a small slap, and then extended this expression to anything causing pain, for example, soap stinging his eyes while washing himself; and let us remember the other child who used the same expression for a dish which had fallen on the ground and therefore for a broken dish, and subsequently for any broken or torn object. Who could ever understand the natural connection between the expression "boom!" and soap, or between the same expression and a torn piece of clothing, without first being familiar with these precedents? And if similar transformations occur before our very eyes within the life span of a single individual, who could ever recognize those transformations which took place over tens of thousands of years in the succession of different races?[3]

Furthermore, observation of how certain expressive conventions are formed in the spontaneous language of deaf-mutes shows that the original connection between sign and meaning may often be purely fortuitous. We saw, for example, that deaf-mutes from a Paris institute said "gymnasium evening" for Saturday evening, or hinted at certain exercises with their arms to signify Saturday, because the physical education lesson took place then. Had the lesson time been changed and the sign left the same, it would have been very difficult to understand its origin.

Therefore it must be acknowledged that the probability of tracing the prehistorical origin of a current root is practically nonexistent. It may well be, for example, that the Indo-European root *ikk* which seems to signify something pointed and sharp (from which we get our "acutus" and "oculus") derives, as some authors have maintained, from an initial interjection of "Lautgebärde" *k-kk,* emitted in the strain of plunging the dagger into the victim. But it is far more likely that this expression had a completely different origin which we will never be able to reconstruct. It is not within the scope of our present inquiry to ascertain the historical origin of single expressions. Our task is to formulate a general theory capable of explaining the origin of language, that is to say, of an achievement that marks the transition from animal to human life.[4]

In the light of present knowledge we believe that the theory we have proposed and expounded is the only convincing one, thus we hope that scholars will accept it as a working hypothesis and test its operative efficacy. We believe that by working in this direction many problems, such as that dealt with by Trombetti regarding the monogenesis or polygeny of language, could receive a new and more fruitful approach. But our most fervent wish is that our essay might in some way contribute toward the creation and general acceptance in Italy of studies in comparative mimicry, a discipline which we believe may produce results at least equal to those obtained by its older and far more fortunate sister.

6. Note on the Problem of Roots

Naiveté of Considering Roots as the Residue of the
Original Language—Glottologic Hypercriticism—
Verbal Meanings Prevail Both in Roots and in Mi-
metic Language—Roots Do Not Represent the Most
Elementary Linguistic Period because They Were
Preceded by a Mimetic Period—Monosyllabic Roots
Are Mostly a Later Stylization of Pictographic
Expressions—Inconsistency of the Thesis that Con-
siders Roots as Pure Grammatical Abstractions—In-
consistency of the Thesis that Denies Any Distinction
between the Period of Roots and the Subsequent
Period—Inconsistency of the Thesis that Aims at
Wholly Discrediting the Theory of the Three Evo-
lutionary Stages—Roots as Signifying Phonemes Not
Derivable from Other Phonemes.

We have already referred to the appearance of early roots without taking
into consideration the difficulties presented by the concept of linguistic roots.
These difficulties had already been perceived by early modern philology and
have been brought to the forefront more clearly by subsequent researchers.
We will now examine the problem of the roots because it will also help to
show how the hypothesis of mimetic origin favors a more comprehensive
approach to old problems in linguistics.

A few historical references will help make things clearer. As is well-known,
ancient Indian grammarians had already observed that syllables with similar
meanings are often common to different words, so that those words may be
considered as belonging to the same family. These syllables were then considered as the "datum" or the "theme" of the word. The Roman grammarians
called such words "roots" by analogy with the name used by the atomists to
denominate the elements forming things. The words of historical languages
were thus considered as being composed of a basic element and of other
formal elements.[1]

When the founders of modern philology discovered roots common to the main European languages and to Sanskrit, some of them believed that by gradually going back from the languages of more recent formation to those of more ancient families (for example, from the romance languages to Latin, and from Latin to the ancient Indo-European mother tongue), we would eventually arrive at the words of a primitive language made of roots only; and because roots are usually monosyllabic, it was thought that the first language must have been monosyllabic. In this way a distinction was made between a "period of roots," or of the constitution of language, and a subsequent period in which the historical languages developed from the original phonemes. Friedrich Schlegel went as far as considering root-words as the result of divine revelation, while the subsequent development of languages was the result of human work.

In conformity with such a description of roots, a genetic classification of languages was then established. The *isolating* languages were thought to belong to the initial stage in the development of languages (for example, Chinese, in which as a rule words are not obtained from the fusion of several elements, but rather are formed by the juxtaposition of monosyllabic roots, with the lexical element predominating over the grammatical).

A second stage was thought to be represented by the *agglutinative* languages (such as the Ural-Altaic) in which words are composed of several roots that are joined in such a way as to allow recognition of the different components. The third stage was thought to be constituted by the *inflected* languages, in which words are formed from the fusion of various roots in such a way as to make the elements composing them unrecognizable for the uninstructed (e.g., the ablative of "mens" becomes a simple adverbial desinence).

This theory, which views the roots of today's spoken languages as the words of a primitive language is obviously extremely naive and transforms the grammarian's abstractions into substantial realities.

In all truth, Pott had already acknowledged, even after the compilation of his dictionary of roots, that roots as we know them today are grammatical abstractions. Nonetheless it was certainly not his intention to wholly deprive the concept of roots of any real meaning.[2]

The hypercritical attitude of later glottologists toward such theories is as misleading as the original naiveté of their predecessors and even results in the complete destruction of what was positive in the old theoretical constructions.

We will now briefly list the most important arguments of these critics, adding our own observations.

(1) First of all—it was said—if we consider the languages of the Indo-European family, we will find that some roots are common to the entire group, but others are only common to a subgroup, that is, only to Latin languages or to Germanic languages, etc.

Even if the supposed "era of roots" came to an end when the mother tongue was being spoken, we cannot explain such a phenomenon.

(At most, this observation shows that the distinction between an era of roots and an era of etymologies should be taken *cum grano salis*. It is a fact that in historical times very rarely do new roots arise, but there is no reason why they should not arise even in the present day, as seems to have happened, for example, with the word "gas" and as continually takes place in baby talk. Moreover, new roots which are to be found in German and not in Latin, or in Slavic and not in Greek, etc., may have been borrowed—as indeed occurs—from languages of other families.)

(2) Similarly to the mentality of infants, the primitive mentality grasps the more concrete and particular concepts first. Verbs express more general concepts than nouns. The concept "to strike," for example, is more general than "stick," for one may strike in various different ways and not always with a stick. If roots are the residues of a primitive language, most of them should have the meaning of concrete things, that is, of nouns, whereas on analysis we find that most of them have verbal meaning.

(It is a fact that in mimetic language verbal forms—those expressing activity—usually prevail; this is so because it is easier to represent through mimicry the action of striking rather than the concept of stick, of drinking rather than water, or of writing rather than pen, etc. Therefore, it is only natural that roots should have privileged verbal meanings, if they arose at a time when the influence of an early mimetic language was more direct.)

(3) The fundamental unit of language is the proposition and not the single word or the single root, which are grammatical abstractions.

In fact, in agglutinative languages it is usually impossible to distinguish between the word and the proposition. For example, in a dialect spoken by the Delaware Indians the proposition "He comes and gets us with a canoe and takes us to the other side of the river" is expressed with a compound word which is also a proposition. This globality of the more primitive languages is confirmed by comparison between the most ancient and the most recent stages of the same linguistic family, for often a multiplicity of words is used in subsequent forms in the place of a previous, more complex, unitary expression. This also happens sometimes in the transition from Latin to romance languages (for example, the form "amavi" may become "ego habeo amatum").

Here too our hypothesis could perhaps give further elucidations. It is very true that only in the course of evolution is expressive globality analyzed and articulated into an increasingly more distinct multiplicity of terms. In fact, original mimetic language may be likened to a painting in which the single parts are not separable from the whole. But when, for practical purposes, the phonetic element accompanying mimetic expression prevailed and became the common expressive medium, the most important analytical process of all linguistic evolution was accomplished: dissociation of voice from gesture and fragmentation of pictographic unity.

Therefore, phonetic roots do not represent—as traditional glottology recognized—the first and elementary stage of linguistic evolution. On the contrary, they were preceded by a mimetic-onomatopoeic period which probably lasted much longer than that which passed between the appearance of the first verbal expressions and the current state of literary language. However, the first root-words were certainly still polysynthetical in character, and the same expression, or at least expressions between which it was difficult to distinguish, could signify rather different concepts such as, for example, pain, fear, enemy, danger, cataclysm, alarm, attention, escape, etc.

In relation to the question concerning whether or not early roots were monosyllabic, it is worthwhile going back to their origin. If we consider affective or imitative expressions still used today (sounds like "tick tock" or "boom" and the like), and still more if we examine certain semiarticulated cries often used by children and young boys (sounds such as "chip-chiri-chipp," "grrfle-brrble-strffle," "broom-broom-broom"[3] and many others which cannot be reproduced with alphabetical symbols), we will have to acknowledge that to describe them as words made of one or more syllables is unsatisfactory; just as it would be out of place to ask whether the noise produced by rain or by a storm is monosyllabic or polysyllabic.

If we wish to maintain our own distinctions, we must claim that early roots were mostly polysyllabic expressions in which certain phonetic groups—rhythmically alternated with symmetrical variations—predominated.

In many cases, therefore, the presumed roots are probably a later stylization of more ancient pictographic expressions. Just as in the evolution of writing primitive signs were gradually simplified and stylized according to the law of minimum effort and to the practical needs of communication, in the evolution of language the same law and the same practical exigencies probably transformed sounds into monosyllabic "roots."

With reference to the arguments we have so far expounded and to others of the same kind, many modern glottologists have deemed it necessary to deny all concrete reality to the concept of roots. It is certainly true—they say—that we find the same roots in numerous words in the same and in similar languages, but this is not proof that they were expressions of a mythical mother tongue. In fact, the letters of the alphabet are also found in many different words, but this does not authorize us to believe that there ever existed a language in which single letters such as *a, b, c, d,* acted as words: letters as much as roots are pure abstractions and not historical realities.

This thesis is comprehensible as a reaction to the naive consideration of roots as the original words, but it overshoots the mark. The comparison between roots and alphabetical letters does not hold well, because in many cases we are more or less able to reconstruct the history of roots. By following their transformations in different languages, we are able to ascertain how phonetic changes come about according to given laws and to account for transformations in meaning as metaphorical variations on the same theme; this is by no means possible for the letters of the alphabet.

In spite of all hypercritical reserve, the affinity between languages that seemed completely different, demonstrated on the basis of the sameness of roots, is historically founded, and this discovery represents one of the most decisive conquests in glottology.

On the grounds of such negative criticism, some scholars subsequently concluded that it was not possible to distinguish a period of roots (that is, a period in which the first signifying expressions were gradually established) from a later period in which new words were continually derived from ancient roots. They believe that language has always developed slowly just as it does today, namely, through the successive modification of preexistent expressions.

For example, Wundt says that if psychic forces in a very distant primal period of language joined articulate sounds in such a way as to form words, if these forces are the same as those that still today govern the life of language, it follows that the original creation of words cannot be a process long concluded and finished, but rather is continually repeated in living language, just as a creative act is renewed every day under our very eyes in the generation of living organisms.[4]

Wundt's comparison proves its author wrong because, if it is true that the earth has a period of incandescence behind it during which no living organism could have survived, it will still be necessary to postulate a point in time for the realization of that transition from inorganic matter to vegetable and animal life and which cannot be ascertained in present natural phenomena. From a philosophical point of view, it is very true that such institutions as the State, language, etc., which represent fundamental determinations in life, did not arise suddenly but are recreated by us every day, and that those same spiritual forces which still today concur in keeping such institutions alive must have been active in the primitive phases of their formation. The philosopher, too, has the right to state that the transition from animal life to humanity did not occur suddenly, but takes place every day within ourselves each time we succeed in mastering our most brutal impulses, thus allowing human consciousness to triumph. But this point of view has nothing to do with the problem which, for instance, Darwin dealt with in his book on the origin of man, nor with the problem we have proposed regarding language origin, it, too, empirical and naturalistic.

From an empirical point of view it is only right and appropriate to distinguish in the evolution of language between an initial mimetic-onomatopoeic period, mainly characterized by natural signs, and a second phonetic period, characterized by conventional signs, and to place the appearance of the first "roots" toward the end of the first period.

In Renan's words: "Qu'on ne dit donc pas: si l'homme a inventé le langage, pourquoi ne l'invente-t-il plus? La réponse est bien simple: C'est qu'il n'est plus à inventer; l'ère de la création est passée." A substantially true statement if by creation we mean the creation of phonetic roots.

Once the reality of a "period of roots" has been denied, it is only natural that some glottologists have maintained that etymological research constitutes the only possible kind of glottogonic inquiry, and that books should be written on language origin in which the problem of the origin is not dealt with at all, and in which everything is reduced to deriving certain words from others with the greatest and most patient erudition.

For our part, we confess we are not satisfied by this disappointing manner of dealing with our problem, and we do not even understand how others—when it is a question of reflecting on the origin—can be satisfied with this never ending retrogression which explains nothing.[5]

Here, too, a comparison with writing may help. When we search for its origin, nobody would be satisfied with ascertaining that, for example, the Gothic, Runic, Armenian, Slavic, etc., alphabets are similar to the Greek, and that they all derive from the Semitic alphabet; and the assertion that the latter, in its turn, must derive from another alphabet, and that from yet another, and so forth indefinitely, would sound absurd.

To demolish without reconstructing seems to be the motto guiding a certain orientation in modern philology. The negative attitude also prevails with respect to the classification of languages according to certain evolutionary stages. Just as a period when men spoke in monosyllabic roots never existed, in the same way it is believed that isolating languages (in which the proposition is formed through the juxtaposition of expressions and the grammatical element is almost completely absent) do not represent a backward stage in linguistic evolution. An increase in the degree of grammaticality is not considered as the result of evolution. Indeed, according to certain sinologists, the Chinese language developed in the opposite sense, that is, from a greater degree of grammaticality in the ancient language to a lesser degree in the more recent language.[6] Similar phenomena may be recognized in various other cases, for example, in the transition from Latin to the romance languages, and even in the more recent English language, where we may note a tendency toward the reduction of grammatical elements. (In our opinion, the limit of these objections lies in their beginning from a confused idea of what is to be understood by "evolutionary tendency." An absolutely straightforward line of development or progress does not exist and never has existed; when we say, for instance, that astronomical doctrines have developed from the Greeks onward, we do not intend to say that the astronomy of the Ostrogoths or that of the Zulus is superior to that of Ptolemy or of Aristarchus of Samos. In order to test whether such criticism is well-founded, we need to establish how much the mentality of less civilized peoples and even social classes has influenced the transition from Latin to the romance languages or from the most ancient Chinese to the most recent—without forgetting that this question concerns complex psychological facts in which contrasting tendencies and dispositions may interfere. I would not say that the psychology of the Romans is intellectually more developed with respect to either the Greeks or Renaissance Italians, but the grammatical compactness of their language corresponds marvellously to the general orientation of these peoples and to the lapidary character of juridical expression.)

The hypothesis that the grammatical element, which implies a more abstract and intellectual mentality, was hardly developed or not at all in the most primitive stage of language is for many reasons a probable hypothesis. Among other things we also believe that the following should be taken into consideration: that the same thing may be recognized in mimetic language (and in the spoken language of semi-educated deaf-mutes) where, exactly as in isolating languages, the lexical element prevails and grammar is reduced almost solely to the order of succession of the single terms of discourse (so that what will be said is "pears three" and not "three pears," "father loves son" and not "son is loved by father").

Critical glottology has the merit of having emphasized that which was artificial and inadequately demonstrated in the assertions of early scholars.[7] The task of the experts should now be to reach new and more comprehensive constructive syntheses.

This task, we believe, will be made easier if the hypothesis of the mimetic origin is taken into consideration and if "roots," in the grammatical sense, are distinguished from "roots" in the logical sense. In the logical sense because their existence is postulated by the logical impossibility of a never ending retrogression. The conceptually precise definition of such roots is in fact the following: meaningful phonemes that cannot be derived from other phonemes.

It goes without saying that not only are these phonemes not derivable *because of* us, but also *in themselves:* that is, not only because of our own incidental ignorance, but also because we suppose that they emerged as directly expressive utterances or as the consequence of their association with particular expressive gestures. In this sense, the "period of roots" corresponds to the period of pictographic language.

BOOK ONE

PART TWO

Historical Survey of Glottogonic Doctrines from the Greeks to the Present Day

1. Antiquity and the Middle Ages

Theological and Mythical Doctrines—Discussions on
the Conventional or Natural Value of Language—
The Natural Origin According to Epicurus—The
Thesis of Hermogenes and Cratylus in Plato's Dialogue—References to a Primitive Mimetic Language—Symbolic Onomatopoeia According to
Plato—Arguments Set Forth by Democritus in Favor
of the Arbitrariness of the Linguistic Sign—The
Conventional Character Proposed by Aristotle—
Reservations Expressed by Alexander of Aphrodisias—Return to Theological Conceptions in the Middle Ages—The Natural Origin According to Saint
Augustine.

As already stated in the introduction, our problem is still today uncertain
and unsettled both at the level of the solution and of the approach best
adopted toward it. Many believe it is a false and ill-posed or insoluble problem
and there are differences of opinion among those who have attempted to
tackle it. For this reason we believe it not without interest to examine the
main solutions attempted from the time of the Greeks through to the present
day.

The problems of the origin and of the essence of language have commonly
been confused: while the first is naturalistic and evolutionistic in character,
the second is philosophical.

The ancients often approached philosophical problems naturalistically
and believed, for instance, that to answer the question about the essence and
meaning of the world, it was sufficient to know the "arché" and to state that
everything derives from fire or water or from the "nous."

Modern thinkers, and especially authors of an idealistic orientation, usually commit the opposite error: they believe they have answered the naturalistic problem of the origin by answering the philosophical problem of the

essence. Indeed, at times they even go so far as to deny the naturalistic problem all legitimacy, as did Humboldt, Steinthal, and Croce, on the basis of the strange motivation that thought and language (or intuition and language) are the same thing, and that thought is not temporal in origin. This philosophical approach is no less naive and fallacious than the naturalistic orientation of the ancients. Let us make a comparison with another area of study: it is obvious that modern research into the structure of the atom cannot suffice to solve philosophical problems concerning materialism and spiritualism, but this does not justify the denial of the importance of such research for the knowledge and progress of mankind. Confusion between the two problems has been more harmful and persistent also because of the fact that not only were certain philosophers ignorant in anything to do with modern science, but they even made a show of their ignorance as though it were something to boast about.

As we see it, in order to avoid confusion and superficial negation, the two problems, the naturalistic and the philosophical, must be differentiated and treated with the method proper to each. Only then will they throw light on each other, for to differentiate does not mean to separate, and it stands to reason that a clearer philosophical consciousness of the essence of language and of the relations between linguistic activity and other spiritual activities, cannot fail to be useful to naturalistic research. Indeed, it is indispensable, for to form an idea of how human language arose we must specify that which is to be intended by language. For example, it could be demonstrated that the false concept that views phoneticity as an essential character of language has often led glottogonic research astray.

In the same way, the evolutionistic problem of origin cannot fail to influence the philosophical conception of language, for to know "how something was born" will also enlighten us as to its essence.

The confusion we have complained of has also created an obstacle restricting a clearer vision of the history of the two problems. All historians who have concerned themselves with this issue, even those of the highest intellectual and cultural standing such as Steinthal, have treated the history of the two problems promiscuously, thus falsifying and confusing the historical perspective. In fact some thinkers, like Herder and Humboldt, achieved noteworthy progress in relation to one problem while maintaining extremely naive views in relation to the other.

The brief history we are about to present is the first that proposes to concentrate on doctrines concerning the origin of language, and to mention philosophical doctrines about essence only in as far as they may help shed light upon ideas relating to language origin.

THEOLOGICAL DOCTRINES. The first solution that comes to mind when searching for the origin of a thing or of an institution which seems mysterious and difficult to explain is that of a supernatural cause. Theological explanations may sometimes be a useful indication of the fact that a given problem cannot be dealt with by the naturalistic method alone; but from a scientific point of view they represent an *ignava ratio* which pretends to offer an explanation while declaring the problem insoluble.

In relation to the problem concerning us here, explanations of this kind are encountered with great frequency from the dawn of speculation through to the thinkers of the nineteenth century.

According to the Bible, God Himself attributed a name to the things He created: He called the light "day," and the darkness "night," the firmament "heaven," the dry land "earth," and the waters that were gathered together "sea," etc. (*Genesis 1:3–14, 8–10*). For the creation He used language—"Dixit Deus: 'fiat lux,' " etc.

In regard to animals, God left Adam the freedom to call them as he thought best and at the same time established that the name chosen should then remain as the appropriate name for that animal: "Adduxit ea [animantia] ad Adam, ut videret quid vocaret ea: omne enim quod vocavit Adam animae viventis ipsum est nomen eius" (which defines two important characteristics of the linguistic sign: arbitrariness at the moment of institution and the necessity of then faithfully maintaining the established convention, which perhaps also expresses the primitive idea that knowledge of the real name of a man or animal implies acquisition of a special power over them).

Therefore language is partly considered as a divine heritage and partly as the creation of Adamitic wisdom. Consequently the problem arose as to why all mankind does not speak the same language: this was explained with the story of the Tower of Babel.

As in all other fields of knowledge, here too the Greek thinkers resolved to leave myth aside in the search for a scientific solution.

As to the doctrines previous to Plato, our information is mostly uncertain and based on documents from a much later period. The most debated problem was whether language existed "by nature" or "by convention."

This antithesis probably first arose in the field of political and moral values when the question was discussed whether a given custom or social institution derived from a logical and natural need or simply from human convention and habit, and thus in the last analysis from prejudice.[1]

PLATO. In Plato's *Cratylus* discussion about the conventional or natural value of language reflects the question, among other things, of whether language faithfully reflects the nature of things. However, for the problem concerning us here, the most important issue is another: whether the connection between the linguistic phoneme and its meaning is natural or arbitrary, and whether primitive language was pictographic (i.e., naturally expressive) or conventional.

We may well understand how at the beginning of philosophical speculation the problem could not be formulated as univocally as it can be today. The first Greek thinkers had not yet completely freed themselves from the mythologism of the earlier, primitive way of thinking, and when they speak of a "natural" bond between words and things they sometimes mean a hidden bond so that, as in the passage quoted from the Bible, there are supposedly "real" names which capture the essence of things and "false" names which do not.[2]

If the following argument expounded by Ammonius and attributed to Heraclitus is reliable, the latter was not very far, under certain aspects, from the same view. In fact, it is stated that just as we possess a given sense for each different sensation, for example, the eye perceives the form and color of objects, in the same way there exists a sense that captures the appropriate name, inherent in all things. Only whoever expresses the *objective name* of a thing really gives it a name; whoever does not do this does not give the thing a name, but simply produces a noise; naming is the task of whoever knows the specific name a given thing is entitled to *by nature,* just as it is the task of whoever sees to capture the particular aspect of each object.[3]

Just as medieval writers believed that the "right price" was the objective property of all merchandise, here the "real name" is considered to be the objective property of all things. A similar concept is expressed in Plato's *Cratylus,* where, with a probable reference to Heraclitus, it is stated that in a false proposition the single parts are also false, and therefore that there exist words which are true and words which are false *in themselves.*[4]

Nevertheless, according to certain documents and written fragments it would seem that Heraclitus believed in the hidden innate wisdom of language, so that etymological analysis and the comparison between words could serve as an indication of the truth of a doctrine.[5]

The thesis of the "natural" origin of language is supported by Epicurus and Lucretius in clearer terms. Not only does Epicurus oppose the theological thesis, he also believes that the first expressive sounds ever were emitted out of physiological necessity and that man then used those initial sounds to name things.[6] The same idea was to be developed by Lucretius. Just as nature induces children to stretch out their hands and point with their finger to the things they can see, necessity forced human beings to use sounds produced spontaneously to form the names of things.[7] Elsewhere, with greater materialistic emphasis, Lucretius states that sounds emitted by human beings are determined by an emission of atoms from the vocal cords.[8] In other words: people experience impressions and images (*phantásmata*) from the external world which provoke an emission of air from the vocal organs, and the air produces sounds as it comes out of the mouth.

According to Diogenes Laertius, Epicurus believed that the presence of things had a direct influence on the vocal apparatus forcing it to produce given sounds. Consequently all words contain some "natural" element comprehensible to everyone.

Once this natural and even mechanical relationship between objects and their names was accepted, the diversity of words in the various languages remained to be explained. Epicurus explains it in terms of the physiological differences between human families: the same object stirs up different affections, images, and sounds in people of different races, just as the same sentiment gives rise to very different expressions in different animals.[9] Sounds first voiced through natural necessity were subsequently stylized through mutual consent and established, to all effects, as words.[10]

Even though their premises were different, the Stoics also believed in a natural relation between objects and their names, considering words as the imitation of the things named.[11]

All the different hypotheses formulated by Greek thinkers about language origin find their most complete formulation in Plato's *Cratylus*. The thesis of the "natural" relation is also more comprehensively and more organically set out here than it is in the later writings of the Epicureans and Stoics.

In this dialogue, Hermogenes' thesis, according to which the names of things are not determined by their nature but rather by convention and custom, and Cratylus's thesis, according to which there must be a natural bond between the name and the thing, are set against each other (383A).

Intervening in the debate, Socrates asks himself what names really are and answers that they are a means or an instrument. Just as the drill is an instrument used to bore holes, and the shuttle is an instrument used for weaving, names are used to express and emphasize the properties of things. The weaver uses the shuttle, but he does not make it: this is up to the carpenter. In the same way, speakers and teachers (the dialectician) make use of names, yet they do not create them: this is up to the "name-maker," the founder of language.

And what does the carpenter have in mind when he makes a shuttle? He takes as his model that which the shuttle is in itself, that is, the concept or idea of the shuttle. In the same way, name-makers must look to the concept of the thing and make sure that the name is appropriate to the nature of the thing named.

No doubt it is true that a Greek word-maker and a barbarian used different syllables for the same concept, but this is of no importance, provided that the names formed corresponded to the thing. In truth, not even carpenters make shuttles with the same wood: what counts is that the instrument, once made, should correspond to the use it must serve. We will have names that are appropriate and names that are not appropriate: Archepolis, for example, is a name which suits the ruler of a city, Agis and Polemarchus the leaders of armies, Eupolemus is appropriate for someone valiant in war, and Iatrocles or Acesimbrotus for skillful physicians.

Syllables must correspond to meaning, but whether a letter is taken away or added matters little. For example, we can call *e, u, o* the letters which have this sound (and here the correspondence between the name and the thing is perfect), but then we also call *b* beta, and here we have added something to the sound, and nevertheless we may say that the name remains appropriate. In contrast, the names would not be appropriate if we were to call impious men Theophilus or Mnesitheus.

Through etymological analysis we are sometimes able to decide whether or not a word is appropriate, but all we do with this method is go back from one word to another, until we eventually arrive at elements that cannot in their turn be derived from other words. It is therefore necessary to search for the origin of these "roots" in another way.

In an effort to solve the problem of the origin of early roots, Socrates asks what we would do to understand each other if we had neither voice nor tongue. And he answers that we would make an effort to answer with signs of the hands, head, and body, as do dumb people. For example, if we wished to designate something light, we would raise our hand toward heaven to imitate the nature of something that rises, and if we wished to designate something heavy, we would bend toward the ground. To designate a galloping horse or any other animal we would make our body look as much like theirs as possible.

Given that this natural mimetic language consists of imitating the things we wish to signify through gestures, Socrates infers that phonetic language also evolved as the imitation of natural sounds. But a difficulty arises here: if this is the way things go, those who amuse themselves by imitating the sounds of sheep or cocks, etc., would name those animals with such inarticulate sounds, whereas when we represent or imitate natural sounds with song or music, this does not imply that we are name-makers or word-makers.

Things have shape and color and may be sonorous, however, it is not with words but with painting and music that we imitate such qualities. The imitation we accomplish through language must therefore be of a different sort. Perhaps the role of language is that of imitating with letters and syllables, not the qualities of things as they appear to us, but their essential characteristics. Now, the letter *rho* seems to be a good instrument for the expression of motion, because in pronouncing this letter the tongue is least at rest and more vibrant than in any other. Therefore we find it in roots expressing movement. *Psi, sigma, phi,* and *zeta* are fricatives and suitable for the imitation of that which may evoke the image of blowing; on the other hand, *delta* and *tau* are compressed sounds which on being pronounced seem to cause the tongue to stop suddenly; while on pronouncing *lambda* the tongue seems to glide, as is evident from the words λεῖα (level), ὀλισθάνειν (glide), etc.

In this way, therefore, it was thought that the founder of language was able to use these symbolic onomatopoeia, that is, associations of certain ideas with certain phonemes, in order to imitate the quality of things through letters.

That things may be imitated through letters and syllables, Socrates adds, might seem ridiculous but on the other hand we do not have anything better to explain the origin of the first names, unless we want to resort to the intervention of the gods, as do tragic poets when in difficulty.

The onomatopoeic theory, according to which early roots are naturally connected with their meaning through their very sound, does not seem false to Socrates, but he is not completely satisfied with it either.

Among the reasons that may be set forth for the insufficiency of this theory, Plato cites two: (1) the number of words that in some way symbolize their meaning through sound is only a small part of those we use; indeed, if we take numbers (which are infinite) as an example, it is not clear how we may find as many onomatopoeic names as are necessary to name them; (2) we cannot deny that at least some words have a sound that does not "resemble" their meaning, such as the word σχληρόν which has a soft and flowing sound and on the contrary means *hard,* and yet, despite the lack of similarity between sound and meaning, on pronouncing that word, we understand it. Hence, we must conclude that what makes us understand meaning in such cases is not similarity, but conventional use. In fact, as Hermogenes had already observed, if we change a servant's name, the new name is not less suited than the former.

The dialogue seems to conclude as follows: many words are derived or composed from others, and in the latter the relation between the signifier and the signified is natural (even if this etymological link may be difficult to trace and may give rise to the abuses perpetrated by the Sophists); furthermore, of the early roots, some have a symbolic onomatopoeic relation to their meaning, but this does not explain them all; consequently we will have to acknowledge that conventional use as well is an essential element in language.[12]

CONVENTIONALISTIC DOCTRINES. The first to have questioned the existence of a natural relation between words and their meaning seems to have been Democritus. According to Proclus,[13] the arguments put forward by Democritus were the following: (1) some words have different meanings even though they sound the same; (2) at times two words different in sound have the same meaning; (3) in different eras different words are sometimes used for the same meaning; (4) certain objects and concepts have no corresponding denomination.

The Abderite's observations are still valid today in demonstrating that the words of currently spoken languages have semantic value in so far as they are conventional signs and not purely aesthetic, that is, directly expressive of value.

In fact, if the meaning of words depended on their sounds, we could not explain how the same item, for example, the Italian word "piano," may signify slowly, softly, flat surface, project, musical instrument, etc.

Furthermore if the bond were natural, how is it that words with different sounds such as wife, bride, consort, uxor, Gemahlin, etc., all signify the same concept?

Finally if, as the Epicureans were later to claim, the impressions we receive from objects provoke sound reactions in us, which then become the names of things, no object would exist without a name.

Having denied the "natural" origin, Democritus thought that in ancient times people had agreed to establish certain linguistic conventions, roughly as they agreed on certain juridical conventions. Epicurus argued against this opinion by questioning the capability of human beings devoid of language of coming to such agreements.[14]

The conventional character of linguistic signs is explained in greater detail by Aristotle. Words, he says, do not have meaning "by nature," but are conventional symbols of the affections (παθήματα), just as alphabetical letters are symbols of vocal sounds. The affections of the soul are the same in everyone, just as the mimicry used to express them is the same. However, vocal sounds are different for different people, just as alphabetical signs are different. Therefore the former (instinctive attitudes) are direct images of the affections and are objective and natural in character, the latter (words), on the contrary, are but the arbitrary and subjective signs of the former.[15]

Boethius expresses Aristotle's view as follows: letters signify sounds, sounds intellectual concepts, and concepts signify things.

These passages are important because Aristotle clearly establishes in them the difference between pictographic signs and conventional signs, and therefore between aesthetics and semantics. To the extent that they are conventional signs, the words of a language are rightly equated to alphabetical writing systems and contrasted with mimetic gestures and the cries of animals.

Aristotle concludes that since words are conventional signs, they can only be considered as the result of an agreement among their users.[16] Why is it that thinkers like Democritus and Aristotle never asked themselves, as Epicurus subsequently did, how it was possible for people devoid of language to agree on the meaning of the words to be used? It is not easy to say. Was it their intention to refer to a silent agreement, devoid of explicit awareness and ratified spontaneously through usage from one century to the next? This interpretation seems a little too modern and we should remember that the ancients did not have our ideas about progress and historical evolution, but sometimes conceived of primitive men as being not less refined and less developed than contemporaries but more enlightened and wiser.

Indeed, Aristotle believed that myths were the storehouse of ancient wisdom. He stated that:

> From the ancients and from very ancient times the idea that the celestial bodies are divinities and that the divine element embraces the whole of nature was handed down through the ages to descendents in the form of myth—and that because all forms of art and wisdom were probably found and lost again many times, those opinions have been preserved as the residues of ancient wisdom in our own times. It is only in this way that we are able to comprehend the patriotism and the ideas of our forefathers.[17]

Therefore the mythical image of ancient men gifted with extraordinary faculties, who had enlightened the human race with their discoveries and inventions, also survived among great thinkers. This is clear, for example, in Plato who, in relation to the question under discussion, speaks of the "founder of language," or of the "maker of names."

Regarding the origin of languages Alexander of Aphrodisias (according to Ammonius's account) held a different view from Aristotle's and maintained that the origin of language is natural and spontaneous.[18]

A passage from the comment to the *De anima* also seems to reveal that Alexander's opinion was closer to Epicurus's than to Aristotle's: the phoneme, namely the word considered as a simple sound, is like the sounds made by animals, an instinctive reaction to an external stimulus. Thus nature has endowed us with the capacity of imposing names upon things. But the choice of words and the relation between a thing and its name rather than being the work of nature is the result of convention. Language is not innate, but, as Dante was also to say, the faculty which creates it is innate.[19]

In conclusion, the Greek thinkers formulated all those solutions to the problem which were subsequently to be repeated in various forms up to the nineteenth century.

They saw more or less clearly that the only way to explain the birth of language as a natural phenomenon was to admit that initially it was directly expressive. In other words, language derives from emotional sounds or signs provoked by physiological necessity as in the case of animal cries, or from the plain or figurative imitation of natural sounds. Furthermore, indications of the special importance of the role played by mimetic gestures and expressions in primitive language are not lacking. On the other hand, the Greek thinkers recognized the inadequacy of doctrines limited to postulating a natural link between things and their names, and with the use of valid arguments, they asserted the conventional character of linguistic signs.

If the reasons put forward to support these arguments are not always convincing, this is because of the preconception common in the classical era that a naturalistic problem such as that of language origin can be solved through pure reasoning, without the support of careful documentation. This is not surprising in relation to an age when the science of nature, as we understand it, did not exist, but it is strange that such a pre-Galilean mentality should still be traced in many modern authors dealing with this problem. What most compromised the approach to the problem among the Greeks was how the distinction was to be intended between "by nature," on the one hand, and "by convention," on the other, where the latter was always considered to be inferior.

Another impediment to a better approach to the problem derives from the confusion, common among Greek authors, between the philosophical problem and the naturalistic.

The concepts of the Greeks that remain most distant from our own way of looking at things, a way derived from the theory of evolution and the idea of historical development, are those which concern primitive man, who was not imagined to be less evolved than modern man. This leads to such cases as Plato's, for instance, who imagined that before the birth of language mankind had a conceptual life similar to his own.[20]

MEDIEVAL CONCEPTIONS. In the Middle Ages there is a return, in many fields, to the mentality characteristic of pre-Hellenic civilization. Theological digressions are frequent and concern such discussions as whether Adam knew the names of all things and whether in general he had been a "perfect scientist."[21] Many authors from this period were to deal at length with the logic and psychology of angels differentiating between "matutinal" knowledge and "vespertine" knowledge and were able to nicely inform us about the language used by the saints in heaven and by God Himself.

At most, the biblical point of view, according to which the power of speech is an original faculty impressed upon the spirit of the first man by the Creator, was accepted. It was thought that the original language was Hebrew (or sometimes Aramaic or Syrian) and that the multiplicity of tongues was God's punishment for the arrogance shown by the construction of the Tower of Babel. Authors who believed in the mysterious, magical force of words, such as words used not only in certain rites but also in exorcisms, were not lacking. Origen speaks of a "occulta quaedam theologia quae universitatis opifici congruat, qua propter nomina sunt efficacia."

Among the more reasonable authors we may remember Gregory of Nissa who held the opinion, later to be accepted by Dante, that God gave man only reason and, therefore, the capacity of creating a language for himself, but that the actual creation of language is the work of man.

But the Middle Ages, in which the mythological mentality is so characteristically mixed with logical reasoning, also preserved the achievements of Greek thought, repeating, and sometimes developing its most important aspects. In Augustine, who was at one and the same time the last great philosopher of the classical era and the greatest father of the church, not only do we find the statement that language is the work of human beings,[22] but also his development of the important concept, attributed to the Stoics, of figurative onomatopoeia. Furthermore, he makes a perceptive reference to the role of gestures and of mimetic expressions in the birth of language. The early stirrings of the spirit, he says, are instinctively manifested through moans and cries and through the various movements of the limbs, so that the sentiments of human beings may be interpreted on the basis of instinctive actions, contractions of the face, the expression of the eyes, and the position of the limbs.[23]

The Aristotelian conception of the conventional meaning of words ("ad placitum primi instituentis") was generally accepted by the scholastics. St. Thomas Aquinas took a stand against Hermogenes' thesis as it was expounded by Plato in *Cratylus,* "quod nomina naturaliter significant quasi sint naturales similitudines rerum."[24]

In his *De vulgari eloquio,* Dante maintains that on creating Adam, God also created the Hebrew language with its words and grammatical forms, but that after the confusion of Babel, the multiplicity of tongues provoked the need for conventional languages, independent of the arbitrary will of single individuals; this led to the language of the Greeks and Romans.[25] Instead, in the famous lines of canto XXVI in *Paradise,* Dante maintains that the faculty of speech is naturally inborn, whereas the single languages are subsequently created on the basis of man's will:

> Opera naturale e ch'uom favella;
> Ma cosi o cosi, natura lascia
> Poi fare a voi secondo che v'abbella.

2. Humanism and the Renaissance

Francisco Sánchez—The Port Royal Grammarians—
Richard Simon—Outline of a General Semantics in
Francis Bacon.

FRANCISCO SÁNCHEZ. The linguistic problems most commonly dealt with during the humanistic period and the Renaissance concern grammar and rhetoric. The rare allusions to the glottogonic issue repeat views that are already familiar, and often the naiveties are such that doubt remains as to whether such views were asserted out of conviction or as a didactic expedient. Some new views, although not free of scholastic preconceptions, are to be found in the work of Francisco Sánchez, nicknamed "el Brocense."[1]

Sánchez makes an attempt at reconciling the doctrine of the natural origin (which he attributes to Plato) with the Aristotelian doctrine of institution *ad placitum*. The former holds true for the original language of the human race, as is stated in chapter II of *Genesis*. Here, names derive from the very nature of things, while this is not true of the other idioms. The explanation of words other than names is to be looked for in etymology, which no doubt is often obscure but not less worthy of investigation because of this. If then the same things are called with different names by different peoples, this is so because the same thing may be considered under different aspects. For example, the Romans derived the name *vento* (wind) from the verb *venire* (to come) while the Greeks call it *anemon* from the verb which means to blow gently; in the same way the Romans derived the word *fenestra* (window) from *phainestai*, the Spanish call it *ventana*, and the Lusitanians *janella*, "quasi parva janua."[2]

Sánchez perceived the following truth much better even than many authors who came after him: that primitive language must have been directly and naturally expressive and that the conventional character could only be the fruit of later development.[3]

He also has the merit of having distinguished between animal cries, which are the symptoms of given feelings, and words, which are conventional signs. Interjections, he says, are not real parts of discourse and cannot be classified as either Greek or Latin expressions, even if they are written with Greek or Latin letters; rather they are manifestations of sadness or joy similar to the cries of birds or beasts, to which, however, no one attributes the power of speech.[4]

THE PORT ROYALISTS. No progress is made concerning the issue under consideration with the *Grammaire générale et raisonnée* of Port Royal, published in 1660 by Lancelot and Arnauld, which accentuates the intellectualist naiveties of the Cartesians.

Our impression is that these grammarians saw things as follows: primitive men, still devoid of language, one day wondered about the best way to communicate their thoughts to others through signs, and immediately they discovered that the best way was through sounds. On emitting various sounds from their mouths, they soon realized that there were some like *a, e, i* which produced a distinct sound without the need of anything else, and they called these *vowels,* while there were other sounds which were clearly pronounceable only in conjunction with the first, and these they called *consonants.*

Syllables were formed from vowels and consonants and words from the union of more than one syllable. But because words, once pronounced, vanish without leaving traces, another kind of sign was invented to make them durable: this is how writing systems arose.[5]

It is difficult to say to what extent these grammarians really believed in their abstractions, and to what extent, on the contrary, their tendency to oversimplify is to be considered as a didactic expedient.

We do not mean by this that the rationalism of the Cartesians cannot at times give excellent results, especially in those definitions in which the clarity and distinction of concepts is of major importance. For example, the remarks made by the Port Royalists concerning the necessary qualifications for a perfect alphabetical system (and which could easily be extended to a semantic system in general) are correct and relevant: that every sign should signify some sound, that is, that no sign should be written which is not pronounced; that every sound should be indicated by a sign, that is, anything which is not written should not be pronounced; that every sign should signify a single sound; and that the same sound should never be signified by different signs.

R. SIMON. The ideas of Father Simon, the famous forerunner in philological criticism of the Scriptures,[6] are not of much interest to our purpose.

To defend himself, he invokes the authority of Saint Gregory of Nissa and others, but his opinions are perhaps akin to those of Lucretius.

According to Diodorus Siculus, he says, human beings, on attempting to speak, first pronounced senseless sounds and only later did they articulate them better to express their thoughts: reason corrected nature and adapted words to the signification of things.

The need to communicate obliged people to invent new words each time they were faced with new objects; so the confusion caused by the construction of the tower of Babel is not surprising: a great many things which were still without a name presented themselves in relation to the work and everyone named them in their own way. The possibility must not be excluded that the adamitic tongue had been forgotten, as Saint Gregory had already maintained, laughing at those who believed that God was the first author of the language, as though He were a master in grammar. God created things and not names, which are the work of man.

God gave man a "reasoning nature" with which to invent languages. This is the sense in which we should interpret the words of Lucretius: "At varios linguae sonitus natura subegit Mittere, et utilitas expressi nomina rerum."

If by "natura" we mean rational nature, Aristotles's views coincide with those of Epicurus.

Hebrew (which in Simon's opinion is the same as Phoenician) was probably the original language, because it is simpler than all the others. Initially no Hebrew word was made of more than three letters or two syllables, and at the beginning monosyllables were probably more numerous than they were later, words were less compound, verb and noun inflections were not numerous, and those which subsequently became desinences were mostly independent little words.

Simon made a praiseworthy effort to free scientific research from the shackles of Biblical influence, but his rationalism did not bring any noteworthy contribution to the solution of our problem.

With different ends, Bacon's empiricism and Vico's historicism stand in contrast to the rationalist view.

FRANCIS BACON. Bacon declares that, unlike Plato, it is not his intention to inquire into the origin of language in order to decide whether, initially, names were established arbitrarily or with a reason: an inquiry which may prove to be fascinating for it seems to delve into the most obscure secrets of antiquity, but which is doubtlessly unreliable and vain.

Nonetheless Bacon contemplates a general semantics, or—as he says—a special grammar of the various types of signs which may be used to represent and symbolize things.

First of all, he says, signs which designate sounds—such as the letters of the alphabet—must be distinguished from those which instead directly designate things (*Characteres reales*).

Concerning alphabetical signs, he asks himself whether it is better to write them as they are pronounced, namely, according to the requirements of a rational semantic system, or whether it is better to accept tradition (a question of some importance for English orthography). He replies that it is useless to adapt writing to pronunciation, since pronunciation itself changes continually.

"Real" characters, which signify things and not words, may be of two kinds: natural signs which represent things by similarity or analogy (*ex congruo*) and conventional signs which signify *ad placitum*.

In fact, mankind has various means of communication at its disposal. Thus peoples speaking different languages may attempt to understand each other as best they can by means of gestures similarly to deaf-mutes. Indeed, through gestures the latter are able to speak to each other as well as to whoever has learned the meaning of their gestures. It is a known fact that in China and in the provinces of the far Orient, use is made of "real" characters, that is, ideograms that symbolize neither letters nor words but things and concepts. Consequently, by resorting to these "real" characters, not only will peoples speaking different languages understand each other, but they will also understand a book composed in such characters, while reading it in their own language.

Gestures and hieroglyphs are natural signs, that is, they signify through similarity and not by convention. Gestures are a kind of ephemeral hieroglyphs: just as words vanish once pronounced, while writing remains, hieroglyphs outlined by gestures disappear, while if painted they last.

As an example of the use of such mimetic gestures, Bacon recalls Periander's anecdote (attributed by others to Tarquin the Proud), which suggests the massacre of the Optimates by cutting the heads off the highest flowers "et non minus usus est hieroglyphico quam si id in charta depinxisset."

Hieroglyphics and gestures are types of emblem which in some way correspond to things, while ideographic characters are arbitrary and accepted through habit as though on the basis of a tacit agreement. In order to write with them we need many, that is, as many as the number of root words.[7]

The lack of clarity which generally reigns over the subject of our inquiry has stopped historians from recognizing the importance of these passages by Bacon. They in fact represent the only notable advance ever made in this field from Plato onwards, and even lay the foundations for that general semantics which Saussure proposes in approximately 1900 and that, up to the present day, has not yet been systematically organized. Just how much more serious, scientifically-based, and up-to-date this Baconian "general theory of signs" is with respect to other later attempts clearly emerges in the comparison with Gébelin's huge volumes or Morris's "behaviorist semiotic."

Bacon has the merit of having emphasized the fundamental distinction between pictographic signs, which signify *ex congruo,* and mnemotechnic signs, which signify *ad placitum:* he saw that the latter generally were not established according to premeditated convention, but rather through habit "tamquam pacto tacito recepta"; he underlined the analogy between mimetic gestures and hieroglyphics; he gave an exact description (which was not easy in his time) of Chinese ideographic writing. Bacon's observations concern the problem of the nature of the linguistic sign more than of its origin, but conceptual clarity in the one field also helps to throw light upon the other.

3. The Eighteenth Century

G. B. VICO. Bacon's ideas had the fortune of being accepted and fruitfully developed with greater philosophical insight by Giambattista Vico, in whose work the problems of the origin and nature of language merge and throw light upon each other.[1]

Still today the difficulties in properly understanding this philosopher have not been overcome. A contemporary of Locke and Leibniz, his vision of the world was anachronistic by default and by excess. His thought system anticipated post-Kantian historicist idealism, but, in many respects, his cultural formation was medieval and humanistic. He had a very slight understanding of the scientific revolution which, after Galileo, occurred in all fields. He had a very low opinion of the Cartesian attempt at founding a rational mechanical conception of the physical world and derided the *Cogito*, comparing it to the jests of a fool in one of Plautus's plays.

As a fervent upholder of the unity of philosophy and philology, he felt the need of collecting great quantities of documentary material to support his theses, but he was seriously lacking in philological sensibility and precision. He cited texts without checking them, often misunderstanding words or twisting them to his own ends, while in fact they meant something completely different, or appealing to evidence destitute of scientific reliability and sometimes to authors who never existed.

Too many pages of the *Scienza Nuova*, in the first version as much as in the second, convey the image of a man of genius who feverishly dashed off his ideas in the urgency of a creative outburst. Vico's style is obscure and suggestive; he uses words in his own way without bothering about being understood, without paying attention to either order or grammar, and without distinguishing between scientifically based views and views that, in the light of more careful criticism, were dubious or arbitrary and false. This is even more peculiar if we consider that, in Italy, we already had the clear and pleasant scientific prose of Galileo.

To this it may be added that Croce, who deeply influenced all Italian scholars after him, is too strong a philosophical personality not to have in some way superimposed his own conceptions upon those of the author we are now discussing. He closely examined, clarified, and brought to attention Vico's philosophical doctrine on art, imagination, and language. But given his slight interest in and understanding of the empirical sciences (which he undervalued owing to prejudices of an epistemological order), he ignored Vico's naturalistic theory language origin.

Vico worked on this issue (which according, to Croce and others is badly proposed, imaginary, and insoluble) fully aware of the difficulties involved and of its importance. Making the most of Bacon's suggestions, he contributed toward the formulation of a solution more than any other thinker before him. No doubt Vico is in the first place a philosopher, but he also combines and intermingles an extremely lively psychological and naturalistic interest in the primitive mentality (widespread among modern ethnologists and psychologists though hardly shared by Vico's contemporaries) with his philosophical interests.

The greatest spiritual conquest of the primitive age was the formation of language. What made such a miracle possible? This problem, says Vico, has cost us too much difficult meditation because, for a proper understanding, it is necessary to forget civilization and enter into the nature of primitive man, still close to a state of almost animal-like wonder and deprived of all language.

In order to draw any positive results from an investigation into the origin of spoken languages, Vico advises that we combine this study with that of the origin of writing, since the two things are naturally connected. In fact, those scholars who have considered them as being separate have had as much difficulty in discovering the origin of spoken languages as of that of writing. The concept expressed here, which we believe favors a scientific approach to the problem, is partly obscured by the strange idea that it is not so much the evolution of writing (which is generally known to us) that may give us some indication as to the origin of language, but rather the origin of language (which can only be reconstructed hypothetically) that may explain the origin of writing.[2]

As is well-known, Vico sets the specific problem concerning language within the context of a more general philosophical conception in which he proposes a close correspondence between "eternal ideal history" (the dialectic development of concepts) and temporal history (philogenetic development). The most simple and primitive form of knowledge is that of sensible impressions; from these we pass on to imaginative representations and finally to intellectual consciousness. Sensations and representations are considered, therefore, in the life of the individual and of humanity at large, as necessary stages in the development of our conceptual formations.

Language, which arose in a very distant era from our own, cannot be a cold, intellectual construction, as the Port Royal followers of Descartes naively believed. Indeed, we may identify three stages in its development.

In the first stage, which we could call mimetic-pictographic, nations were still almost completely mute and made themselves understood by resorting to acts or objects which were naturally related to their ideas; in the second stage, which Vico calls heroic and poetic, the first emotional and onomatopoeic sounds were formed—in this stage arose the first articulate, strongly rhythmical, and almost sung language; it was only in the third stage that the "parlare epistolare," that is, vulgar prose was developed, created by the common people of heroic populations.[3]

In Vico the characteristics of these three stages do not always emerge as clearly as we ourselves have outlined. Having noted the analogy between spoken languages and writing, he then seems to mistake analogy for identity and treats writing systems as though they were spoken languages and spoken languages as though they were writing systems.

For example, he says that "the Egyptians narrated that, throughout the whole of their history, they had spoken three languages . . . they said that the first was hieroglyphic or sacred or divine; the second symbolic or made of signs, in other words of heroic exploits; the third epistolary used to communicate the current needs of life to those distant from them."[4]

Three spoken languages are mentioned, but in reality it would seem that Vico is describing three kinds of writing systems, that is, of means suited to communication among people distant from each other. The first is pictographic and reproduces the objects to be signified; the second, ideographic, in which the hieroglyphics become symbolic signs; and the third is made of conventional signs, either syllabic or alphabetical.

At this point it is worthwhile to remember that Vico, as were the authors of his time generally and unlike modern scholars, was not in a position to deal with hundreds of thousands of years of human evolution, but by referring to biblical chronology dated the creation of the world 3253 years before the foundation of Rome. While we believe that the birth of language is many thousands of years anterior to the invention of writing, Vico thought that the two events were contemporary. He established a probable correspondence, from a temporal point of view also, between the first mute language made of mimetic gestures and the first pictographic writing systems; second, between imaginative and poetic language and ideographic symbol writing; and third, between vulgar and prosaic language and alphabetical writing.

The expression "to speak through writing" or "to speak through hieroglyphics" is used by Vico to designate the mimetic mode of signifying an object by outlining it in the air. He says that all nations initially spoke through writing, that is, they used a kind of mimetic design. Just as the mute express themselves through gestures or by pointing to objects, in the same way it was common necessity for all nations at their beginnings to speak through hieroglyphics, before becoming familiar with the use of articulate language.

With bold intuition Vico believes that there are traces of this mute primitive language in ancient traditions and reports various examples: Idantura, king of the Scythians, replied to Darius, who had threatened him with war, with five "real words," namely, he sent him a frog, a mouse, a bird, the prong of a plough, and a bow. According to Vico's both acute and arbitrary interpretation, the frog meant that that king was born from the land of Scythia just as frogs are born from the land when it rains; the mouse, that he had built his house, as mice do, where he was born; the bird meant that he had been a fortunate man, that is, he was free and not subject to the religion of others; the plough, that he had cultivated the land; and the bow, that in his land he had dominion over arms and with these arms he intended to defend it.

Another example of mute language is reported by Thucydides: to a foreigner who marvelled at the fact that Sparta was not surrounded by walls, a Spartan replied by pointing to his breast, almost as though to say poetically: "The walls of Sparta are our breasts!" Another Spartan, in answer to someone who wanted to know how far the borders of the state extended, replied by hurling a lance, as though to say: "Our empire extends to the point reached by this lance." Another example is offered by Tearco, king of Ethiopa who, in reply to the ambassadors of Cambyse who wishing to subordinate him had presented him with gold vases, answered by refusing the gold and by firmly drawing an arrow on his bow, to signify that it was not gold but warlike virtue that made a prince estimable. Yet another example is the gesture, already cited by Bacon, which legend attributes to Tarquin the Proud but which probably goes back to more ancient times. "Heroic emblems" also belong to the same kind of primitive forms of expression through mute signs. These are symbolic signs used by the ancients in various circumstances, for example, to secure the boundaries of their estates, or for the assertion of their rights in general (the use of trade-marks on the products of craftsmanship, medals, etc.). They also include, for example, family emblems which were a kind of "armed" language of families, and military banners which were an "armed" language of cities. Such emblems arose in an era destitute of articulate spoken languages, when human beings, not knowing how to communicate through speech, used real words, like those of Idantura, or picture speech, like the sacred language of the Egyptians.

Vico was also aware of the totemic symbols used by primitive peoples. He maintains, with admirable insight for his times, that the Indians too used hieroglyphics depicting animals, plants, and flowers through which they identified the lineages of their families, "a use which equals that of family arms in our world."[5]

In the Middle Ages or, as he says, in the new barbarian era, nations became dumb again of vulgar speech, so that no information has reached us concerning, for example, the Italian, French, and Spanish languages of that era; Latin and Greek were learned only by priests, and modern languages did not exist.[6]

Given Vico's rather confusing approach to the discussion of language and writing, Nicolini's interpretation of the expression "nazioni mutole di favella volgare" [nations dumb of vulgar speech] as "illiterate nations" would appear to be acceptable.[7]

But Vico's opinion, which in truth is extremely rash, clearly emerges from his letter to Gherardo De Angelis of 26 December 1725 in which he asserts that in the Middle Ages, owing to the confusion of as many languages as were the nations that overran Italy, the Latins and Barbarians did not understand each other, so that, "the dumb language had to return among the Italians. As we have shown this was used by the first noble nations whose authors, before the advent of articulate languages, had to explain themselves in the manner of dumb persons through acts or objects naturally related to their ideas." Vico, therefore, does not refer to illiterate peoples but rather to peoples using a mimetic language.

Vico believes that there is an essential affinity between poetic fables, dumb speech, and hieroglyphic writing systems, because they are all representations common to poets and painters, that is, direct expressions and not conventional expressions, so that even a dumb person, devoid of speech, could depict them. In fact, the same expressions of mimetic language mentioned above could be signified by designing hieroglyphics: Idantura's drawing of a frog, a mouse, a bird, etc.; Tearco's design of gold vases turned upside down on the ground and an arm drawing an arrow with a bow, and so on.

In the second era phonetic language begins to form with onomatopoeia and interjections. This is exemplified by various (though not always acceptable) etymologies: for example, the name Jove became Zeus among the Greeks as an imitation of the noise of lightning, and Ur (preserved in the Greek Uranos and in the Latin Uro) among the Orientals from the noise of fire. Interjections are monosyllabic sounds articulated in the surge of violent passions. An example is the expression of surprise and fright "pa!," provoked by the first thunderbolts, which repeated in "pape" became an attribute of Jove and the other gods, as is obvious in Jupiter, Diespiter, Marspiter. Consequently, the gods were called "patres" and their activities "patrare." Another residue of words derived from interjections is present in the ancient "pipulum" and "pipare," meaning complaint and to complain, which must have derived from the interjection "pi! pi!"

The first expressions must have all been monosyllabic, as we still see nowadays among children who through babbling render words monosyllabicly. Almost all pronouns and particles are monosyllables (*a, ab, e, ex, de, di, ad, in, sub, se, prae, ob, am*, etc.) as well as many of the more usual words such as *sol, lux, nox, os, cor, pes, vox, nux, fax, ver, nix, nos, lac, mel, bos, sus, grecs, rus, res, sal, vas, as, es, sta, i, da, dic, fac*, etc. (we could easily observe, today, that more than one of these derives from non-monosyllabic words).

The transition from expression through mute gestures to articulate words must have been very difficult for those ancient peoples who had never yet heard the human voice and whose vocal cords were very hard.

Just as stammerers, when they have difficulty in pronouncing some word help themselves by drawing out the voice in song, those primitive men sent out their voices by singing.

Diphthongs testify to such initial singing: they abound in primitive languages similarly to vocalizations and sing-songs in certain barbaric populations, for example, as in the Chinese languages. The latter, in fact, do not have more than three hundred articulate expressions, but by variously modulating their sound and tempo, a very high number of hieroglyphic words are composed and pronounced through song.

In this way, words formed from monosyllabic sounds were drawn out in song and became redundant, only to be shortened again in civilized speech. Numerous examples of such contractions are available in Latin and in Italian poetry.

That languages began with song and that primitive man spoke in rhythmic verses also emerges, in Vico's opinion, from the fact that the most ancient literary documents of all peoples are written in verse: for example, the ancient maxims of the Sybils and the responses of the Oracles, which were sung in heroic verse; and the most ancient laws and histories of the Teutons, Persians, Chinese, and American Indians. Traces of such a tradition are recorded by the most ancient Greek and Latin writers who used rhythm that was almost poetic in their prose as did the Fathers of the Church, with the return of the barbaric age, so that their prose had an almost sing-song quality about it. It is common knowledge that Vico, owing to the cultural conditions of his time and environment and to the excessive fervor of his temperament, sometimes made rather surprising mistakes, rendering the recognition of so many of his brilliant discoveries more difficult. A significant example is his observation regarding the poetry which flourished at his time in German Silesia. A province, he says, almost wholly populated by peasants, and whose verse he takes up as an example of the spontaneous popular poetry characteristic of barbaric and primitive nations, while in reality it was the product of those Silesian baroque poetic academies of the seventeenth century that imitated Italian "marinismo."[8]

Because of the need felt by the first primitive men to transfigure every-thing through their imagination and to personify their feelings, mute expres-sions were transformed into fables or personified as divine figures. Before having a conventional word to indicate the year, these primitive peoples would indicate, with a sickle or with their arm, the number of times they had har-vested in order to signify the corresponding number of years. Therefore, Saturn the God of Time was pictured with a sickle, personifying the passing of the years.

Numerous poetic and mythological images were created in the same way: Jove to signify the thundering sky, Saturn to signify the sown earth, Ceres to signify grain, and so on for all of the three thousand gods referred to by Varro.

Since all concepts and objects of daily life such as the Sky, Sun, Earth, Grain, Time, etc., were deified, Hesiod's theogony may be considered as a glossary of Greece's first language, and Varro's three thousand names as a vocabulary of the first language of Lazio.

These initial languages were not a collection of conventional signs, but of images and fables, and they corresponded to the hieroglyphics of the sacred writing of the Egyptians. Mimetic hieroglyphics, the ideograms of picto-graphic writing systems, family emblems, and mythical representations have this in common: they are *universals of the creative imagination*. In fact, the human mind needs to rely on something constant, and the first men, not yet being capable of scientific or even intelligible concept-formation, felt the natural necessity to invent *poetic figures*.

Not knowing how to form the botanic concept of "grain," they created the poetic image of Ceres, and in the place of the abstract concept of "time," they shaped the image of Saturn. Through such personifications the ancients explained all the facts of history and nature. All the heroes of daring feats were called Hercules; all the inventors of ingenious devices, Mercury Tris-megistus; all the creators of folk songs, Homer (this procedure is still evident today in children who attribute to all men of a given type or profession, the name of the first man of that kind they ever met). These *poetic universals* are models or ideal portraits created by the imagination owing to the poverty of the intellect.

Therefore poetry was the mother tongue of the human race, and the first men were, by nature, sublime poets. By nature and not artifice, for poetry was not born as the result of the idle search for pleasant inventions, but from necessity among unrefined peoples, in whom sense and imagination prevailed over reason. Their whole life was unconsciously poetic, so that the events which unfolded under their eyes, seen through a perturbed mind, became legend, and the whole of nature was populated with infinite demons.

EVALUATION OF VICO'S LINGUISTICS. General linguistics includes, as we have seen, two fundamental issues: one is philosophical and concerns the nature or essence of language; the other is naturalistic and concerns its origin.

In relation to the first Vico maintains that language is a poetic creation of the imagination which arose at a time when the intellectual faculties of man were still weak.

One of the merits of Vico's conception is that it also throws light upon the empirical problem, because it shows how language, which would seem to require a sublime and complex spirituality, arose at a time when human minds still intellectually weak and unrefined were however exuberant in the senses and the imagination.

This view would have been more fruitful had Vico distinguished between the semantic value and the directly expressive value of languages and had he attempted a philosophical definition of the mnemonic sign, inquiring into the relation between memory and imagination (a relation he perceived when he defined the imagination as "either dilated or compound memory").[9]

Concerning the ancient problem whether the relation between the sign and its meaning is natural or conventional, Vico tends toward the first solution. Nonetheless, he does not deny the role played by convention, for he sometimes speaks of conventional words in contrast to real and natural words.

To make things clearer, we may interpret his view as follows: primitive mimetic language was pictographic and was naturally related to its object; phonetic language began through the imitation of natural sounds, but subsequently the conventional element prevailed.

The vulgar languages, he says, do not signify through conventional signs. Because they derive from the original directly expressive languages, they too have a natural origin.

But if a natural connection exists between words and their meaning, why can the same thing be signified by different phonemes in the various languages? Vico, as others before him, answers that the same object observed by men different in temperament and custom was perceived in different ways.[10]

Vico's assertion that language and writing have an analogous essence, and that the best way of understanding the origin of spoken languages is by connecting it with the study of the origin and development of writing systems, indicates, in our opinion, better than almost any other thinker before or after him, the most fruitful direction to follow in this kind of research.

As we have seen, Vico found a few indications, or suggestions, in Bacon. However, after these two thinkers, the idea was not as fully developed as deserved. It was only with Saussure that the issue was to be taken up again, when he mentions the advantages to be gained by studying the nature of language together with that of other semantic systems. Saussure's advice corresponds perfectly to Vico's idea of describing spoken languages, mimetic expressions, writing systems, family emblems, military banners, and commemorative medals.

The idea that mankind resorted to a mute language made of mimetic signs (briefly referred to by Plato, Saint Augustine, and others) before the advent of phonetic language, and that this hypothesis throws the best light on the problem of the origin of language, finds development and organic unity in Vico's thought system more than in any other thinker, be he ancient or modern.

Here, too, as elsewhere, Vico—who had always esteemed the art of finding more highly than that of proving—is brilliant in his intuitions but not very rigorous in his demonstrations. Vico's identification of and even confusion between language and writing does not help toward making the doctrine any clearer; however, his conception of mute expressions as mimetic hieroglyphics shows how we may consider the pictographic gesture as the common antecedent both of the spoken word and of writing. In fact, as mentioned earlier, according to modern scholars the correlation between primitive graphic signs and mimetic gestures is obvious.

Numerous authors, from Plato onwards, have also maintained the other hypothesis, that phonetic language originated from onomatopoeia and interjections. Vico, however, attributes a more legitimate function to these two elements (which modern scholars believe insufficient by themselves to explain the origin of language) which are not used to explain the beginnings of language, but rather the transition from mimetic to phonetic language. Vico believes that the first stage of this transition, which he recognizes as having been extremely difficult owing to physiological causes also (the "very hard fibers" of primeval man), consisted in the emission of voice through song, and strengthens his hypothesis with reference to the chants and vocalizations of certain barbaric languages. It is truly amazing how this philosopher, despite the scarceness of positive information accessible to his time and milieu, anticipated certain learned modern glottologists (such as, for example, Jespersen) who, through different arguments, reached analogous conclusions.[11]

This is true not only concerning Vico's observations on the monosyllabic nature of roots, but also on the two opposite tendencies described in the historical development of phonemes. He calls the first tendency broadening (from the monosyllable to the polysyllable) and the second shortening or contraction, so that there is a transition from certain very long archaic word-propositions, not yet analytically articulated, to the shorter and more distinctly separate modern expressions. Vico's views on the nature and "guisa del nascimento," or modality attendant upon the birth of language, acquire greater universal meaning and philosophical dignity because of their connection with his discoveries relating to poetry (as the mother tongue of the human race) and to the imagination (as a necessary phase in eternal ideal history). But historical truth and impartiality are badly served if, on underlining Vico's philosophical discoveries, we set aside as irrelevant his remarkable discoveries concerning the empirical origin of human language; worse still if the problem itself is declared to be falsely put and unworthy of study, on the basis of the suspiciously philosophic argument that since language is an eternal category, it is vain to look for its origin. Thus we believe that despite excellent studies on the subject from Croce onward, our own detailed approach may actively contribute toward a more comprehensive and balanced estimation of Vico's linguistics.

Passing from the study of the *Scienza Nuova* to other empiricist and rationalist doctrines of the seventeenth and eighteenth centuries, we mainly find ourselves faced with immature conceptions that repeat the old motifs and are inferior to what had already been said on the subject by the Greeks.

LOCKE. Locke studies the problem in a chapter of his book *Essay Concerning Human Understanding*.[12]

He begins by saying that God, having established that man was a social animal, provided him with organs suited to the emission of articulate sounds. Since the pleasures and advantages of society are not possible without the communication of thought, it was necessary for man to discover some external sensible sign through which his invisible internal ideas could be made known to others.

Nothing was more suited to such a purpose than those articulate sounds which man found he could produce with great ease and variety.

Words were used as signs of ideas not because of some natural connection between those sounds and the ideas (which would have led to the development of a single language), but because of a voluntary imposition, through which a given sound was assumed arbitrarily as the mark of a certain idea.[13]

Since they were arbitrary signs, at the origin of language it was impossible to know without an explanation what a given sound meant. For example, had Adam created the words "kinneach" (jealousy) and "niouph" (adultery), with the intention of communicating to Eve that he had noticed that their son Lamech was sad because of his wife Adah, these sounds would not have been immediately comprehensible.[14]

But Locke was not so much interested in the origin of language as in its epistemological value, so that immediately after the quoted passage, he underlined the difference between names designating complex ideas of mixed feelings (e.g., "jealousy"), and those designating concrete substances (e.g., "gold"). Given that the epistemological issue is not our concern here, we will not follow Locke's analysis any further.

LEIBNIZ. Though on a higher level, even the observations of this thinker are not very helpful for our own purposes. With reference to the words of Locke, Leibniz begins by saying that God, having made man a social being, granted the latter the faculty of language.[15] As to the question of whether the origin of language is natural or conventional, Leibniz opposes the scholastic view of purely arbitrary institution and remarks that even if words were not determined absolutely by natural necessity, this does not mean that they were established arbitrarily. He hypothesizes the probable existence of an original "Adamitic" language, common to all human beings, in which the formation of words was the combined result of natural and physiological causes and of a wise and worthy choice made by the first Author.

The reasons motivating such a choice include convenience and practicality (as with the construction of algebraic numbers); the natural reasons are those based on the imitation of sounds.

With a probable reference to *Cratylus*, Leibniz goes on to discuss the onomatopoeic symbolism characterizing certain letters of the alphabet. He avers that the ancient Teutons, Celts, and other populations of the same family probably used *r* to express vehemence; the letter *l*, instead, for something softer (such as in "lenis," "lentus," "labi"); the sound *a* and *ah* seemed naturally associated with the idea of a light breath of air, and probably gave rise to the words, "aw," "aer," "aura," "haugh," "halare," etc., and since water also gives the impression of something fluid, the sound *ah*, rendered more material in *ahha*, signified "water."[16] In short Leibniz, like many others, yielded to the temptation of these attractive and unreliable etymological hypotheses.

The Adamitic language was predominately natural; languages derived from other languages are the result of a choice and are intermingled with the element of nature and chance present in the languages they presuppose. Equally artificial are the so called *lingua francas* which act as auxiliary languages among different nations.

Leibniz also hypothesizes the existence of languages that are completely artificial, such as Chinese and the languages invented by George Dalgarno and Wilkins.[17]

It was only natural, with the spreading of interest in the social sciences and the flourishing of the natural sciences, that in the eighteenth century numerous authors should have felt the need to face the problem we are dealing with in this book. However, the glottogonic doctrines of that century and of the following are generally disappointing and disorientating. And this is so not only because we are too often faced with doctrines that are immature and inferior to those elaborated by the Greeks two thousand years before, but especially because of the total lack of continuity in development from one author to the next. Authors like Condillac, De Brosses, and Stewart, who deal with the problem with a reliable method, intelligent views, and at times with brilliant intuition, are not lacking, but their efforts almost always remain isolated and each begins to speculate again from the very beginning on his own account, ignoring what was achieved by others.

CONDILLAC. Despite the disorganized eclecticism of his ideology, Condillac, who in other respects was influenced by the English empiricists, displays a certain confidence in method and originality of views in his research into the origin of language.

He opportunely connects the problem to the study of those operations through which we relate signs and ideas.[18]

We must not believe, he says, that the ideas behind numbers, separated from their signs, are clear and determinate. The name given to single numerical concepts enables us to distinguish between them, and the same is true of philosophical ideas. We need signs in order to think.

Even if a man wished to make some calculations for himself, without communicating them to others, he would still have to use signs. It was the use of signs that enabled the development of memory, imagination, and intellectual comprehension.

Before the advent of conventional signs, memory was aided through signs dictated by circumstance. The first natural cries were not signs, but after having repeatedly experienced the same feeling followed by the same cry, people associated one with the other, so that on hearing that cry, they would also experience the same feeling. In this way, that cry came to take on the function of a sign.

If we compare these reasonable propositions made by Condillac to Morris's far-fetched definitions, we can only conclude that modern neopositivist writers, if they do not feel up to coping with such personalities as Vico or Hegel, would do well at least to read the not too demanding authors of the French Enlightenment.

The first language, continues Condillac, probably only consisted in contortions, violent agitations, and natural cries.

Resorting to a common mental experiment, he imagines that two children, soon after the Flood, get lost in a deserted place before becoming familiar with language or signs. If they had remained apart their cognitions would have been limited to simple perceptions, but as they lived together each of them was soon to notice that his companion's feelings were accompanied by certain calls, gestures, and movements of the body, and this enabled them to help each other in case of need.

As time passed, they learned to repeat those cries and gestures at will with the purpose of signifying their feelings to each other. Thus, initial natural manifestations became models for the creation of new signs.

Primitive men did not suspect that the human voice could be far more variously modulated and articulated than those few natural cries, and consequently they opted for "action language" which was easier and more natural than phonetic language.

Owing to its very simplicity, this language of gestures and movements seriously obstructed the development of oral expression. In fact, many centuries were to pass before the advent of articulate language, so that a language intermingled with words and actions was used for a considerable period.

On this point Condillac observes that, with respect to ourselves, a language of gestures and actions is more widespread among the Orientals, whose temperament is suited to a more vivacious and immediate form of expression. As proof of this he refers to the following examples from the Bible: a false prophet shakes his horns of iron to signify the defeat of Syria (*I Kings 22:11*); Jeremiah hides his linen waistcloth in the cleft of a rock near the Euphrates (*Jeremiah 13:4*); Ezekiel portrays the siege of Jerusalem on a brick (*Ezekiel 4*), weighs his hair and his beard on a balance (ibid., 5:1), takes the furniture away from his house (ibid., 12), etc.

The ancient oracles expressed themselves through action language as emerges from the words of Heraclitus: "that the King, whose oracle is in Delphi, neither speaks nor keeps silent, but expresses himself through signs."

Action language was sometimes called dance, and this is probably what is meant in the biblical passage where David is said to dance before God's ark.

The art of dancing was of two kinds: one was called "dance of gestures," the other "dance of steps." The second derived from the first and served to express happiness and rejoicing.

The first words to spring from action language preserved its character: similarly to the alternate movements of the body, the voice was raised or lowered at perceptible intervals.

For a long time voice and gestures were intermingled, with natural variations in the inflections of the voice as in the emphasis of gestures.

Still today, even when we do not know a language well, the inflections of the voice help comprehension and the same phoneme often expresses different feelings according to intonation. For example a mere "ah!" may signify pain, disappointment, admiration, pleasure, fear, delusion, sadness, etc., depending on the emphasis with which it is pronounced.

For a long time there was no other way of expressing the concepts of "I want," "I love," "I hate," if not by pronouncing the thing desired, loved, or hated with a particular tone, and by making one's feelings understood through emphasis of sound and gesture.

In Greek tragedy choreographic movements (stylization of action language) and music (stylization of expressive sonority) were an essential part of the representation.

In ancient times particular importance was attached to the rhythmic and harmonious word, and speech was accompanied by carefully studied gestures. Sometimes song and gesture were divided between two different actors: thus it seems that, for the performance of one of his plays, the poet Livy Andronicus asked that his verses be recited by a slave, while he acted out the gestures.

This is how pantomime probably arose. A distinction was made between three kinds of gesture: those destined to portray tragedy, comedy, or satire.

As performances could not be enhanced by expressions of the face, covered as it was by a mask, a far more emphatic gesticulation was necessary. Consequently ancient actors would have seemed frantic to our eyes, while ours would be considered cold and unexpressive by them.

It was not so easy for the ancients to become accustomed to expressing, through words alone, those sentiments which they were used to expressing by force of gestures, movements, and unruly calls. The insistent repetitions, abundance of pleonasms, and in general the sublime and at the same time emphatic style of the Bible and of Oriental poetry can be explained by the need to find a substitute for the directness of gestures.

Condillac also observes a certain correspondence between hieroglyphic writing and the earliest languages and maintains that the two modes of communication influenced each other. Initially hieroglyphs directly reproduced the thing signified, subsequently they became symbolic, so that, for example, the sign of a "hare" could signify shyness, a "billy goat" impurity, and an "ant" prudence.

In speech it was natural to resort to the symbols used in hieroglyphs, and when drawing hieroglyphs use was made of the tropes of spoken language.

As we can see, with excellent psychological insight Condillac espied a plausible picture of the birth of language by appropriately relating a number of accurate observations. If his documentation seems incomplete, we must remember the imperfect state of the information then available, and be grateful that he never gave in to those fanciful deformations of the facts, so common among some of his contemporaries.

Nevertheless, the beneficial influence exercised on the French thinkers by the English empiricists and by the revival of the natural sciences did not counterbalance the rationalist tendencies to which the French were inclined by nature and tradition.

DE BROSSES. De Brosses,[19] for example, made a conscious effort to stick to the facts and his description is one of the most complex and accurate available on our argument. Despite this, however, the tendency toward intellectualistic oversimplification is present throughout all his work.

The construction of our organs, he says, is determined by nature so that the effect follows on naturally from the cause, and an organ cannot produce any other effect beyond that allowed by its structure: man cannot fly because he does not have wings, and he is able to walk because he has feet. (This argument highlights how much our vision of the world and of nature has been changed, in all fields, by evolutionistic theories.)

The natural articulations of the voice, which are the necessary effects of the structure of the vocal organs, are the initial elements of all languages. As these early articulate sounds were few in number, human intelligence had to variously combine them in order to form words. The choice of letters used to form the name of an object was determined by the nature of the object itself. Whoever gave a name to a soft object for the first time had to use a soft sound and not a sharp one, similarly to a painter who uses the color red to paint a red flower and the color black for a piece of coal. A savage who hears the shot of a cannon for the first time will refer to it by making a booming sound and not by imitating the chirping of birds.

Thus a primitive, organic, and physically inevitable language is probably common to the whole human race, while the words used by all the nations in the world are but ramifications from that common trunk. This primitive language was directly and indirectly subject to amplifications and alterations which produced a number of different languages, but the latter also share more or less in the inevitable character of the original language.

It is up to the scientist to analyze the mechanism of languages, to distinguish between that which derives from natural necessity and that which is added arbitrarily, and to show how we passed from one meaning to another.

De Brosses, therefore, describes the organ of the human voice, the number, form, and functions of its parts. He believes it possible to demonstrate that elementary sounds, namely, vowels, consonants, and accents, are a mechanical effect of that structure and could not have been different, in quality and number, from what they are. (It is strange that he did not even ask himself why the number and quality of elementary sounds should greatly differ from one language to another, and why alphabetical sounds common to certain peoples have the effect of inarticulate expressions on others.)

He then attempts to identify the relations between natural sounds emitted by the human voice on the one hand, and certain sensations, feelings, physical and moral objects on the other, and lists the various ways in which the first roots arose. Some were the result of direct imitation, like the terms "cuccú," "fracas," "claque," "siffler," "clangor," "tonnerre," etc. Others were the result of symbolic imitation, by attributing a soft, sharp, dull, fast sound to soft, sharp, dull, fast things, etc. Other roots were formed by choosing groups of letters that naturally conveyed the idea of a given property. For example, the phoneme *st* conveys the idea of stability ("stay"), *fl* of something fluid ("fluo," "flatus," "flame"). Still others were formed through a correspondence between a sound and that part of the vocal organ involved in producing it. For example, the phoneme *gheu, go,* is present in "gullet," "gola," "gorge," "gurgle," "glottis," "guttur," "garguero," "gargarismo," etc.; the dental sounds in "dens," "odòn," "tzan," etc.

Words that include the letter *m* are the most suitable to signify the mandible ("mâchoire," "maxila," "mastico," "mordeo," "manger," "manduco," "mentum," "maschera," "mask").

Since the lips are the most external part of the vocal organs, the labials indicate what one wishes to keep away from oneself, such as in "pouah!," "vae!," "fi!" The aspirates express pain and surprise as in "heu!," "hélas!," "uh!," "eh!," and sometimes joy as in "ha-ha-ha," "hee-hee-hee."

All words are either formed in this direct manner or through derivation from preceding words.

Working through the genealogical filiation should eventually lead us to the reconstruction of the first language. But since this language does not belong to the historical languages, we must look for it among the first sounds emitted by children.

Before learning how to articulate words, the infant's language consists wholly of interjections. His whimpering and cries at birth are no more than interjections. These indicate moods, so that names referring to the affections of inner feelings are the first and most ancient and may be considered as invariable residues of primitive language.

The easiest and therefore the first articulate words ever pronounced by the child are the labials. In fact, these consonants can be traced in the infant expressions "mamma," "pappa," "ninna," "am-am," in all times and places.

Any child left to himself would start speaking with these syllables, for they are formed almost automatically upon moving the lips.

Immediately after the labials, the dentals "tata," "tete," "toto," "dada," etc., are pronounced. Not only interjection and onomatopoeia, but also accentuation, inflection, and intonation are all part of natural language. Through such devices a single syllable may correspond to different expressions, to the extent that we could envisage a language in which the diversity of words consists almost solely in the variety of accentuation and intonation.

These expressive elements are more important in the most ancient languages and in the primitive languages than they are in modern languages. In fact, as conventional terms gradually prevail, emphatic accentuation decreases. Nature rests when art goes into action.

The origin of words that express the impressions of feelings and that refer to sounds is easily explained; in contrast, it is more difficult to explain the origin of the names of objects that strike the sense of sight, which is very different from the sense of hearing.

A noise is produced when we touch, taste, or even smell something, so that sound associations are possible, but sight does not produce noise. For this reason, says De Brosses, visual perceptions do not enter at all into the primitive system of word-making. (Modern scholars have reached the opposite conclusion: in animals, primitive men, and children the sense of sight is the most acute, ready, and useful for training and plays a more important part in primitive expressions and communication than even the sense of hearing.)

Sometimes even visual impressions can be signified through figurative analogies, as when we say that a given color is dark, bright, or loud, but such an expedient is imperfect and not always possible. Thus to convey visual impressions human beings had to resort to the imitation of sounds which was almost as immediate and natural a form of expression, though it more heavily involved conscious will.

What primitive man did not succeed in communicating through the voice, he roughly designed with a bit of color: this led to the development of writing systems. (De Brosses imagines this process as follows: like the good school teacher who takes chalk in hand to make his lesson clearer from a didactic viewpoint, the cave man intermingled his discourses with little explicative figures. If, for example, he wanted to say "A raven flew away and rested on the top of a tree," he would first imitate the croaking of the bird, then he would express the flight with a "frrr! frrr!" and eventually take a piece of coal and draw a tree with a raven on top. . . .)

In the author's opinion, pictographic representation preceded the word whenever objects could not be easily signified with imitative or affective sounds. He also mentions *en passant* that, in certain cases, design could be substituted by gesture. (Instead of saying, as would seem natural, that the first language was entirely made of gestures and directly expressive sounds and that a conventional phonetic language was developed only after many centuries and writing systems after yet another very long period, De Brosses believes that phonetic language is the most primitive and places gesture and writing at the same level, indeed he considers gesture as a surrogate of pictographic writing.)

In order to demonstrate the priority of pictographic writing over phonetic language, he remarks that conventional signs require greater reflection than immediate representation. Therefore the first stage consisted in roughly sketching the outline of objects, so that once greater familiarity was acquired with the concept of the thing, it was easier to establish a conventional name for it.

A few wise observations on writing systems follow: the first elements do not derive, as is generally thought, from the necessity of communicating with people at a distance. It was easier for primitive man to believe he could fly rather than fix his own words and transport them from one place to another. Early writing systems are simply pictorial representations of visible objects.

The necessary stages in the evolution of these writing systems are outlined as follows: (1) reproduction of single objects: a man, an animal, a tree; (2) a series of objects with the aim of communicating an event which has taken place; (3) material objects with symbolic meaning: a skull means death, a lion means force, etc.; (4) hieroglyphs or conventional ideograms; (5) syllabic writing; (6) alphabetical writing.

All these types of writing can be classified under three headings: (1) direct representations; (2) symbolic representations; and (3) conventional phonetic writing systems. The first refers to that which strikes the external senses, the second to the feelings, the third to conceptual reflection.

De Brosses collected carefully and intelligently a great amount of material observed by travelers and ethnologists to support his theories. He refers to primitive knot writing, he delves into Egyptian hieroglyphs (yet to be deciphered in his own time), and rightly notes that ideographic writing, as with Arabic numerals, has the advantage that it can be read by everyone in his own tongue.

He believes that the need and capacity to communicate through phonetic or graphic signs is intimately inherent in man, so he does not doubt that if children were to grow up in isolation without ever hearing a single word, they would spontaneously create a language of their own. Indeed, if four groups of children were left alone in four different parts of the world, they would produce languages very similar, if not identical, to each other, because these languages would be formed according to the same principles. But the small initial differences would subsequently become increasingly marked owing to the successive influence of a great many other factors. De Brosses also acknowledges that there may exist languages different from phonetic language. A people which expresses its ideas through graphic signs without using the voice, or which, instead of drawing shapes on paper, expresses itself with the fingers and with gestures of the hand, as deaf-mutes do, is not inconceivable. We could even have a population of blind deaf-mutes who express themselves through the mere contact and pressure of the hands, as do deaf-mutes when communicating in the dark.

Despite obvious faults (the most striking being the tendency to oversimplify and to state too often that "on ne peut douter" when instead a doubt would have been more appropriate), De Brosses's writings are among the best written in his time; and certainly no one before him had developed the ancient thesis of language as originating from affective and imitative sounds with so much detail or had backed it with such a great amount of documentation.

The invention of writing and the origin of language are considered to be almost contemporary in the mechanistic theory just expounded as well as in Vico's idealist and historicist approach. However, several reasons induce us to believe that human beings used some form of language tens and probably hundreds of thousands of years before the invention of writing. Firstly, we must remember that in the prehistoric era, progress in technology was slow, and by no means comparable to the rhythm of the modern era. Furthermore, there is an enormous separation between the almost animal way of expressing oneself with the body and voice and the far less spontaneous use of external expedients for designing figures. Everyone carries his voice with him, while, on the other hand, the use of external expedients, which are not always readily available, requires a greater capacity of premeditation. Moreover, emitting an "ah! ah!" or a "bow! bow!" or pretending to fly by flapping one's arms does not require a much greater skill than that possessed by anthropoids, whereas to draw even the rough outline of an animal, a clearness of vision and manual dexterity not possessed by all is necessary. But it seems to us that the most decisive proof is this: there exist still today hundreds of millions of illiterates in the world. Little more than half a century ago, ninety per cent of the population in certain regions of civilized countries such as Italy, Russia, Spain, and Greece were still illiterate, while in a country with such an ancient civilization as China, illiterates exceeded 99 per cent of the population. Therefore, up until 1800 A.D. the use of writing was the prerogative of an extremely limited part of humanity, while, on the other hand, a population so primitive and uncivilized as not to possess a language from time immemorial does not exist. To this we must add that there are or have been illiterates who have fulfilled important social functions, not only as heads of the family or as tribal leaders but also as sovereigns of large states, while a man destitute of all phonetic or mimetic language could not be a useful member of any human society.

To form an idea of the confusion which dominated (and still largely dominates nowadays) in the treatment of our problem, it will prove instructive to look at the works of Court de Gébelin and of Monboddo (in their time highly evaluated and renowned), which we consider as two outstanding monuments to bad taste and poor scientific method.

COURT DE GÉBELIN. The most important work by Gébelin, *Monde primitif*, devotes a good part of its many pages to the origin of language and to the reconstruction of a "dictionary of the original language."[20]

His method is very simple: he says that the analysis of any language at all immediately reveals that it is composed of words and that the words are composed of letters. Therefore the letters of the alphabet are the material out of which all languages are made; they are immutable and are the same in all the world.

Letters are divided into vowels and consonants. There are seven vowels and fourteen consonants. The first man ever to have spoken used these twenty-one elements which formed the unchanging basis of all languages. Every letter has its own natural meaning: each vowel expresses a given sensation and each consonant a given idea. Just as the painter uses colors to portray the exterior aspect of all things, man used alphabetical letters to represent, without any difficulty, the qualities of objects. Man walked because he had legs and spoke because he had a mouth.

Since the basic words, namely, the twenty-one letters, were not sufficient, they were united in twos and threes to compose monosyllabic words of one, two, or three letters, as well as bisyllabic words. These four kinds of combinations produced a sufficient number of words to wholly construct the language of the primitive world. The number of words was subsequently increased by using certain words not only with their literal meaning but also in the figurative sense.

All languages in the world are modifications of the same roots and the roots are none other than the words of the first language.

It is on foundations such as these that the author reconstructs his "dictionary of original language." It is sufficient for him to analyze a word of any language whatsoever to then find the same root—with a few modifications—in all other languages.[21]

Gébelin's weighty and pretentious book, in which all the world's languages are examined with the method we have described, is a caricature of intellectualistic oversimplification. That this book should have met with wide success is not only explained by the common, vulgar (though temporary) tendency of writing too much, but also by the tenacious rationalist tradition of the French grammarians from Port Royal onward.

What a difference between Gébelin's heavy, academic foolish talk and the casual and even unpretentious remarks of such brilliant men as Rousseau and Diderot!

Rousseau says:

Toutes nos langues sont des ouvrages de l'art. On a longtemps cherché s'il y

avait une langue naturelle et commune à tous les hommes; sans doute il y en
a une; et c'est celle que les enfants parlent avant de savoir parler. Cette langue
n'est pas articulée, mais elle est accentuée, sonore, intelligible. L'usage des
nôtres nous l'a fait négliger au point de l'oublier tout à fait. Etudions les
enfants, et bientôt nous la rapprendrons auprès d'eux. Les nourrices sont
nos maîtres dans cette langue; elles entendent tout ce que disent leurs nour-
rissons; elles leur répondent, elles ont avec eux des dialogues très bien suivis;
et quoique elles prononcent des mots, ces mots sont parfaitement inutiles; ce
n'est point le sens du mot qu'ils entendent, mais l'accent dont il est accom-
pagné.

   Au langage de la voix se joint celui du geste, non moins énergique. Ce
geste n'est pas dans les faibles mains des enfants, il est sur leurs visages. Il
est étonnant combien ces physionomies mal formées ont déjà d'expression;
leurs traits changent d'un instant à l'autre avec une inconcevable rapidité:
vous y voyez le sourire, le désir, l'effroi naître et passer comme autant d'éclairs:
à chaque fois vous croyez voir un autre visage.[22]

Though he dealt with the issue only on occasion and not exhaustively,
Rousseau has the merit of having seen very distinctly that the natural language
of man is directly expressive, that is, a language of sounds and affective
gestures. From a theoretic point of view his fault lies in not having distinguished between spontaneous physiological reactions and intentionally communicative attitudes.

   Diderot makes a few brief but suggestive considerations on our topic in
his *Lettre sur les sourds et les muets (à l'usage de ceux qui entendent et qui parlent)*,[23]
in which he deals with various issues in aesthetics, rhetoric, and linguistics.

   On describing "inversions," that is, indirect constructions, from a grammatical and aesthetic point of view, he attempts to clarify his thoughts by
examining "how languages were formed." Since we cannot go back to the
origin of language, we may help ourselves by imagining a man who, denying
himself the use of articulate sounds, makes every effort to express himself
through gestures alone. From the succession of his gestures it should be
possible to infer the order of ideas that appeared as the most natural and
suited to primitive man.

   Continuing the mental experiment of his "muet de convention," Diderot
correctly distinguishes between the character of pantomime and the language
of gestures: the first renders an action, the second a discourse (we would say:
the first has an aesthetic character, the second a semantic character). He also
suggests two methods for the study of mimetic language: (1) a mental experiment like that of his "muet de convention"; (2) direct observation of deaf-
mutes. Observation of the mode of expression of unschooled deaf-mutes
should give some indication as to the birth of primitive language.

   As an effective example of mimetic expression, Diderot points to the case
of an actress who, to render Lady Macbeth's obsessive remorse, moves without speaking, like a somnambulist, and rubs her hands as though they were
still stained with blood.

   For a better understanding of the nature of mimetic expression, Diderot proposes that we follow the action of a play with our ears blocked, or that we translate spoken discourse into mimetic discourse.

Finally, he underlines the importance of directly expressive elements among the ancients. The Greeks and Romans declaimed their verses by almost singing them and accompanied their recitation with a musical instrument. In Cicero's view, verses which were not backed up by song seemed to be prose. However, the ancients modulated their voices at rhythmic intervals even in prose, so that our own kind of recitation would have seemed inexpressive and discordant to them.

Neither Rousseau nor Diderot dealt specifically with the problem of the origin of language. Indeed, the former, in other writings, expressed his perplexities in the face of this issue and its difficult solution. Let us now pass on to examine the work of a writer who devoted the best part of his life to the problem of language origin.

MONBODDO. In 1773 James Burnett Lord Monboddo published a work in six volumes on *The Origin and Progress of Language*[24] which aroused a great deal of interest all over Europe and was translated into German with a preface by Herder. Monboddo begins by saying that no author, ancient or modern, had so far dealt with the subject specifically, that it was a completely new and unknown field which he had the merit of being the first to explore, dedicating to it many years of study and patient work. Nevertheless, in the course of his work he discusses Plato's *Cratylus* at length and mentions studies by Condillac and De Brosses, who certainly could have enlightened him as to how to treat his subject more reasonably. But he declares that he is familiar with only one extract by Condillac and that he sees no use in studying him more carefully, because Condillac deals mainly with the faculty of the intellect and devotes only a part of his book to language; as for De Brosses, Monboddo does not even mention his name but simply refers to a "French author" who wrote a book of little value on the mechanism of languages.

Language is defined by Monboddo as the "expression of concepts through articulate sounds," adding that when we speak of the language of the eyes or of gestures or of other signs, the word "language" is used metaphorically and not scientifically.

This is an instructive example of the determining role that an initial conceptual definition may play in the development of a line of inquiry. Monboddo did not realize that with such an approach his research was to be totally devoid of interest and importance, from the very outset. Our interest does not lie in how human beings learned to modulate their vocal cords so as to produce articulate sounds (a problem to which he devotes all his attention), but how they managed to construct a semantic system in order to fix their ideas and communicate among themselves. It is of little consequence whether in the signs then used, cries, songs, gestures, actions, or other elements prevailed.

Monboddo dwells on the question of whether language is a gift of nature or a product of human art. He supports the second thesis, but to avoid contradicting the Bible he grants that primitive man received language through science, but that as a consequence of original sin he then lost this gift and had to re-invent it on his own. In fact, if language were a natural gift, children would know it as soon as they are born, without the need to learn it gradually. Pronouncing articulate sounds may seem easy to us, since we do it from birth, but in reality it is a difficult art and takes a great effort to learn (as we see, for example, with deaf-mutes who must be trained to speak).

The various positions and movements of the vocal cords in the pronunciation of alphabetical letters are anything but natural; in fact, certain consonants which seem completely natural to a given nation cannot be pronounced by foreigners.

With reference to Rousseau's aporia, according to which language could only have arisen after the constitution of society but no society could have been possible without language, Monboddo maintains that societies without language are possible and exist. There exist whole nations of savages who do not know how to speak. Of particular interest to him are the orangutans whose habits he describes by referring to Buffon's natural history.[25] Their bodies are similar to our own, both internally and externally, with a few small variations (just as among the various human families) which, however, do not determine a specific difference. They walk upright and not on all fours like other savages, they have long white venerable beards, they build huts in trees, use sticks as weapons, live in societies and have a sense of honour, justice, and modesty. Sometimes they kidnap negro women making them slaves for their own pleasure and for work. They have their own culture, are intelligent, can easily learn to play the flute, harp, and other instruments; they have vocal cords similar to our own, but do not know how to speak. In conclusion Monboddo believes that the existence of orangutans is the most obvious proof that human societies devoid of language exist.

What is more, he continues, there are various species of political animals, for example, beavers, which live in villages of twenty to twenty-five small houses and form state communities of one hundred and fifty to two hundred individuals, work in harmony, fell trees, construct dams, and set up storage houses.

Animals, living in societies without language much as orangutans and other savage populations do, may communicate in rudimentary ways through inarticulate calls, eyes, and gestures.

From the example of deaf-mutes, we know that through gestures both feelings and ideas and be communicated. In this connection Monboddo reminds us of the high degree of perfection attained in Rome in the art of pantomine. Before the invention of language, human beings were probably able to signify some of their feelings and conceptions through inarticulate calls, imitative sounds, and gestures. However, we must exclude the idea that the art of mimicry was brought to the same level of perfection as among the

Romans. Even if we were to accept such an absurd hypothesis, mimetic communication had the disadvantage that it could not be used in the dark or while hunting or fishing. The use of imitative sounds was necessarily restricted, because they could only signify sonorous objects. Communication through painting and signs could have been possible but would have been slow and difficult and only suitable for the rendering of visible objects.

Monboddo goes on to examine Dr. Blackford's hypothesis, an intelligent and cultured man from Edinburgh, blind since childhood, who believed that man's first language had been music. This hypothesis does not seem plausible to Monboddo. Musical language without articulations could not have satisfied even the most simple needs of a primitive community, though he does recognize the fundamental importance of stress and intonation in both ancient and barbaric languages.

Primitive inarticulate emotional cries probably became more effective with the addition of intonation and musical rhythm, but the decisive step took place only with the rise of articulate sounds.

In Monboddo's opinion, to interrogate oneself on the origin of language is equivalent to asking oneself how man learned the difficult art of pronouncing the letters of the alphabet. His reply is that man learned to talk from beasts.

He maintains that man generally learned various arts from animals; he learned how to spin and weave from spiders, to construct dams from beavers, and to sing and speak from birds.

He knew a negro child who assured him that her people's music imitated the song of birds. Since such birds as the cuckoo, the raven, and especially the parrot produce almost alphabetical sounds, he believes that the art of phonetic articulation is the result of imitating the sounds made by such animals.

We cannot establish whether verbs, nouns, or some other parts of speech were invented first, for original articulate sounds were complete propositions which as such expressed a given need or mood. Furthermore, it is not possible to maintain that roots were invented first, as primitive languages do not include either compound words or words derived from previous words, and therefore do not have roots.

It was only later, with the intervention of the art of grammar, that we learned to modify a given word, adapting it to various meanings, and to create compound words.

Over-long words were artfully simplified and embellished, so that they were rendered more pleasing to the ear and more suited to their meaning. The creators of language, that is, writers and grammarians, perfected language and made it more beautiful with the aid of rational rules and methods, as may be seen from Greek, Latin, and Sanskrit.

Without going into greater detail, these references should suffice in giving us an idea of Monboddo's book to which he dedicated so many years of his life. Some good observations and plausible theories in relation to specific topics are not lacking here and there. However, especially in the part concerning language origin, Lord Monboddo gives the impression of being an English gentleman accustomed to having even his most eccentric and fanciful ideas listened to with deference.

The fact that such heavy, laborious, and muddled books as these should have enjoyed wide favor in the academic world up to the present day has contributed largely to the discrediting of inquiries into language origin, as the over-hasty opinions of many contemporary scholars make obvious.[26]

4. The Nineteenth Century

Dugald Stewart—Importance of Sympathetic Imitation in the Origin of Language—Importance of
Mimetic Language—Herder—Identification of Linguistic Capacity with Thought Capacity—Surviv-
ing Theological Tendency in Herder—F. Schlegel—
Cesarotti—Manzoni—Grimm—Jaeger—Steinthal—
Renan—Linguistic Innatism.

STEWART. A complex, well thought-out doctrine on the essence and origin of
language, founded on a great quantity of documented observation, was elaborated toward the end of the eighteenth century by Dugald Stewart.[1] Before
setting to work on my historical survey, I was only familiar with this author's
account of the life and works of Adam Smith.[2] As a philosopher, Stewart was
a mediocre follower of Reid's school, which had forsaken good sense for fear
of being criticized by the followers of common sense.

Though a mediocre philosopher, Stewart was an excellent psychologist
and intelligent observer, and one of the rare authors ever to have said something new on our subject. He identifies a natural language and an artificial
language. Basing himself on one of Reid's observations,[3] he notes that the
formation of an "artificial" language or, as we would say, a language composed of conventional signs, presupposes the existence of a natural language.
It was necessary to agree on what conventions were to be used in order to
establish artificial signs, but this was impossible without having signs to act
as the medium of communication.

He cites a passage from Dr. Ferguson who says that if we consider the
language of highly civilized nations, their invention will seem to surpass human capacities and appear to be miraculous. The error consists in comparing
two extreme points in evolution (namely, animal life devoid of language and
civilized humanity). In contrast, it is advisable to imagine society in its infancy
and then consider the successive stages in the gradual formation of languages.

It is not a question of verifying historically the various phases in linguistic development, but of tracing the way the mind proceeds in the use of artificial signs. Stewart makes this point with the intention, among other things, of allowing the religious-minded the freedom to believe in an original divine institution of language. In our eyes it is important because he distinguishes between the naturalistic point of view, which formulates hypotheses on the evolution of the human faculties, and the historical point of view, which, for the case in question, would require an impossible documentation. As we know, confusion of these two points of view has led many contemporary scholars to believe that our topic cannot be dealt with scientifically.

To convince ourselves of the expressive importance of "natural" signs, he suggests that we read to a child one of Aesop's fables, first in a monotonous tone of voice without taking our eyes away from the book (so that communication may only be accomplished through the conventional meaning of words), and then by livening it up with facial, gestural, and voice expressions.

The connection between our feelings and external appearances is obvious; in fact, people with a good memory for faces, and authors of treatises on pictorial technique, have observed that all emotions and mental operations have an expression of their own so that certain habitual feelings leave a trace on the face.

Moreover, man seems to be gifted with an instinctive aptitude for interpreting certain facial expressions, gestures, and intonations of the voice. A child understands the meaning of a smile, or of a severe glance, or of a sweet or threatening sound in the voice much sooner than acquiring such knowledge through experience of the connection between a feeling and its manifestations. If interpretation were the result of experience, there is no reason why a child should understand natural signs before conventional signs.

Why does an infant smile on seeing his mother smile? How does he know that her smile corresponds to a feeling of affection and happiness? Why is he able to reproduce that smiling expression without the need of looking at himself in the mirror?

Stewart resorts to the concept of *sympathetic imitation* elaborated by Adam Smith in his *Theory of the Moral Sentiments.*[4]

In Smith's opinion, sympathetic imitation is the mechanical effect of an illusion of the imagination. When we see someone about to receive a blow on the leg or arm, we instinctively withdraw the corresponding part of our own body as though to protect ourselves, and if someone is wounded we instinctively feel sorry for him. If we look at a sick person covered in ulcers we experience a sense of discomfort and something like physical compassion. An acrobat dancing on a cord causes us to instinctively bend and balance our body as though to maintain our equilibrium, and when we go bowling we bend our body and follow the ball's course as though to direct it.

Stewart recognized the potential importance of the "law of sympathetic imitation" in explaining the origin of language. He defines as "sympathetic" imitation that which is based on our instinctive imitative faculties and which manifests itself mechanically and independently of the will.

We find enjoyment in imitating the actions and attitudes of others, without the intervention of reason: in the words of Horace, "ut ridentibus arrident, ita flentibus adflent humani vultus."

An actor does not need a mirror in order to know which expression of the face and body corresponds to the feeling he wishes to represent. Even when we are alone and remember a certain feeling which we represent to ourselves, our facial expression instinctively manifests it.

The imitative instinct is remarkably important in education, and especially in language learning among children. Imitation is more spontaneous and more effective in the child than in adults: an English child taken to Russia or Arabia will pronounce the corresponding languages correctly after a short time, while an adult will not succeed in doing this even after a prolonged stay. Even the moral bond between the citizens of the same nation is not conditioned by climatic and biological causes as much as by the imitative instinct.

In Stewart's opinion, this same instinct explains the contagious effect of certain physiological and pathological manifestations, such as yawning, laughter, hysterical convulsions, as well as the diffusion of such feelings as fear, aggressiveness, and religious enthusiasm.

On this point he cites a passage by Dr. Gregory who reveals an uncommon capacity for psychological penetration with respect to his times:

> We say and do many things through pure imitation. While not yet fully aware of what he is doing, the child imitates all he sees and hears. Similar to this in a certain sense is that other kind of imitation, sudden and violent in character, which causes individuals as well as whole nations to go mad. Through this sort of contamination, sad, happy, and ridiculous feelings pass from the face of one man to the breast of all. The fervour of the battle and the hope of victory that emanate from the face of the captain lights up thousands of breasts. On the contrary, the very same soldiers, struck by the terror of a single man, may shamefully flee. The frenzy of certain fanatics spreads in a similar fashion: people who believe they are healthy and mock expressions of insanity, may become possessed by that very madness simply by seeing and hearing these mad men. Certain hysterical and epileptic nervous diseases have a similar effect and are strangely contagious through sight alone.[5]

Stewart does not exclude that a feeling may at times be communicated to others even without the mediation of an exterior sign, that is, through a mysterious mental influence, or, as Bacon asserted in his *Silva Silvarum*, through a kind of magic transmission from the spirit of one person to the body of another. In this connection, Stewart recalls the recent experiments by Mesmer. Modern experiments seem to confirm the possibility and reality of similar telepathic experiences.

Stewart also considers certain customs as natural, which though common to very different populations are founded in nature itself: for example, the custom of showing respect by making way for someone, of standing up when the other person enters, of bowing the head in sign of approval, and the etiquette and formalities observed in certain social environments in general. He also recalls the mimetic language of the deaf and dumb and points out that two deaf-mutes, who spend some time together, soon understand each other even if they belong to two different nations. Finally, the instinctive tendency of human beings to communicate among themselves through natural signs is confirmed by the existence of a *lingua franca,* composed of gestures, in use among the Indians of North America. He documents this in a paper read at the American Philosophical Society (Philadelphia 1819) and in another one concerning an expedition undertaken in 1819 and 1820 from Pittsburgh to the Rocky Mountains.[6]

Passing on to artificial signs (this is the weakest part of his theory), Stewart believes that they were established by mutual agreement. As ideas gradually multiplied, the imperfection of natural langauge began to make itself felt and, consequently, man resorted to artificial language. When artificial languages (those made of conventional signs) were later perfected, natural languages declined, so that in the current state of civilization it is not easy to recognize the latter's function and to rediscover its use.

Even the ancients, who cultivated the science of natural signs with great success, as is evident from the diffusion and perfection of Roman pantomine, needed to study a good deal to acquire that art, or better still to rediscover their natural bent for it.

Artificial signs may be divided into visible and auditory signs. The first included those which, in Polibius's opinion, were used by the Greeks to communicate letters by means of burning torches, as well as the system of signals generally thought to have been introduced by James II into the British navy.

If human beings had been unable to hear and speak they would have spoken through visible signs alone. These however have the drawback that they cannot be used in the dark or when the interlocutor is too far away. Auditory signs have the advantage of being able to easily attract the attention of the interlocutor even when his eyes are turned elsewhere and of allowing more rapid communication. According to Stewart, it has been calculated that two thousand letters may be pronounced distinctly in a minute. Furthermore, modulations and inflections of the voice may also confer, to a certain extent, an immediately expressive character to arbitrary signs.

Stewart's intelligent and documented treatment of the nature and origin of language represents, in my opinion, the best of what has been done in this field after Bacon and Vico up to the present day.

It is surprising that his observations and ideas hardly influenced the numerous scholars who treated the same subject after him in various ways. In part this may be due to the fact that Stewart's excellent observations were watered down with a great many other less convincing considerations on the formation of the parts of discourse, on etymologies, on the affinity between languages, etc., which were presented as part of a vast though all but well-founded "philosophy of the human spirit."

But the main reason is to be looked for, I think, in the insecurity of method which still today dominates these studies as well as the psychological and moral disciplines generally, making profitable collaboration and progressive development difficult.

HERDER. The thinkers of German Romanticism, who toward the end of the eighteenth century and during the early decades of the nineteenth century meditated on problems concerning language, exalted manifestations of individuality, such as sentiment and poetry, in contrast to the abstractions of the rationalists, and saw in language a significant example of spontaneous spiritual creativity. Thus they prepared the way for a new philosophical and historical conception. However, as to the question of language origin, they tended to deny the very problem, reducing it to that of its essence, and when they could not deny it, they took refuge far too easily in vague theologizing conceptions.

This tendency can be noted in Herder who nevertheless does not lack in ideas of great interest, which exercised their influence on subsequent scholars.

He concentrates specifically on our problem in *Abhandlung über den Ursprung der Sprache* and in *Ideen zur Philosophie der Geschichte der Menschheit*. The former was written in 1760 and presented in 1761 in Berlin to the Royal Academy of Sciences, which had proposed a competition on the following subject: "Imagine a group of people abandoned to their natural faculties. Would they be capable of inventing language? How would they arrive at such an invention?"[7]

He begins with the observation that, if seized by pain, a suffering animal as much as the hero Philoctetes will scream and groan without the intention of communicating their condition and would do so even if they were to find themselves on a desert island. But, just as a cord of a musical instrument vibrates in relation to another cord, in the same way those spontaneous manifestations arouse interest in whoever listens to them.

This is a language of nature, common to all the individuals of a given animal species. Atavistic residues consisting in inarticulate cries, laughter, sighs, tears, etc., are also present in human beings. They are physiological manifestations, which do not yet have a precise and univocal meaning (e.g., ah! and oh! may have numerous different meanings), but which are singularly suited to expressing the affections and passions. They acquire great expressive importance in music, dance, and ancient poetry, as we see in Greek tragedy where these three arts form a harmonious unity. "Natural language" exercises a greater influence than cerebral expressions on children, women, the common people, and on all those animated by delicate and profound sentiments.

Despite this, Herder adds that he is surprised that certain philosophers should have believed they could explain the origin of human language with these animal cries. In his opinion they are expressions of an essentially different nature: all animals possess a natural language, but none, not even the most perfect, possess the initial rudiments of human language. (Herder is indeed correct in noting the diversity between physiological manifestations and linguistic expressions, but he does not see the importance of the former in the development of the latter. Moreover his refusal to acknowledge the essentially identical nature of mimetic language and phonetic language impeded him from recognizing those linguistic rudiments which are not wanting even in the animal world.) Children, he continues, display their feelings like animals by emitting sounds, but the language they learn from human beings is something completely different.

In his *Essais sur l'origine des connaissances humaines*, Condillac had asserted that two children in isolation, before becoming familiar with the use of signs, would learn to connect their thoughts and instinctive cries to the repetition of like circumstances. But, observes Herder, without the use of signs and without expression, thought is not possible. How could these children connect thoughts they did not have to their physiological manifestations? Condillac (who influenced Rousseau) supposed, therefore, that words and thoughts arose on the basis of preexistent thoughts.

Human beings are the only living creatures gifted with language. But what is the essential difference between animals and man? The difference is this: animals act through unconscious instinct; man, on the contrary, is conscious of what he does. For this reason, Herder believes he can identify man's linguistic capacity with reason or reflective discernment *(Besonnenheit)*, that is, with the awareness that man—and man only—has of his own actions and states of mind. Consciousness is the sum of all our spiritual faculties: intellect, imagination, reason.

Man is exercising his capacity to reflect when he succeeds in isolating an image from the swarm of impressions passing through his senses, fixing his mind on it, and contemplating it with serenity and clarity.

(That consciousness, or self-awareness, is in some way an essential requirement of any one of our states of mind is an important concept in critical and transcendental considerations. It is similar to the concept expressed by Kant when he said that the statement *I think* dominates all our states of mind—but in a naturalistic context the appeal to transcendental concepts is out of place. Moreover Herder is not as clear as he could be because, on the one hand, he separates the impressions of the senses too definitely from representations, and, on the other, he does not seem to distinguish between images, expressions, representations, and concepts.)

Through what device, Herder asks himself, does the recognition of the image take place in man? Through a distinctive sign *(Merkmal)*, which remains in him as the mark—the marker or tag—of his reflection. This mark is the word of the soul. With it human language is invented.

Man, for example, may feel the need to become familiar with sheep. His senses reveal them to him as being white, soft, and woolly. His spirit intent on reflection searches for a distinctive sign. The sheep bleats; here then is the sign. The property of bleating stands out from the others and remains impressed on the mind. On seeing the sheep again, man observes it and looks for the distinctive sign. He recognizes it and says: you are that which bleats. Bleating, perceived by man as the mark of the sheep, becomes an interior evocative vocable, that is, the name of that animal. The first human language is no more than a collection of such names.

According to Herder, most of those who have dealt with the origin of language have searched for it outside the only place (that of theoretical reflection) where it could have been found. Some have searched for it in a more perfect articulation of the voice, as though parrots were gifted with language. Others in animal sounds, as though the neighing of the horse were discourse; others in the imitation of natural sounds, as though mechanical and monkey-like imitation were language; and, finally, others averred that language emerged by convention, which led to the absurd conclusion that, before the advent of speech, human beings established among themselves a sort of semantic contract.

Herder takes his stand against Suessmilch who had written a treatise upholding the divine origin of language.[8] Divine origin, he says, is contradicted by the fact that to comprehend divine teaching we need reason, yet we cannot conceive reason without language.

However, a theologizing tendency also persists in Herder since he identifies language with reason, and reason is given to man directly by God (i.e., without gradual development). Language was not gradually developed through many generations but was immediately perceived by the first man ever to have formulated the first thought. Herder, in fact, begins with a theory commonly accepted in his time and which ignored the naturalisitic theory of evolution: namely, that Nature identifies itself with wisdom and divine providence and proceeds through preordained rational designs. Man, he says, was created for language. Human nature requires language; the materials, form, and shape of language concur for such a purpose, expressive signs were set up and coordinated for such a purpose.

This spurious method of the "final causes" is based on the assumption that all that which exists is programmatic in "nature" and has a specific end. For example, we say that as man knew how to take shelter from bad weather better than other animals, he was able to survive even without being covered in a natural fur; in contrast, Herder would say that as man does not have a natural protection, he was "created for clothes."

Giving a far too exclusive priority to phonetic signs, Herder asserts that hearing is the path to the soul and that only through hearing can man take in the language of nature, his teacher, and that without hearing he would not have invented language.

The leaves of trees rustle and whisper, the stream babbles as it flows, the waterfall roars, so that the tree will be called "the rustler," the stream "the babbler," the waterfall "the roarer." Nature made these markers echo in our ears and in our souls.

But not all objects have a sound. Where do the words for soundless objects come from? How did man gain the art of transforming into sound that which is not sonorous? The explanation is to be found in the association, or as Herder says, in the concomitance of certain impressions. There are cases where we cannot avoid associating a given visual impression to a given sound. For example, the perception of immediate visual rapidity is given by the word "Blitz" (flash) thanks to its short quick sound.

Herder repeats and develops analogous concepts in his *Ideen zur Philo-sophie der Geschichte der Menschheit.*[9] Similarly to Smith and Stewart, he believes that the "instinct of imitation" is particularly important. It is not the result of intellectual elaboration, but rather it is the immediate product of "organic sympathy."

The faculty of experiencing sentimental vibrations and of re-echoing them finds maximum expression in children. Actions, gestures, feelings, and thoughts unconsciously pass from us to them through a sort of direct spiritual assimilation.

The same thing happens in primitive and savage peoples who are still close to nature. As natural mimes, they vividly imitate all that is narrated to them and all that they wish to signify, and they display their expressive capacity in dances, games, and discourses. Their imagination conceives the image through imitation: the treasures of their memory and language are made of such signs.

From these extracts it would seem that, according to Herder, the first language arose in part through a kind of direct telepathic transmission and in part through instinctive mimicry. But he, too, like many others does not believe that mimetic and pictographic expression constitute a proper language. Despite all the mimicry, he says, primitive man would still not have attained the character peculiar to our species: reason. Without the incomprehensible link between vocal breath and other factors so different from it, the structure of the human brain and organism would have remained backward and incomplete.

As proof of the essential importance of phonetic language he refers to the mentality of deaf-mutes who, though living in a world of gestures and other expressive signs, behave like children or "human animals." They act on the basis of analogy to what they have seen and not understood and, despite their wealth of visual impressions, they are not capable of true conceptual comprehension. (From this example it is evident how the habit of being content with hurried observations may induce even men of great genius into obvious errors. If Herder had consulted an expert in this specific field, he would have been able to ascertain that, for many deaf-mutes, the lack of phonetic language is not an impediment to the attainment of a spiritual and conceptual life as elevated and complex as that of other human beings.)

In Herder's opinion, conceptual life can only be reached through that "miracle of divine institution" that is language. The miracle thanks to which colors, feelings, and thoughts are expressed through sounds, so that a breath of air from our mouths becomes a picture of the world, is the work of divinity.

That joy and pain become sound and that what our ear hears makes our tongue move is an admirable tendency introduced by the Creator when He united body and soul.

As we have already noted, the philosophical approach—which, as in Humboldt and Croce, invokes the universal character of expressive activity—and the theological approach show certain affinities in their neglect of the problem of the origin of language. Herder started out by attacking Suessmilch's theological solution to the problem but in the end rounds off his arguments with a theological and transcendental interpretation of the a priori nature of his *Besonnenheit.*

FRIEDRICH SCHLEGEL. We also wish to mention briefly this author who in 1808 published his famous essay on *Über die Sprache und Weisheit der Inder,* where in chapter five we find a few references to our problem.

The hypotheses, he says, which have so far been put forward on the origin of language would have proven untenable or would have been completely different had they been founded on positive historical investigations rather than on arbitrary intuitions.

The preconceived idea that language, and in general the spiritual development of humanity, began everywhere in the same way is totally false. The differences between one linguistic family and another are so great that it will always be possible to find a language to exemplify a theory, whichever it may be.

How did Sanskrit arise? Or, if it too is a derived language, how did the Indo-European mother tongue arise? According to Schlegel, the sure answer to such a question is that it did not initially arise from uniquely affective and imitative sounds that only later underwent rational elaboration. Indeed, Sanskrit offers proof, if this is needed, that the human condition did not begin everywhere with animal obtuseness but that a definite reflective consciousness existed from the very beginning, at least in our own lineage. Sanskrit is in fact a work of reflection even in its early elements.

To sum up, Schlegel supports the strange idea that inflected languages, such as Sanskrit, arose through direct divine intervention, while agglutinative and isolating languages have a natural or, as he says, animal origin.

It is easy for us, today, to remark that instead of accepting the hypothesis of a sudden and miraculous rising of a rationally elaborate language, Schlegel should have concluded that neither Sanskrit nor any other grammatically similar language may be viewed as the primitive form of human language; but we must also consider the fact that our ideas on this subject have undergone the decisive influence of two scientific conquests unknown in this scholar's time: chronological calculations which shifted the appearance of man on the Earth from 4,000 to 500,000 years before Christ; and naturalistic theories of evolution which eased the way for the eventual abandonment of the idea of continual miraculous intervention.

M. CESAROTTI. The doctrine of De Brosses was followed with intelligence, equilibrium, and linguistic precision by Cesarotti.[10] Single languages, he says, either arise or derive spontaneously from others. They arise spontaneously when they develop through natural impulse, as does the language of two children raised separately.

All words may be classed as either mnemonic terms or representative expressions: the former recall the object, the latter in some way depict it. For this reason the former may also be called cypher terms and the latter figure terms. The former have only a conventional and arbitrary relation with ideas, the latter a natural relation.

Natural terms may be divided into another two subgroups: those which depict the object itself either whole, summarized, or indicated, and those which designate an object through the representation of another object which symbolizes it.

Man carries a natural and in a certain sense a uniform language from birth, which serves as a common basis for all the languages of the world. Initial expressions imitate natural sounds or give the object a name similar to the sound that object conveys.

In addition to direct onomatopoeia we have symbolic onomatopoeia and on this matter Cesarotti recalls one of his own pages, written in a rather self-indulgent Latin though not without elegance (which, however, contains echoes from an Augustinian passage quoted above):

> Nimirum inter litteras et certas rerum proprietates, eas praecipue quae ad auditum ratione aliqua referuntur, arcanam analogiam natura statuit; quam sagax animus arriperet, eaque ductus ad res ipsas exprimendas quam proxime accederet. Enimvero cum litterae in pronunciando aliae aegre exploduntur, aliae elabuntur atque effluunt, nonnullae abblandiuntur organo; nonnullae vehementius impingunt. Quaedam se caeteris facile agglomerant; reluctantur quaedam; cum sibilat haec, illa frendit, altera glocitat; nonne propemodum clamitant esse se certissimas notas analogis corporum proprietatibus exprimendas ab ipsa natura constitutas? Itaque dentales litteras constantibus rebus et firmis; gutturales hiantibus et laboriose excavatis fluidis laevibus, volubilibus liquidas; asperae ac rapidae vehementiae caninam; anguineam sibilae celeritati notandae, natas et conformatas verissime dixeris.

Initial onomatopoeic terms then became the roots of other expressions which were used to indicate objects in some way related to these initial onomatopoeic terms. Consequently an early expression may include numerous derived significations. In some of these, the similarities and relations to the root are still obvious, while in others the greater the distance from the source the greater the deviation from its meaning. Thus it is not easy to rediscover the initial meaning.

Developing one of De Brosses's examples, Cesarotti observes that the sound *st!* expresses stability and that the Latins used it to intimate silence and standstill. From this sound were derived the terms sta! stator (epithet for Jupiter, catcher of fugitives), exstor, resto, adsto, consto, constantia, praesto and praestantia, substo and substantia. Furthermore: stabilis, statuo, constituo, therefore, statuto and constitutio, destituo, substitutus, prosituo and prostitutione. And to continue: statue, stirrup, stabulum and stable, stallion and stall. Star, stellion, stellionate (and in Greek stéreos and sterno); stalk, stipulate, stipulation, style, stock, stupor, stupid, etc.

Taking the suggestive effectiveness of sound as his starting point, Cesarotti identifies words that are more or less beautiful. Thus "flumen" is more beautiful than "potamós"; the Italian "acqua" (water) and the French "vague" "which are like water in the mouth" are better than "hydor," etc. The words *"orgoglioso"* (proud), *"baldanzoso"* (bold), "tracotante" (haughty) are nice because, with their full vowels, strengthened by the appropriate consonants, and with their multiple syllables they express the idea of audacity. Equally good are the words "umile" (humble), "timido" (shy), "stupido" (stupid), which with the thinness of their vowels correspond to the wretchedness they signify.

As may be seen from these few examples, Cesarotti is especially concerned with the aesthetic and literary problem of good style more than with the naturalistic issue. As to the topic of our own investigation, no more than a few appropriate observations on affective and onomatopoeic expressions are to be found in his writings.

MANZONI. Manzoni makes references to our problem in a few notes published posthumously by Bonghi and Sforza.[11] They consist of numerous comments, made in a hurry and never put into order, with numerous repetitions and sentences left unfinished.

Since his work (as well as that of Rosmini who influenced him) is of interest to us for our purposes, we will attempt to organize these fragments into an organic whole as far as this is possible.

Manzoni distinguishes between the problem of essence and that of origin, as we ourselves have also done, and asks himself first of all what the essence of language consists of, or, as he puts it, by virtue of what property is each language the one it is. And he rightly replies that only use, that is to say, a tacit convention accepted and observed by a given group of persons, makes languages what they are. Even when the verdict contrasts with the authority of venerable writers or does not seem to be confirmed by analogy with the other words and forms in our language, only the usage of a term or of a grammatical rule will tell us whether they belong to the Italian language or not.

As to origin, he maintains that language cannot be a human invention and to demonstrate this he takes Condillac's doctrine into consideration.

The French philosopher (and with him Degérando[12]) imagined two youths isolated immediately after the Flood and still completely destitute of language. In the first place, each of the two recognizes in the other a being similar to himself, and when one sees the other perform acts that he too is in the habit

of performing, he guesses his thoughts by analogy. For instance, one youth
may see the other flee and realizing that he does so because he is afraid of
some ferocious beast, he also flees. Or, one of the two may produce an
instinctive cry for the lack of an object he needs and makes efforts to get it,
and the other is touched by this and instinctively comes to his assistance.
Initially there is neither the intention to signify nor the capacity of using or
understanding signs, but with the repetition of the same circumstances, the
two become accustomed to attaching a certain impression to a given cry, and
therefore to recognizing the feelings of the other through such signs. Finally
they use these signs to communicate their feelings to each other.

Manzoni remarks that the whole hypothesis is groundless because it presupposes human beings destitute of language, while all the peoples we are
aware of know how to speak, even the most primitive, and there is no trace
of people destitute of language either in the testimonies of travellers, or in
historical works or legends. Condillac's error consists of considering the word
as incidental and secondary and not as essential and necessarily as old as
humanity itself. He made man out to be a beast that one fine day began
inventing words.

In order to speak of human reason as the inventor of language, we need
to discover what operations can be carried out by reason when it is destitute
of language. We need to verify whether reason is capable of operating once
it has been deprived of the word.

But if the word is the very means through which reason observes and
searches for the causes of what it has observed, through which it interrogates
itself and gives itself an answer, if the very impressions of the senses cannot
become the object of reasoning without the word, how can we imagine men
who observe and reason while being destitute of language?

Condillac himself had acknowledged elsewhere that if we did not have
names we would not have abstract ideas and we would not be able to reason,
in other words, we would have no idea of identity, similarity, and dissimilarity.
We would not be aware that certain actions are similar to others, that certain
cries are repeated in a similar fashion and in similar circumstances; we would
not be able to carry out all those more or less explicit forms of reasoning
attributed by Condillac to his two imagined youths. Condillac insists on postulating the existence of a language before its invention. When his youth
observes his companion, tries to understand who he is, distinguishes him
from other objects, recognizes him as similar to himself and wonders what
his feelings are, he has no need of inventing language because he already
possesses it.

In Condillac's opinion all our knowledge of the external world is produced
exclusively through our sensations. Nonetheless, he acknowledges that his
imaginary subject may form an idea for himself of what another person feels.
But is it not obvious that through our own senses we may know what we
ourselves feel, but not what another person feels?

Indeed, a man provided with senses but devoid of general concepts would be incapable of establishing any kind of link or of making a comparison between one phenomenon and another and, therefore, between a sign and its meaning.

A real man, such as those we are familiar with, is certainly able to understand what another man feels and wants from his cries and facial expression, but not Condillac's man. There is nothing strange in supposing that two human creatures who do not understand each other through words, may succeed in understanding each other, even if imperfectly at first, through gestures and inarticulate sounds. This actually happens when two men meet for the first time without knowing each other's language. Nonetheless, they speak to each other: initially they are unable to understand each other through words, because they do not share common words, but in spite of this they understand each other, because each man has his own words through which he is able to reason and realize what the other is making an effort to convey.

Condillac says that his two imaginary human beings, devoid of language and therefore of intellect, gradually become accustomed to linking a given sign to a given meaning. This is like saying that a blind man ends up seeing an object because it passed in front of him several times.

A real man, instead, already gifted with his own language may gradually come to understand a language that was previously unknown to him, because he is like a diviner who eventually succeeds in getting a clearer idea of the form of an object which at first appeared indistinct to him.

The fact that still today, when necessary, people prove to be skillful and prolific in deriving new words from existing ones, while they are poor at and adverse to making up completely new phonemes, is proof for Manzoni that man is not made for inventing language, but only for modifying and adapting a preexisting language to his own ends.

Condillac and his teacher Locke are convinced that their doctrines are based on facts; but the fact is that human beings have the faculties necessary for understanding and conveying words, whereas they do not have the faculty for inventing them. Consequently, the only reasonable hypothesis is that man originally learned language from a teacher who was not a man. And this is just what *Revelation* teaches us: in the beginning God spoke to man's first ancestors and in this way communicated the act of speech; He had given them the faculty of speech together with life. *Revelation* teaches us that, subsequently, confusion came about in the original language, and that this led to the rising of different tongues.

Manzoni's main argument, namely, that it was necessary to reason in order to invent language but that it is not possible to reason without the use of words (or of other signs), is substantially identical to the argument maintained by Herder, Humboldt, Croce, etc. However, while the idealists assert the impossibility of the temporal origin of language in support of the universality of categories and apriority of linguistic activity, Manzoni uses the same argument to demonstrate the supernatural origin of language and appeals to the testimony offered by the biblical account which he unquestionably considers as a competent authority in scientific questions.[13]

Manzoni is in a good position to criticize Condillac's contradictory sensism, but he does not realize that a philosophical error does not invalidate all the empirical propositions by the same author. To acknowledge the existence of sensations totally devoid of conceptual references may be an epistemological error; this however does not impede us from stating that, at the psychological and naturalistic level, an animal feels but does not think, meaning that feeling prevails over reasoning.

Psychology teaches us that not only do we have association of ideas, but also of sensations and subconscious reflexes. If a dog sees a piece of meat, its stomach secretes gastric juice, and if the meat is shown to it several times while ringing a bell, that ringing alone will then suffice to provoke the secretion.

If it were true that primitive man could not become accustomed to associating a sign with a given meaning, the same should be true of children as well. A baby reasons even less than primitive man and yet he gradually comes to understand the expressions and words of those who surround him. According to Manzoni's argument, a baby cannot learn how to speak without the use of the intellect, and he cannot use the intellect without already possessing a language.

If Manzoni had worked on his notes, he would have produced a clear, acute, and enchanting treatment of the issue in question in keeping with his conceptual prose, even if his logic, so scrupulous and formally impeccable, is too often led astray by highly irrational basic assumptions.

M. J. GRIMM. After the works of Stewart, De Brosses, and Condillac, M. Jacob Grimm's dissertation *Über den Ursprung der Sprache (1852)* (which in its day aroused a great deal of interest throughout the whole of Europe and was made known in France by Ernest Renan) proves to be disappointing.

Grimm underlines the difficult nature of the subject and expresses his doubts about the possibility of a solution. One would have to go back a lot further in the history of humanity than has so far been done: the most ancient literary monuments, whether they be Sanskrit, Zend, or Hebrew, come thousands of years after the era of the birth of language (today we know that it was hundreds of thousands of years after).

He rightly believes that science must aim at explaining the marvels of nature in the terms inherent in nature itself and he demonstrates that language is not transcendental in origin but the result of human work.

If Psammeticus's experiment were possible, the two children would not pronounce a single word, for language is not innate, so much so that a Russian child raised in France speaks French and vice versa.

To the question as to how primitive man invented language, he replies by identifying three levels of development: The level of the creation of early roots, the level of inflections, and the level extending beyond inflections. (Such a description of linguistic evolution seems rather oversimplified to us today. If anything we could identify the following: an initial stage of purely instinctive animal movements and cries; a second stage of immediate picto-graphic expressions; a third stage of predominantly mimetic conventional expressions; a fourth in which expressive sounds begin predominating over gesture, though the grammatical element is limited to the organization of phonemes and their accentuation; a fifth stage in which grammatical dis-tinctions are indicated with appropriate small empty words; a sixth in which inflections begin to emerge, etc.)

In Grimm's opinion the first language was melodious, long-winded, and made of short vowels and simple consonants. Each alphabetical sound had its own natural value which was determined by the organ that produces it. Vowels were feminine and consonants masculine, etc.

In his essay Grimm indulges far too often in vague statements, without ever bothering to specify their meaning or to back them up with appropriate arguments. His lack of commitment in dealing with the subject emerges, for example, from the following words: "We may be surprised with good reason that neither Classical nor Indian antiquity tried to solve or even posed the question of the origin of language" (from which it would seem that he was totally unaware of all that the Greeks had done in this field).

In truth, on comparing *Cratylus* to this little nineteenth-century treatise, our impression is that if studies in etymology and the genealogy of languages have progressed, not only has there not been any progress concerning our topic, but on the contrary, we have never again reached the same level as the ancients.

Though the monadic and discontinuous treatment of the subject also persists among other writers of the nineteenth century, some effective im-provements are achieved thanks to a broader and more precise knowledge in the field of ethnography, as well as to the general progress of naturalistic studies and to the clarifying influence of evolutionistic theories. We have already mentioned some of Darwin's interesting observations in his study on expressive manifestations. He also devotes a few pages to our problem in his *Origin of Species* where he compares the faculties of man with those of animals. He does not doubt that language originates from the imitation and subse-quent modification of natural sounds, with the help of signs and gestures. He recalls that special form of imitation which we have called pre-aesthetic and observes the inclination of monkeys, idiots, and primitive peoples to imitate all they see and hear. Articulate language is peculiar to man, but together with animals man also shares the capacity to express his feelings through inarticulate cries as well as through gestures and movements.

G. JAEGER. Jaeger[14] begins by saying that it is easier to form an idea of how the first men spoke by studying the languages of animals rather than those of modern man, and that a zoologist would be more competent than a scholar of comparative grammar to formulate a hypothesis concerning primitive language. He believes that the transition from the most developed animal state to the appearance of language is immediate or, at any rate, more direct than the transition between primitive man and civilized man (in our opinion it is probably more correct to speak not of two, but at least of three important transitions: from anthropoid apes to *homo alalus* in which the first rudimentary mimetic-pictographic language arises; from *homo alalus* to prehistoric man, gifted with a language made of conventional mimetic-phonetic signs; and lastly from prehistoric to modern man).

Jaeger then makes some interesting suggestions regarding affective cries. As the strongest and most diffused animal feeling, sexual excitement stimulates natural groans and calls from human beings and animals, which then become calls of attraction and invitation for individuals of the other sex.

The sexual cry is already, to an extent, a means of communication, and therefore it already possesses one of the essential characteristics of language. The importance of the sexual instinct also results from the simultaneous physiological development of the voice and sexual organs: insects develop their vocal organs only when they are sexually mature; when birds sing and the rooster calls, we will observe a swelling of the genital organs. As to man, the tone of his voice changes with puberty.

Affective cries subsequently become a means of communication. For example, a cry of anguish is often understood as a danger warning even by animals belonging to different species. But, as Steinthal rightly observes, we must discover whether those cries were emitted with the purpose of warning others, or whether, rather than a piece of intentional communication, they represent an instinctive manifestation only subsequently interpreted as the sign of a dangerous situation. If we do not make this distinction, even the noise produced by the footsteps of the advancing enemy could be called "language."

Jaeger at least did not fail to perceive the importance of pre-aesthetic imitation, as emerges from what he has to say about certain birds that readily imitate other voices and songs: they do this without a purpose, if not as a simple display of vitality.

Another important element of expression is constituted by the sounds and cries of a maternal nature, such as those of the mother hen calling together its chickens; such cries and sounds become increasingly varied and specific in animals living in social groups.

Musical talent, that is, the capacity of enjoying, remembering, and repeating certain modulated series of sounds, also plays an important role in the formation of language.

Nonphonetical expressions have had at least a preparatory importance. When a question of indicating an object in a specific place, a gesture, a glance, or the movement of the limbs were enough to identify it. This kind of gesturing was already perfectly developed in monkeys. The dog that wags its tail, the horse that stretches out its ears, the monkey that designates an object with its head and hands are already capable of communicating.

Finally, Jaeger notes that anthropomorphic monkeys possess very developed imitative skills but, in contrast, their phonetic skills are scarce. He concludes that human language arose when a microcephalic species of anthropoid apes, only capable of communicating through affective cries, developed into early man who distinguished himself from his ancestors, at the somatic level, by his macrocephaly, at the linguistic level, by his onomatopoeic talent, and at the intellectual level, by his capacity to use his imitative talent for the purpose of communication. Originally, phonetic language was not as independent from mimetic language as it is today; indeed, words and gestures were but two complementary elements of the same means of communication.

The scientifically more mature mentality of the nineteenth century protected Jaeger from the superficial a priori approach of numerous previous writers, despite the fact that the documentary material at his disposal was still rather inadequate.

STEINTHAL. At about the same time Steinthal also wrote an essay entitled *Der Ursprung der Sprache*,[15] which however proposed no more than a critical examination of the main doctrines on language from 1770 to 1870. Steinthal is an idealist (belonging to the same current of thought as Herder, Humboldt, Renan, Croce, Vossler) and judges as "superficial" the conception of language as a sign system developed by mankind to communicate representations which preexist in the mind, independent of their linguistic expression.

Given that without language, according to this author, neither representations nor concepts, nor any other conscious activity, are possible, he denies that the problem of the temporal origin may be proposed. (We have already commented on the philosophical character of this point of view which is incapable of distinguishing between the problem of the essence and that of temporal origin.)

Nonetheless it is curious that all those authors who deny that the problem should be posed or declare it insoluble, and they are quite numerous, cannot avoid dealing with it and attempting a few more or less obvious hypotheses once they become interested in linguistic issues. Consequently, Steinthal too says elsewhere that originally the body and soul of men were so interdependent that all psychic impulses caused an echo throughout the whole body and provoked reflex movements in the respiratory and vocal organs. Sympathy between body and soul, very strong in the child and in the savage, became a means of expression in primitive man, so that all his impressions were manifested with a given sound and accent.

Spontaneous sounds accompanying a given impression were subsequently associated with that impression, so that it was enough to hear that given sound in order to recall the impression. In this way the sound became a link between the image produced by the direct impression and the image preserved in the memory; it acquired a meaning of its own and became an element of language.[16]

On glancing at the volumes of the glottological review directed by Steinthal and Lazarus, I was struck by a letter from a reader, a philologist, who asks for explanations concerning Steinthal's theory on language origin. The hypothesis that linguistic roots were derived from reflex motions of the vocal cords and assumed as the signs of representations is the only one, he believes, able to explain language origin, but it still seems too general and inadequate to explain the specific form of the single roots; it does not explain for instance why the root *i* signifies to go and the root *sta* to stop.

I was meditating on these problems, says the above-mentioned reader, when I came across an article on the language of gestures in an English review: it had no scientific pretensions though it was written by an expert on the subject. The writer maintains that deaf-mutes use a mimetic language that corresponds perfectly to our own phonetic language. To signify, for example, "this object is not wet," first they point their index finger toward the object, then they shake their head in sign of negation and finally they touch the dampness of their tongue with their finger. Thus we are not dealing with a pantomimic representation, but precisely with a composition made of a certain number of signs connected in such a way as to form a proposition.

The reader asks whether we know how the association of gestures to corresponding representations comes about and what the relation is, for instance, between the shaking of the head and the concept of negation.[17] He also proposes a great many other questions which however do not interest us here.

Steinthal replies by acknowledging that the hypothesis is currently too general and he maintains that the limitation of natural sounds, and not just of reflex movements, may have influenced the creation of roots. However, he denies the possibility of indicating physiological causes for individual meanings. Paraphrasing Job, he says that he would like to ask those who claim they can establish the natural meaning of a given phoneme the following question: "Were you present when the first articulate expression issued from the breast of silent men? Or did someone record for you the history and memory of the original roots which broke forth from human lips hundreds of thousands of years ago?"[18]

As may be seen, though Steinthal began by asserting that no form of consciousness is possible without language and that there is no sense in interrogating oneself about its origins, he was soon led to formulate hypotheses regarding the origin of language and ended up by developing a cautious agnostic attitude.

RENAN. Renan's essay,[19] written with his usual grace, though not without rhetorical overtones, is one of the most instructive pieces of writing available on our subject, even though his conclusions are unacceptable.

He frequently refers to the paper by Grimm and recalls other German scholars of the same period. As is well-known, Grimm had acknowledged three successive ages in the development of languages: (1) the monosyllabic and isolating age, which is grammatically the poorest. In this phase objective notions are signified by full words, and relations by small empty words; (2)

the age of inflections, where empty words lose their autonomy and become root endings and an imposing grammatical structure is developed; (3) lastly a stage in which speakers, incapable of adopting such a logical and laborious structure, prefer using words to signify that which was previously indicated with endings ("amabor" in German becomes "ich werde geliebt werden").

In Renan's opinion transition from one grammatical type to another is not admissible. Zoologists, he says, have acknowledged the impossibility of arranging animals in a single linear series in which the same type is gradually perfected from the polyp through to man; they acknowledge instead the existence of a multiplicity of distinct primitive species. The same thing is true of languages. (Today the biological comparison seems to invalidate Renan's thesis rather than support it.)

According to the author, the invention of language was not the result of prolonged effort, but rather the expression of primitive intuition. The need to signify one's own feelings and thoughts to others is natural in man.

If animal cries are spontaneous, why should man's speech not be considered as spontaneous? Man did not choose speech (i.e., the use of articulate sounds as signs of ideas) as something that would be useful to him, he did not choose his eyes to see with. It would be absurd to consider the application of eyes to sight or of ears to hearing as a discovery; not less absurd is it to call an "invention" the use of words as a means of expression. It is wrong to imagine an initial state in which man did not speak and then another state in which he was able to use language: man was gifted with the use of words from the very beginning just as he was gifted with the use of sight. (Against Renan it would be easy to observe that, in truth, not even the eye was created at the beginning with the wave of a magic wand. Indeed, the stages of its development are among the most instructive.)[20]

It is rather strange that Renan was never aware of the difference between the use of words and the use of the senses. Man sees because he has eyes, but to have a mouth is not sufficient in order to speak (if it is true that animals have a mouth but do not speak). Whoever has eyes can see without going to school, but languages must be learned. Language is a complex system of conventional signs and not the immediate function of an organ or faculty.

According to Renan, man is able to use signs and interpret them. By the same logic, to the question as to how the most complex arts and human institutions arose, we could reply that man created them because he had the faculty of doing so. We would do well to be constantly on our guard against such conceptual "passe-partouts."

Renan was deceived by a great truth asserted by the Romantics against naive and cold rationalism: the spontaneity of spiritual creations. He rightly emphasizes the expressive superiority of popular spoken language over the pedantic exercises of the grammarians and ridicules Duclos who, in his commentary to the Port Royal grammar, believes he is correcting the continual "inconveniences" of spontaneous language.

Most appropriately he remarks that deaf-mutes, before learning the mechanical system supplied to them at school, create and use a language of their own spontaneously, which is a thousand times more expressive.

He concludes that primitive man constructed a linguistic system with perfect ease and from the very beginning, an enterprise that seems prodigiously difficult to contemporary eyes.

Renan forgets what every artist knows from his own experience: that even spontaneity can be achieved only through years of work. Like the German Romantics, he too indulges in a mystical conception of spontaneity. The true author of spontaneous works, he says, is human nature, or if we prefer, the Prime Mover of nature. The child learning his own language does not have greater difficulty than a plant or animal reaching its full development. God is present everywhere, but hidden: an Infinite Force that acts while the individual soul is absent or asleep.

As is often the case with Renan, a happy intuition becomes an uncautious error. Instead of saying that in the course of the centuries primitive man created his own pictographic language, and that in the course of still other centuries those directly expressive gestures and sounds became conventional signs, Renan has no doubts that such a grammatically elaborate language as Latin or Sanskrit arose suddenly, almost as though through Divine illumination.

That which induces him to postulate the originality, stability, and independence of linguistic families is the singular tenacity with which each family maintains its characteristic grammatical form; something which, as we shall see, has led even contemporary authors into error.

He says that Chinese, which is all lexicon and hardly any grammar, and Sanskrit have nothing in common except the purpose of communication.

Every language is definitively imprisoned in its formal structure. In spite of continual contact with other people, Semitic languages, for example, have preserved their extremely unpractical writing system, devoid of vowel sounds, for thousands of years.

(To accept that the formal structures of languages are not subject to any kind of evolution seems an absurdity to us today, at the same time, however, it would be interesting to search for the reasons behind the unquestionable tenacity of different grammatical types. I think that one of the reasons is this: lexicon is a collection of single signs, while grammar is a set of rules indicating how those signs should be combined. By rough comparison with numeration systems, we could say that numbers, for example our own numbers from zero to nine, correspond to lexicon, while the rules of the decimal system correspond to grammar. Now while we may easily become accustomed to a change in the name of single numbers, by calling "quattuor," for example, what before was called "tessera," it is not easy to accustom ourselves to the use of a binary system instead of the traditional system. In the first case, it is enough to keep the new term in mind; in the second, one must get used to a different way of reasoning.)

Although he set the problem aside, Renan also made a few references to hypotheses on language origin. For example, he claims that, on analyzing the most ancient languages, one is led to the conviction that the primitive form of language did not yet distinguish between verbs, adjectives, and nouns (this contradicts Renan's negation of grammatical progress); and that imitation and onomatopoeia were generally used to form calling words—the language of the first human beings was the echo of nature in the human consciousness. On the whole he denies the problem of origin and tends toward a kind of linguistic innatism; his French acuteness rendered absurd the most profound but also the most nebulous conceptions of the German Romantics.

5. More Recent Theories

Our problem falls into discredit more and more during the final decades of the nineteenth century and the first half of the twentieth century up to the essays by Ginneken and Paget. On the one hand, authors who believe they have found the key to the enigma but whose doctrines only they find convincing are not lacking. On the other, the intolerance of those who do not believe the problem worthy of scientific consideration is increasingly frequent.

Help in examining the glottogonic issue more comprehensively could have come from evolutionistic theories, an orientation promoted by August Schleicher, though he deserves to be remembered more for his approach than for the results attained.[1]

Schleicher rightly insists on the empirical character of this research and asserts, similarly to Vico, that to know a thing is to know how it became what it is.

He proposes an inquiry into linguistic evolution from its very beginnings, doing for language what Darwin did for biological evolution; however, he did not succeed in developing his idea.

Diversity among currently existing languages was too great to conclude that they have a common origin, at least from the point of view of vocabulary or lexicon. Schleicher limits himself to saying about language origin that primitive man discovered how to produce meaningful expressions through onomatopoeic sounds and mouth gestures, and that such expressions were no more than isolated and grammatically unrelated phonemes.

WUNDT. Let us now take a look at some of the more significant among the many recent authors (upon whom history has not yet had time to operate its inexorable and timely selection).

Wundt, who collected extensive and well-examined material on language as well as on various other modes of communication, and described this data with acute and balanced psychological observations, asserts on numerous occasions that our problem is insoluble and "metaphysical."[2]

He avers that the hypothesis of a condition whereby man was not only destitute of language, but also of the capacity for producing it, is completely worthless and without meaning in the light of scientific reasoning.

Words were not originally created once and for all back in the distant past, but rather are the result of a process which is continually repeated in living languages, so that the need arises to study current languages and not lose our bearings in conjectures that cannot be verified. (This is equivalent to saying that a man breaks away from animality each time he dominates his instincts, which would render the research carried out by Darwin and other biologists completely useless.)

However, not even Wundt was able to fully abstain from glottogonic hyotheses. Elsewhere he says that language must have arisen from oral mimicry (*Lautgebärde*), in other words, from the instinctive movements of the mouth accompanying the expressive movements of the body. He adds that only when we recognize that phonic displays were the product of reflex motions will we invalidate the naive claim that primitive words were the intentional imitation of sonorous impressions.[3] In the last edition of his *Grundiss der Psychologie,* edited in 1918, Wundt goes as far as to maintain that children could create a primitive language without the teaching and influence of others, just as deaf-mutes sometimes construct a mimetic language by themselves. Sentiments could be included in mimetic expression, representations could be communicated through physical gestures or by pointing to certain objects or by outlining them in the air (*Luftmalerei*). The origin of phonetic language could be explained as the result of a process of differentiation, so that the hypothesis is that "gestures made by sounds" were gradually selected from a multiplicity of gestures and expressive movements.

Wundt's plausible propositions did not influence scholars as much as they should have. They were put forward too hastily and without methodical demonstration, so that they took on the appearance of more or less probable subjective hypotheses.

More decidedly negative is Vendryes' attitude.[4] In his opinion, most of the authors who had dealt with language origin in the past century had only succeeded in producing a series of errors. The problem is hopeless because even the most ancient languages we know of no longer have anything primitive about them and do not offer us any indication as to the rising of language. Not even the languages of savages can help us on this point, because their languages are as complicated as the most complex civilized languages. (Coming from a linguist a similar statement is rather strange. Vendryes was probably deceived by the lexical exuberance characterizing the less developed languages.)

We oscillate between extreme negations and the most naive discoveries. For example, Raoul de la Grasserie is convinced that subjective onomatopoeia, based on a certain synchronism between the movement of phonation organs and of the signified object, must be opposed to the old concept of objective onomatopoeia, which is only achieved in rare cases. According to this hypothesis the sound m, for example, represents a state of rest, of not going beyond oneself, and therefore the first person pronoun, while t implies a movement toward the exterior and is suited to signifying the second person, etc.[5] (As the reader will remember, explanations of this kind have been offered on many occasions from Plato onwards.)

An analogous discovery is Callet's who believed that the mystery of language could be unveiled by postulating an acoustic pre-phase in which the "voice of the species" had a primitive semantic function and gave rise to the embryos of basic roots.[6] (It is highly probable that the primitive affective sounds of the human horde, perceived by an outsider had the effect of a "voix d'espèce" similar to the barking of dogs or the miaowing of cats, but we cannot see the advantage of calling "voices of the species" what others call physiological displays, natural voices, cries, and the like.)

It is not surprising that Assirelli thought he could ascertain the definitive failure of all attempts at discovering the origin of language.[7] He insists, as did Wundt and many of the more serious scholars, on the principle that the same forces and laws active in the evolution of historical languages must have been active from the very beginning. He claims that the most recent attempts at finding the origin of language, that is, those of the past few decades, are different and new with respect to any previous attempts, for once the genetic question is left aside, they search for the beginning and proof of the origin itself in the evolution of language.

(We have repeatedly observed: as a rule, new words in historical languages derive from the modification or combination of preexistent roots, and if we accept that linguistic creation was originally of the same kind, we will inevitably fall into an infinite process of regression.)

H. PAUL. A predominantly, if not coherently, negative attitude is also taken up by Paul. He deals with the origin of language in a chapter of his book entitled *Prinzipien der Sprachgeschichte,*[8] though a more appropriate title would have been *Psychology of Language,* given that the approach is more naturalistic than historical.[9]

In chapter nine he proposes to search for the conditions of the original creation of language in the nature of contemporary human beings. Given that the spiritual capacity of modern man is vastly superior to that of primitive man, he strangely deduces that the capacity to create language must also be more developed and perfect today than it was in the beginning (in reality, the contrary is true: the spontaneous and instinctive faculties are less powerful in modern man than they were in primitive man).

He denies that two periods may be identified in the development of language (an original period of the roots and a later period in which, as a rule, language develops from previous phonemes). But he then admits that there must have been a direct link between the object and the word in the original language and enumerates a number of terms that have an onomatopoeic and affective sound. He also acknowledges that the meaning of an expressive term would often become clearer if accompanied by gestures and that, in the beginning, the development of phonetic language was parallel to that of mimetic language and that only at a later stage could gesture be dispensed with.

In reality Paul is not very interested in our problem and is not concerned about coordinating his casual observations in a more satisfactory manner.

A. PAGLIARO. One of the Italian linguists to have investigated the most diverse and complex problems of linguistics with the most fervor is Pagliaro. At first his attitude toward our problem seems completely negative. In fact, he believes that all attempts at forming an idea of the original language should be considered absurd because of the total lack of documentation.[10] The problem of language origin is identical to that of the origin of man and for this reason it cannot be examined seriously. We may look for the etymology of an Italian word by comparing it to Latin or to words of other Indo-European languages, but we are not in a position to go any further. Any documentation of linguistic activity at our disposal does not go back any further than the fourth millennium B.C.; the belief that we are able to discover what happened in the preceding millennia on the basis of such material is completely absurd.[11] But not even Pagliaro was able to stop himself from meditating on the topic of our inquiry and of formulating a few reasonable hypotheses. He says, for example, that once the sound sequence accompanying a sensation acquired a certain stability, it was not difficult to recognize in it the acoustic translation of that sensation, so that such a translation could be assumed as the signal of that sensation. A more complex state found expression in a more extended and complex phonic and, perhaps at the same time, mimetic sequence. The articulate voice in all its variety accompanied that sensation as allusively as possible whenever the need to represent it arose.[12]

REVESZ. One of the attempts at solving our problem which encountered most favor in the academic world (which does not always correspond to the world of intellectuals) is that by Revesz.[13] He calls his new doctrine "contact theory." By "psychic contact" Revesz intends the intentional communication of feelings and spiritual inclinations such as to provoke an appropriate reaction in the receiver.

The need for contact with one's own similars may be limited to the need of physical closeness without yet reaching mutual comprehension; however, as this need gradually acquires psychic characteristics, the contact is spiritualized and becomes the need for communication and comprehension.

In Revesz's opinion, affective and imitative sounds should be excluded from the prehistory of language. It stands to reason, he says, that the intention to communicate would be absent in these manifestations. They have a mere symptomatic function, that is, they designate states of mind but do not communicate them, and they only become linguistic symbols when associated with the intention of entering *into contact* with others. Consequently, he claims that such manifestations did not play a constructive role in the formation of the phonetic system. He distinguishes between purely physiological manifestations and linguistic "preforms" such as *calling sounds*. The latter already reveal traces of the intention to establish contact, even though the specific characteristics of language, namely, articulate sound, symbolic nature, and grammatical structure are lacking.

The calling sound ("Zuruf"[14]) is an inarticulate, sonorous, and originally instinctive emission addressed to a group, more or less with the purpose of obtaining the satisfaction of one's desire. A typical example: sounds made by the mother hen while calling its chicks; and the great variety of sexual calls.

Children commonly use these sounds to attract their mother's attention as well as that of the other members of the family and to make it understood that they do not want to be left alone. They are also common among primitive man, whereas in civilized populations they are only occasional.

A further degree in the development of the calling sound is the invocation ("appel," "Anruf"). While calling sounds are anonymously addressed to anyone present, invocations are addressed to specific individuals and are imperative in character. Calling sounds are emitted under the influence of a hereditary instinct, while invocations are individual in character and arise as the result of individual experiences. For example, a kitten that, with imploring eyes, communicates its desire for a piece of the meat we are cutting is already expressing an "invocation." Another essential feature of invocation is locative indication. Even an animal can indicate the location of the desired person or object through the expression of its eyes and through its movements. Primitive signs of invocation are directly expressive and are understood without conventions.

The three essential functions of invocation are: the imperative, the indicative, and the interrogative.

Awareness of the gradual transition from instinctive manifestations to more intentional ones is one of Revesz's strong points. However, it is not clear why we should attribute so much or even, exclusive importance to calling sounds or to invocations. There are numerous other instinctive phonetic and mimetic displays which over a period of time gradually become intentional and form elements of communication.

To give an example among many: shrinking, stooping, and making oneself small in front of a stronger presence which is at first an instinctive expression of fear and defence, may subsequently become a symbolic gesture of homage, such as the bow and prostration.

Revesz makes a few plausible observations on the birth of music.[15] When primitive men wish to communicate at a distance, they resort to short, almost inarticulate sounds, or to modulated cries. The same device is also used by civilized populations of the alpine and sea regions (e.g., the Tyrolese yodel). This tradition has a physiological explanation: in order to emit a loud call easily recognizable at a distance, the voice is gradually strengthened and made more acute and then eventually lowered until it slowly vanishes.

Revesz sees in these calls a sort of transition from verbal communication to music. Of the same kind, he adds, are the rhythmic sounds that human beings often use to accompany their work.[16] (He could have just as well remembered the modulated calls of some of the pedlars, or "rag and bone men," still today recognized more through intonation than by syllabic meaning.) Revesz concludes that invocations were roots common to language and music, but this does not justify his preference for them with respect to other analogous expressive displays.

Of greater interest to us could be Revesz's deliberate attempt to examine arguments that support the priority of a prevalently mimetic language, done in order to demonstrate on the contrary, the priority of phonetic language; but his argument is very weak.

He avers that the mimetic theory is based on the hypothesis that in the beginning man reacted to his impressions and states of mind through movements more than through the voice, whereas, in reality, all living beings gifted with a voice express their emotions both through movements and through the voice (the observation is correct, but it only shows that primitive language was probably accompanied by vocal sounds as well). He adds that sonorous expression is more important than mimicry in birds and monkeys (this is true for birds, but completely false for anthropoid apes).

Continuing, he states that in man the physiological conditions necessary for both mimetic and acoustic expression are the same, so that gesture could represent an antecedent stage with respect to speech. But the consequences of such a hypothesis are so absurd that one cannot understand how a serious scholar can accept it. The absurd consequence is the following: that primitive men would have had to communicate with each other like deaf-mutes, when, on the contrary, they were not deaf but gifted with all the senses.

No one has ever asserted that primitive men were deaf, but they probably preferred mimetic language for they needed an immediately comprehensible language without prior convention, and the potential of direct mimetic communication is by far much greater than that of affective and imitative sounds alone. This is easily proven with experiments.

In relation to this subject the following episode narrated by a French tutor of deaf-mutes is instructive: in November 1939 an unschooled deaf-mute enters into the classroom around evening and directs himself toward the switch to turn on the light. His school friends stop him and explain through gestures that the enemy is flying over the city and should they see that light they would drop their bombs and kill them all.

If we attempt to express all this without gestures, that is, solely through affective and onomatopoetic sounds, no one would make anything of it. In contrast, the following gestures were used by those youngsters: to designate the aviators and to give the impression of a gliding flight, they stretch out their arms and move bending to the right and to the left. To signify the dropping of bombs they rapidly move their closed first downwards and then open it suddenly keeping their fingers opened wide and curved, and to indicate the explosion, at first they hold their arms tightly against their breast fist against fist, and then they violently open them wide; they subsequently represent the fatal effect by simulating a fall and remaining on the ground with limp bodies and stiff hands. Finally, staring at the imprudent student, they frown and make a warning gesture with a pointed finger.[17]

Revesz asks once more: when, out of necessity, averbal Paleolithic man searched for a way of making himself understood, why should he have been contented with as imperfect a means as mimicry, which can neither be used at a distance nor in the dark, while phonetic communication offered him far greater advantages? (As though to ask: why should Paleolithic man have been contented with such imperfect arms as stones and clubs, when the bow, arrows, crossbows, and perhaps even rifles would have offered him far greater advantages?)

Revesz's essay is rich in erudition and developed systematically but, in our opinion, it reveals that not even modern scholars possessed an appropriate method for the scientific treatment of our topic.

6. Gradual Recognition among Modern Linguists of the Importance of Mimetic Expression

Van Ginneken—Alphabetical Signs as the Analytic Breakdown of Inarticulate *Clicks*— Authoritative Acknowledgment of the Importance of Visual Language—Priority of Mimetic Language Defended with Inadequate Arguments—R. A. S. Paget—Retrospective View of the Historical Survey.

Indeed, there has been progress, especially in the sense that modern authors have increasingly acknowledged the importance of the mimetic element. Van Ginneken and Paget have supported the mimetic origin of language with particular commitment and enthusiasm.

VAN GINNEKEN. Following the work of Meillet as well as that of Nikolaj Trubeckoj, Jacques van Ginneken attempted to reconstruct the archaic languages of humanity and consequently to form an idea of mankind's original language.[1]

In the first part of his book he expounds a thesis on how the articulate sounds of our languages were formed. He asks himself how the idea emerged of inventing signs, in themselves destitute of meaning, and of grouping them together in such a way that they could signify anything. Signs destitute of meaning are basic phonemes designated with alphabetical letters.

He recalls that Karl Bühler compared linguistic phonemes to the signaling flags used by sailors to transmit messages from one ship to another. But he remarks that those flags already existed and were used for other purposes as well, so that it was then possible to think of using them as signals by combining them. But *a, b, c* taken separately are of no use. How did the idea of using them as expressive elements arise?

He thinks he has found the solution to the enigma: alphabetical sounds are the analytic breakdown of *clicks,* that is, of semi-articulate, inspirate clicking sounds produced by a sucking movement innate in all human beings.

All children instinctively begin producing such movements within the first few days of birth, accompanying them with certain mostly labial or dental inspirate sounds which in all world languages give rise to interjections.

For example, as had already been noted by Vendryes, Jespersen and others, in French and various other languages (Italian included), there exists an inspirate *t* that expresses doubt and surprise, its repetition *tut-tut* (at times accompanied with the shaking of the head) means disapproval; an inspirate *f* that expresses a sense of pain, etc. Of the same kind is the clicking sound produced by the tongue against the palate, used for urging on horses, whereas in baby talk it signifies "horse" and "to ride"; in addition, there is a labial *click* imitating a big kiss, though softer and shorter, and which on being quickly repeated is used to attract cats and other domestic animals.

During the first six months of life the child emits a great number of these *clicks* mechanically; after six months, it produces normal expired consonants together with the *clicks,* and very soon after the first year they become more prevalent.[2]

Van Ginneken notes that these inspirate sounds, labials, dentals, alveolars, palatals, velars, and laterals become lexical phonemes in certain primitive languages of the Caucasian areas and in South Africa.

He is convinced that the first phonetic language ever to have been used by prehistoric man was made of *clicks* joined together according to the rules governing the syntax of the isolating languages. It was only at a later stage that our alphabetical phonemes derived from these semi-articulate sounds.

We could object, with regard to Van Ginneken's observations, which are certainly not without interest, that his initial question "How did the idea of using alphabetical letters as a means of communication arise?" attributes substantial reality to grammatical abstractions. How can one imagine that human beings "employed" letters of the alphabet in order to speak? Human beings emitted cries, screams, groans, etc., in other words, they emitted instinctive sounds, sometimes inspiring air, sometimes expiring it. Subsequently certain sounds became more distinct and more constant as the result of communicative needs, and grammarians schematized and classified them into vowels and consonants. But still today, especially in popular spoken language and in words pronounced in the surge of passion, the sounds we pronounce are very different from those catalogued by grammarians. Van Ginneken dwells upon one type of instinctive sound only, and it is not clear why wailing and shrieks, whistling, coughing and yawning, laughter and crying, etc., should be of less interest than *clicks* to the linguist investigating the origin of language. Nonetheless Van Ginneken has the merit of having stressed the importance of those particular manifestations which, by combining facial mimicry and voice emission, may have facilitated transition from the predominance of mimetic expression to the predominance of phonetic expression.

The idea Van Ginneken put forward with such enthusiasm of the priority of "visual" signs over "acoustic" ones deserves far more attention in relation to our own interests.

Citing numerous authors, he shows that the original importance of visual language is increasingly acknowledged by modern scholars. For example, basing himself on M. V. Negus's anatomical and physiological researches, M. P. Fouche maintained, at a linguistic congress in Rome,[3] that the phonetic function of the larnyx is secondary and was only acquired after a long period of refinement. Therefore, it is probable that human beings used a gesture language for a long period of time which was only substituted with phonetic language much later.

The importance of mimetic language has been increasingly acknowledged by French academics thanks to the influence of Lévy-Bruhl and of Marcel Jousse. To persuade ourselves of this, all we need do is compare two linguistic dissertations in a volume on *Psychology* compiled under the direction of Professor Dumas. In the first (1922) written by L. Barat and Ph. Chasline, mimetic language is not even mentioned, but in the 1933 edition M. A. Ombredane gives this expressive form a place of honor.[4]

The Chinese philologist Tciang-Tceng-Ming is convinced that all linguistic data, from the sinologist's point of view at least, confirm the priority of visual language.[5] He divides the history of Chinese writing into four periods, each with its own characteristic development. The first three are thought to derive wholly from the language of gestures, and only in the fourth does the acoustic element assert itself. With particular reference to the Yins inscriptions,[6] he demonstrates that the ideograms of that era, in most cases, do not reproduce objects but fix descriptive gestures in their general outlines and are often incomprehensible if their derivation is not kept in mind. Finally, he compares quite a few of those ancient morphograms to the gestures used by the Indians of North America and discovers some surprising affinities. (We do not believe that this is necessarily proof that writing derives from gesture, for both gesture and pictographic design quite often do no more than reproduce a characteristic aspect of the real object. However, derivation is sometimes evident for other reasons.)

Both our Chinese philologist and Van Ginneken seem to pass from correct observations to an untenable conclusion. They inform us that there is no trace of phonetic reference in any of the ancient Chinese characters; if the people of that time had in fact used a phonetic language similar to our own, or even a language of semi-articulate sounds, there would have been some trace of this practice in ideographic signs. Therefore, those ideograms arose at a time when human beings only expressed themselves through gestures, because an acoustic language did not yet exist. (On the basis of such reasoning one might say that: as the writing of Hebrews does not include vowels, their language is composed of consonants only!)

In Van Ginneken's view, if acoustic *clicks* had existed in that era, they would have appeared in writing. The same is true of ancient Egyptian vowels: had they existed they would have manifested themselves as they subsequently did during the centuries preceding the Christian era, in other words, as soon as they appeared. (We think that the idea that the Egyptian language was originally devoid of vowels is untenable.)

In relation to De Brosses, we listed above the various reasons for believing that the invention of writing occurred tens and probably hundreds of thousands of years after language was first used.

That there is no phonetic reference as a rule in primitive pictographic and ideographic writing systems is not proof that those writing systems are antecedent to language. This absence can be explained by the fact that phonetic writing requires a greater capacity of abstraction and analysis than pictographic writing. In fact, still today, less-civilized people draw a tree, a man, a hut to signify the corresponding concepts, but they would not be capable of analyzing the words they use in terms of their alphabetical components.

Van Ginneken has the merit of having assembled a vast and convincing bibliography to support his theory of the priority of mimetic language, but then he weakens it with a few serious and naive mistakes.

He claims, for instance, that phonetic language only arose around 3,500 years before Christ, and that in China the phonetic element of language only appeared toward 1200–1300 B.C. All this contradicts a great deal of scientifically ascertained data and enormously distorts historical perspective. This renders incomprehensible the gradual evolution from pictographic language to a language in which conventional mimetic signs predominate, through to phonetic and literary language, where the latter, though the product of a long process of elaboration, certainly developed before 3500 B.C.

These differences are not trivial. In fact, according to a reasonable calculation made by Kainz,[7] human language emerged during the low Pleistocene age, that is, from 400 to 500,000 years before Christ, when the use of fire and stone implements was already known.

In conclusion it can be said that Van Ginneken defended a thesis that was plausible with arguments that were not always well chosen.

PAGET. The same thing may be said of the work of Sir Richard Paget.[8] According to Paget, primitive man expressed himself instinctively through mimicry of the entire body, and especially of the face. Mouth movements unconsciously accompanying all expressive motions, and which could have influenced the larynx and other vocal organs, should be considered as a special case of facial mimicry.

He examines certain letter groups in detail and shows that they are an effect of oral mimicry. For example, as already observed by I. R. Firth, the letters *sl* are produced by sliding the tip of the tongue backwards and have a pejorative meaning, the *str* group has an analogous meaning even in words of different etymology; in most linguistic families the sounds *ku, gu,* and *hu* signify something raw, empty, and tubular, which corresponds to the form of the lips on pronouncing them. In English more than eighty percent of the monosyllables beginning in *sp* have a meaning which corresponds to the mimetic expression of the lips on pronouncing them.

It seems highly probable, he says, that if a group of children were abandoned before they knew how to speak and formed an isolated community, they would start communicating with each other through mimetic movements of the body and face joined to unconscious articulate sounds, and this would then give rise to a phonetic language. The language spontaneously created by those children would necessarily have roots similar to the principal languages in the world, for they all derive from the same source.

He believes that primitive oral mimicry was so obviously signifying that sight alone was sufficient to interpret it, just as deaf-mutes still today read lips. (Paget does not seem to be aware of the essential difference between directly expressive signs and conventional signs. A deaf-mute can certainly read "menin aeide thea" on our lips but if he does not know Greek he will not understand its meaning.)

Paget also believes that his theory on the mimetic nature of the human word could offer a rational basis for the development of the art of giving mimetic expression to thought. He recalls that around 1920 the famous mime Severin announced to the readers of "Comoedia" his project of making pantomime the universal language of deaf-mutes; but more daring than Severin, Paget believes that his theory offers the possibility of establishing on solid foundations a universal auxiliary language made of gestures. For this purpose and with the help of some of his collaborators, he assembled a dictionary of about two thousand signs which were to express everything that was generally needed in the everyday affairs of life. In our opinion, Paget did not live up to the level of his happy intuition in the subsequent development of his ideas.

The hypothesis of the mimetic and pictographic origin of human language, suggestively referred to on numerous occasions—from Plato's *Cratylus* to the works by Paget and particularly to those by Van Ginneken—has not yet received treatment that is theoretically sound and consequently it has not been accepted by most linguists;[9] nonetheless, in our opinion, it is still the only hypothesis on which a tenable solution to this extremely difficult problem can be founded.

CONCLUDING REMARKS ON DOCTRINES. If we now take a retrospective view of our survey, we will soon realize that the topic of our inquiry has seriously engaged the mind of numerous scholars, including such great thinkers as Plato, St. Augustine, Bacon, Vico, etc. Indeed, this is remarkable in relation to a problem which, in the words of an illustrious scholar, is thought to be so absurd "as to deserve a special clinical-psychiatric ward, such as exists for those who are obsessed with perpetual movement."

On the other hand, we are forced to recognize that too many of the scholars who have dealt with the problem have done so unconvincingly, and that in most cases the progressive development of ideas from one thinker to another, so much admired in the evolution of modern natural sciences, is found to be lacking.

The solutions, continually repeated and alternated, can be reduced to a few basic types: the theological solution, the rationalistic solution based on conventional institution, the onomatopoeic and mimetic solutions. To these we must add the variously negative attitudes of the Idealists and Skeptics.

In spite of the fact that the same attempts at finding solutions are repeated, there has been some progress, even if this had been due only to the influence of more mature scientific conceptions in other fields.

The theological solutions, described by Plato as being far too easy, are taken up again in the Middle Ages and slowly emerge with laborious argumentations right through to the whole of the nineteenth century, but subsequently they are almost completely abandoned. The conventionalistic thesis attributed to Democritus, which denies the existence of a natural link between word and meaning, contains an important truth regarding the nature of the linguistic sign, and a naive error regarding its origin.

The fact that the problem of the conventional character of language has not yet been perfectly clarified even today emerges from the most recent discussions on the subject. For a greater understanding we must distinguish the conceptual problem from the temporal one, the appearance of the first roots from later evolution, and we must recognize that primitive language must have been directly expressive in character and that the conventional aspect is the fruit of natural evolution, noticeable not only in language but in all spontaneous semantic systems.

Without such explanations the observations attributed to Democritus become incomprehensible, for they presuppose that primitive hominids, destitute of language, in fact established a conventional code among themselves.

Thanks to modern historicism and evolutionism and, even more, to ethnological studies, there no doubt has been a noteworthy advancement in our views on the mentality of primitive man. No one today would attribute the mentality of civilized human beings to primitive hominids, as did not only the Port Royalists but also such an author as Gébelin at the end of the eighteenth century.

Another important step forward is represented by the Romantics who contrast to the Rationalists, accentuate the spontaneous character of linguistic creation. They also have the merit of having insisted, as Condillac and others had already done before them, on the inseparability of sign and concept against those who had considered language as a mere external means for the communication of concepts that already exist inside us without expression; but as for the origin they show a clear preference for nebulous mystic conceptions.

The idea of derivation of language from affective and imitative sounds (which is the first and easiest hypothesis that comes to mind for anyone intending to support the natural origin theory) recurs frequently in ancient and modern thinkers. It has been amply developed and enriched by various authors who have also added tropes, onomatopoeia, invocative cries, sexual calls, rhythmic calls accompanying work, intonations, affective modulations, inflections, and so forth.

Finally, as van Ginneken rightly emphasized, noteworthy progress is represented by the increasing recognition of the importance of mimetic language, made possible by the scrupulously documented studies of modern ethnologists.

As to the solution that we ourselves have formulated, almost all assertions proposed in the theoretical part of this work were subsequently traced here and there in some previous doctrine. No doubt, had we been fully aware of the attempts carried out by other scholars from the very beginning of our inquiry, we would have reached our conclusions more easily; but it is just as true that we would not have appreciated former doctrines without first formulating our views from our own theoretical standpoint.

There is, in fact, a reciprocal influence between science and the history of science: on the one hand, all new theories present themselves as the mature product and almost inevitable point of arrival of preceding theories, and on the other, preceding doctrines are chosen, highlighted, and graded according to the perspective proposed by current theory.

The extent to which a historical view changes according to different points of view can be seen by comparing this survey to that outlined by Croce in the appendix of his *Estetica e linguistica generale* (Aesthetics and General Linguistics). It is only by taking into account the theoretical point of view accepted by Croce that one may understand, for example, his opinions concerning the linguistics of Romanticism. In the same way, it is only through the criteria of evaluation that we ourselves have employed that we have been able to rectify in a negative sense traditional views on Gébelin and Monboddo, and in a positive sense those on Bacon, Vico, Condillac, and Stewart, etc.

BOOK TWO

On the Nature and Essence of
Language: Principles for a
General Linguistics

1. Object and Method of Our Inquiry

Dialectic Union of Positive Science and Philosophical Inquiry—Union of The Two Methods as Distinction and Not Confusion.

In the first book of our work we concentrated on clarifying the problem of language origin from the point of view of the natural sciences; in the second book we now propose to examine the philosophical problem of the essence or nature of language.

In the first book we asked ourselves how human language arose; here, instead, we will ask ourselves "What is human language?" Or better: what is its specific value and function among the spiritual activities of man? How is it most comprehensively described so as to outline the problems of general linguistics with greater precision and better results? What relation is there between linguistics, aesthetics, and logic?

Here a doubt may arise: would it not have been more logical to work in the reverse order—namely to deal with the philosophical problem of the essence initially and with the naturalistic problem of origin later? Indeed, it could be claimed that we must first know what language is and only after that will it be possible to inquire into its origin.

But, if we look into the problem carefully, the opposite thesis is just as legitimate (and just as unilateral): first we must be informed about the concrete facts of language and its historical development, and only then will it be possible to understand its nature. How can we speculate on the definition of language without knowing anything about the way it manifests itself or about the "way it was born?"

But if knowledge of the facts is essential for an adequate approach to the philosophical problem, and, on the other adequate hand, if it is not possible to consider the facts without having first clarified the concepts philosophically, how will we free ourselves of this vicious circle?

This is one of those cases of reciprocal implication which are always present whenever we are not simply dealing with two distinct concepts but with two phases or aspects of the same concept. The conflict derives solely from the unnecessary separation of facts from concepts, that is, of positive inquiry from philosophical investigation.

To make things clearer we may distinguish between scientific inquiry in which empirical considerations dominate while philosophical elucidations remain in the background, and philosophical inquiry in which greater emphasis is placed on conceptual investigation; but a positive science that does not presuppose and make use of philosophical concepts does not exist and never has existed, and the same can be said for philosophy which continually refers to positive facts more or less explicitly.

However, the dialectic union of science and philosophy that we are here proposing is not to be understood as an indistinct confusion of the two terms and methods. It is a fact that when the empiricists of the eighteenth century, the positivists of the nineteenth century, and a host of modern authors, such as the neopositivists of the circle of Vienna and the American neopragmatists, attempted to apply the methods of the natural or of the physical-mathematical sciences to the field of philosophy, the results were completely negative; and not a single philosophical concept exists which can be said to have been developed in such a perspective. On the other hand, whenever the positive facts have been treated with the philosophic method (not only the so-called philosophy of nature of Schelling and Hegel, but also many other unfounded abstractions of the idealists) the results have even been worse, if we believe that delirium is worse than vulgarity.

In contrast, the two approaches should be united in the sense that, even though they remain distinct and respond to different demands—philosophical and empirical—they must in any investigation converge toward a single end. In reality, these two opposite demands have hardly ever been felt and satisfied in equal measure; indeed in some authors we perceive the lack of speculative vigor, in others a lack of positive concreteness.

Let us take as an example *The Critique of Practical Reason,* one of the most brilliant and altogether most accurate and well thought-out works of philosophical literature available, and we will have to admit that rigorous conceptual commitment and profound speculative intuition find no correspondence in an equally serious, vast, and controlled positive foundation. No doubt there are references to specific concrete facts, and they could not be lacking, but at the most, they are implied or mentioned as examples without methodical preparation or control.

Had Kant been convinced that a moral theory loses all significance when it does not seek to understand the concrete actions of mankind, and therefore had he felt the need to document through methodical observation the moral customs of different times and countries whose speculative foundations he was searching for, his work would not have had that abstract character which has so often been criticized. Had he done this, he would not have failed to recognize the importance in our moral life of animal needs and impulses, passions and affections, traditions, economic interests, juridical and social orders, etc., and, in short, the whole of his conception would have been more faithful to life without losing in conceptual profoundness because of this.

On the other hand, if we consider the works of those psychologists, ethnologists, and sociologists who in the last fifty years have also made human actions and traditions their object of study (from the works by Wundt, exemplary in their own way, to the very well-informed works by scholars such as Lévy-Bruhl, Durkheim, etc.), we will have to acknowledge the opposite shortcoming. Through admirably organized work, these authors offer us a limitless quantity of facts concerning the moral customs and conceptions of different people—facts which are carefully collected, documented, checked, and classified—while, on the other hand, their conceptual apparatus is extremely inadequate. So inadequate that these works are certainly able to satisfy our erudite curiosity, but as to our inner spiritual orientation, they are inconclusive.

One of the philosophers who most felt the need of not separating facts from values, or—as he used to say—of not separating certainty from truth, was Vico; but we know that owing to both personal and circumstantial reasons his documentation is anything but reliable.

The two most important scholars of Italian idealism were not lacking either in conceptual intuition or in aptitude or taste for accurate documentation. Nonetheless, as a reaction against the banalities of positivism and because of aprioristic prejudice, they relegated naturalistic research to the limbo of "abstract logos" and "pseudo-concepts." Consequently, their works are extremely distant from achieving the union of science and philosophy that we would like to see realized.

For our part we have tried—far more in this work than in the previous one—to get close to this unity, and we hope that on examining it, scholars will dwell not only on the specific hypotheses and theories we have formulated, but also on our method.

We truly believe that if others, fresher and more suited to the task, propose to achieve the union we have longed for, this in itself will be a valid contribution toward lifting philosophy from the degradation and discredit into which it has now fallen.

2. Formulation of the Problem

The Omnipresence of Philosophical Categories Does Not Enable Characterization through Concepts of a Specific Reality—It Is Wrong to Ask Whether Language Is Art or Thought—Linguistic Issues Are Semantic in Character.

Specific philosophical problems are usually formulated as follows: what is art? what is science? what is justice? In our case, therefore, we should ask ourselves: what is language?

But this way of formulating such problems may give rise to misunderstandings and errors. Philosophical concepts are constitutive aspects of the thinking subject and—differently from empirical concepts—they concern the whole of reality, because thought is constantly present in anything we talk about. This is the reason why we may imagine a world without trees or metals, whereas we cannot conceive a universe without concepts, representations, sensations, etc., if not through naive abstraction, because without such conceptual instruments, we would receive no information whatsoever about the universe.[1]

But if philosophical predicates are universal there can be no sense in asking whether a given reality or institution has aesthetic or logical or practical value, for none of these values could be absent.

For example, it is said that Plato's *Phaedo* and Machiavelli's *Principe* are works of reflection, and they certainly are for whoever searches them for the reply to a conceptual problem. But if I take no interest in their truth and abandon myself to the powerful personal accent used by the authors to express their inner world, *Phaedo* and *Principe* become works of art. And there is nothing to stop others from considering those same works from other points of view, evaluating their moral value, or considering them from a purely philological point of view as language texts, etc.[2]

The same thing is true of that millenary and complex institution we call language. In fact, language may be legitimately considered from a philological point of view as a documented collection of words used in a given period by a given people, or from an aesthetic point of view as the creation of images and expressions (as did Croce), or from an abstractly logical point of view (as did ancient syllogistics or as the modern supporters of linguistic analysis do with an over-elaborate algebraic apparatus), or even from a moral and political point of view (as we citizens of Trieste did under Austrian rule, when our language appeared to us as a political right and an ideal we had to fight for).[3]

What we are saying is that the question "what is language?" acquires its most precise meaning only from the problems that linguistics proposes to explain.

According to most modern linguists the specific function of language, which is more or less explicitly implied in glottological research, is neither logical nor aesthetic, but semantic.

But while treatises of logic and aesthetics abound, works that deal systematically with problems of semantics are scarce and unsatisfactory.

3. The Concept of Semantics and the Constitutive Elements of Aesthetic Synthesis

Croce's Definition of Intuition is Negative rather than Positive—Memory Transforms Sense Impressions into Aesthetic Images.

In the pages that follow, we will specify the concept of semantic activity, showing that it is a characteristic aspect of aesthetic activity and a necessary premise to the formation of logical concepts.

Croce's theory, according to which art is pure intuition, has helped to clarify some aspects of the aesthetic problem, but it has also raised questions. Even if we accept his theory in its general outlines (in the sense that what matters most in the work of art is not the truth of concepts but the lyricism of images), the value and function of creative image-making remains obscure.

We have already mentioned the difficulties that may arise on formulating the aesthetic problem with the question "what is art?" However, leaving this aside, Croce's answer is still negative rather than positive: art is intuition, and intuitions or images are not sensations, they are not scientific concepts, neither are they utilitarian nor moral volitions.

But what are they? Croce insisted on emphasizing the essential difference between the tumult of sense impressions and emotions that excite us, and the image or aesthetic representation of those impressions. But what does such a difference consist of? What difference is there between our sense impressions (when, for instance, while going for a walk we experience the impressions of the sun and wind and the noises and smells of the countryside, similarly to animals) and the image we form of such impressions on contemplating them?

According to the theory we wish to propose, the difference is between the mere experience and the transfiguration accomplished by memory on re-evoking what we felt. The act of memory elevates us, placing an ideal distance between ourselves and that which we experience, a distance which at times is even perceived while that very experience continues.

That light in us, that cathartic liberation we experience when we succeed in contemplating that which is happening inside us, derives from the evocative act of memory. An act which gathers the multiplicity of our impressions and emotions within the unity of its synthesis. Memory makes aesthetic contemplation possible by operating the first *synopsis* of the uncoordinated elements of the senses: this is symbolized well in that Greek myth which names Mnemosyne the mother of the Muses.

4. Documentary Memory and Poetic Memory

Immediacy and Subjectivity of Sense Impressions—
Memory as a Transcendental Act, Necessary for the
Consciousness of Sensation—Objectivity of the Doc-
umentary Memory and Subjectivity of the Poetic
Memory—Analogy Between Aesthetic Synthesis and
Scientific Synthesis—Classicism and Romanticism,
Epic Poetry and Lyric Poetry as Elements of Aes-
thetic Synthesis—Sense and Memory as Sources of
All Expressive Activity.

Let us better define the reciprocal relation uniting this conceptual triad: sensation, memory, intuition.[1]

That which is recognized through the senses is always something immediate. Immediacy and simplicity were already asserted by Aristotle when he
explained that perception by the senses is always true, for error can only
arise from that which is composite, and sensation as such consists of a single
element and not of a relation among diverse elements. If the sweet wine I
am drinking seems bitter to me, my sensation is not wrong: the taste is really
bitter.

The same thing is acknowledged by Kant when he states that if we leave
aside the case in which numerous sensations succeed each other, sense impression only lasts an instant.[2]

In fact, we need a certain amount of time to become familiar with a
scientific work or a work of art, first we learn one thing and then another,
so that we may say: "I do not yet know this whole work, but only part of it,
and I will only formulate an opinion once I know it more fully." But no one
would say: "I do not know yet whether the taste I experience on drinking
this liqueur is sweet or bitter because I've only drunk half a bottle." Sensation
is immediately present in its wholeness, otherwise it does not exist. It is pure
intensity without extension.

Insofar as it is pure immediacy, sensation is at the same time absolute subjectivity: I can think your thought, but I cannot feel your sensation. We may think of memory as the opposite and necessarily complementary aspect of sensation. It is pure continuity, pure extension, an empty form gathering tangible content. The objectivity of mnemonic recording contrasts with the subjectivity of sensation.

If experience were totally devoid of memory, we would not know anything: we cannot grasp sensation in its immediacy, but only as contemplation and memory of that which we have experienced.

Memory is usually defined as the faculty of reproducing representations. This definition lends itself to misunderstanding: it may lead us to believe that the sole function of memory is to preserve preexistent representations, and that we can have images without the complicity of the mnemonic act. In contrast, what we should say is that memory is a formative activity whose function is described not only by the verb *retinere* but also by *apprehendere*.

However, we must distinguish between the memory of the chronicler and that of the poet. The theory we have proposed does not suggest that images are mnemonic registrations of objective facts, which would mean confusing poetry and chronicles, but it considers the poetic image as the unitary synthesis of memory and sentiment.

Chronicle-like or documentary memory deprives the affective and sense content of its subjectivity, transforming it into objective registration, while poetic memory merges with the subjectivity of impressions and affections.

Nevertheless a documentary exigency is always implicit in poetic creation: the need, that is, of that intimate sincerity which makes the poet a scribe of his own heart as he writes what is dictated to him, so that he considers his work as a testimony to which he cannot arbitrarily add a single syllable.[3]

In order to clarify the nature of aesthetic synthesis a few references to other synthesis operated by cognitive activity may help. Let us take as an example our knowledge of the laws that govern the physical world. Here too we are able to identify two constitutive aspects: on the one hand the observation and description of phenomena, and on the other the arrangement of observed facts in a logical and mathematical perspective. Observation gives us the various elements that make up the content, and the conceptual framework assembles that content into a unified form.

The two constitutive aspects of synthesis characterize two different types of science: the descriptive, in which empirical description predominates, and the rational in which conceptual rigor predominates; but neither of the two can ever be absent, for empirical content would be blind without conceptual light and a conceptual schema would be empty without phenomenal content.

In our opinion the dialectic of aesthetic activity is perfectly analogous: sense and affective impressions give us the multiplicity of content which the mnemonic act assembles in the unity of its form.

Here also the two elements characterize two different types: romantic art, in which sensual intensity and emotional content prevail; and classical art in which perfect formal contemplation prevails; but both are equally necessary, for the sensual without contemplation would be blind, and the contemplative act without sensitivity would be empty.

Therefore all real works of art must be both romantic and classical. They are romantic insofar as they must express an intense and spontaneous life of sense and affective impressions; and classical insofar as they must dominate the tumult of the passions and sensations in the serenity of contemplative re-evocation.

The distinction between *lyric poetry* and *epic poetry* has similar implications, however different the psychological emphasis. The lyrical character of art is the subjective character of sensibility, its epic character is the objective character of memory.

The predominance of one of the two aspects may be indicative of two merits, but also of two dangers in art.

When aesthetic synthesis is successful we admire the intensity and intimacy of sentiment in romantic and lyrical art, and contemplative perfection in classical art; but when synthesis is not perfectly successful, unbridled sentiment is excessive, and in the opposite case, form without sentiment is cold and impersonal.

The two inferior aspects of synthesis present themselves in all their crudity in spurious art (detective stories and the like) where contemplative serenity is replaced by the purely sensational element (libido and bloodshed) on the one hand, and by the pure curiosity of a chronicle where all we want to know is how the story ends, on the other.

The danger of classical art is the impersonality and coldness of chronicle-like reproduction and of mnemonic imitation; the danger of unrestrained lyrical impetus is the exaggerated emphasis of sentiment.

These two constitutive elements of synthesis are necessary not only for the creation, but also for the comprehension of the work of art and therefore for aesthetic judgement: a person blind from birth cannot enjoy the beauty of a painting for he is incapable of making that sensible content his own. But philological preparation, the mnemonic continuity of traditions, the knowledge of facts implicit in the work of art are no less necessary. Good taste will not suffice to understand a poem, one must also be familiar with the language in which it is written. Erudition without sensitivity is insufficient, just as sensitivity without the necessary preparation is insufficient.[4]

Sensitivity and memory are the two sources of all expressive activities, bringing about in all fields a dialectic opposition analogous to that between romanticism and classicism.

In linguistic descriptions the classical point of view unilaterally stresses the mnemonic aspect, that is, tradition, holding that the writer should model his expressions on so-called language texts, while the romantic point of view appeals to spontaneous popular sensibility. Glottogonic theories that consider interjections and affective calls as forming the origin of language emphasize the affective and sense element; whereas those theories that consider on-omatopoeia as the source of language accentuate the importance of imitation and mnemonic reproduction. The same can be said in relation to mimetic expression, so that we distinguish affective gestures, which are the physio-logical reaction to given impressions, and imitative gestures which are the mnemonic reproduction.

Finally in writing, or better still in expressive signs (phonetic, graphic, or mimetic) generally, we may distinguish between pictographic signs which refer to the most immediate impressions, and the mnemotechnic which refer to a conventional code, preserved by the memory.

But in all these cases one element never appears completely without the other. A gesture or affective cry, an "ah! ah!" caused by pain will not become an expressive interjection if it is not in some way contemplated and remem-bered; on the other hand, even the most frigid and least affective expressive sign, for example the Morse code, must still refer to impressions of the senses, for without that reference memory would have nothing to remember. Memory and sensitivity cannot therefore be considered as two different and auton-omous acts, but quite simply as two phases and aspects, distinguishable but not separable, of the same expressive activity.[5]

5. Problems of Artistic Technique and of Language

Distinction between Intuition and Expression—Artistic Technique as Semantic Activity—Technique as Aid and Support for Artistic Creation.

The aesthetics of pure intuition has identified intuition with expression. It asserts that if the artist does not know how to express his image he only has the impression that he possesses it, while in fact he does not.

This assertion may have some value as a reaction to the widespread opinion that overestimates technique, naively maintaining that we could all be skillful painters or sculptors with practice and manual ability in handling colors or a chisel.

It is true indeed that the chisel is not everything, though it does count. If it were true that it will suffice to have an image in one's head to know how to express it, then it will also suffice to remember a symphony perfectly in order to know how to play all instruments without exercise.

Technique, which is in a relation of continual reciprocal action with artistic creation, would not find adequate recognition in an aesthetic theory which considers the creation of the poetic image as an unanalyzable miracle.[1]

In our opinion, our attempted analysis of the constitutive elements of aesthetic synthesis can shed light on the problem, enabling us to formulate a more exact conceptual definition of artistic technique.

If, as we have said, the aesthetic image arises when a multiplicity of sense and affective impressions is contemplated in the ideality of memory, our natural way of communicating an image to others will be this: make him feel those impressions so that on assembling them in his memory he is able to reproduce the image.

If I have a given hue of green and blue in mind and I want to communicate it to you, I will have to mix the colors of the palette to obtain that particular shade and then arrange them in such a way as to give them the specific visual impression I have in mind. In this way colors become *expressive signs*, that is to say, stimuli capable of producing those particular impressions which on being taken in by the memory will form the image. Technique consists in the ability to arrange these stimuli.

Naturally the importance of this activity will vary greatly according to the different cases. If the image one desires to communicate is a black profile on a white background, far less ability and training will be required than for the "Last Judgement."

The aesthetics of pure intuition correctly affirms that a work of art can neither be appreciated nor evaluated if we do not recreate it in our mind. Thus the reader or spectator accomplishes the same process of unification and transfiguration of impressions as that already accomplished by the artist; the same, but with different degrees of effort! The artist relies on himself alone, while the spectator relies on the artist, allowing himself to be carried away on the wings of the latter.

The sense impressions have already been clearly circumscribed for the spectator who must do no more than assemble them in his contemplative act. On the contrary, only through a good deal of pain and hard work will the artist achieve that unitary vision which his sentiments urge him to create. In fact the mechanical reproduction of impressions in their shapeless and un-coordinated multiplicity is one thing, and the vision of the artist is another. If, while admiring a landscape, we experience at one and the same time the smells of the countryside, the noise of a train, the unpleasant humidity in the air, pangs of hunger and concern for our son's health, it is plain that this uncontrolled jumble has nothing to do with the work of art.

The artist must bring forth the impressions and emotions that enter his painting. More than communicate a completely finished vision to others, technique helps him fix his vision in outlines that are continuously less im-perfect.

Artists gifted with such a plastic imagination as to be able to work out and polish their creation through interior work alone are rare, just as sculp-tors capable of creating works of art directly out of marble, as did Michel-angelo at times, are rare.

In most cases a sculptor uses clay. This enables him to provisionally fix a vague or partially elaborated image, experiment with this image, modify it, change his mind, and search for a more and more adequate expression of his sentiments.

Sculptors, painters, and musicians thus avail themselves of technique not only to communicate images they already have in mind, but also to "see better inside themselves," that is, technique provides support for their cre-ative work.

6. Aesthetics and Semantics[1]

Technical Impossibility of Giving Immediate Expression to Most of Our Inner World—Language as Indirect Communication—Arbitrary Character of Linguistic Signs—Linguistics as a Special Case of Semantics.

We have said that the natural and direct means of communicating a pictorial image to others is that of choosing and arranging colors in such a way as to produce the corresponding impressions. But if the necessary colors are missing from the painter's palette and if for some reason he cannot procure them, he will not be able to communicate his image to others.

It is a fact that we are often just like a painter without colors with respect to a great part of our inner life. We take moving images into our memory which painting cannot express, we re-evoke the rustling of leaves and the freshness of the air, our thirst, yearnings and emotions, which all go to form, when possible, a unitary picture in our mind. But to communicate all this we would have to transmit the memory of our sensations and states of mind through mental suggestion.

Similarly to the images of form, color, and sound, we should also directly communicate the images of smell, taste, tactile impressions, etc., by impressing the corresponding physical sensations on the spectator; but it is plain that the liveliness of such a sensation, which involves our sensitivity as such far too violently, would impede the act of contemplation.

Given that adequate technical means for the conveyance of most of our images are not available and that our physiology does not permit the immediate expression of such violent and complex impressions as those made by a hurricane, a fire, or a surgical operation, man is obliged to resort to the use of the indirect technical devices.

This is how language arose. Unlike the colors of painters and the sounds of musicians, the phonemes of language do not have an immediately expressive function. Rather the latter are an indirect device for recalling an image to the mind, like the memory trick of tying a knot in a handkerchief which does not in itself represent the book I am supposed to return, but only reminds me of it.

As we have seen, the pictographic or directly expressive element originally predominated in language also, but neither mimetic expression nor affective cries are as directly communicative as painting. The image of a burn can be signified by a scream of pain, a convulsive movement of the hand and face, but certainly not by reproducing the corresponding sensation in others.

The conventional and therefore "arbitrary" character of linguistic signs used today emerges, as has often been observed, from the fact that a single concept, for example, a number, can be signified in different languages with completely different phonemes or with other signs chosen *ad placitum,* as occurs in writing and coded languages.

What ensues from this is that the linguistic sign is not comprehensible to anyone who is not familiar with the conventional meaning of that sign. This gives rise to the necessity of approximative translations from one language to another, a necessity peculiar to linguistic expression and which is not found in either music or painting.

For these reasons Vossler's so called glottologic idealism, which following in Croce's footsteps identified semantics with aesthetics, brought more confusion than clarity to the problems of linguistics and has not generally been followed by the more competent scholars.[2]

7. General Theory of Expressive Signs

Definition of Expressive Signs—The Various Types of Expressive Signs—Antithesis Between Aesthetic Signs and Conventional Signs—Mnemotechnic Signs Remind Us of a Different Content from the Sense Impression Produced by the Sign—Affinity between chance Signs and Conventional Signs—The Beginnings of Grammar and Syntax—Consolidation of the Rules of Grammar—The Problem of Immanent Rationality and of Unconscious Natural Finality.

Ferdinand de Saussure has the merit of having explicitly stated that language falls within the broader sphere of semiological institutions in general. He calls the science that deals with (or should deal with) such institutions "semiology," and compares spoken language with writing, the mute alphabet, military and nautical signs, and with certain conventional courtesy forms (*signes de politesse*).

Therefore, he says, we must conceive a science that studies the life of signs in social life, a science of which linguistics would only be a part.[1]

We could ask ourselves why he did not then develop at least an outline of this *general semiology*, instead of mostly limiting himself to simply collecting information about language and writing. But we must remember that Saussure wrote at a time when the need was felt to react against the over-general ideas and hasty syntheses of preceding linguists, and he was mainly interested himself in the accurate observation and recording of concrete facts.

The situation in linguistics today is very different; special studies abound and, in contrast, greater conceptual clarification is required. Developing the suggestion made by the Swiss linguist, we will now attempt to explain the concept of general semantics of which linguistics is a special case.[2] To achieve this we will first attempt a definition of the expressive sign and then enumerate the different types of signs, indicating the characteristics peculiar to each.

As already stated, the expressive sign may be defined as a stimulus predisposed in such a manner as to produce sense impressions capable of giving rise to given images or representations. Since concepts as well (whether they be mathematical, physical, or philosophical) can only be expressed and communicated through representations, expressive signs are necessary for the communication of both images and concepts.

By *sign* some authors mean every representation which is in some way connected or associated with another: hence symptoms of disease (dealt with by medical symptomatology) are usually called "signs," and the Stoics said that smoke is a *sign* of fire or that the massing of clouds is a *sign* of rainy weather. But to place different concepts into the same group on the basis of verbal similarities can only bring about confusion.

The semantics we are concerned with only deals with signs that express and communicate images and concepts and which are therefore called *expressive signs*.

Among the criteria used for the classification of expressive signs we may list the sensory organs through which signs are perceived, so that visual signs may be distinguished from the auditory, etc.; the devices through which signs are produced (flags, gongs, etc.); the context in which they are used (military signals, maritime signals, etc.). We believe it more appropriate to base our own classification on the relation between signs and meaning (i.e., on the different ways in which the signifying function is accomplished).

On the basis of these criteria we may identify the following sign types:
(a) *Immediate aesthetic signs.*

This category includes directly expressive devices as they are used in the arts, such as the colors of painters and the sounds of musicians, in which the image is the product of the immediate (i.e., not mediated) contemplation of the sign.

This expressive technique is characterized by the absolute prevalence of the intuitive element over the conventional. Conventionality, which is the law that regulates communication through arbitrary signs, is no less than a shortcoming in art.

Another characteristic is the unity and globality of expression. Aesthetic synthesis does not allow for analytical isolation of the single component parts, which is only possible by abstraction at the theoretical level. Just as that which Aristotle said about the State is true for all living organisms (i.e., that the whole comes ideally before the parts), it is also true for the work of art. In a portrait, for example, the expression of the eye, mouth, hands, etc., are obviously global expressions, and by concentrating our attention on one particular rather than on another, we accomplish an act of abstraction which must not break up the unity of expression.

Croce's view of language is one-sided and inadequate for he considered it solely from an aesthetic point of view and coherently stated that the reality of language is to be searched for in global discourse and not in single words. Indeed, to his mind, words were no more than abstractions devoid of independent meaning, on a par with the letters of the alphabet.

(b) *Immediate conceptual signs.*

This category includes, for example, numerical signs (e.g., single numbers intuitively indicated with a corresponding number of dots, or direct pictographic signs that signify a given object—house, tree, dog—by picturing that object itself).

Meaning is more generic and less determined in these signs than in aesthetic signs, and the arbitrary component already begins to emerge. For example, number five may be signified not only by arranging five dots in different ways, but also by substituting five small stones ("calculi") or five dashes for the aforementioned dots. Similarly, in pictographic signs it is not always necessary to use an identical sign to signify the same object.

Indicating mimetic gestures, as when one points to one's own eye to signify "eye," or to a red object to signify "red," are similar to this type of sign. Finally, this group may also include "writing through real objects," when symbolic meaning does not prevail over direct meaning.

(c) *Chance mnemotechnic signs.*

The technique used in conventional signs is antithetical to that used in aesthetic signs. In relation to the latter the content of the mnemonic act is formed of impressions directly produced by the sign, but in the mnemotechnic sign the content to be remembered is different from the sense impression produced by that sign.

It would seem that the menhirs, dolmens, and cromlechs of the neolithic age belong to this category.

Their function is carefully described in a biblical passage referred to earlier. After the waters of the Jordan had opened to let Israel pass, Joshua made his men erect a monument at that point with a pile of rocks so that—according to the text—their children would be induced to ask: what do those rocks mean? and their fathers would reply by narrating the memorable event.

These signs aim at producing an impression that is to strike the attention, thus inducing us either to remember a given fact or to interrogate others about it.

We cannot here speak of conventional signs in the proper sense, because not only is there no code containing the key to the established conventions, but the same sign may be used for an indefinite multiplicity of meanings. We are still dealing with non-systematic signs established at random, according to the specific situation.

Nevertheless there are affinities between chance signs and conventional signs: the "natural link" between sign and meaning is absent in both, whereas the institutional and interpretative elements are necessarily related in both cases.

Knot writing systems such as the Peruvian Quippus and message sticks represent a further development in these signs: to the mnemotechnic element is added the conceptual (which we have already discussed) as well as the pictographic and symbolic. We shall now consider these latter aspects.

(d) *Chance pictographic signs.*

In these signs meaning is the product of a natural association with the sign. This group includes onomatopoeia, interjections, mimetic expressions, and pictographic writing, all of which are spontaneously invented in specific circumstances for communication purposes.

For instance to signify "death" we may mimetically imitate, without preestablished rules, stiff arms or a collapsing body, draw a skull or a tomb, hum a funeral dirge, etc.

"Real object writing systems" also belong to this group when they are chance—symbolic in character and not conventional.

We said that our classification represents ideal types, this means that one and the same element may belong to different types.

The painting of a dog on the wall of a prehistoric cave may either be considered as an aesthetic sign or as a pictographic sign depending on whether that which prevails is the mere taste for individual representation or the need to symbolize a more general, magical meaning. Similarly, the same little mimetic scene may sometimes be considered quite simply as artistic representation and at other times as objective informative communication.

(e) *Traditional pictographic signs.*

These are either direct or symbolic pictographic signs established by traditional use as fixed symbols. Noteworthy examples are hieroglyphic writing systems and mimetic hieroglyphics.

In the evolution of these signs symbolic and figurative expression progressively predominates over direct expression.

To signify, for example, the concept of sovereignty, first we could draw a king on a throne with his sceptre and crown, and then we could abbreviate the symbol by simply drawing either the crown or the sceptre.

As time passes the abbreviated and stylized symbol may become incomprehensible to the uninstructed. The need thus arises for a "code" which establishes the meaning to be attributed to the signs in use in a given community.

In contrast with artistic expression (where synthetic unity is anterior to the parts), in the case in question single signs are preexistent to the whole, and expressive synthesis is obtained from the composition of the parts.

In the context of a painting, an eye, a nose, or a tree do not have expressive value in themselves, but they acquire such value within the harmony of the whole; in writing systems, on the contrary, single signs already have a semiological value of their own and synthesis is only a subsequent product.

A certain degree of systematization and coordination begins to emerge in pictographic signs. Primitive polyvalency which enabled a single sign to signify water, drinking, thirst, etc., is followed by a certain distinction between the parts of discourse, and sometimes several signs unite to produce a more complex meaning. For example, the sign for man and that for woman put together mean marriage; or, "day here" means today, "day behind" (past) means yesterday, and "day ahead" (after) means tomorrow. Reiteration of the same sign will have an augmentative value ("water! water! water!" means pouring rain). Special signs are adopted for comparatives and superlatives. A constant order in the arrangement of signs acquires a semantic function and, for example, numbers as a rule are placed after the noun to which they refer, adverbs after the verb, etc.

In conclusion, pictographic signs represent the initial stage of what was to evolve into grammatical and syntactical rules.

(f) *Conventional signs through natural evolution.*

As we have seen, various factors coincide over a long period of time causing signs to gradually lose their primitive expressive character and take on a conventional value.

We have also identified the main factors that determine such a transformation. In the first place, a change in circumstances, so that the natural association obvious at the moment of initial institution subsequently becomes unrecognizable (e.g., the uncovering of the head loses its original meaning of servile subjection to become a simple gesture of greeting).

Moreover, the characteristics of the material used (as we see by comparing the engravings of cuneiform signs with the strokes of Chinese signs), the practical need for simplification, and the taste for aesthetic stylization also contribute to the development of writing systems. In these semantic systems analytical distinction among the parts of discourse and observance of constant rules generally become more and more important. This group includes mainly ideographic writing systems, conventional mimetic languages used by the primitives and deaf-mutes, and especially phonetic languages.

(g) *Semantic systems through conventional institution.*

By this we mean sign systems deliberately established with the purpose of acting as a means of communication among those who recognize and refer to the accepted conventions. These signs may be considered as the rational and systematic development of chance mnemotechnic signs, though such development took place over thousands of years. In fact chance signs, as we have defined them (piles of stones and the like), were in use as far back as prehistoric times, whereas intentionally conventional systems are the recent product of intellectual civilization.

In this group we must distinguish between first degree systems, in which the sign indicates its meaning directly (e.g., numerical and geographical signs and conventional gestures), and second degree systems (such as syllabic and alphabetical writing systems, which designate phonemes, which in their turn indicate a representation or concept. In the first case it is enough to know the sign in order to understand the meaning; in the second, in addition to the sign, it is necessary to know the language to which the sign refers.

For our own purposes, however, we may group the two together as their signifying technique is the same. The most common systems of artificial signs include: telegraphic signs like those of the Morse code, telegraphic codes, cypher writing systems, alphabetical and numerical digital signs, algebraic symbols, musical notes, and finally, artificial languages such as Esperanto (however much their roots may be drawn from historical languages).

It is interesting to note how the semantic technique of artificial systems can be very similar to that of signs established by natural evolution. For example, the technique of a theoretically established cypher alphabet may be almost identical to that of the Roman alphabet, which evolved naturally from a previous pictographic writing system after having first passed through the Semitic alphabet.

This shows how in age-old historical institutions immanent rationality sometimes gives results similar to those obtained on the basis of well thought-out determination.

We do not deny, however, that there is some difference between the rationality of deliberately established semantic systems and the rationality of language and sign systems in general which have arisen spontaneously: artificial systems are obviously more rigorously rational, more abstract, less individualizing and less immediate and, therefore, aesthetically less evocative than natural systems. As their function is more rational, that is, more suited to communication purposes, artificial systems may be more helpful than natural systems in conceptually defining the essential and necessary characteristics of mnemotechnic systems.

8. Essential Characteristics of Mnemotechnic Systems

Grammatical Evolution and Perfecting of Semantic Rules.

Let us ask ourselves the question: What are the essential requirements of a semantic system for it to be rationally suited to communication?

As we have often observed, especially in relation to the rationalization of alphabetical writing systems, these requirements include the following:

(a) *Each sign must correspond to one meaning only.*

If a single sign has several meanings as in the case of the phonemes of historical languages—if, for example, in the case of numerical symbols, the same number arbitrarily signifies both *zero* and *nine*—its semantic function will obviously be compromised.

(b) *For each meaning there must be one sign only.*

In fact, a plurality of equivalent signs would complicate the system to no advantage.

To this we may add:

(c) *A distinction must be made between the phase of institution and that of semantic application.*

This aspect of semantic systems has sometimes made them resemble juridical systems which are characterized by the distinction between legislative power (the phase of institution) and executive power (the phase of interpretation), where the latter must respect that which is established by the former.

In art the two phases tend to merge into one, and in the case of directly expressive signs (such as the colors of painters or the sounds of musicians) artists do not have to respect a conventional code. In contrast, in conventional semantic systems single signs are not created during the phase of application. Consequently, certain scholars have declared that sign use is not arbitrary. But there is a misunderstanding here. The sign is "arbitrary" at the time of institution and not at the time of application.

(d) *There must be certainty about the code to be applied and perfect continuity from the time of institution to the time of application.*

For the interpretation of a text it is obvious that we must know what code should be applied.

The need for continuity derives from the very nature of the mnemonic act, in itself a product of continuity. When semantic continuity is interrupted—as occurred in Etruscan inscriptions—the system remains undecipherable for a certain period of time, if not for ever.

In cypher communications continuity is entrusted to a code or *key*, and to dictionaries and language texts in the historical languages.

(e) *There must be rules for the creation of new signs.*

As man needs to express an indefinite multiplicity of new meanings, a rational system cannot limit itself to assembling a given number of signs into a code.

As regards the most rational semantic system, that is, that made of numerical figures, Archimedes has the merit of having devised a numerical system in his *Arenarius,* based on numerical powers, with which a number of any size may be signified.

In language an analogous though not identical function is performed by grammatical rules. On the basis of the latter, new words are obtained by joining several roots; and various terms, expressing different relations or values of the same concept, may be formed from a single root.

By following the historical evolution of grammar in its general outlines, we are able to observe how methods for the creation of new expressions are gradually perfected. In order to signify the nominative and the accusative, the singular and the plural, the past and the future, the comparative and the superlative, etc., at first use is made of affective accentuation and pictographic expression, of word arrangement and repetitions, but subsequently small auxiliary words are formed (the "empty words" of the Chinese grammarians). The plural, for example, is formed by adding a symbol meaning "plus," the past tense by adding a symbol meaning "behind" or "yesterday," the future with a symbol meaning "I want" or "I must." Furthermore, new signs are created through compound words and metaphorical extension.

In inflected languages the small *empty* words merge with the *full* ones, giving rise to prefixes, suffixes, and desinences.

In certain artificial languages, for example Esperanto, an imperfect but extremely interesting attempt has been made at establishing a dictionary made of roots rather than of proper words, and then at indicating the rules for the formation of an indefinite number of words through the union and modification of those roots.

Other qualifications we might list seem less essential: the immediate recognizability of one sign with respect to another, the practicality of execution (painted signs are easier than engraved signs, etc.), durability of the material, etc.

The characteristics we have just listed are obvious and generally acknowledged. Nevertheless, it is important to define them carefully, bearing in mind the modest but essential nature of their function, so as not to confuse, as so often occurs, the semantic concept with the logical, aesthetic, or juridical concept, etc.

9. General Conclusions on Expressive Signs

Two Fundamental Classes: Pictographic Signs and Mnemotechnic Signs—Primitive Lack of Distinction between Artistic Expression and Semantic Communication.

On reexamining the various groups listed, we may observe that all expressive signs fall within one of two fundamental and contrasting classes: either the more or less directly expressive signs or the mnemotechnic signs.

Returning to the ancient problem of whether the relation between sign and meaning is natural or conventional and arbitrary, we could say that in the former class it is natural, and in the latter it is conventional.

However, the value that the two terms have for us is very different from that which it had for the ancients. That which is valid *by nature* was considered by the latter to be rational, while *convention* implied something inferior and designated lack of rationality. For our part we have attempted to define the rationality proper to conventional signs, and we believe that it is always symptomatic of some progress in critical inquiry when an aspect of spiritual activity (which was initially considered to be a shortcoming and negative) reveals a positive value: thus imagination, once only considered as having a negative influence on knowledge, subsequently proved to be the source of aesthetic value. Utilitarian interest, considered morally as a negative aspect of egoism, proved to be a category of economic value.

Aesthetic signs are a characteristic example of "natural" signs. The very sense impression of the sign becomes the content of the contemplative act, and because there is perfect unity between form and content, it would not be possible to express the same content through different devices.

An example of "arbitrary" signs is the purely mnemotechnic signs (like the knot in a handkerchief) in which the content of the mnemonic act is different from the sense impression produced by the sign, and therefore the same content may be remembered by different signs.

Artistic technique belongs to the first type, the technique of communication through conventional writing systems belongs to the second. At the dawn of civilization there was often a lack of distinction between expression and communication, between art and writing.

As evidence of this we may look at the residues of such lack of distinction and consider that the aesthetic element is still very important in the most ancient writing systems, on the one hand, and that common respect for traditional stylizations is of no small importance in the most ancient works of art, on the other.

Subsequently communication technique was increasingly distinguished from intuitive expression. Technique in the arts was to be considered coarse and defective when using stereotyped models, and was perfected the more it suited the individuality of the image. In contrast, communication through conventional signs was perfected as signs became static, impersonal, and univocal.

10. Characteristics of Linguistic Signs

Difficulty in Making Linguistic Signs Fall within One of the Two Fundamental Classes—Language Corresponds Imperfectly to the Demands of Semantic Rationality—Language is Inadequate for the Expression of Man's Inner Life.

If, on the basis of what we have said so far about expressive signs in general, we now examine the characteristics of linguistic signs, we will soon realize the difficulties involved in classifying them as belonging to either one or the other of our two basic categories, that is, as either aesthetic signs or conventional signs.

We have already seen that the words of language cannot be considered as immediately expressive aesthetic signs, because in order to understand them one must be familiar with the relative code, that is, the vocabulary and grammar. But the historical languages do not even satisfy the demands of conventional semantic systems.

In fact we stated:

(1) That all signs must correspond to one meaning only.

On the contrary, homonyms, that is, one and the same phoneme with different meanings, are very common in all languages, just as one and the same desinence is commonly used for different forms even in the rigorous grammar of Latin.

(2) That for every meaning there must be one sign only.

On the contrary, synonyms are common in language. Not only are they used to indicate varying shades in meaning, but they are also used indiscriminately. This will not seem strange if we consider that even in certain number systems, such as that used by the ancient Romans, the same number can be signified by different signs.

Similarly pleonastic grammatical forms in conjugations and declensions as well as superfluous morphological agreements are common in language.

For what reason—from a semantic point of view—is there more than one declination and one conjugation? Why are there so many irregular forms? Why is the use of diminutives, forms of endearment, and pejoratives, and in general prefixes and suffixes so varied and arbitrary?[1]

(3) That there must be a distinction between the time of institution and that of application.

In languages, such a distinction is valid in a somewhat elastic manner. The speaker is certainly faced with a certain *corpus iuris,* but on using it he modifies and renews it and his intervention does not exclude the creation of new lexical elements and forms.[2]

(4) That there must be certainty and consensus regarding the code.

On the contrary, there is nothing more uncertain than linguistic codes, based as they are on contrasting texts and dictionaries and above all on that uncertain, ever-changing, and wonderful code that *usage* is.

(5) That there must be fixed rules for the creation of new signs.

Here too, in the last analysis, linguistic legislation is entrusted rather to usage, a capricious tyrant that follows different rules in identical cases, sometimes maintaining the same signs and expedients over thousands of years, other times transforming or abandoning them after a few years.

We may thus conclude our analysis as follows: the semantic system of language only satisfies the requirements of both aesthetic signs and mnemotechnic signs very imperfectly. Indeed, in a certain sense we may assert that, because of its very nature, human language is incapable of giving adequate expression to most of the images and representations concerning inner life.

As already mentioned: if it were impossible for a painter to use colors, he might resort to indirect allusion by appealing to his listener's memory, but even the most accomplished literary skills will be inadequate to render and communicate the images of a painting or symphony.

Now there is no reason to believe that words signifying emotions and feelings such as hope, fear, etc., or sensations such as smells, tastes, and tactile impressions should be more suited to evoking the corresponding images. If such terms as "violet" or "orange" only express the corresponding images in an indirect and approximative fashion, we cannot see why such terms as "to love," "soft," "fearsome" should be more adequate.

In order to understand the difference between the direct experience of emotional life and its indirect description, it will suffice to think of dreams. When we dream, whether while sleeping or daydreaming, we do not express in words: "I'm trembling with the cold, I feel faint, I'm down in the dumps," but rather we relive the images of what we felt. The poet could achieve the painter's immediacy only if it were technically possible to fix his dream and convey the memory of his sensations and feelings to others through some kind of hypnotic suggestion.

From all this it would seem, therefore, that language is an extremely obscure and inadequate semantic system.

Moreover it may be observed that written language is even less efficacious than the spoken, for it is lacking in the gestures and positions of the body, the laughter, the tears, the cries, and infinite intonations of the voice that animate spoken language.

11. Expressive Function of Verbal Musicality

Poetic Language Transforms the Technical Medium into an Expressive Element—How in Certain Codes the Form of Writing Systems Becomes an Expressive Element—Expressive Importance of the Graphic Form in Chinese Literature.

We said that linguistic signs may be considered as indirect signs which do not depict the object but only recall it. But every medium can in its turn become the content and element of expression.

If I represent a child dressed in red against the green background of a meadow, the words "child," "dressed," "red," etc., are indirect devices, that is, they are stimuli for symbolizing representations different from the sounds of those words. But if I represent the cries, gossip, and talk of human beings, such sounds and words are no longer mnemotechnic signs for me, as their sound and meaning merge into a single image.[1] And if I represent myself in the act of speaking, while enjoying the sound and the rhythm of the expressions I pronounce, such expressions are one with my intuition.

Because of the need experienced by all artists of overcoming the material limitation of the technical medium, the poet listens to the sonorous sensuality of his own words and in this way reaches the immediate union of image and expression.

The function of rhythm, assonance, and rhyme is just this: to transform the technical medium that the word is into an expressive element.

Actors and actresses are also means used in communicating to the public scenes imagined by the playwright. They are imperfect means that render imperfectly that which the poet has imagined. But an author who is born and lives for the theatre, such as Molière or Goldoni, may already have in mind, in the very act of conceiving his work, the figure, gestures, and voice of the first lady or of a leading actor, so that what may have been considered as a technical means in fact becomes the expressive element.

The same thing may also happen, after all, with such technical media *par excellence* as are writing systems and typographical characters. For a thinker who is not a writer of poetry, the characters with which his book is printed are mere means, but for an aesthete such means may well acquire expressive importance. In carefully illustrated manuscripts, the form of the text acquires the dignity of art and often constitutes a single form of expression with the text.

That rhythm and sound have a similar function in poetry seems to be confirmed by that which occurred in classical Chinese literature. On studying its history we are struck by the excessive importance attributed by the Chinese man of letters to the beauty and style of the graphic signs. But considering that Chinese ideographic writing is not writing in our sense, that is, it does not imply a necessary reference to the words of a phonetic language but is a language in itself (in which signs have the same function as the expressive words of our own languages), one may suppose (if I may take the liberty of putting forward a hypothesis in a field which is not my own) that for the Chinese scholar, the graphic form of the sign is as intimately connected to its meaning as word meaning is to sound for us. Thus the harmony and beauty of graphic signs acquired for the Chinese an expressive importance comparable to the musicality of verse in our own poetry.

12. The Role of the Poetic Imagination in the Creation of Languages

Figurative and Imaginative Use of Preexisting Sounds—The Popular Imagination as a Creator of Images—But Only Expressions Accepted by Use Are Incorporated Into Language—The Semantic Criterion Is the Only Decisive One.

From the preceding considerations it is clear that the phonemes of language, especially those of poetic language and of language spoken in a state of excitement, not only have an indirect and conventional semantic function, but to a certain extent they also assume the function of aesthetic signs.

In the sonorous expression of our languages as well as in the pictographic expression of the graphic language of the Chinese, the technical means becomes in its turn the object of contemplation and becomes part of that union which includes intuition and expression.

But even leaving this aside, though language mainly has a semantic function, it may also be considered in its aesthetic or logical aspect. Let us now look at the importance of the aesthetic element in the creation and development of languages.

To this end, it is enough to observe how language is continually modified and enriched with new expressions. As we speak we seek out those linguistic signs that are most suited to that which we wish to express. We impress our own particular tone and accent upon words and sentences, we use certain words giving them a different meaning from the usual and sometimes we form expressions or even completely new words.[1]

In some cases new expressions have the character of deliberately established semantic conventions as in technical and scientific language or abbreviations formed from initials; but in most cases they are formed through the figurative use or imaginative combination and modification of existing expressions. Whoever molded the term "malingerer" to signify one who has escaped the dangers of the front, or "beau" for "young gallant," or "Latinorum" for doctoral or incomprehensible Latin, or "red tape" for cumbersome bureaucratic procedure not only created new linguistic *signs,* but also new expressions and images.

Sometimes these new expressions originate from the writer's name as in the word "Dadaism" (from the infantile expression "dada") invented by Tristan Tzara (1916) and still other words mentioned above. This is how a great part of the suggestive terminology of Freud's imaginative psychology was developed: *Oedipus complex, censored dream, weaning of a sick person,* etc.; but as a rule new expressions are created by the inexhaustible popular imagination.

Just as certain verses or certain images created by a poet often become the common heritage of cultured people, in the same way certain proverbs, sayings, and expressions created by the "genius (or special vocation) of language" become the heritage of the whole nation.

On going over the history of words and sentences we immediately become aware of the part played by need and of the part played by aesthetic taste.

This is where Croce's doctrine is correct, for he identifies art and language, and aesthetics and linguistics, which is of no small account. But Croce's doctrine is mistaken when he holds that aesthetic activity is the only one involved in the creation of language, disregarding the special importance of semantic activity.[2]

Semantic activity creates a system of signs which are not directly expressive but which act as conventional signs, even if conventionality is not the result of deliberately established institution.

If it is true that speakers continually create new images it is also true that only a minimal part of these new expressions come to form part of the common linguistic heritage. Now, what is the necessary qualification for the transformation of these expressions from fleeting individual expedients into living cells of the linguistic organism? Obviously this: that they be favorably received by use. All the most sensible observations of grammarians, men of letters and people of good taste, are vain: when the new expression is welcomed by use it becomes a part of language, and when it is not accepted, it disappears.

Years ago a kind of referendum took place in the University of Rome's newspaper which aimed at substituting some other word for the unaesthetic but successful term "ordinario" (full professor) used to signify one who holds a chair. A great number of more suitable terms were proposed from various parts, not without excellent historical and philological motivations and sometimes with refinement of taste, but none was accepted by use; so, despite bad taste, everybody continues saying "*ordinario* of classical philology," "*ordinario* of rational mechanics," and we all understand what is meant.

Even grammatical errors are legitimated by use. The first to have said or written "vota socialista" (vote socialist) probably did so because he did not know how to speak correctly. Today everybody says or writes "vota communista," "vota liberale," etc., and the expression is well-received as an elliptic adverbial expression not without effectiveness.

There are many expressions that today seem unpleasant and hardly in conformity with the characteristics of the Italian language. For example, "post-telegrafonici" (an expression which includes what in English is designated with the terms "post-office clerk" and "telegraph operators" and which instead almost sounds like "those who come after the telegraph operators"), or—as one can read in a column in the Rome "Messaggero" —*Colloqui autotranviari* (which could mean trams talking to themselves), but good or bad as they may be, if they are accepted by use they will quite rightly become part of the Italian language. Years ago Umberto Saba pointed out to me that the Italian "autobus" is a grammatical error, for the "bus" of "omnibus" is not at all a desinence meaning "coach." He was right, and yet the word has become part of usage and has now entered the Italian vocabulary. To give another example: according to what they tell me, the Italian word "titoismo" (as opposed to leninismo, stalinismo, etc.) was invented by the Slovenes of Trieste who had little experience in Italian linguistic usage. In Italian, in fact, we do not say "cattolicoismo," "cesareismo," "petrarcaismo," "platoneismo," or "tomaismo"; nonetheless it is highly probable that use will prevail, that the grammatical error will become the rule, and that the correct expression "titismo" will sound like an incongruity.

But to say "a given term has become part of usage" implies that a meaning has been attributed to that term through tacit consent, or convention, and this is exactly what happens in every tacit or explicit semantic invention.

The fact that a new linguistic term does not become part of language until it is accepted by use means that the necessary and sufficient qualification of linguistic creation is neither aesthetic, nor logical, nor historical (which may represent legitimate concomitant factors), but rather pure semantic convention.

13. Antithesis between Semantic and Emotional Requirements in Language and Writing

---

Example of the Language Adopted in Israel—And of Jewish Writing—Abundance of Polyphony and Homophony in Hieroglyphic and Ideographic Scripts—Analogous Phenomena in the Writing of Modern Man—Examples from French and English—Drawbacks of Irrational Spelling—Reasons Given to Justify It—Rationality of German, Spanish, and Italian Spelling—The Rationalization of Writing Systems and the Concept of Semantic Rationality—Confirmation of the Antithesis between Semantic Perfection and Aesthetic Requirements—Rationality in Linguistic Formations and the Problem of Finality in Nature—Creative Ingeniousness and Imperfect Rationality of Natural Formations—Contrasting Characteristics of Natural Formations and Intellectual Constructions.

A certain degree of antithesis may be observed between semantic demands and what have been called the concomitant factors. Where emotions have less weight, semantic demands make themselves felt in an almost absolute manner. For example, numerical cyphers and, in general, the symbolism of the mathematicians represent perfect sematic systems such as would satisfy all the needs listed above; this too was one of the reasons why certain scholars subsequently confused semantic rationality with logical rationality. In writing systems established intentionally, such as the Braille alphabet for the blind or Morse Code, semantic rationality also asserts itself without the interference of emotional considerations.

On the other hand, in spoken languages and in historical writing systems there is antagonism between contrasting requirements. A typical example of the prevalence of historical and emotional motivations over semantic rationality is provided by current events in the state of Israel.

Certain citizens from different parts of the world who spoke different languages up to the moment in question felt the need to adopt a common language. Three solutions seemed to be the most rational and practical:

(1) "Yiddish,"[1] or a language already used by millions of Jews from Eastern Europe, a language which has an age-old history behind it and which has produced excellent literary works and poetry, even in recent times;

(2) German, or the cultural language most widely known and most easily understood by the majority of citizens;

(3) English, which would present notable economic and political advantages, and which is already acquiring prestige as an international language.

But the reasons of the heart prevailed and the ancient, solemn language of the Bible was adopted, that is, a language as difficult to learn as it is inappropriate for the satisfaction of everyday needs in modern society. It was chosen and is today fluently spoken by most of the population and by all the young people, overcoming difficulties greater than those that Italians would have to face should they get it into their heads to adopt Latin as their everyday language.

More significant still was their choice of a writing system. For practical reasons it would have been advisable to write modern Hebrew in a Latin alphabet, opportunely adapted (not very easy no doubt, but not impossible). Instead the choice fell upon the ancient Hebrew script which goes back to the period of the Achaemenids. It still preserves many of the characteristics of a primitive syllabic writing system, and its characters seem more suited to being engraved with the chisel or stylus rather than being outlined with pens.

Given that, as a rule, almost all the vowel signs are missing, quite a number of difficulties and uncertainties emerge.

If in an Italian text we were to find, for example, "mgrh" we could read "magra," or "magre," or "migra," or "megera" trusting to the context for the right choice.

If we were to express the initial lines of the *Divine Comedy* in this sort of writing, we would write roughly the following:

Nl mzv dl kmin di nvstrh vth
    mi rtrvbi pr vnh slvh vskvrh
    Kh lh drth vih arh smrith.[2]

The problem of the rationalization of Hebrew writing was debated at length: for our part, we do not have the competence necessary for deciding on the extent to which its obvious semantic irrationality is counteracted by aspects of a different nature.

It is only natural that numerous cases of the two opposite pathological phenomena should be found in ancient writing: several signs for a single meaning (or sound) or a single sign for several meanings (or sounds). For example, in hieroglyphic and ideographic scripts a given sign that may have initially signified "eye" may subsequently mean by extension "sight," "wakefulness," "surveillance," "science," "power," etc. In the transition to phonetic writing systems the symbol "eye" could therefore come to signify the syllable "eye" but also the syllable "si" (sight) or "wa" (wakefulness) or "sur" (surveillance), etc.

In cuneiform writing a single sign may represent fifteen or even twenty different phonemes.

The opposite phenomenon may also have an analogous cause. In the transition from ideography to phonetism the symbol "camel" could have been chosen to indicate the syllable "ca"; but at other times "caribou" or "castle," etc.[3] were chosen, so that we end up with a multiplicity of symbols for the same phoneme.

Stranger still may seem the fact that we should encounter these semantic inconsistencies in the writing systems of the most modern civilized people. They generally derive from the more tenacious conservative spirit of the written word as compared with the spoken, so that from a semantic viewpoint irrational spelling is often a reminder of ancient pronunciation. In French, for example, the sound "s" may be symbolized with *s* (savoir), *ss* (chasse), *c* (cinq), *ç* (ça), *sc* (acquiescer), *x* (dix), *t* (nation); and the sound "k" with *c, q, k, ch, cc, cq*. In the same language we may have double letters in writing even when the double consonant sound is not pronounced, for example, "sottise," "souffrir," etc.

The phoneme "sên" can be written in more than eight different ways: "sain" (healthy), "saint" (saint), "sein" (breast), "seing" (signature, signum), "cinq" (five), "ceint" (past participle of "ceindre"), "sin" (as in e.g., sincère), "Sains" (geographical name), etc.[4]

Things are even worse in the English writing system which, from a semantic viewpoint, is one of the most irrational in the world, second perhaps only to Tibetan.

Its forty-four alphabetical sounds are signified by more than five hundred symbols and combinations of letters, and the same symbol may be read in a number of different ways; for example the syllable "ough" is read as /u:/ in "through," as /ou/ in "though," as /ɔ:/ in "thought," "ought," "brought," as /au/ in "plough," as /ʌ/ in "rough," "enough." It is immediately obvious that many inconveniences derive from this state of affairs. Many foreigners who have learned English from technical and scientific handbooks know how to read it but do not understand it when spoken, just as many workmen who emigrated to English-speaking countries know how to speak the language but not how to read it. Moreover, the great quantity of homophones make consultation in a dictionary difficult, so that for each entry compilors often resort to the complicated expedient of enumerating all words similar in sound and different in spelling.

The irrationality of writing systems is sometimes the cause of inconveniences from a historical point of view as well. It often prevents us from establishing how a given word found in ancient scripts was pronounced, so that we are unable to form an adequate idea of ancient poetic harmony. For example, we do not know how "ertha," "erdha," "erda," "thri," "dhri," "dri," etc., were pronounced in ancient high German.

Numerous proposals have been made of course to rationalize French and English spelling, but for various reasons they have never been accepted.

One of the most plausible reasons is this: on reading a sentence in French or English we immediately notice a series of words that are similar in pronunciation but written differently (e.g., "tant" and "temps," "il devait" and "ils devaient"), an advantage which would be lost with rationalization. Against such an argument one could observe that this "advantage" is not active in the spoken language, and no serious inconveniences result. Furthermore, the function of our writing systems should be that of rendering the sounds of words by breaking them down into their alphabetical elements, and not of rendering a complex syllabic phoneme, as occurred instead in archaic scripts.

Historical and etymological reasons seem to carry greater weight. If "sañ" were the written form in French for "sang," "cent," "sens," and "cens," the etymological reference to "sanguis," "centum," "sensus," and "census" would be lost, which would make recognition of these words by non-French speakers less easy.[5]

However, the main obstacle that stands in the way of a radical rationalization of writing systems, even today, is of an aesthetic order. In fact a page in French or English, written in the glottologic alphabet, would initially prove to be repellent to the eye and even illegible for anyone used to traditional spelling.

The situation is different for German, Spanish, and Italian spelling systems, for they are among the most rational. In Italian it would suffice to introduce two signs for the c (pronounced as in the English chip and cat) and for the g (pronounced as in the English geranium and goat), two for the s and the z (soft and hard), one for sc (pronounced as in the English shore) and for gn (pronounced as in the English Kenya), and to abolish the h and the g and a few other expedient forms.[6]

Had there not been far more serious and urgent problems to deal with at the present moment, one of our Education ministers could have easily introduced an orthographic reform such as to make Italian writing a model of simplicity and rationality, and we believe that we would not have to fear greater inconveniences than those which came to be verified when the Renaissance spelling of such words as "iustitia," "scripto," "extrahere," "hoggi," "excellentia," "ynno," "thosco," etc.[7] was abandoned.

We have dwelt upon these facts and concepts in order to impress them on the readers and on ourselves, for we believe they can clarify two problems which are not without importance for our own purposes.

The first concerns the very concept of semantic function and rationality. This is anything but a difficult concept, but it has often been misunderstood and badly defined, thus giving rise to confusion and error in relation to problems of logic as much as to those of semantics.[8]

From our observations on writing systems it would seem that semantic rationality substantially limits itself to the restriction of homonyms and synonyms. Therefore, the institution of a perfect semiological system would seem to be a very different and more modest affair than the institution of a system of logico-mathematical concepts.

The second problem, upon which these facts and concepts may throw some light, is that of the antithesis between semantic perfection and aesthetic and emotional demands in language.

We spoke above about the *poverty* of language, pointing out the deficiencies proper to this expressive instrument; but we confess that after having written those pages we were tempted to act like Socrates in *Phaedrus* who, after having rattled off some very nice arguments to demonstrate the uselessness of and harm caused by love, felt the need to purify himself and to implore forgiveness from God for his blasphemy.

All we need do is remember the verses of a poet or the pages of a great prose writer or simply listen to the picturesque spoken language of the common people to experience the expressive power of that divine and human institution called language.

We do not mean to say by this that the poverty and deficiencies mentioned above were invented by us; on the contrary, we are convinced that they are effective imperfections inherent in the very nature of language—semantic imperfections which nonetheless are often overcome and counteracted by values and merits of different kinds.

If semantic perfection is successfully contradicted by emotional and aesthetic aspects[9] even in alphabetical writing systems, which are formed of no more than a modest and circumscribed system of a few dozen signs, how much more likely is this to be true of such an infinitely more complex system as spoken language.

If we consider the unpremeditated and non-individual way in which language is formed, what should surprise us are not the deficiencies of language, but rather its rationality. The scholar who meditates on the origin and essence of this human activity often experiences a similar impression to that provoked by the "miracles of nature."

How were primitive men (who did not yet possess a rational device enabling them to come to agreements) able to create such a marvellous system of rationally connected signs? We encounter analogous and even more mysterious problems in each phase of our studies on nature: how is it possible for bees and termites to set up such wise political societies?

As is obvious, we are dealing with the ancient problem of the finality of nature, out of which metaphysicians have construed the teleological argument (a problem dealt with by Kant in his *Critique of Judgement* and which Darwin formulated in naturalistic terms).

It might prove instructive to set the problem of immanent linguistic rationality alongside the broader issue just mentioned, for it is certainly easier to become aware of our activity in the creation of language than of unconscious creative forces operating in nature.

The contrast we have observed in language between a genial structure and numerous imperfections and deficiencies also emerges not only in institutions created by primitive man, but also in the social life of insects as well as in the very conformation of living organisms.

If we consider even superficially the structure, for example, of the human eye, the comparison with a camera (the crystalline lens corresponds to the photographic lens, the iris to the diaphragm and the retina to the sensible film) is spontaneous.

But here too, if on the one hand we ask ourselves with religious wonder how it was possible for a similar apparatus to be formed (which, owing to its complexity in structure and function and capacity of adaptation and recovery, does not find an equal among human achievements), on the other hand we may observe a number of deficiencies and almost a generous neglect of mechanical rationality.

Certainly no optician from the Zeiss laboratories would have constructed such a uselessly complex system of lenses as that formed by the cornea, the aqueous humor, the crystalline lens, and the vitreous humor, and nobody would have ever thought of using such inappropriate material as albumin, mucoid, physiological humor, and the like in the construction of lenses, just as no intelligent entrepreneur would have put on the market so many faulty apparatuses as the eyes of the far-sighted, the short-sighted, of persons suffering from astigmatism, etc., and eyes so easily weakened by trachoma, glaucoma, cataract, etc.

According to a fine observation made by Bergson, one of the most characteristic differences between the way animal nature operates and human behavior does is this: animals mainly reach their objectives by using their own organisms as the instrument and means of production (the spider spins its own spittle into a web, bees and termites use a secretion from their bodies as architectural material, etc.), whereas man has always availed himself of external instruments and materials, from the primitive tools of stone-age man to modern machinery.

If we compare the two most important existing semantic systems, that is, language, which arose at a time when man was still steeped in animal life, and writing, which developed in a more advanced age, we will note an analogous difference.

Mimetic and phonetic language still have the character of spontaneous natural productions. Expressive signs are produced directly by the organism itself, like the web of the spider and the wax of bees. On the other hand, writing is engraved in stone or marked out in some other external material.

We may say of language according to Schelling, that which is true of all natural organisms: on the one hand, they seem to proceed in a blindly irrational manner, but, on the other, we cannot deny their immanent rational finality.[10]

To sum up we may say that language is a sign system that has developed naturally over thousands of years from preceding pictographic expressions; that in language, however, immediately expressive elements such as the tone and inflections of the voice merge with the semantic elements, and the emotional and aesthetic requirements are added to the semantic. As in all institutions with roots in primitive societies, individual contributions are eventually submerged by collective activity and, more than a premeditated rationality, that which emerges is the immanent and unconscious rationality of a natural process.

14. Artificial Languages

Natural Diffidence in the Face of Such Experiments—Esperanto—Problems in Linguistics and the Comparative Study of Artificial Languages.

The need to communicate among people who speak different languages has led to the partially spontaneous and partially artificial development of auxiliary languages: the *lingua franca,* or common language, used for commerce among Europeans, Turks, and Arabs;[1] the so-called *creole* languages, which arose from European languages spoken by some peoples of color; *broken English,* used in West Africa; *pidgin English,* used in the far East, and many others based on Portuguese, Spanish, and French.[2]

Numerous projects for the development of international auxiliary languages were proposed in a completely different context, especially in the nineteenth century, when Latin was losing its function as a universal scientific language. Not only did these projects aim at creating a communication system that was supranational, but they also aimed at greater rationality, thus avoiding the excesses, disorders, and abuses of historical languages.

It is only natural that a man with a certain degree of culture should feel an instinctive aversion toward such experiments. It is as though he were dealing with someone who wishes to build a woman in plastic in spite of the fact that so many beautiful women already exist in the world. We confess that a few years ago our own attitude on the matter would also have been wholly negative. How can we think of replacing—we would have said—a live language, which has acquired meaning and flavor through the centuries-old cooperation between poets and writers and through the unlimited ingeniousness of the common people, with an artificial product?

But since it is not correct to give too much weight in conceptual questions to our likes and dislikes, we have tried to orientate ourselves better and form a more documented idea of the value and meaning of those experiments.

The first thing that strikes us is the great number of such projects and the seriousness and authority of many of the scholars who have concerned themselves with the problem.[3]

Just as the creole languages are simplifications of the traditional languages, in the same way Leibniz had already proposed a kind of creole Latin for international use. For his part, Peano had created and used his *Latino sine flexione (1909)*, which presented the advantage of being easily understood by anyone with a certain degree of culture, though it remains inferior to Merlin Coccaio's macaronic Latin from the viewpoint of aesthetic value.

The fact that there exist numerous projects tells us that the problem is of great topical interest. Nevertheless we remain perplexed, for while the general aim of such projects is that of performing a unifying function, they risk having the opposite effect. In fact, should we have to choose an auxiliary language from the historical languages, we would be faced with not more than six or seven possible contenders; on the other hand, should we have to choose from the artificial languages, we would be faced with more than fifty projects.[4]

The first project to have had a noteworthy application was Msgr. J. M. Schleyer's *Volapük*,[5] which in a short period of time was accepted by several thousands of supporters, though after no more than a decade it declined and was surpassed by other projects.

The greatest success was attained by Esperanto. It was proposed in 1887 by the physician and learned Polish Jew L. L. Zamenhof and very soon gained the support of important personalities and of diverse international boards and associations.[6] It became increasingly widespread between 1924 and 1936, but, having fallen out of favor with Stalin as well as with Fascism, it was eventually banned by Hitler in Germany as well as in the occupied countries. After the Second World War the movement flourished again attracting a considerable number of supporters in the Western world as much as in the communist countries.[7]

The success of Esperanto is due to the fact that it is efficient and easy to use. For a person of average culture a few hours will suffice in fact to learn the grammar, about ten days to understand it completely, and a couple of months to speak and write it correctly.

That Esperanto does not lack in expressive effectiveness would seem to emerge from the large number of literary masterpieces which have been translated, and which, according to the experts, succeed in conveying the original meaning often less inadequately than other translations.[8]

The history of artificial languages may prove useful for anyone wishing to form a well-founded concept of the nature and essence of language, for it almost enables us to observe *in vitro* the way in which a language comes into existence and develops.[9]

For example, to clarify the problem whether it is useful to consider language as a system of expressive signs or as the creation of aesthetic images, it will help to ask ourselves what Dr. Zamenhof's aims were when he elaborated his project.

He certainly did not intend to offer us a collection of the images populating his imagination (which is the task of poets and artists), but rather a semantic system (i.e., a code of systematically coordinated signs) suited to expressing our representations and concepts with the greatest possible evidence and precision.

The goals and methods proposed by Msgr. Schleyer, Dr. Zamenhof, and others who elaborated similar projects correspond perfectly to the procedure adopted when a group of people arrange to use a given semantic system, such as a telegraphic code or a system of arithmetic or algebraic symbols.

The common qualifications necessary for the formation of such systems include: a code containing a certain number of signs and their meanings (vocabulary), rules for joining the various signs (syntax), and rules for the creation of new signs so that codified signs may always be modified in the same way (grammar).

Naturally projects for auxiliary languages must also take account of other requirements such as euphony, intuitive immediacy, ease of learning, etc. (which are all active elements in the spontaneous development of historical languages also).

To conclude our considerations we should remember that whether a given auxiliary language asserts itself or not does not depend on the advantages it presents or on its intrinsic merits as much as on the will to adopt it. In the final analysis, this will determine whether a given project will simply remain a project or become an effectively spoken language.[10] This, too, is proof of the conventional character of linguistic signs.

Before continuing our inquiry, we will now recapitulate what has so far been expounded in the second book of this volume. We resolved to develop a general linguistics able to describe the essence and nature of language, and the relationships between linguistic activity and the other fundamental activities of man.

On considering language as a system of expressive signs, we felt the need to define the concept of "sign" by analyzing the constitutive elements of aesthetic synthesis.

The aesthetic image arises from the transfiguration of our sense and emotional impressions accomplished by memory. Therefore, artistic creation requires the lyrical intensity of the passions on the one hand, and the serenity of recollection on the other: romantic art corresponds to the predominance of emotional intensity; classical art to that of contemplative serenity.

This analysis has enabled us to explain the function of artistic technique: in painting and music technique consists of the ability to arrange the stimuli best suited to stirring up those impressions which, once received by memory, will form the image.

But since a great part of our inner world cannot be communicated in this direct fashion, man was forced to make use of indirect expressive devices, resorting to the use of *signs* able to elicit the memory of our experiences. This is how language arose.

Passing on to the classification of expressive signs we identified the following types: immediate aesthetic signs, immediate conceptual signs, chance pictographic signs, chance mnemotechnic signs, traditional pictographic signs, conventional signs established through natural evolution, and conventional signs established through premediated institution. Each belongs to one of two fundamental classes: immediately expressive signs (aesthetic and pictographic) and mnemotechnic signs. The function of the former is based on sense impressions received during mnemonic contemplation, and the function of the latter is based on the act of memory which must re-evoke previously experienced impressions.

15. Logic and Semantics
(Thought and Word)

All Semantic Systems Are in Some Way Languages—
Thought Does Not Exist without Symbols.

We have examined the relation between aesthetics and semantics, that is, between artistic activity that produces images and the activity that forms expressive signs, and we saw that semantics is a constitutive component of aesthetic activity. Signs do not create images but serve to fix them, in other words, to represent them and to communicate them to others.

The sign, we said, is a stimulus predisposed in such a way as to produce in us and in others a given representation, directly or by means of conventional associations. The sign therefore has an instrumental function, and the ability of arranging expressive signs constitutes the technique of the arts.

We shall now examine the relation between semantics and logic, between symbols and concepts, or, to adopt a traditional terminology between words and thought. To avoid misunderstandings we should specify that by the term *word* or *language* we intend *any* group *whatsoever* of signs or symbols. Instead of spoken words we might be dealing with graphic signs, such as Chinese ideograms and algebraic symbols, or mimetic signs or musical notes and the like.[1]

Neglect of such an obvious specification has been the cause of many useless discussions; by language some intended only phonetic language, while others understood it in a broader sense. That we are perfectly capable of thinking without using phonetic words even mentally is certain. It will suffice to think of deaf-mutes. If the deaf-mutes have not been instructed in phonetic language but master a well developed mimetic language, they are still able to reason and carry out difficult calculations.[2] The development of thought does not require the use of spoken words, but it does necessarily require the use of expressive signs. Gerard Harry describes with excitement the scene when, after many fruitless attempts, he succeeded in making the blind and deaf-mute Helen Keller understand the value and use of expressive signs[3] "Ce jour là le voile se déchira qui lui cachait l'univers."

Even before that memorable day Keller in some way represented her impressions and sentiments to herself. She had some vague inkling not only of the sensations of hot and cold, of taste, etc., but also of hunger, fear, of her volitive impulses, etc. What she lacked was the means of fixing those fleeting and imprecise representations for herself as well as for communication with others.

If it is only a matter of recalling concrete representations, such as animals, trees, or houses, conventional signs are less important. It will suffice to remember just a few of the representations used by Keller which, somewhat schematized, acted as symbols for similar representations. But as soon as we pass from more concrete perceptions to more abstract concepts and judgments, the necessity of signs becomes obvious. How could we formulate the judgment, "I like sweet things more than bitter things" if we did not have conventional signs at our disposal to fix those representations? Even more obvious is the necessity of conventional signs in logico-mathematical thought. Just to mentally formulate the concept of a number or of equivalence we need symbols. It is not possible to formulate even the most simple mathematical judgment such as: "four is greater than three," "two is smaller than four," "two plus one is equal to three," etc., without making use of symbols. Conventional meanings of signs must be respected as the development of logical thought proceeds, as we pass from the more simple concepts to the more complex. There should not be one sign with different meanings nor several signs for one and the same meaning; in other words the law of semantic rationality must be observed.

16. The "Improper" Identification of Semantics with Logic

In Peirce—In G. Calogero—Reasons for Such Identifications—Semantic Coherence, A Necessary But
Not the Only Condition for Logical Thought—Examples of Semantic Non-Observance—Examples of
Logical Incoherence—Progress in the Logico-Mathematical Disciplines Does Not Consist in Semantic
Perfection.

The fact that logical reasoning cannot be formulated without using symbols and without accepting conventions has persuaded certain scholars that the essential condition of all logico-mathematical reasoning is no more than this: that established conventions should be respected, in other words, that semantics and logic, words and thought are to be recognized as the same thing.

This identification, which is also suggested by the ambivalence of the Greek term "logos," was perhaps implicit in Parmenides' conviction that what is, what can be thought, and what can be said are the same thing.[1] It also led to the peculiar idea that just as some judgments and concepts are true and others false, in the same way there exist "true words" and "false words."[2]

Language was commonly considered by the grammarians of Port Royal, and in general by the Cartesian school, only from the abstract and rational point of view. Leibniz, falling under the Cartesian influence or, rather, in-duced by the same rationalistic mentality, also worked in the same direction. Of the authors that are closer to us, Hilbert is one of the scientists who most contributed to confirming the identification of logic with semantics. His stud-ies have been of fundamental importance for the logical systematization of mathematics.

In order to avoid the difficulties that arise from considering the objects of mathematics as either real or ideal, he resorted to extreme formalism, stating that the objects of the theory of numbers are solely *signs*. In this way the whole of mathematics becomes a sort of sublime chess game in which conventionally fixed *signs* are moved in the place of pawns in accordance with accepted rules.[3]

The identification of logic with semantics was also supported by Peirce who exercised a vast influence on a great part of American and world thought.

We cannot think, he says, without signs . . . all and any thought is essentially a sign and precisely a sign of a linguistic character.[4] What is most important is that his "semiotic tables" propose a classification of signs and at the same time of all possible judgments.

In Italy, Guido Calogero formulated the same identification of logic with semantics, working in another direction. What is traditionally called logic he says, in reality is no more than crystallized language. Analytical logic is no more than a collection of verbal schemes which, on the basis of the presupposed constant identity in the meaning of certain words, studies the necessary semantic implications that arise from the relation of such words to others. For this reason Calogero considers the principle of non-contradiction, the foundation of analytical logic, as a semantic principle that only concerns the use of words, and not as the principle and norm regulating thought.

One of the reasons why, in Calogero's opinion, the principle of non-contradiction cannot be considered as the norm of correct thinking is this: a norm—that is, a precept—only makes sense if there exists the possibility of not respecting it. For example, the precept "do not steal" presupposes that theft is possible and that there are people who break the rules. But since no one can think that which is contradictory, that presumed norm supposedly dictates what everyone does and must not do.

According to this line of reasoning when to exhort someone we say, "be a man," that person could reply "I am and will be a man in any case"; but it is our intention to remind him of his duty of being *more of a man,* in other words of developing to a higher degree the qualities we believe essential in a man. In the same way when we say to someone, "be logical," we wish to exhort that person to exploit the essential qualities of the human mind to a greater degree. Certainly nothing of that which thought concretely thinks is contradictory, but often we believe we have thought something without actually having done so, that is, we did not think it out thoroughly and with perfect coherence.

When Kant asserted, on the one hand, that the principle of cause is an intellectual concept which only applies to phenomena and never to the noumenal object, and on the other, that the noumenon is the *cause* of phenomenal appearances, his thoughts were not contradictory, but rather he did not think at all, in other words, he did not think out his thoughts in their organic wholeness.

It seems to me that Calogero's argument disregards one of the most important principles of philosophical logic, one upon which Hegel particularly insisted: the reality of our thinking is not *being* but *becoming,* and, in the becoming of thought, a finality, that is, a goal to reach, a "must be" is always implicit. What we call unsound reasoning, error, or evil is never something positive, but always indicates the non-being, the non-accomplishment of a task that should have been accomplished.[5]

In Calogero's opinion, all that Aristotle achieved with his logic was to give a full and systematic expression to the need to establish some fixed points in the linguistic game. Aristotle's so-called logic only gives us rules concerning language, that is, it fulfills an essentially grammatical function.[6]

Calogero's position is interesting because it is similar and nevertheless, in a certain sense, contrary to the position taken up by Peirce and subsequently by Neopositivism. Both Peirce and the Neopositivists tend to overestimate semantics, identifying it with logic, whereas Calogero tends to undervalue analytical logic by lowering it to the level of semantics.[7]

Let us attempt to get a better understanding of the reasoning behind such identifications. As we have already said, in order to utter even the simplest of mathematical judgments a whole series of semantic conventions are necessary. To assert, for example, that $3 + 2 = 5$ we must respect the convention that the sign $+$ means addition (with all the implications of this concept), that $=$ means equality, that 2 means $1 + 1$, that 3 means $2 + 1$, etc. If in the course of our argument we were to change conventionally established meaning without realizing it and attribute, for example, the meaning *"one"* to the sign 2, or the meaning "greater than" to the sign $=$, our judgment would prove to be false. But if we remain faithful to established conventions, then it seems that the judgment must automatically prove to be correct.

In accordance with Hume and not with Kant, modern epistemology has acknowledged that all mathematical judgments are analytical, and that what is requested of the mathematician is essentially this: that he should not fall into contradiction and that he should remain coherent with his premises.[8]

But since, on the other hand, no one can think that which is contradictory, it was concluded that if semantic coherence is fulfilled, so is conceptual coherence, and that semantics and logic are one and the same thing.

This false conclusion was also formulated because there was no clear conception of the semantic essence of language, of the prerequisites proper to all semantic systems, and of the meaning of "semantic coherence": concepts which we have endeavored to clarify in the preceding pages.

Semantic coherence is a necessary but not sufficient condition of logical thought. In fact it is based on the pure continuity of memory, while logico-mathematical coherence requires coherence of concepts. The difference is evident if we compare two cases, one in which error derives from semantic incoherence, the other in which it derives from conceptual incoherence.

As Goethe did not have perfect knowledge of the Italian language, he interpreted Manzoni's words "i percossi valli" (the attacked trenches) as meaning "le percorse valli" (the travelled valleys). This is an example of semantic non-observance and to correct his error it would have been enough to show him a dictionary of the Italian language.

Errors deriving from logical incoherence can be discovered a priori solely on the basis of reasoning, but semantic deficiencies can only be discovered by documenting them. When certain theologians support simultaneously the theses of predestination and of the freedom of human actions, they are making an error at the conceptual level and not in vocabulary, an error of logic and not of semantics. Or, to give an example from the history of mathematics: the Pythagoreans sinned against logic if it is true that they wished to remain faithful to the corpuscular concept of numbers (as a set of "calculi" or "psafoi" or extensive monads) even after having discovered that if each of the two sides of a right-angle isosceles triangle were equal to one, the hypotenuse would be equal to the root of two; this root cannot be expressed with a given number of monads, not even if we were to admit that the monad is subdivisible in its turn into a certain number of smaller monads (i.e., not even using fractional numbers).

Indeed, to correct this error it would not have sufficed to consult a dictionary of the Greek language, but rather the very concept of number would have had to be changed, freeing it from all references to corpuscles.

The difference between semantic value and logical value is also confirmed by the way progress comes about in the two different fields: progress in logico-mathematical disciplines does not simply limit itself to linguistic and semantic perfection (i.e., to the elimination of homonyms, synonyms, and similar inconveniences) but rather is obtained by elaborating new abstractions and new concepts, by discovering new identities, by passing from a logically imperfect definition to a more rigorous one, by reducing an antecedent theorem to a special case of a more general one, and so forth.

If the elaboration of mathematical concepts were to take place solely on the basis of semantic principles, the great mathematician would only need to be gifted with a broad, tenacious, and exact documentary memory, and not also with a brilliant intuition for unsuspected conceptual relations and with deductive rigor—qualities that are rare and to our eyes worthy of admiration.

17. The Conventional Character of Semantic Systems and of Logical Systems

Logical Postulates Were Described as Conventional to Avoid the Difficulties of Innatism and Empiricism—Logical Postulates Are Not Set *ad libitum* But Have an Operational Justification—Requirements of the Semantic Criterion and of the Logical Criterion Are Different—Precedents of the Semantics of Neopositivism—The Semantics of Tarski—Scientific and Philosophical Interest in Rectifying Methodological Errors.

Confusion between semantic conventionality and the conventionality of logical postulates also contributed to bringing about the illusion that semantics and logic were identical.

As is well-known, modern logicians and mathematicians consider the premises (definitions, axioms, and postulates) at the basis of logical systems as arbitrarily fixed conventions. Given that the premises of a semantic system as much as those of a logico-mathematical system are accepted by convention, and furthermore that in both cases the validity of later propositions uniquely depends upon their faithfulness to the accepted premises, it has been concluded that the two systems are one and the same thing.

It is not difficult to recognize that such a conclusion is the result of a misunderstanding based on external similarities. In order to convince ourselves of this it will suffice to think about the reasoning behind the creation of the conventionalistic theory of mathematical postulates. After the criticism of Hobbes, Leibniz, and others, it was no longer possible to accept the Cartesian concept of the "intuitive evidence" of postulates. On the other hand, to consider the latter as being drawn from experience presented a number of difficulties. By experimental truths one intended provisional empirical observations such as, for example, that animals living in water are oviparous. These are not necessary truths and must be abandoned as soon as a new observation proves them wrong (e.g., in our case as soon as we realize that dolphins are viviparous). Thus it was not easy to put a proposition of this kind on the same level as the propositions of mathematics.

To avoid the difficulties of innatism and of immediate evidence, as much as the difficulties involved in considering axioms and postulates as simple empirical observations, such axioms and postulates are viewed as being accepted by convention. This conception was later consolidated by the appearance of new mathematical systems that did away with one or the other of the traditional postulates.

But how and why are those given "conventions" chosen and not others? To answer this question we will consider three cases:

(1) Let us exclude the transitive property of equality, accepting, by convention, that if A = B, and B = C, C is not equal to A. Once this has been accepted, we immediately perceive, however, that it is no longer possible to construct a logico-mathematical system. Therefore, this principle appears as the absolute condition of all possible quantitative sciences.

(2) Let us exclude, instead, Archimedes' postulate: given two sizes there is always a multiple of one greater than the other. At first sight this may also seem to be a universal principle and such that we cannot logically imagine that given, for instance, the numbers 10 and 3, we do not have a multiple of 3 greater than 10. Nevertheless, G. Veronese has shown that a perfectly logical geometry can be constructed, quite apart from Archimedes' postulate. But even if Archimedean geometry is beyond criticism from a logical point of view, it has proven to be useless in the interpretation of experimental phenomena.

(3) On the contrary, non-Euclidean geometries that exclude the postulate of parallels have not only proven to be logical constructions beyond criticism, but they are also fruitful in the interpretation of physical phenomena.

Therefore the premises which we take as our point of departure are not chosen *ad libitum,* but rather some of them are necessary conditions of all scientific constructions and others are confirmed by experience, that is, only as far as the conclusions that can be deduced from them prove to be fruitful in the interpretation of experimental reality.

Semantic conventions are completely different. When we agree on using the phonetic sign "ten" or "decem" or "deka" or "dieci," etc., to signify the number 10, we are simply establishing an association between a sign and its meaning, allowing ourselves to be guided by historical tradition, by euphony and the like, without the need for any special logical or physical-mathematical considerations.

We have already listed the essential features required by a semantic system. On the other hand, the requirements of a system of axioms and postulates are completely different: namely, logical compatibility between the various propositions; independence, that is, propositions cannot be deduced from each other; elimination of superfluous premises; and finally, logical completeness of the system.

The main cause for confusion between semantics and logic is the concept that the sole value of language is in its logical function.[1]

This is an obvious but excusable error made by the grammarians of Port Royal, by the Cartesian school, and not less obviously, though less excusably, by modern Neopositivists who, after Vico, Croce and Vossler, still consider language only in its logical function without even suspecting that it may be considered from a different perspective.

Misled by this preconception, Descartes, in a letter to Mersenne, expounded the project of a universal language easy to learn and capable of helping the human intellect in the formulation of judgments. His description is so clear and precise that it seems impossible that he should have been mistaken.

The philosopher then proposed, as though they were the same thing, a project for an international language with simplified and rationalized grammar (similar to that which was later to become Esperanto) and at the same time a project for a combinatorial calculus like the *ars magna* of Raimondo Lullo—or like mathematical logic which, making use of algebraic symbolism, was later to be elaborated by Peano, Russell, the Warsaw school, etc.

Leibniz acted on the same misunderstanding. All his life he dreamed of a *lingua characteristica universalis* which was to be a rationalized language and at the same time an *ars combinatoria* and a *calculus philosophicus*. He described this language in terms of an alphabet of human thought, for, by combining its symbols, it was to be possible to formulate and automatically discover all possible judgments, just as all the words of language are formed through the combination of alphabetical signs. Therefore, Leibniz proposed a kind of international *pasigraphy* (that is, a system of graphic signs which, similarly to Arabic numbers and algebraic symbols, could be understood by people speaking different languages), as well as a development and renewal of analytical logic.[2]

This new art was to render our arguments as stable and definitive as mechanical laws ("quod velut mechanica ratione fixam et visibilem et, ut ita dicam, irresistibilem reddat rationem").

Leibniz added that algebra, as it was ordinarily intended and which was so highly considered (and rightly so) was only a part of the art he had in mind. However, taken as it was, it was impossible to make errors for it placed the truth before our very eyes just as a printing press impresses a design on paper. Leibniz was convinced that the time would come when the new instrument he had proposed would enable us to formulate conclusions about metaphysical problems (God, the soul, etc.) which would not be any less certain than the conclusions currently formed about geometrical figures and numbers. With these grandiose and naive dreams Leibniz anticipated, in the good and in the bad sense, modern attempts at language analysis, mathematical logic, and certain applications of computing machines. However, as regards the philosophy of language, his only merit is that of having absurdly pushed the rationalistic point of view to the extreme.

The misunderstanding we have tried to define becomes even more explicit in certain modern language analysts who currently speak of "linguistic rules," "semantic rules," and "logical rules," as though they were the same thing. To say, for example, that the validity of an empirical proposition cannot be the result of a simple logical analysis, Tarski was later to say that such validity could not be decided on the sole basis of "linguistic rules." He explicitly states that the relation between his semantics and positive linguistics is the same as that between pure and applied mathematics, and he expected his doctrine to be accepted and followed by linguists. The latter, however, ignored it completely, and rightly so.[3]

Similarly, Carnap also described logical concepts such as *consequent, contradictory, compatible,* etc., as purely semantic terms.

In the next chapter we will make a more thorough examination of one of the most famous works representing this approach and we will see what advantages may be obtained by science from the uncritical identification of logic with semantics.

We have dwelt on this problem in order to demonstrate that the identification of semantics with logic is an error. It produces a false perspective of the very categories themselves, that is, it is a methodological error. Indeed, errors of this kind have a far greater and more harmful influence on the progress of thought than specific errors.

An example of a methodological error is the belief that the way a naturalistic event is to manifest itself can be deduced a priori (that, for example, we can decide whether or not an illness is contagious without the aid of observation). This error favored the propagation of a great many pseudo-sciences and prevented the development of the modern natural sciences for more than a thousand years.

The consequences of a specific error, even one of great importance (e.g., the error of pre-Galilean physics according to which the continuous intervention of force was necessary to keep a body in motion), are never so far-reaching, general, and difficult to correct as the consequences of a methodological error. To rectify an error in method, in fact, we need something more than the accuracy of single observations or the rigor of single arguments. In other words, what we need is a change in our way of thinking, which is something slow and difficult to achieve.

18. Charles W. Morris's "Behaviorist" Semiotics[1]

Convergence of European Neopositivism and American Pragmatism—A Scientific Definition of the Sign—Positivist Denial of Self-Consciousness—Academic Creation of New Sciences—Trained Dogs and the Classification of Signs—Transition from Irrational Philosophies to Science—The Pseudo-Mathematical Apparatus used by These Authors—Carnap's Hairsplitting.

Morris's semiotics is a general theory of language, a "theory of signs," as well as a universal logic of scientific, artistic, etc., discourse. In American universities it is considered as a scientific approach of fundamental importance. Given that Morris's doctrine together with others of similar orientation are also received with great favor in Italy, and that philosophy professors who substitute the classics of European thought with the teaching of such doctrines are increasingly numerous, we believe that a careful examination of Morris's doctrine will be of some interest.

Morris originally proposed to unite European Neopositivism and research as it was carried out by the Cambridge analytical school and the methods of traditional American pragmatism. In his turn he exercised a noteworthy influence on certain Neopositivists and particularly on the logico-linguistic analyses of Rudolf Carnap.[2]

As authors belonging to the same line of thought only too often do, Morris declares his intention of substituting the "empty verbosity" of traditional philosophers for the rigor of logical analysis and scientific method. His allusion is to the limits of the philosophical works of such authors as Aristotle, Spinoza, Kant, etc. However, being more liberal than other Neopositivist scientists, he does not really believe that philosophy is to be eliminated altogether and thinks he can assign it the task of formally systematizing results achieved by the sciences.[3]

He describes his science as behaviorist (or in Italian "comportamentistica" according to Ceccato and other importers of similar elegant turns of phrase[4]) for having refused such "mentalistic" terms as sensation, representation, concept, thought, etc. (which smack of ancient metaphysics), and he accepts the pragmatic principle which holds that a proposition has meaning only if verifiable through observation of the behavior of the organism or object in question. In truth, I do not see how we can observe anything without referring to our sensations, representations, and concepts. However, even though I do not understand, I will report faithfully.

Since science is made of propositions and propositions are made of language, Morris, like many other modern methodologists, is convinced that we may broaden our comprehension of all contemporary problems—intellectual, literary, cultural, individual, and social[5]—through the scientific analysis of language. But language is made of words, of symbols or signs, and this leads to the necessity of a *general theory of signs.*

It is a question of formulating a scientific definition of the concept of *sign.* Definitions proposed by the Neopositivists generally oscillate between the rationalistic formalism of pure conventionalism and oversimplified forms of empiricism that draw their concepts wholly from common use.

Morris judges the conventionalistic method as being too abstract. He believes that in order to define a term we must take into account its use in effectively spoken language and then rationalize such use to obtain a scientific definition.

Thus he examines various cases of the use of the term *sign:* the color or pallor of the face is a *sign* of a state of mind, music is a *sign* of a given sentiment, the Parthenon is a *sign* of Greek civilization, wet roads are a *sign* that it has rained, a black ribbon is a *sign* that someone has died, the whistle of a train is a *sign* that the train is about to leave, etc.[6] After having put together this fine collection of examples, Morris attempts to formulate the beginnings of a scientific definition.

Here it is: "If something, A, controls behavior toward a goal in a way similar to (but not necessarily identical with) the way something else, B, would control behavior with respect to that goal in a situation in which it were observed, then A is a sign."[7] According to this definition, if, for example, we see a child playing with a loaded gun (A) or a drunk driving an automobile (B), our reaction could be similar, that is, that of facing or of avoiding the danger. Now, according to the definition, we should say that the child (A) is a sign.

That this definition is perfectly useless is soon realized by the author himself who therefore makes an effort to render it even more scientific.

And here is the result: "If anything, A, is a preparatory-stimulus which in the absence of stimulus-objects initiating response-sequences of a certain behavior-family causes a disposition in some organism to respond under certain conditions by response-sequences of this behavior-family, then A is a sign."[8]

To form an idea of the rigorous nature of this definition we must ask ourselves what the meaning is of that interpolated clause "under certain conditions." It obviously means that the definition is not valid if not "in certain cases" (which are not specified), that is, that sometimes it is valid and sometimes not, which is just the opposite of what is required of a definition.

Furthermore, what does "a certain behavior-family" mean? What is the criterion that enables us to judge whether or not two behaviors are related to the same family?

And again, in Morris's opinion, the concept of *sign* implies that of *stimulus*, which is defined as follows: "that which causes a muscular movement or a glandular secretion in an organism." From this it would follow that if someone reads or listens to a page of poetry that reveals a world of images and concepts, those words, spoken or written, are not *signs* if the muscular contractions and the glandular secretions they presumedly provoke cannot be ascertained.

It was perhaps to avoid consequences of this kind that Morris took care not to speak of the effective "responses" of an organism, but only of a *disposition to respond*. But his American critics already remarked that a "disposition to respond" which does not manifest itself in externally verifiable events or occurrences is a *"mentalistic"* concept inadmissable in a *behaviorist* science.

It is easy to see that even Morris's second definition is both too narrow and too broad. Too narrow because, as we have seen, signs *par excellence*, namely, words and writing, are not always included; too broad because it may include a great many things that nobody would call *signs*. For example, if a mother with a paralytic child, on seeing a group of lively youths playing, were to remember her own ailing son, sigh, and then head for a shop to buy him a small gift, thus starting off a "response-sequence," those youths would consequently be *signs* of the paralytic! How was it possible for Morris to formulate such an irrational concept and such a laborious, strained, and altogether ambiguous and narrow definition—so distant from the usual simplicity and precision of the exact sciences he so much admires?

The reason seems obvious to us: his decision to keep to external behaviorism and to investigate such spiritual activities as logical thought, artistic expression, and language only by taking into consideration muscular movements and physiological manifestations deprived him of all possibility of understanding the essence, or, if we prefer, the nature of semiological activity.

Morris (like other authors with a similar orientation) got it into his head that to practice science all we need do is observe the external world, as though minerals, plants, and animals were real things while we ourselves were nothing. This makes one want to shout at him the Augustinian warning *in te ipsum redi!*— return (to look) within yourself and tell me whether you are a secretion or a living person!

According to Morris, all that which acts as a sign is characterized by three special relations: to the person using the sign, to the other signs of the same system, and to the symbolized objects. This leads to no less than three new sciences:

(1) *Pragmatics*, which studies the set of "expectations" that the sign arouses

in the user. It is immediately obvious that we are dealing here with a science of unlimited possibilities. The sight of smoke, for example, may sometimes provoke the expectation of fire, on other occasions it will be related to a locomotive, and on still others to a cooking dinner, etc.

(2) *Syntactics*, which concerns the formal relation of a symbol to other symbols (or rather of a meaning to other meanings). For example, the sight of smoke usually provokes the expectation of fire (even if in some cases there may be smoke without fire). Moreover, to shout "fire" in a crowded public place usually provokes panic. This will lead to the formulation of such syntactic-behavioristic rules as: "when you see smoke expect fire," and "to shout *fire* provokes panic." This new science can establish "that certain expressions containing the term 'smoke' logically imply other expressions in which the term 'fire' appears and these, in turn, imply new expressions in which the term 'panic' is present."[9] According to Morris, this link between the symbols "smoke," "fire," and "panic" constitutes the "structure of the logical relations between symbols." As we can see, syntax is even more spectacular in scope than pragmatics, since it studies all possible associations between all possible symbols.

(3) The third new science is *semantics* which should be an empirical science that describes the different types of signs and the relations between signs and their meanings.

Passing on to the classification of signs, Morris divides them into four types: indicators, describers, appraisers, and prescribers, which correspond to four types of *significata: locata, discriminata, valutata,* and *obligata.*

Instead of explaining the meaning and value of these distinctions with examples taken from human language (which according also to the Neopositivists is the most outstanding example of a semiotic system), the author believes it more "scientific" (that is to say, more worthy of *his* science) to address trained dogs.

Let us suppose, he says, that a hungry dog is subjected to the following preparatory stimuli:

I_1 which induces it to look for food or water (without specifying which of the two) in a hiding place we will call 1.

I_2 which induces it to look for food or water in a hiding place we will call 2.

D_1 which specifies that the object to be searched for is food.

D_2 which specifies that the object to be searched for is water.

A which determines the dog's choice univocally. When there is a doubt between the two possible meanings, A determines which of the two is to prevail.

For example, if the dog is simultaneously presented with two groups of stimuli I_1D_1 and I_2D_1 it would be uncertain as to whether it should search for the food in 1 or in 2. If instead it is presented with the two groups AI_1 and I_2D_1 it will know that the first group must prevail over the other so he will look for the food in 1.

Finally P prescribes how and after what movements the dog is to search for its gratification. For example, PAI₁D₂ will stimulate it to search for food in ɪ after having circled three times.[10]

The signs I, D, A, and P, that is, indicators, describers, appraisers, and prescribers, are called "lexicatives." Those which correspond to the question mark, parentheses, or conjunctions, as in the Latin *et* and *aut*, are called instead "formators."[11] (Morris may have meant *formal signs.*)

Then there are complex signs or "ascribers" which join signs together and correspond to what in languages are called propositions.

Ascribers are divided into designatives (formed by an indicative sign and a descriptive sign), for example, "that is a deer"; appraisives ("that deer is beautiful"); prescriptives ("come here!"); and formatives ("that round table is not square").

Finally these signs may have four different uses: informative, valuative, incitive, and systemic.[12]

Morris concludes his work convinced that his distinctions may replace the rather forceful epistemological distinctions of traditional philosophy (like those, for instance, between Kant's analytic and synthetic judgments) and proposes his own scientific classification of all human activities and disciplines.

The criterion adopted consists of combining the four different modes of signification with the four uses of the semiotic function so that sixteen fundamental types of discourse are obtained, according to the following table:

Mode	*Use* informative	*Use* valuative	*Use* incitive	*Use* systemic
designative	scientific	fictive	legal	cosmological
appraisive	mythical	poetic	moral	critical
prescriptive	technological	political	religious	propagandistic
formative	logico-mathematical	rhetorical	grammatical	metaphysical

Kant, poor man, spent his whole life defining and characterizing mathematics, physics, morals, and art in his three critiques, while Morris, in no time at all, lays down the encyclopedic foundations of all human disciplines. For our part, however, we must confess that we find the abuses and incongruities of his classification rather disconcerting.

For example, why is *"fictive discourse"* evaluative-designative, poetic discourse evaluative-appraisive, and mythical discourse formative-appraisive? Why is *cosmological discourse* systemic-designative and *metaphysical discourse* systemic-formative?

We very much appreciate the typically American idea of placing "propagandistic discourse," in other words publicity, among the fundamental human disciplines together with art, science, morals, and religion.

Something rather particular about Morris's semiotics is that it is not clear how it should be classified according to his own indications. In so far as it deals with the rules according to which signs (and therefore words and propositions) are to be used, it should belong to *grammar* (incitive-formative discourse); in so far as it is an empirical science it should belong to informative-designative discourse; in so far as it investigates the formal structures of discourse it should belong to the logico-mathematical sciences; but in so far as it examines and establishes the value and range of all other disciplines, it should fall within critical discourse, or, better still, philosophical-metaphysical discourse.

Morris states that the number of linguists and other scholars who have followed the direction indicated by his semiotics is quite considerable and mentions Edward Sapir, Alan Gardiner, Leonard Bloomfield, Manuel J. Andrade, etc.

I am unaware of what discoveries were made by these authors, but I do not believe that any problem of linguistics or of any other science has been explained or ever will be thanks to Morris's methods.

I would finally like to draw the reader's attention to the rather peculiar use made of what would seem to be mathematical formulae and which the scientists belonging to this line of thought are happily spreading throughout America and Europe. Anyone with even a superficial knowledge of the scientific disciplines is aware of the usefulness of the symbols and formulae of mathematics and physics in formulating a synthetic, precise, clear, and intuitively effective exposition; they often enable us to express in a few lines what would otherwise require whole pages. On the other hand, the pseudomathematical apparatus used by Morris does nothing but express in a long-winded, laborious, imprecise, and confused manner that which could have been stated better in a more simple common language.[13] This habit reminds us of the methods used in his day by Professor Francesco Orestano in Italy and his "formula of ontological integration."[14] Twenty years ago, when Orestano occupied a position of great importance in official Italian philosophy, I believed it my duty to examine some of his works and reveal their pretentious nullity.[15] Time subsequently proved me right in my evaluation, just as, I am sure, it will prove me right in my current "untimely" criticism of behaviorist semiotics.[16]

The use and abuse of cumbersome mathematical techniques is common today even among authors who, though incompetent and unintelligible in problems of philosophy, have given some personal contribution in other fields.

Let us consider, for example, Carnap's distinction between "objective" (Objektsprache) and "syntactic" language. The proposition "Aristotle is a Greek philosopher" is an example of *objective* language, while the proposition "Aristotle is a pentasyllabic proparoxytone" is an example of *syntactic* language. In the second case, says Carnap, the word refers to itself and is used in the sense of autonymy (in other words, the judgment is referred to the same phoneme in the second case, whereas in the first case it refers to a meaning different from the phoneme). This logico-mathematical distinction is in fact as clear as daylight, but here is how it is examined and explained by its author: "In the context of the relation between objective language and syntactic language we may consider a field B of objects whose properties may be described by a language-object S_1. If we admit that an objective property E_1 is referred to B, and a syntactic property E_2 is referred to S_1, so that if E_1 refers to an object, E_2 refers to the expression that indicates the object, E_2 is, in that case, the syntactic property coordinated with E_1, and the latter is an objective property, even if it is genuinely a syntactic property." If we simplify Carnap's rather complicated formulations, three kinds of propositions emerge:

(1) Objective ("23 is a prime number").

(2) Syntactic ("*twenty-three* is an apocopated polysyllable").

(3) Quasi-syntactic ("*twenty-three* is a number"). The latter may be transformed into the proposition: *twenty-three* is a word indicating a number.

In Carnap's words: the proposition that attributes property E_1 to an object A is a *quasi-syntactic* proposition, if it may be coordinated with an effective syntactic proposition that attributes property E_2 to an indication of A.

Continuing in the same direction, he examines the following five propositions:

(1) "ω" is a type of rule.

(2) "ω" is a letter.

(3) "*Omega*" is a letter.

(4) "*Omega*" is not a letter but a word formed of five letters.

(5) In the fourth of the previous propositions the object in question is not the *omega* as in the third proposition, that is, it is not the ω as an alphabetical sign, but rather *omega* as a linguistic expression.[17]

Some of the admirers of such subtleties have remarked that without Carnap's distinctions the fifth proposition would not have been definable. Anybody can see how much damage this would have brought about in philosophical research.

Let us give yet another example of the fruitful discussions provoked by distinctions of this kind: with the intention of transforming *pseudo-objective* propositions into purely formal and therefore "scientific" discourse, Carnap asserted that a proposition of the type "yesterday's conference dealt with Babylonia" can be usefully transformed into the following more accurate proposition: "the word 'BABYLONIA' or other equivalent words came up during yesterday's conference." The American mathematician Haskell B. Curry objected, on the contrary, that one could very easily suppose that the conference dealt with the breeding of polar bears and that in the course of his speech the lecturer made a joke in which the word "babylonia" appeared.[18]

Compared with the loftiness of such concepts and problems, it is only natural that the concepts dealt with by "metaphysical" philosophers such as Aristotle or Hegel must seem quite silly.

I would like to observe again that in most cases Carnap's laborious distinctions and constructions, like those of other authors working in the same direction, are not false. Nonetheless, however true or false they may be, they have no value whatsoever in the clarification and thorough examination of philosophical problems.

The person who acquires some familiarity with their cumbersome symbolism and has the patience to follow their minute analyses step by step will soon realize that, all things considered, the concepts proposed are all but difficult. It is the way they are presented which makes them seem very abstruse indeed, thus leaving inexpert readers surprised and dissatisfied.

19. The Linguistics of Abstract Idealism and of B. Croce

Historical Background of Croce's Theory: Herder—
Individuality of Linguistic Expression Asserted by
Herder—Spirituality of Language in Humboldt—
But Spirituality, Essential to Every Human Produc-
tion, Cannot Be Considered as a Characteristic Fea-
ture—Humboldt Denies the Distinction between the
Origin and Subsequent Development of Language—
Universalistic Claims Favor Innatist and Theological
Solutions—Antinomy between Individuality and
Universality of Language—Mystic Conclusion—De-
nial of the Problem of Language Origin in Stein-
thal—Myth Explains the Essence in Terms of Tem-
poral Origin, Abstract Idealism Confuses the
Question of the Origin with That of the Essence—
Complexity and Organic Unity of Croce's Concep-
tion—Identification of Representation, Expression,
and Language—Uselessness of Lexical Studies—
Unique Individuality of the Word—Negation of Uni-
ty in Language—A Universal Language Cannot Be
Created—Grammatical Rules and Phonetic Laws
Are Devoid of Scientific Value—Technique Is of No
Importance in Artistic Creation—As It Is a Spiritual
Category, Language Does Not Have a Temporal
Origin—Contradiction in Croce's Concept of Cate-
gory—The Individuality of Intuition Contradicts Its
Communicability—And Renders It Unexpressible
and Not Intuitable—Pure Universality and Pure In-
dividuality Are Abstract Elements in Concrete Ex-
perience—Croce's Denial of Mathematics and the
Natural Sciences—The Empirical Nature of Con-
cepts Cannot Be Eliminated—The Inadequacy of
Translations Derives from the Diversity of Linguistic Conventions—And from the Different Musical

Expressiveness of Words—Refusal to Recognize
Technique Derives from the Lacking Analysis of Intuition—And from the Presumed Insuperable Individuality of Expression—Merits of Croce's Aesthetics.

After having examined the identification of semantics with logic and the
confusion it can cause, let us pause to reconsider the identification of semantics with aesthetics which has found its most complete and definite formulation in the doctrine of B. Croce.

Firstly, we will consider the historical background of Croce's theory. Herder, in his dissertation on the origin of language,[1] had already identified
consciousness with language. Language and consciousness *(Besonnenheit),* he
says, are the same thing. Man sees a lamb, he perceives it as being white,
docile, and woolly. Undisturbed by the violent immediacy of instinct, man's
spirit looks for a characteristic sign: the lamb bleats. He sees the lamb later
and hears his bleating again. The man recognizes it: you are the bleater. The
bleating sound, perceived by the spirit as a characteristic of the lamb, becomes
the *name* of the lamb. Language is no more than the collection of such names.

Herder refuses the intellectual conception of language. Language does
not come into being in salons among cultured and elegant people, but in
that place where the senses, crude astuteness, passion, and inventive brilliance
reign; where the various faculties and spiritual forces are not yet perfected
and differentiated, and life throbs with the urgency and immediacy of instinct.

He also insists on the individual character of linguistic expression, emphasizing that diversity in situations, sentiments, and pronunciation prevents
unity and favors the multiplicity of languages. Strictly speaking, a language
is never the same in men and women, in father and son, in the aged and in
the child. Every person has a different language from that of others just as
his own body and face are different.

In *Kaligone* Herder asserts that the beginnings of human speech through
tones, gestures, and the expression of sensations and thoughts through images
and signs was no more than a rudimentary form of poetry, just as it still is
today among savage populations.

Herder's writings are rich in interesting intuitions: in contrast to the
intellectualism of the French he accentuates the spontaneous, primitive, individual, and poetic character of language. He acknowledges the semantic
and symbolic function of language and, at the same time, stresses that its
most important function does not lie in extrinsic communication, but rather
in providing a necessary moment of self-consciousness.

Nonetheless, these reasons are badly coordinated and at times they are
expressed in a form which is overemphatic and imprecise, so that even the
author was dissatisfied with them in his later writings.[2]

Similar ideas were developed with greater philological and philosophical
competency by Humboldt. He made the famous statement that language is

not a kind of finished product, but something in continual development, something that arises and dies away. It is not a product, but rather continuously active production; it is not a completed work (*érgon*), but an activity (*enérgeia*). In short, according to Humboldt language is nothing but speech.[3] These words express a truth of great significance, but at the same time they can lead to errors and confusion.

The truth concerns the general philosophy of the spirit rather than the science of language. Post-Kantian philosophy, and especially the philosophy of Hegel, has the merit of having insisted on the distinction between *doing* and *done*, a distinction ignored by coarse intellectualism. To understand poetry, for example, it will not suffice to contemplate works from the past as they appear fossilized within the classifications and rules of literary genres, for on the contrary poetry is something we must feel intimately, experience in its becoming, understand as spontaneous activity.

This is also true of the activity carried out by the mathematician, the moralist, the politician, etc. It will never be possible to understand the intimate nature of any human activity by simply judging it from the outside in the light of preconceived rules derived from the dead past.

Given that the principle set forth is so universally far-reaching, it is not useful in the specific characterization of linguisitic activity. We must beware of answering specific questions with propositions that become inconclusive because of their very universality.

Humboldt acknowledges that a speaker is always tied to a given tradition and does not create his expressions arbitrarily. He says that not only does speech as it is currently spoken exist, but also speech as it was spoken in the past, that is, a reserve of words and a system of rules.

This touches on an issue of fundamental importance: that of the relation between *thinking* and *thought*, between *doing* and *done*, which in linguistics is specified as the distinction between the time of institution and that of semantic application. But here too Humboldt is generalizing and denies that there is a difference between the beginnings of language and the continuous creation of later development. He says that language is constantly conditioned by previously existing linguistic material.

But how did language originate? How did man begin speaking as he left the animal state? Humboldt replies that there is no difference between origin and development. He maintains that not only is the language of today both fluid (speech) and fixed (that which was spoken), but already in the most primitive language words belonged to whoever pronounced them as well as to whoever listened to them and understood them. Thus the empirical problem of the origin is considered vain and is consequently avoided.

Humboldt continues: Given that man can only be conceived of as a thinking being, as such he must also be conceived of as a speaking being—from the very beginning. Man is immediately endowed with language which cannot be explained as the work of the intellect.[4]

As we can see, universalistic confusion comes close here to innatist and theologizing naiveties.[5]

Humboldt insists on the reciprocal implication of thought and word: without language neither concepts nor, more generally, objects perceived by the spirit are possible. Language is the organ that produces ("bildet") thought. It is the matrix (Geburtsstaette) and organ of thought. Just as the eye is the organ of sight, language is the organ of thought. Language arises with thought and thought only develops through the union of intellectual activity and sound.

Note that it is one thing to acknowledge the sign (linguistic, graphic, or mimetic) as a necessary component of consciousness and another to identify it with consciousness itself. We should also remember that Humboldt does not take non-phonetic signs into consideration, for he attributes to sound a universality which does not belong to it.

For Humboldt, understanding and speaking are only two different effects of the same spiritual energy. Children learning how to speak do not merely deposit words in their memory and repeat them in a parrot-like fashion, rather the growth of their language capacity corresponds to an increase in their general development. This is well said, but it would have been more correct to acknowledge that receptive memory and mechanical imitation do also play a role, and that they must then aid and support the development of a more intimate understanding.

Humboldt seems to believe that mankind received the gift of language through the grace of God: the song of the nightingale originates from its breast, and man too is a creature that sings, but he unites thought and sound.[6] Among the merits of this author, we should emphasize his sharp awareness of the antinomy between the individuality and the universality of language. He asks himself how it is that speakers understand each other and thus overcome their uniqueness even though they each express their own individuality.

He replies that many things, but especially language, induce us to believe that diversity among individuals is not essential, that in reality separate individuals do not exist, but that on the contrary individuality, in other words, the external division among single individuals, is only a phenomenal manifestation of the unique human spirit. He believes that language hints at a point beyond itself where single individuals reveal their identity, and where language has its source.[7]

These concepts are neither superficial nor unfounded, but they are not yet sufficiently developed and clear. They produce a rather vague and uncontrolled mystical conception: individuality, he concludes, is the principle of human existence and since language takes us beyond that which is individual, it also takes us beyond that which is human.

Humboldt's ideas were accepted both in their positive and negative aspects by Steinthal, an illustrious and worthy scholar of linguistics and its history.[8]

Before Humboldt, he says, when language was merely considered as a collection of phonetic signs, the problem of the origin was formulated in the question concerning how people came to use phonetic signs in order to communicate their representations and concepts and preserve them in their memories. But once Humboldt had taught us to conceive of language as spiritual production, the problem became another: how does linguistic activity develop from lower psychological manifestations? What role does it play in overcoming the state of animal stupor and how does linguistic activity relate to the totality of the spirit?

The difference between the naturalistic view of temporal origin and the philosophical view that investigates the continual dialectic passage from obscure animal sensations and passions to clarity of expression could not have been better defined.

Nevertheless Steinthal's shortcoming, common to authors of similar orientation, consists in his belief that philosophy must devour and annihilate science.[9]

Darwin, for example, dealt with the naturalistic problem of evolution from the animal to the human state and came up with his theory of natural selection. It is obvious to all that the objection that we constantly leave the animal state each time we dominate our instincts or overcome the tumult of the emotions and disorderly sensations is completely out of place. Mythologists thought they had solved the problem of the essence by giving some sort of an explanation in terms of temporal origin; for example, to the question concerning the essence and function of evil and pain, it was replied that once evil did not exist, but was the consequence of a fault committed. Something of this mentality is still easily recognizable in the *archè* of the Greek natural philosophers. Philosophic explanations in terms of abstract idealism are similar to myth turned upside down, for they aim at explaining the naturalistic and temporal origin by talking about the essence.

Steinthal does not deny that certain expressions may have arisen from reflex movements and from instinctive onomatopoeia, nonetheless the gap must be bridged between physiological manifestations such as laughter and tears, on the one hand, and speech, on the other. Paraphrasing *Job*, Steinthal says he would like to ask those who think they can identify the emotional impulse from which a given phoneme arose the following question: Were you present when the first articulate sound issued from the breast of primitive man? And, had you been present, would you have understood what was being said? Who preserved for you the history and memory of those original roots which hundreds of thousands of years ago came forth from human lips?

Croce has the merit of having eliminated any imprecise and confused aspects from the ideas of the German Romantics, and of completing them with Vico's notion of poetry as a primitive stage in spiritual evolution. In this way he developed an orderly, clear, and organic conception of language.

Croce's *Estetica* (Aesthetics) bears the ambitious subtitle *Linguistica generale* (General Linguistics). In fact, this philosopher is convinced that, in so far as they are sciences, aesthetics and linguistics are not separate but rather one and the same thing.[10]

Art is intuition, intuition is expression (that which the spirit represents and expresses to itself) and linguistic expression is no less than art.

The old and outmoded conception of language considered the latter as a system of conventional signs. However, in Croce's opinion, language is not a means, but the idea or representation itself; something which can never be conceived of as being separate or distinct from intuition. On perceiving one's own state, the corresponding words are inwardly pronounced: "I'm hungry, my body feels heavy, this animal frightens me."

Indeed we may experience confused sensations and emotional impressions and not know how to express them. However, art is not sensation but intuition, that is, a contemplative act through which our mysterious inner feelings are raised to expressive clarity.

Consequently, De Amicis gives bad advice when he encourages young people to study dictionaries. Whoever lives intensely, contemplates, and thinks, precisely because of this, has all the language he needs. There are better things to do than learn nomenclatures. We have the world itself to study and read: *verba sequentur*.

Speakers must have something to say, in other words, they must have some sort of culture. Culture, which is a necessary condition of expression, concerns all one's spiritual experiences and includes all eventual grammatical and lexical notions. Therefore, such notions will only form one of the many premises of expression but will never correspond to expression itself.

The words of a dictionary are conventions (i.e., practical acts), but as soon as a convention is translated into language, that is, as soon as it is used by a speaker, it ceases to be a convention and becomes a natural fact, which every speaker elaborates in his own way. Words acquire a particular meaning for each individual, indeed in each expressive act.

There are no such things as two identical words: "si duo dicunt idem, non est idem." Intuition is an unrepeatable individual act.

This is the reason why the translation (which postulates the separability of content and form) of poetry is impossible. Translations are either ugly and faithful or beautiful and unfaithful: in the first case we are no longer dealing with poetry but with a mere philological aid, in the second with new works which only vaguely resemble the original.

For the same reason, the unity of language (which the Italian purists believed they could obtain by taking certain language texts as their model—and the followers of Manzoni referred to Florentine linguistic use) is a false conception.

Furthermore, the concept of a universal language, such as that contemplated by Leibniz or that which is thought to be realized with *Volapük* or with *Esperanto*, is completely unfounded.

This idea will always remain a utopia of the most foolish sort, for it is full of contradictions; in fact, given that the linguistic act is absolutely individual, a presumed universal language either will not be a language or it will not be universal. If two or more men agree to name bread with the sound "puk" and to say "I want" with the sound "ro" so that "ro puk" would be the translation of "I want some bread," they will not have invented a language. In so far as they are effectively spoken, the sounds "ro puk" will acquire a special meaning each time they are pronounced; they will always be new and unique expressive creations.

It must be firmly kept in mind that concepts such as vowel and consonant, syllable and word, Italian word and Greek or German word, are no more than abstractions, and that similar to all empirical concepts, they have neither scientific value nor a precise meaning. These classifications are clumsy and convenient though they sometimes prove useful for reference to a specific set of concepts and problems. At the same time, however, they must be overcome if we are to reach concrete reality.

Neither grammatical laws nor lexical repertoires, let alone phonetic laws, have any kind of scientific value. The external classifications of glottologists cannot stand up to a rigorously critical linguistic theory which aims at showing that the human spirit is effectively the sole cause of all expressive forms. Some scholars believe that the study of grammar, vocabulary, and language texts favors artistic creation because it helps to master expressive technique. Furthermore, if technique does not coincide with art, it is indeed necessary to art, for it is one of its constitutive elements.

Croce, on the contrary, firmly states that practical or technical elements are never part of the process of artistic production; spontaneity dominates from beginning to end and the concept of technique is as alien to aesthetics as it is to artistic criticism. Technique plays a role once the creative process has been accomplished—that of materially fixing the artistic vision in the memory, or it may precede the creative process as a datum, but it will not succeed in penetrating it and effectively becoming part of it.

In Croce's opinion, identification of language with poetic expression also has the merit of eliminating the old problem of language origin according to which language is an institution which arose at a given point in history and is therefore contingent. In contrast, Croce believes that language is a spiritual category and does not come into being in the historical sense.

There has never been a primitive period in the rise of language, for it has always existed, given that development is not conceivable without creation. Primitive creation and daily speech are one and the same thing.

As with all seriously thought out doctrines, Croce's philosophy has the precious fault that it can only be judged by taking account of all the concepts forming his thought system. As we have already thoroughly examined it elsewhere,[11] we will here limit ourselves to simply listing the reasons why we do not find Croce's linguistic theory acceptable:

(1) Croce's concept of spiritual categories is inadequate and contradictory: on the one hand, he states that his four categories correspond to essential and omnipresent activities, that is, they concern the whole of reality, while on the other, he acknowledges alogical intuition and amoral economic action, thus denying the universality of both the logical and moral categories, which he then reduces to special concepts that at times exist and at other times do not. In truth neither "pure" intuition, nor "pure" economic action, nor "pure" mathematics exist, or these activities can only be considered *pure* by abstraction (which amounts to the same thing). A logical element exists in

every intuitive act and cannot fail to exist, but when we take this act into consideration from an aesthetic point of view, we are disregarding its logical value.

(2) Consequently, the concept of the absolute individuality and unrepeatability of the intuitive act is also untenable. Croce asserts that a translated verse is always a new work, an individual expression which cannot be compared with others, but had he been consistent he should have said that even the same verse, pronounced by two different people, and therefore with a different accent and with words that stir up different reminiscences and images, is never "the same." To read a work of art means to reduce it to the level of presuppositions and content for a new possible intuition. The *Divine Comedy* as I picture it is not what Dante pictured with his fervid, mystical, and partisan imagination, just as it is not what Schopenhauer, who considered it inferior to Petrarch's *Canzoniere,* pictured.

Croce states that the concept of artistic plagiarism is contradictory, because the new work either is not art, or it is a new work which cannot be compared with any other. However, he did not realize that the concept of the re-creation of the work of others is just as contradictory.

Furthermore, since our moods change so that at each moment we are someone else, our images are never "the same," intuition is elusive in its individuality, and therefore expression—as Croce understands it—is by definition unexpressible. In order to overcome the contradiction, we must acknowledge that the objectifying act of the empirical concept (through which we attribute to the image identity and continuity with itself) is not an arbitrary act accomplished for the sake of convenience, but rather an absolute condition of all knowledge, a necessary act, without which intuition itself cannot exist.

We do not have purely individual intuition on the one hand, and purely universal abstract concepts on the other. Rather every cognitive act is always both an individual and a universal experience. My knowledge of Newton's laws is experience, and my knowledge of the *Divine Comedy* is experience. However, within the single experience we may distinguish dialectically between two different values: artistic value, in which the individual personality pulsates more intimately, and scientific value which fulfils our need of universal truths.

(3) Not having recognized the dialectic nature of categorial values, Croce modelled his theory of pseudo-concepts drawing on the epistemology of empiricism and of pragmatism (in which theory has a completely different scope and meaning).[12]

According to Croce, concepts in the natural, physical, and mathematical sciences have no cognitive value at all; rather they are arbitrary constructions developed uniquely for practical purposes. This is the reason why when a scientific concept seems imperfect and inadequate, Croce does not bother about making it less imperfect and less inadequate (as scientists have always done) but simply rejects it as a pseudo-concept.

(4) Finally, having accepted the concept of intuition uncritically and non-

dialectically, Croce was not able to analyze its constitutive elements or recognize it as a synthesis of sense impressions and memory.

On reexamining Croce's linguistics, we soon realize that he denies that words are conventional signs, for he denies the very concept of word: Croce refuses to grant all concepts of experience any cognitive status whatsoever.

But the fact is that any intuition we discuss must be the object of our thought and experience. In other words, not only is it intuition but also concept, to the point that Croce and his followers (such as Vossler) do away with concepts such as *word, phoneme, Italian language,* etc., on the one hand, but continually use them and could not avoid doing so, on the other. Whoever thinks makes continual use of empirical concepts, and this is not so for the sake of convenience, but because it is absolutely impossible to formulate a judgment without them. No doubt the concepts of experience are contingent and relative and change continually in content, but this does not mean that they are not necessary. The content of moral laws also varies according to time and place, but this does not contradict the universality of the moral need: river-banks change continually, but a river without banks is inconceivable.

It is true that the translation of poetry is always inadequate, but this is not due to an alleged insuperable individuality of expression (otherwise it would be impossible to communicate any image at all, including pictorial and musical images). The relative impossibility to which Croce is referring depends, rather, upon the particular character of linguistic signs.

In fact a language is not an abstractly established rational semantic system; rather, it is the result of millenary historical evolution. The words of two different languages, which have arisen in different environmental and cultural conditions, do not designate the same group of representations. Even interjections and imitative expressions differently stylize the natural impressions to which they refer (so that, for example, the "ding-dong" of English bells become "tsiang-tsiang" in Chinese and "kiling-kiling" in the Manchu language). Certain distinctions common to one language are absent in another: in Italian for instance, "you," is expressed with "tu," "voi," "lei," "ella," whereas Latin only had the "tu" form, and in certain languages the Italian first person singular personal pronoun "io" is expressed with different words according to the speaker's social class. Word order, morphological agreements, and syntactic constructions vary from one language to another and the figurative use of words also varies greatly, [13] so that in fact it is surprising that we often find, if not perfect conformity, at least a remarkable similarity in meaning between the proposition of a language and its translation.

On top of this, linguistic communication contains directly expressive elements such as accentuation, intonation, and the general musicality of discourse, so that the words of a language carry with them a whole range of associations and meanings.

That these, and not the presumed unrepeatability of intuition, are the reasons for the impossibility of perfect translations also emerges from the fact that some works of art may be rendered more perfectly and others less so. For example, novels and plays in which the artistic vision emerges especially from the representation of characters and from the succession and unwinding of dramatic situations are "more translatable" than lyric poetry. In fact, in spite of his theory, Croce was able to enjoy and intelligently appreciate the beauty of Ibsen's dramas and of Tolstoy's novels even though he was not familiar with either the Norwegian or Russian language.

Moreover, the unsuccessful analysis of the concept of intuition renders impossible a clear formulation of the concept of artistic technique. In fact, Croce does not distinguish between directly expressive signs and conventional signs, between the way a painting or a symphony is communicated to others and the way a story is communicated. It is not true (as Croce would have it) that when one perceives one's own mood the corresponding words are always pronounced inwardly. On the contrary, one can easily represent the image of a sentiment to oneself and not find suitable words to express it. Just as it is possible to clearly form an image of a flower or a mechanical tool without knowing the names of these objects. This is the reason why Italian poets, from Petrarch to Leopardi through to Carducci and Pascoli, were often skillful philologists and studied their language assiduously, even if one poet may have preferred to study language using dictionaries, another by reading good writers, and yet another by making use of popular speech.

The need for memorizing words and grammatical conventions clearly emerges in the study of ancient languages and of foreign languages and is evident in artificial semantic systems, for example, in cypher codes and algebraic symbols; but whether we are dealing with a mother tongue or foreign language or cypher established by convention, the qualifications proper to semantic systems are always the same.

Croce denied technique all importance in the process of creation, for in the light of his notion of intuitive individuality, he would not accept that two images could be compared, or that one image could be considered as being more encompassing and more profound than another. In reality, however, the artist continually compares his images and expressions and passes from vague outlines to more elaborate representations. Technique and creation interact so that the artist, after having conceived something, fixes it on paper or on canvas, which helps him to see better and to pass from a poorer and more imperfect representation to another that satisfies him more.

In spite of our fundamental reservations, Croce's *Estetica* is an important achievement. Of particular interest is the clear distinction established between the aesthetic value of a work and its logical, moral value, etc. Also interesting is the stance successfully taken against those evaluations which emphasize the value of content instead of form, and which, instead of appreciating the beauty of a work of poetry, give excessive importance to the ideological, moral, or social content.

Even if it has not failed to contribute toward the clarification of our problem, Croce's linguistics is less valuable thanks to his emphasis on the spirituality of linguistic creation and on the undeniable function of the poetic imagination in such creation.

That Croce dedicated himself less to linguistic problems than to other areas of study also emerges from his history of linguistic doctrines: by contrast to the constant, scrupulous, and sometimes meticulous passion characterizing the work of this erudite researcher, he often speaks of works he does not know directly, limiting himself, as he confesses, to consulting the reference book by Steinthal.

Summary and Conclusion

On examining the relation between logic and semantics, that is, between thought and words, in the first place we observed the impossibility of formulating a logical judgment, even if only mentally, without symbols (phonetical or other) and without established semantic convention; this has led some scholars to the conviction that semantic and logical coherence are identical.

On considering the reasons behind such identification, from Descartes to the modern analyzers of language, we saw that it has its roots in a purely intellectual conception of language, and that it does not stand up to more thorough examination.

It will suffice to compare a case of semantic noncompliance (for example, a mistaken translation) with a case of logical incoherence to realize that we are not dealing with the same function, but rather that coherence in sign use is a necessary but not sufficient prerequisite for logical thought. The difference between the two values becomes even more evident by comparing linguistic evolution with the development of logico-mathematical constructions.

Conventionalist theories elaborated by Hilbert and other modern mathematicians have contributed to the identification and confusion of the two concepts, but it is immediately obvious that the "conventionality" of logico-mathematical axioms and postulates demands an operational justification and has very different requirements from grammatical and lexical conventions.

Given that in this book we have attempted to outline a *general theory of expressive signs*, we felt it our duty to examine Morris's semiotics which, in fact, presents itself as a universal classification and theory of all possible signs, and which is considered by many as the most important modern doctrine on our subject; we have also explained the reasons why we disagree with the approach and method employed by this author.

Finally, we examined the linguistics of romantic idealism and of Croce, both of which may be considered as the unilateral antithesis of positivistic doctrines.

As to Herder, Humboldt, and Steinthal we emphasized those aspects which were subsequently to be developed and unified in Croce's theory:

indistinct identification of words and consciousness, spirituality of language, individuality of expression, and rejection of the problem of the origin.

We have shown how the concept of the unrepeatable individuality of intuition is untenable, even though Croce developed most of his corollaries from it: the impossibility of translation, negation of the idea of unity of language and grammatical rules, etc. Finally, we criticized his doctrine of pseudo-concepts on the belief that experience cannot be disregarded.

As a conclusion to our inquiry we may state that language is a semantic system which has evolved naturally, over thousands of years, from preexisting directly expressive modes of communication; that in language the direct elements, such as mimetic expressions, modulations and inflections of the voice, merge with strictly semantic elements; and that aesthetic and emotional needs sometimes dominate over semantic requirements. As in all institutions with their roots in primitive societies, the contribution of individuals is submerged by collective activity at the level of linguistic creation also and, similarly to the products of nature, an unpremeditated but immanent and unconscious rationality is present.

In our investigation we have attempted to take into due account all the valid aspects of aesthetic and of intellectual linguistics. We have insisted on the difference between semantics, aesthetics, and logic, while at the same time we have acknowledged that the use of expressive signs must be considered as a necessary prerequisite for both aesthetic synthesis and logical thought.

Having reached the end of our work, we hope that our theoretical and historical research into the glottogonic issue, together with our research into the relation between semantics, aesthetics, and logic, may contribute toward our focusing more clearly upon the philosophical and psychological problems concerning language, thus putting an end to the irritating alternation between eccentric theoretical constructions and sterile negations.

APPENDIX

The Problem of the Origin and Nature of Language in Plato's *Cratylus*

1. Confusion, Prolixity, and Bad Taste in Current Diction

Plato's Work Has Reached Us Deformed by Later Interpolations and Revisions.

The most important document of Greek thought on our subject is Plato's *Cratylus*. However, it seems to me that the text of the dialogue, in the form it has reached us, is unworthy of Plato. The weak, verbose, and useless parts prevail over the others, argumentation sometimes insists on that which is obvious, sometimes it overlooks evident difficulties, and far too often the transition from one argument to the next is uncoordinated. Paraphrasing the expression "Quandoque dormitat Homerus," we soon realize that even Plato had his off moments, but *Cratylus,* which polemicizes against Heraclitus and his followers and makes obvious references to the theory of ideas, must have been written more or less in the same period as *Theaetetus,* that is, at the time of full maturity of this philosopher and artist[1]; yet its shortcomings are more numerous than in any other of Plato's works. Three-quarters of the dialogue consists of an interminable, graceless enumeration of etymologies, part of which are obviously outlandish and listed with the intention of satirizing the abuse made of that method of research by certain Sophists, other etymologies are completely beyond reproach, and still others could have easily been accepted in Plato's day and in fact do not distinguish themselves from etymologies presented on a more serious note by the same philosopher in other dialogues. Thus the satiric motive seems unjustified and arbitrary, and the lack of clarity surrounding the author's intention gives the impression of lack of reliability.[2]

In this case also, the critics have spoken of "subtle" Socratic irony[3]; but I refuse to believe that Plato spent his time awkwardly repeating the same type of joke for pages on end and numerous times in each page, without making even the slightest degree of progress in conceptual inquiry.

This of course does not mean I accept Schaarschmidt's opinion[4] (which Benfey and Lehrs opposed very convincingly) that the dialogue is not authentic. The most likely hypothesis would seem to be that the work belongs to Plato, but that several parts have been ruined and deformed by later interpolations and revisions.[5] As for the etymologies, Plato may have discussed them in a few pages, recalling some of the more convincing and mentioning, even if jokingly, others which were either uncertain or odd, to show how easy it is to exaggerate in this field, as did Procius and other Sophists.[6] Some post-Aristotelian grammarian, from an era in which disquisitions of the sort in question were fashionable, may have taken advantage of this to display his erudition by adding dozens of other examples to Plato's list, strung together in one way or another.[7]

The fact is that after reading so much nonsense in *Cratylus* it is not easy to form a clear idea of the important concepts proposed in it on the nature and origin of language. We will now briefly summarize the book.

2. The Essential Content of the Dialogue

We ask the reader to forgive us if, in order to avoid destroying the organic unity of our observations on *Cratylus*, we repeat some of the things already said in the *Historical Survey*.

Cratylus's first thesis (set forth by Hermogenes) is the following: names of things are not the result of mere convention. Indeed, between the name and the thing named there must be a natural bond (383A). To this Hermogenes replies by proposing the opposite theory: that nothing has a name of its own, determined by its own nature, but rather the only reason for the existence of names is convention and custom; this is true to the extent that if we change a servant's name, the new name is no less correct than the earlier one (384D).[1]

Participating in the debate, Socrates observes that Hermogenes' opinion seems to correspond to Protagoras's, namely that things do not have a definitive essence but are such as they seem to each of us (386A). If however we grant that things have a nature of their own, names also—it seems—should correspond to this nature. But what are names really? They are a means or instrument. Just as the drill is an instrument used to bore holes, and the shuttle is an instrument used for weaving, names are used to express and emphasize the essential character of things. The weaver uses the shuttle, but he does not make it: this is up to the carpenter. In the same way, speakers and teachers (the dialectician) use names, yet they do not create them: this is up to the "name-maker," the founder of language.

And what does the carpenter have in mind when he makes the shuttle? He takes as his model that which the shuttle is in itself, that is, the concept or idea of the shuttle. In the same way, name-makers must look to the concept of the thing and make sure that the name is appropriate to the nature of the thing named.

No doubt it is true that a Greek word-maker and a barbarian used different syllables for the same concept, but this is of no importance, provided that the names formed correspond to the thing. In truth not even carpenters make shuttles with the same wood: what counts is that the instrument, once made, should correspond to the use it must serve (387E, 390).

We will have names then that are appropriate and names that are not appropriate: Archepolis, for example, is a name which suits the ruler of a city, Agis and Polemarchus the leader of armies, Eupolemus is appropriate for someone valiant in war, Iatrocles or Acesimbrotus for skillful physicians (394C).

Syllables must correspond to meaning, but whether a letter is taken away or added matters little. For example, we can call *e, u, o* the letters that have this sound (and here the correspondence between the name and the thing signified is perfect), but then we also call *b beta,* and here we have added something to the sound, and nevertheless we may say that the name remains appropriate (393D, E).

On the other hand, the name would not be appropriate if we were to call impious men Theophilus or Mnesitheus. A long train of more or less unfounded and sometimes obviously comical etymologies follows.[2] In short, it is acknowledged that, at most, etymologies explain the meaning of a word by deriving it from other words, and that in this way we are bound to arrive at elements that cannot in their turn derive from other words. It is therefore necessary to search for the origin of these "roots" in another way (421E, 422C).

To solve this problem (which from a certain point of view may seem to be the real problem of language origin) Socrates asks himself what we would do to understand each other if we had neither voice nor tongue. And he answers that we would make an effort to answer with signs of the hands, head, and body, as dumb people do. For example, if we wished to designate something that is light, we would raise our hand toward heaven to imitate the nature of something that rises, and if we wished to designate something heavy, we would bend toward the ground. To designate a galloping horse or any other animal, we would make our body look as much like theirs as possible.

Given that this natural mimetic language consists of imitating the things we wish to signify through gestures, Socrates infers that phonetic language also evolved as the imitation of natural sounds (423B).

But a difficulty arises here: if this is the way things go, those who amuse themselves by imitating the sounds of sheep or cocks, etc., would name those animals with such inarticulate sounds, whereas when we represent or imitate natural sounds with song or music, this does not imply that we are "name-and word-makers."

Things have color and shape and may be sonorous, however, it is not with words but with painting and music that we imitate such qualities (423D).

The imitation we accomplish through language must therefore be of a different sort.

Perhaps the role of language is that of imitating, with letters and syllables, not the qualities of things as they appear to us, but their essential characteristics.[3] In order to understand how this occurs, we must examine the elements composing words, that is, syllables and letters (424C).

Now, the letter *rho* seems to be a good instrument for the expression of motion, because in pronouncing this letter the tongue is least at rest and more vibrant than in any other. Therefore we find it in roots expressing movement such as ῥεῖν (flow), φορά (movement), τρόμος (trembling), ῥυμβεῖν (vibrate), etc. *Psi, sigma, phi,* and *zeta* are fricatives and are suitable for the imitation of that which may evoke the image of blowing, on the other hand, *delta* and *tau* are compressed sounds which on being pronounced seem to cause the tongue to stop suddenly; while on pronouncing *lambda* the tongue seems to glide, as is evident from the words λεῖα (level), λισθάνειν (glide), etc.; by contrast, on pronouncing *gamma* the gliding of the tongue seems to be stopped so that we have the words γλίσχρον (glutinous), γλοιῶδες (gluey), etc.; and lastly *nu,* pronounced by placing the tongue toward the back of the mouth, gave origin to such words as ἔνδον (inside) and ἐντός (within).

The vowels *alpha* and *eta* designate greatness and length respectively (whence μέγας and μῆκος) because the letters are large, *omicron* expresses rotundity (γογγύλον) and *iota* anything sharp and thin, etc.

In this way, therefore, it was thought that the founder of language was able to imitate the quality of things through letters (426C–427D).

That things may be imitated through letters and syllables, Socrates adds, might seem ridiculous but on the other hand we do not have anything better to explain the origin of the first names (426D), unless we want to resort to the intervention of the Gods, as do tragic poets when in difficulty.

The onomatopoeic theory according to which the roots that precede words are naturally connected with their meaning through their very sound does not seem false to Socrates, but he is not completely satisfied with it either.[4]

Of the many reasons that may be set forth for the insufficiency of this theory, Plato cites two: (1) The number of words that in some way symbolize their meaning through sound is only a minimal part of those we use; indeed, if we take numbers (which are infinite) as an example, it is not clear how we may find as many onomatopoeic names as are necessary to name them (435B). (2) We cannot deny that at least some words have a sound that does not "resemble" their meaning, such as the word σκληρόν that has a soft and flowing sound and on the contrary means hard, and yet, despite the lack of similarity between sound and meaning, on pronouncing that word, we understand it. Hence we must conclude that what makes us understand meaning in such cases is not similarity but conventional use (434C, 435C).

Regarding the problem whether language operates by nature or by convention, already debated by the pre-Socratics, Plato's dialogue seems to conclude as follows: many words are derived or composed from others, and in the latter the relation between the signifier and the signified is natural (even if this etymological link is often rather difficult to trace and may give rise to the abuses perpetrated by the Sophists). Furthermore, of the early roots, some have a symbolical onomatopoeic relation to their meaning, but this does not explain them all; consequently we will have to acknowledge that conventional use as well is an essential element in language.[5]

The epistemological issue (how we come to know things) and the metaphysical issue (whether things are in themselves unchanging essences or whether everything flows incessantly) are intimately connected, as is to be expected, to the more properly linguistic issue and predominate toward the end of the dialogue. Since Plato has dealt with these issues in far greater detail in other dialogues, I will now only briefly discuss his theory of error, and his treatment of the relation between words and thought.

3. Cratylus's Theory of Error

The Relation between Words and Thought.

All names, Cratylus repeatedly says, are appropriate, given that they are names. And if someone was to call a person who does not know how to speak Goodspeaker, we could not maintain that this name is false, but simply that it is someone else's name. Indeed, it is completely impossible to utter that which does not exist. Since that which is false does not exist, it cannot have a name and cannot be expressed. And if someone, pointing to Cratylus, were to say "this is Hermogenes"; or indicating a man, "this person is a woman," would not he be saying something false? No, he would simply be uttering sounds at random. And would not these sounds be false? No, they would be mere noises without meaning as though someone were beating a bronze pot (429B-430A).

According to Aristotle, on the contrary, Cratylus affirmed that it is impossible to say anything that is true and that corresponds to reality; because at the very moment of utterance, reality is already changing. This is the reason why Cratylus was interested in the idea of giving up the use of language altogether and limiting himself to pointing at things with his finger. But there is no trace of this in the dialogue we are examining.

Perhaps the authentic maxim maintained by the follower of Heraclitus was this: that it is impossible to pronounce any proposition whatsoever; either a true one, for the reason put forward by Aristotle, or a false one, for the reason put forward by Plato. In this way the two proofs complement each other.

This problem, which is closely connected to the linguistic issue, is dealt with toward the end of the dialogue. Socrates observes that if we know the nature of things through their names, it should follow that if we do not know the appropriate words, we do not even know the things. But, on the other hand, when names did not yet exist and the founders of language were about to formulate them, how were they able to do so if they did not know the things (438B)?

Plato solves the difficulty by arguing that in order to learn the true nature of things it is not necessary to know their names. Instead, it is sufficient to examine entities in themselves and through their mutual relations; furthermore, he maintains that this way of knowing things is far better than through names, which at the most may give us an image that is more or less similar to the entities themselves (438E–439B). Thus it would not be very wise to trust blindly in those who gave names to things for the first time (and who in most cases did so by basing their decisions on changing appearances). It would be preferable to thoroughly investigate the things themselves (439–440D).

4. Topicality and Importance of the Concepts Treated in the Dialogue

> *Nomo* and *physei*—Distinct Separation between Institution and Application—Appearance of Early Roots—Symbolic Onomatopoeia—Theory of Error and Rationality of Reality—Separation between Thought and Representation.

Let us now briefly evaluate the concepts treated in *Cratylus*.

(a) The distinction between that which is valid by convention and that which is valid by nature may be considered as one of the most important conceptual distinctions elaborated by early Greek thinkers. All that which depends on subjective will and changeable appearances is valid by convention; whereas all that which has absolute value is valid by nature because it corresponds to objective reality. We may say that through this opposition the Greek spirit acquires consciousness of its historical mission: that of freeing human thought from the abuses of the magical and mythological pre-Hellenic mentality, so as to assert the universal value of science.

The terms "nomo" and "physei" reflect the orientation of the Greeks toward objectivism: the ideal of science is to let things speak without adding anything which is contradictory because the subject is expected to understand objects while at the same time excluding itself. If our concepts are to be of any value, it is necessary that they no longer be ours, that we objectify them, that is to say, consider them as ideas existing outside ourselves; such was Plato's conclusion.

In *Cratylus* Socrates reluctantly acknowledges the importance of conventional use in language, and precisely because of such awareness, he mistrusts language. He considers language the cause of error and encourages us to pay attention to ideas, which are eternal, without letting ourselves be led astray by language, which changes.

In modern philosophy of language the distinction between the "conventional" and the "natural" element should indeed take on a different meaning; that is to say, that of a distinction between two equally necessary aspects. Those philosophers who neglect the conventional element on the grounds that it is devoid of spiritual value have not yet completely overcome the ancient conception.

Nevertheless, one of Plato's merits is that of having dwelt on the question as to whether the relation between the signifier and the signified is natural or conventional, and of concluding that both elements are necessary.[1]

(b) It is in general a good philosophical norm not to consider human institutions and activities as simple facts, but to investigate them genetically in their development, and to keep in mind that the same mental categories that were active originally must remain active even now, for nothing that the spirit possesses remains inert, but rather each acquisition represents a further achievement.

From this it follows that the epistemological criteria used to judge the work of a person presenting a completely new mathematical theorem is not different from that used by whoever studies such a theorem in the work of the master, reorganizing it on his own account; just as there is no epistemological difference between creating a work of art and understanding it as we rework it in our own spirit. For this reason, one of Humboldt's outstanding merits was to insist that if we wish to understand the essential value of language, we must not consider it as "érgon," but as "enérgeia," because real language is what we continually create through speech. But then Humboldt made an error—as we have already seen—when he applied his principle abstractly, leaving aside the more legitimate empirical distinctions and assimilating at the level of theory things that in reality are different; he was followed in this direction by quite a few modern authors.

Vice versa, Plato's over-rigid distinction between the work of the "founder of language" and that of the user of words, which are in reality two aspects of the same process, may be considered to be a mistake.

However, the empirical distinction between the way new words are created in historical languages, that is, by deriving them from previous words, and the way early roots must have come about is very important. This emerges, for example, from the fact, unanimously accepted by glottologists, that as the Italian language developed over the centuries very few new roots have been introduced, if any at all. Thus one of Plato's merits is that of having perceived the difference between the development of the historical languages and the way we may suppose early roots came into being.

Even the hypothesis of the possible derivation of Greek words from bar-

barian words, which could have provided a basis for the discussion of the genealogy and kinship of languages, is also of some importance, even if Plato's
text is obscure and uncertain on this point. The same can be said of the attempt at comparing words of different dialects, modern words with more archaic words, and even of the attempt at identifying some of the more common phonetic modifications.

As we have seen, the part concerning etymologies is the most confused
and probably the least authentic. No doubt, however, Plato recognized the
importance of etymological investigations as well as the difficulties and dangers they involve—something that can only be confirmed by modern scholars,
even if with different arguments and completely different experiences.

(c) Regarding the difficult problem of the development of the early roots
of phonetic language, the first hypothesis that seems to occur to Plato is that
of divine intervention or of superhuman powers. Nevertheless, he refuses to
resort to such a convenient expedient and thus avoid the question, and, at
the risk of committing an error, proposes to attempt a scientific solution.

He pictures a group of human beings completely destitute of language
and on asking himself how they would communicate with each other, he concludes that mimetic expression is the most natural form of expression. References in this sense were later to be found in Saint Augustine and in many
modern authors, and—as we have seen—the idea deserved further development.

Plato dwells upon it appropriately with the aim of showing that the most
natural form of expression is that of representing things by imitating them;
that is, what we may call pictographic expression. Working in this direction,
he formulates the hypothesis, debated through to the present day in various
forms, that language originated from the attempt at imitating natural sounds
with the voice.

But Plato is soon presented with the objection that the inarticulate
sounds used to imitate the bleating of sheep or the crowing of cocks are not
words. Therefore, he makes a comparison—that could still be useful today—
between the way images are represented in the various arts and their representation through linguistic expression. It should be noted that Plato, who
generally supports an intellectualistic conception of language, is here encouraged by the very argument to liken linguistic creation to works of art. A
tree may be represented to us through painting in such a way that we see it in
front of us immediately, while the word "tree" cannot do as much. Plato limits himself to deducing that onomatopoeic imitation must be, therefore, by
its very nature, completely different from the imitation of animal sounds, because the former is an indirect and, as it were, symbolic form of imitation.

He believes that single letters recall certain impressions by association, so
that, for example, r expresses motion through its vibration, the aspirates are
suited to the imitation of blowing, etc. In any case the onomatopoeic theory
as expounded in Cratylus is far superior to what Max Müller called the bau-
bau theory, and it is rather odd that modern psychologists with their similar

theories, even if different in approach, should not have remembered this precedent in Plato.[2]

Nonetheless, as already mentioned, Plato is not satisfied with the onomatopoeic theory. He cites a few decisive reasons why he does not believe that this theory can adequately explain the birth of language and concludes by acknowledging, even if unwillingly, the necessity of explaining numerous words on the basis of conventional use. He quite rightly cites numbers as an example of the latter: that the number eighty should be called "eight-by-ten" by one population and "four-by-twenty" by another is the result of conventional use and not of onomatopoeic or "naturally expressive" factors.

To consider conventionality, as did the Greeks, as something irrational and negative is an obvious flaw in Platonic theory, but it is a fact that not even most of our contemporary authors have freed themselves from this error. The naive pragmatic theories on the "conventionality" of certain mathematical and scientific concepts are still today accepted by the majority as valid. Furthermore, apart from those few and incomplete references made by myself,[3] no attempts have been made to construct theories relating to the positive value of spiritual activities capable of creating conventions: activities which are dialectic moments essential both to the practical spirit (volitive attitudes, custom) and to the theoretical spirit (of which they constitute the pre-logical and pre-aesthetic stage in mnemonic signs).

(d) The theory of error as expounded in *Cratylus* (which should be compared to what is said in *Euthydemus*, 285E) anticipates the idealistic theory of error as the non-being of thought. In truth, this opinion reported by Plato could seem more appropriate to a follower of Parmenides (for whom the non-being does not exist) than to a follower of Heraclitus (for whom the non-being is a phase in becoming). But Plato relates Cratylus's doctrine to the skeptical and Protagorean interpretation of Heraclitism. Just as the phenomenism of Protagoras appears to be an *ante litteram* caricature of idealism, the theory of error of the Platonic *Cratylus* may be considered as a caricature of Hegelian theory. Proof of this correspondence lies in the fact that scholars who still today confuse the idealistic negation of exterior objective reality with the Protagorean negation, then interpret the idealistic theory of error, similarly to Cratylus, as the denial of the very possibility of committing error.

The apparent similarity between the doctrine supported by Cratylus and that of idealism is even more striking in errors that concern analytical or deductive propositions (according to Greek logic, these are the only scientific propositions). For example, to someone maintaining that the part is greater than the whole, one might rightly reply: you did not think that proposition because it is unthinkable, rather you pronounced words without thinking anything; just as Cratylus asserted that in false judgments sounds are emitted without meaning.

Socrates' confutation, which defines truth as correspondence between the name and external object and error as non-correspondence, does not at all exhaust the argument. At another point in the dialogue (385B, D) dealing with the theory of error, argumentation is so weak that it has not escaped the attention of even the less critical commentators. It is stated that in a false proposition the single parts must also be false, so that words are consequently either true or false in themselves. In this passage, if it is authentic, the naivety of Platonic objectivism is at its peak. But more probably this peculiar conception of names that are true or false in themselves is not to be attributed to Socrates, but to Cratylus or to some other follower of Heraclitus; I believe this is the most likely hypothesis because of the nature of the concept as well as by comparison to a passage by Ammonius, who attributes the following argumentation to Heraclitus:

> Just as we possess a particular sense for each different sensation (the eye, for instance, is the sense that perceives the form and color of objects), there exists a sense that captures the appropriate name, inherent in all things.

Ammonius states that only he who expresses the objective name of a thing really names it whereas he who does not do this does not name that thing, but simply produces a noise; it is precisely the role of whoever knows to find for each thing the specific name to which it has a right by nature, just as it is the task of whoever sees to observe the specific character of each object.[4]

This view recalls pre-Hellenic conceptions which more or less presuppose that the name is an objective property of things. We are told, for example, that Adam had the gift of knowing the true name of each animal, or that knowledge of occult names confers a special power over things.[5] This view is distant from our own way of thinking, though it is no more naive than the conception of medieval thinkers who considered the "right price" as an objective property of each commodity, or of popular thought that considers qualities as an inherent property in objects, independent of the subject that perceives them.

(e) When toward the end of *Cratylus* (438B) Socrates asks himself how it was that "name-givers" were able to invent the names of things if to invent them it was first necessary to be familiar with the things in question, which was only possible through names, he touches on a problem which was to torment many thinkers for centuries and which, among others, was dealt with by Rousseau in *Discours sur l'inégalité parmi les hommes*.

The problem has not yet even today been clarified satisfactorily. Humboldt thought he had found the solution in identifying language and thought and Croce improved on Humboldt's conception by defining language, after Vico, not as thought but as the expressive and imaginative element essential to thought. If correctly understood, Croce's suggestion may contribute toward the solution of the problem, for it helps us to understand how primitive man, rich in sense and fantasy but poor in concepts, was all the same able to lay the foundations of language. However, we saw that Croce's theory was wrongly understood so that it became merely philosophical and brought more confusion than enlightenment, denying the empirical problem of language origin all legitimacy.

The attitude of glottologists working in the direction indicated by Croce may be understood as a unilateral reaction against Plato. Plato was wrong in imagining that mankind had a conceptual life similar to our own before the advent of language (422E), and in placing (according to the orientation of his system) thought on one side and its representation on the other. If by "word" we mean all concrete representations, Socrates' advice to search for truth in things, beyond words, may be viewed as a formulation of the Platonic ideal of abstract rationalism: to reach the universal by depriving it of all individualization; to think without expressing oneself, as when we close our eyes to see better.

Conclusion

Concluding our examination of *Cratylus,* we believe that, from the point of view of its conceptual content, this dialogue is one of the most lively and important of Plato's minor works, and is still today a useful stimulus in studies on the origin and nature of language. Perhaps no other Platonic dialogue has been commented on and discussed as much as this one. If the concepts dealt with have scarcely been acknowledged and are little understood by the historians of philosophy as much as by glottologists, this is mainly due to the fact that the dialogue has reached us in a confused and corrupt form—a form very distant from the original clarity, harmony, and urbanity of Platonic style. For this reason it did not seem a waste of time to reexamine it carefully in an attempt to separate the grain from the chaff and to better highlight its undeniable merits.

Notes

BOOK ONE : Part One
INQUIRY INTO THE ORIGIN OF LANGUAGE

Introduction

1. Here are some of the numerous examples of this negative attitude: "In whatever period it may be considered, language always appears as the inheritance of a preceding age. . . . The act through which names were given to things . . . may be conceived, but it has never been ascertained. . . . For this reason the problem of the origin of language is not as important as some claim it to be. In fact it is a problem that should not even be posed: the only real object of linguistics is the normal and regular life of an already constituted idiom" (cf. F. de Saussure, *Cours de linguistique générale*, Paris 1916, p. 107).

Wundt calls "metaphysical" all research that does not concern itself with the laws governing the development of languages that actually exist but rather concerns itself with the question of the origin. Our science (psychology), he says, cannot concern itself with this kind of research: "A point of view external to language, the hypothesis of a state in which man was not only destitute of language but necessarily also of all those skills through which language is produced; from the point of view of our science this hypothesis is empty fiction, it has no use and is meaningless given that it removes the conditions that render the very existence of language possible" (cf. W. Wundt, *Völkerpsychologie*, Leipzig 1904, vol. 1, p. 614).

In the third international congress of linguists, various authors, including van Ginneken, Uhlenbeck, Schrijnen, etc., took a stance against all hypotheses on the origin of language "about which we do not and cannot know anything" (*Atti del III Congresso internazionale di linguistica*, Lemonnier, Florence 1935).

"The problem of language origin," says Vendryes, "remains outside the scope of our science. It is a part of studies on the origin of man and of human societies and should be studied together with the primitive history of humanity" (J. Vendryes, *Le langage*, Paris 1921, p. 8).

"The origin of language is not a linguistic problem—as Giulio Bertoni has also maintained—but, if anything, it is a philosophical and theological problem" (*Enciclopedia italiana*, under the entry "linguaggio").

And Pagliaro: "The problem of the origin of language, which has worried psychologists and linguists so much, is insoluble for it is closely connected to the problem of human origins. . . . The problem is legitimate only in terms of the origin of single languages; but, all things considered, it is mere fiction, since the immense period of prehistory is not within our range" (Ibid., Appendix II [1948], vol II, p. 209).

2. In the second part of this book, we will examine the problem of the relation between word, thought, intuition, expression, and sign.

3. From this point of view language can be likened to an ideographic writing system similar to Chinese writing. In the latter, in fact, graphic signs do not necessarily

refer to the phonemes of language, as in our own writing system, but rather each sign directly recalls a given concept or a given image. A message formulated in ideographic script can be read and understood even if one is not familiar with the spoken language of the writer. (A Japanese person, for example, can read a Chinese text without knowing the language.) Therefore this writing system is a language in which graphic signs are used instead of phonetic signs. However, it was developed by men of learning for use by a caste of scholars. Many years of study are necessary to learn it, so much so that, in that Ancient Empire, to be instructed in this system of ideograms was one of the most important prerequisites in order to rise to a position of power in state bureaucracy.

4. *Discours sur l'inégalité parmi les hommes.*

5. Most of the authors who had dealt with this problem up to the first half of the nineteenth century based themselves upon the chronology of the Jewish people and assumed that the Earth was approximately six thousand years old. Today it has been possible to calculate that certain rocks date back to more than one thousand eight hundred million years, that mammals have been living on the earth for about fifty million years, and that living beings similar to man (Heidelberg man) existed approximately four hundred and fifty thousand years ago. Calculations are based on the rate of disintegration of certain chemical elements such as uranium, actinium, and thorium.

Since we know with precision that, for example, a gram of uranium takes a million years to produce a seven-thousand-six-hundredth part of a gram of lead, when we find uranium encircled with lead in a geological stratum, we are able to make an accurate calculation of that stratum on the basis of the proportion between the two elements.

6. Steinthal is also of the opinion that the institution of language is perhaps the greatest miracle after the creation of living beings (see *Werke*, Stuttgart 1827, p. 187). In fact, the former represents, as we have said, the transition from animal to man, just as the latter represents the transition from inanimate material to organic and animal life.

7. Pointing out the different perspectives according to which the problems of linguistics may be viewed, Saussure rightly compares them to questions pertaining to the juridical system which is both a descriptive science as well as a history of institutions (Saussure, *Cours de linguistique générale*, pp. 117–18). But his distinction between *synchronic* linguistics (which should correspond to a naturalistic description) and *diachronic* linguistics (which should correspond to a historical survey) does not seem to grasp the heart of the matter. In fact, we may have descriptive laws (like those of phonetic mutations) concerning phenomena in their temporal (diachronic) development and historical or philosophical considerations concerning facts that occur together at a given (synchronic) moment.

8. K. W. von Humboldt, *Einleitung in die Kawi-Sprache*, Berlin 1841, pp. LXXIV–LXXVI.

9. K. W. von Humboldt, *Über die vergleichenden Sprachstudien*, Berlin 1903, sec. 13.

10. Unjust causes were in fact defended with tricks of this kind. For example, at the philosophical congress of Milan in 1928, on expressing his hopes for a regime with greater respect for the freedom of its citizens, Martinetti was answered that freedom is an eternal and inalienable possession that lives *in interiore homine* and that no regime can violate it.

11. E. Renan, *De l'origine du langage*, Paris 1858, p. 90.

12. Ladevi-Roche, *De l'origine du langage*, Bordeaux 1980, p. 14. Similar opinions expressed by Saint Augustine and Saint Thomas are re-echoed in Dante's famous verses: *Par.*, XXVI, 130–32.

13. G. D. Whitney, *Oriental and Linguistic Studies*, New York 1873, p. 279.

14. G. E. Lessing, *Gesammelte Schriften*, Stuttgart 1886, X, pp. 4–5.

15. J. Grimm, *De l'origine du langage*, with a preface by E. Renan, Paris 1859.

16. I explain the inadequacy of epistemology in the sciences of intuitionism, pragmatism, and historicism in *La filosofia del Croce* (Croce's philosophy), Milan 1946, pp. 217–40.

17. G. Curtius, *Zur Kritik der neuesten Sprachwissenschaft*, Leipzig 1885, p. 145.

1. How the Origin of Language May Be Explained by Studying the Origin and Evolution of Writing Systems

Pictography and Mnemotechny

1. G. Fano, *La filosofia del Croce*, p. 172.

2. In H. Wuttke's words (*Geschichte der Schrift und des Schrifttums*, Berlin 1872, p. 11): "The fact that the same concept could be expressed through language as well as through figurative writing [diese Zweiseitigkeit des Namlichen] induced early grammarians to meditate on that essence which is at the basis of both expressive techniques."

3. According to Steinthal: "The formation of writing systems came about in relation to laws of the human spirit: laws we encounter among the various populations insofar as they are human beings" (*Die Entwicklung der Schrift*, Berlin 1852, p. 51). And Philippe Berger: "Comme les langues les écritures sont des organisations vivantes soumises aux lois de la transformation" (*Histoire de l'écriture dans l'antiquité*, Paris 1891, p. IX).

4. *Odyssey*, XI, 77; XII, 25. A famous example of expression through *real objects* comes from Cato the Elder, master of dramatic expression, who during a meeting of the senate hurled a handful of fresh figs and said: "Tam prope a muris habemus hostem!" Expressions of this kind, consisting of a mixture of words, gestures, and real objects, are not rare among Italians.

5. Ibid., IV, 131. Cf. G. De Sanctis, *Il messaggio figurato degli Sciti a Dario* (The figurative message of the Scythians to Darius), in *In memoria lui Vasile Parvan*, Bucharest 1934, p. 110. The Bible, too, recalls various cases of real messages. Not without lugubrious effectiveness is the episode, reported in *Judges 19:29*, in which a citizen asks for revenge against the murderers of his wife by cutting up her body into twelve pieces and sending a piece to each tribe "in omnes termines Israel."

6. Richard Andree collected a great number of such examples in his *Ethnographische Parallelen und Vergleiche, I: Merkzeichen und Knotenschrift*, Stuttgart 1878.

It is the custom, for example, among the inhabitants of the Malay Archipelago to place warning signs and exorcism signs in their fields to stop strangers from entering their property. Pumpkins with a neck and big body, hanging from a pole, mean: "May whoever enters my field be struck with swelling of the belly." A pole with braided palm fibers means: "May he be struck by an intestinal worm *(involvulus)*."

When hunting the Tungusi are in the habit of communicating through arrows or signs on trees. A crossed arrow pointing upward means: "I've gone far away." Pointing downward: "Beware of being hit!" A branch placed across the track means: "Don't follow me!"

Letters of challenge are in use among the Batacchi people. They are hung on the hut of the adversary and foretell fire and murder as vengeance for blood. They are composed of a bundle of coconut fibers (which are used as bait), a flint, and various arms.

George Schweinfurth reports that the Assanti or Niam Niam, a cannibal people of the Upper Nile, once, on being threatened by an enemy incursion, placed some corn-cobs, the feather of a chicken, and an arrow on the road as a warning; it probably read: "If you dare trample on our corn-cobs or steal our chickens, you will die by our arrows."

According to custom, the inhabitants of Sumatra communicate their feelings through symbolic gifts: a pinch of salt, of pepper, and a small piece of betel, which mean respectively: love, jealousy, hatred (cf. K. Weule, *Vom Kerbstock zum Alphabet*, Stuttgart 1921, pp. 58ff. This is a modest little book belonging to a popular scientific collection, but in fact it is richer in personal and intelligent observations than certain much bigger volumes).

7. We have records of various real object letters by these people. For example, a prisoner of the tribe sent a message to his wife consisting of a rock, a piece of charcoal, a dried ear of wheat, and a rag. It signified: "My body, which was once hard and strong like a rock now lives through days as black as charcoal. I will become as thin and dry as this head of wheat and I will be reduced to a rag." As we can see real object writing often makes use of symbolic meanings which may gradually become conventional signs (Weule, *Vom Kerbstock zum Alphabet*, p. 74).

8. Among the Chinese, too, real object writing was sometimes connected to a phonetic element. For example, the sovereign would send the exiled subject a ring ("huan") as a way of exhorting him to return, playing on the fact that the syllable "huan" also means return (Chavannes, in "Journal Asiatique," IX, 18, Paris 1901).

9. Weule, *Vom Kerbstock zum Alphabet*, p. 11. A similar attitude has often been noted in the way children and the common people listen to fairytales and legends, that is, fully believing that they are true stories.

As a rule we might say that the lack of distinction between reality and fantasy characterizes the aesthetic "state of grace." For the poet in the act of composing poetry, what we will eventually call his work of art is in fact the true story of his soul, and unlike the decadent constructors of aesthetic decorations, he will never resolve to write "pure" poetry, that is to say, poetry devoid of truth and faith.

10. D. Diringer, *L'alfabeto nella storia della civiltà* (The Alphabet in the History of Civilization), Florence 1937, p. 23; cf. M. C. Burkitt, *Prehistory*, London 1925, pp. 193ff.

11. R. H. Mathews, in "Journal of the Anthropological Institute," xxv, p. 153. U.S. scholars have put together a fine collection of primitive pictographic and ideographic materials. See in particular the 4th and 10th volumes of Washington's "Annual Report of the Bureau of Ethnology."

12. E. Clodd, *Storia dell'alfabeto* (History of the Alphabet), Turin 1924, p. 58.

13. The letter was communicated by the prince of Wied. Cf. W. Wundt, *Völkerpsychologie, Die Sprache*, Leipzig 1904, vol. I, 1, p. 240.

14. For other numerous examples of North American native pictographies, see H. R. Schoolcraft, in *The Red Man of America, 1851*, I, table 62.

15. Weule, *Vom Kerbstock zum Alphabet*, p. 9.

16. Referred to by Diringer, Wundt, Clodd, etc.

17. On the function of determinatives see below, chap. 3, sec. 6.

18. Egyptian writing, one of the most brilliant creations of pre-Hellenic civilization, is fundamentally ideographic, and, as a rule, each sign corresponds to a concept and to a word. Nonetheless syllabic signs are used here and there as auxiliary signs. Strangely enough, however, as many as twenty-four of these are monoconsonants, which would tempt us to say that the ancient Egyptians had already made the revolutionary discovery of alphabetic writing. However, this cannot be stated and not so much because as did the Semites, the Egyptians probably overlooked vowels and used the same sign for "ra," "re," "ri," etc., but because they only used these auxiliary signs when they did not have the appropriate ideogram. The alphabet existed but they were not aware of it; that is to say, they were not aware of the enormous practical advantage which could have been obtained by basing the entire graphic system on monoconsonantal signs. These considerations may offer a few clues for a better understanding of the origin of the alphabet. In fact, given that twenty-four alphabetic signs already existed in Egyptian writing, it would have sufficed that another population, no longer burdened by traditional use, adopt that writing system favoring

monoconsonantal signs and after a period of time the revolution would have been accomplished on its own, quite unintentionally. Given that use of monoconsonantal signs as alphabetic signs ("ra," "re," "ri," for "r") is only possible in a system that overlooks vowels, such as the Phoenician and Hebraic writing systems, etc., it is not improbable that the transition took place through the mediation of a Semitic population, as the ancients believed. Nevertheless, it is surprising that, as close as it got to the target, Egyptian writing did not accomplish the decisive step but remained at the ideographic stage for millennia, from the Ancient Empire through to the Ptolemies. Ancient oriental civilizations, especially the Egyptians and Chinese, reveal a disconcerting mixture of creative intelligence and irrational attachment to ancient customs. This is difficult to understand if we do not keep in mind (as I have tried to illustrate in my study on *Teosofia orientale* [Oriental Theosophy]) the important role played by the passive observance of handed down custom, characteristic of animal life, in all primitive civilizations.

19. The same more or less approximative method is to be found among such primitive populations as the Yoruba, the great populations of oriental civilization, and among the Aztecs. The puzzles invented by the latter are rather complex and imprecise; for example, they would outline the shape of lips ("te-n-tli"), a road ("o-tli"), a house ("cal-li"), teeth ("tlan-tli") to signify the word "teocaltitlan" (man of the church).

Mnemonic Signs

1. *Genesis 9:12–17:* "Arcum meum ponam in nubibus, et sit signum foederis inter me et inter terram. Cumque obduxero nubibus caelum, apparebit arcus meus—et videbo illum, et recordabor foederis sempiterni."

2. "Ut sit signum inter vos: et quando interrogaverint vos filii vestri cras, dicentes: - Quid sibi volunt isti lapides? - respondebitis eis: - Defecerunt aquae Jordanis ante arcam foederis Domini, cum transirent eum: idcirco positi sunt lapides isti in monumentum filiorum Israel usque in aeternum."

3. Numerous examples are quoted in Andree, *Ethnographische Parallelen*.

4. The witches of ancient Babylonia used charms made of knotted cords. Furthermore, both the Greeks and the Romans attributed a magic influence to knots, raising their power to bind and strangle to the status of symbol.

5. Garcilaso de la Vega, *Historia general del Perú*, Cordoba 1617. Cf. H. Jensen, *Geschichte der Schrift*, Hannover 1925, p. 10. The deciphering of the Quippus was entrusted to specialists called "quippucamayocuna," that is to say, "knot officials."

6. They were also called "tally boards" and in medieval Latin they were called "taleae," or "tallia," which leads to the Italian *taglia*. They were commonly used in almost all European countries to record calculations, debts, incomes, etc. (Jensen, *Geschichte der Schrift*, p. 82).

7. Weule, *Vom Kerbstock zum Alphabet*, p. 63.

8. One such message, from the Mundaingura tribe, was shown by an ethnologist to members of a tribe near Dalebura who understood, at least in part, the conventional meaning of those signs (Weule, *Vom Kerbstock zum Alphabet*, p. 64).

9. Jensen, *Geschichte der Schrift*, p. 9.

10. "Alle ihre Arten stellen sozusagen einen unfruchtbaren Ast an dem Baume des Schriftsystemes dar" (Weule, *Vom Kerbstock zum Alphabet*, p. 23).

11. Reported in "Annual Report of the Bureau of Ethnology," xix. Cf. Diringer, *L'alfabeto nella storia della civiltà*, It. Trans., p. 570.

12. From a report by the Jesuits in the 17th century, we learn that Indian children of North America transformed Christian prayers into pictures drawn in charcoal, symbolizing the more characteristic words, as a way of learning those prayers better (Ibid., p. 563). The same method was used in certain Indian chronicles of the Pre-Columbian era. One of these, by the Delavari Indians, begins with the Indian story

of the flood, which could be summarized as follows: "Gigantic fish are human beings. The lunar woman saved them with her boat. Nanabusc, the God of resurrected life, arrived." These concepts are expressed in three little verses and are remembered by three figures (Weule, *Vom Kerbstock zum Alphabet*, p. 14). More recent are the so-called "winter calculations" of the Dakota. Each year was marked by an important event such as an epidemic, death, successful hunting, etc., represented by a symbol. For example, the chronicle about the solitary Dog is composed of numerous symbolic signs forming a spiral shape. A black disk with two stars represents the solar eclipse of August 7, 1869; thirty vertical lines in three columns represent the death of thirty Dakotas killed by the Assarocas in the winter of 1800, etc., etc.

13. When, to write my book *Teosofia orientale*, I needed to consult certain philosophical and religious texts from India, I was struck by the peculiar way in which those doctrines had been handed down orally through very short little mnemonic verses *(Sutras)*. For example, the entire *Vedanta* doctrine is contained in Badarayana's 555 *Sutras*, which however are incomprehensible without the help of extremely detailed comments. Not only are the verses in themselves incomprehensible, but they do not even aim at being understood; their purpose is to furnish cues to the memory. (As though to help us remember the beginning chapters of the Bible we had to learn short little lines such as the following: "Creation and rest," / "Man and woman in the garden," / "Sin and punishment," / "Killing of the brother," etc.).

In truth owing to the pedantry and lack of intelligence in teaching methods, those little verses are sometimes used to highlight unimportant words such as: at this point, therefore, faced with, especially as, etc., which out of context are rather disconcerting.

This method is exactly the same as that used in mnemotechnic pre-writing systems, and like the designs in such writing systems those verses also presuppose previous training. The same thing may be said of the hexagrams of the ancient Chinese *Book of Changes (I Ching)* which will be discussed in the pages that follow.

I do not know whether this has been studied by specialists in Oriental literatures, but only they will be able to decide whether ancient mnemotechnic designs influenced the method of summarizing verses, or whether they both developed independently from the same pre-graphic and pre-literary *forma mentis*.

14. C. Meinhof, *Zur Entstehung der Schrift*, in "Zeitschrift fur ägyptische Sprache und Alterthum," 1922, p. 49.

15. Clodd, *Storia dell'alfabeto*, It. trans., p. 27.

16. Weule, *Vom Kerbstock zum Alphabet*, p. 60. The frame AB represents a house. The umbrella-shaped figure C represents the girl who is writing. The lines crossing each other signify sadness. The dotted line at the top is the attribute of women: a pigtail. The fact that frame R is not closed like AB should mean that the persons living there (FG) are far away. Figure F, it too characterized by a pigtail, means Russian woman. That we are dealing with a woman is also obvious from the skirt H, which is wider than the others. The stripes (s) at the top joining F and G denote the affection uniting husband and wife. Lines K and L symbolize the love of the Jucagira, line J that crosses over her starting from F means that the Russian woman's (F) influence is an obstacle to the love of the person who is writing. The curved line M means that the girl's thoughts will never abandon her loved one. O represents a Jucagiro whose thoughts (N) are turned toward the girl. P and Q are two sons of the couple F and G.

We have included this letter among those communications in which the mnemotechnic element still predominates, for it seems that the symbolic meaning of the lines and figures will only be remembered if first explained and cannot be understood through systematically conventional signs.

Chinese Writing

1. Jensen, *Geschichte der Schrift*, p. 30.

2. The national religion of the Chinese, Confucianism, the apotheosis of a sober, practical, and prosaic mentality, is also in contrast with the mystical fervor and imaginative exuberance of other oriental religions. As with the Greeks, who compensated for the coldness of their over decorative national mythology by resorting to mysteries of oriental origin, whenever the Chinese felt the need for a more intense religious feeling, they turned to India.

3. Cf. W. Grube, *Geschichte der chinesischen Literatur*, Leipzig 1909. For the *I Ching* see *Sacred Books of the East*, Oxford 1882, vol. 16. Equally the *I Ching*, trans. by C. de Harley, Paris 1897. For Chinese writing in general see B. Schindler, *Die Entwicklung der chinesischen Schriftbildung*, in "Ostasiatische Zeitschrift," year iv; and Schindler, *Die Ausgestaltung der chinesischen Schrift, ibid.*, year vi.

4. Marre, *Manière de compter des anciens avec les doigts des mains*, etc., quoted in Diringer, *L'alfabeto nella storia della civiltà*, p. 719ff. For further information on primitive numbering systems, see pp. 103f.

2. The Pictographic Elements of Language
Interjections and Onomatopoeia

1. Bopp observes, for example, that the element "i" characteristic of the optative as in the Greek φέροιμι (I would like to bring) refers to the root "i" which signified "to go" and then "to desire"; and that the future ending "-sio" (as in δείξω for δείχσιω) refers to the two verbal roots "i," "to walk," and "as," "to be"; so that desire was originally signified intuitively as going toward the desired object, and the future action was designated as desired action with the addition of a particle that signified "to be."

2. This list is taken from a table of fifty-three terms collected by J. Jrie Sendai and in part reported by Wundt, *Völkerpsychologie*, vol. 1, p. 299.

3. From M. Müller, *Letture sopra la scienze del linguaggio* (*Lectures on the Science of Language*, 1861), It. trans. by Nerucci, Milan 1864, p. 374.

4. Müller, It. trans., p. 378.

5. vv. 742–55. The attempts made by certain naturalists to express the songs and warbles of birds through alphabetic signs are of little interest. See J. A. Naumann, *Naturgeschichte der Vogel Deutschlands, 1822–33*, vol. 2, p. 368. The song of the nightingale, for example, is expressed like this: "ih ih ih wati wati wati wati / quoi wati quoi quoi quoi / Quoi qui ita lu lu lu lu lu / lu lu wati wati wati." More interesting, if anything, are the transcriptions that are to be found here and there in the popular verses of which Naumann gives various examples.

6. O. Jespersen, *Die Sprache*, German trans. by R. Hittmair, Heidelberg 1925, p. 131.

7. Already in their first year of life and even before knowing how to pronounce words, children sometimes imitate the various sounds they hear around them. The writer V. Baum, who despite the too intentionally eccentric character of her novels is gifted with an uncommon power of observation and intuition, says this about a child: "Much before he knew how to say mummy he collected sounds by imitating all the noises he heard: the dog's barking, grandfather's sighs and mutterings, the creaking of the door, the tap-tap of the housemaid's plushy slippers, the sizzling of frying pans on the stove, etc." (*Marion*, French trans., p. 269).

8. Müller, *Letture sopra la scienza del linguaggio*, It. trans., pp. 375–76.

9. T. Benfey, *Geschichte der Sprachwissenschaft*, Munchen 1869, p. 404.

10. K. Bühler, in *Atti del congresso internazionale di linguistica*, p. 170.

11. E. W. Middendorf, *Das Runasimi oder die Kechua-Sprache*, Liepzig 1890, p. 125.

12. Hammer enumerates as many as 5744 words to designate the camel (Müller, *Letture sopra la scienza del linguaggio*, It. trans., p. 392).

13. Müller, *Letture sopra la scienza del linguaggio*, It. trans., pp. 365–66.

14. "Rava" however derives from the root "ru," from which we get the Latin "raucus" and "rumor," the German "rufen" and the Sanskrit "rud" (to scream). The element "ru" probably has an onomatopoeic origin, not however in relation to the "cra-cra" of the crow, but rather to murmuring or buzzing sounds.

15. These arguments however are double-edged, for while on the one hand they show that elements of imitative origin are fewer than would seem, on the other hand, they also show that in these words the onomatopoeic influence which is added to the thematic element is continually operative in language.

Abstract Language and Concrete Language

1. For example, the inspirate *s* (to signify pain or irritation), the inspirate *h* (to signify surprise or fright), and the sound expressing dissatisfaction, regret, and negation which the English render approximatively with *tut** or *i'ck** (cf. Jespersen, *Die Sprache*, pp. 408–409). Of the many expressive sounds that cannot be rendered alphabetically we may remember the whistle and other sibilant sounds used to indicate surprise, admiration, etc.; the labial sound imitating the kiss, certain palatal and clicking sounds to indicate that a certain dish is delicious, etc.

2. Müller, *Letture sopra la scienza del linguaggio*, It. trans., pp. 181ff.

3. Differences among articulate sounds have been roughly grouped as follows: alphabetic differences determined by the vocal organs more specifically involved, differences in length, intensity, rhythm, tonality and timbre.

4. K. Bücher, *Arbeit und Rhythmus*, Leipzig, 4th ed., 1908. The author enumerates some of these characteristic calling sounds on page 192: "hau-hau" used by the Ihosai, "yo-ho!" and "ho-ho!" used by the Kuli Indians, "hu-hu-ahu!" by the Chinese, "na-sa-aye-onaaaa!" by the Japanese, "haha-e!" by the New Zealanders, "haha!" "hihi!" "hehe!" used by the Negroes of Tanzanyika, "ho-ho-be ii!" by the oarsmen of the Elba, "ai-da-da!" used by the Burlachi of the Volga, etc.

5. Grimm, *De l'origine du langage*, pp. 39ff.

6. *Atti del III Congresso internazionale di linguistica;* the letter *i* means quick, little, tiny, acute; *o* static, big, distant; *a* present, real, wide; *u* spiritual, exciting; *e* appearance; *h* affirmation; *k* force, decision, tenacity; *n* inertia; *l* liberty, mobility; *r* movement, force; *s* consistency, hardness; *m* hesitation, discretion; *d* tranquil appearance; *p* and *f* vivacity; etc.

7. Cf. Bühler, *L'onomatopée et la fonction représentative du langage*, in *Psychologie du langage*, edited by Delacroix, Cassirer et al., Alcan, Paris 1933, p. 107. In the same way we could mention the German words "kribbeln," "krabbeln," "wimmern," "flimmern," "haschen," etc.; and the English words "slip," "slop," "slur," etc. In Firth's opinion, despite their not having a common etymology, the English words beginning in *sl* or *str* are analogous in that they are unconsciously associated to the idea of sliding.

8. R. A. S. Paget, *L'évolution du langage* in *Psychologie du langage*, edited by Delacroix.

9. Saint Augustine, *De Dialectica*, quoted in Müller, *Letture sopra la scienza del linguaggio*, vol. 2, p. 354.

10. M. Grammont, *Traité de phonétique*, Paris 1933, p. 413.

11. To say "tongue" Polynesians say "elelo," Malayans "leda," certain African populations "ludimi," the inhabitants of Mozambique "limi." For "mouth" the Mongols say "am," the Samoyeds "namo," Malayans "mulut," certain South African pop-

ulations "mulam." To say "to eat" the Chinese say "nam," the Javanese "mangan," Tahitians "amu," the Madecs "human," the people of Surinam "nyam," Australians "nomang," etc. For "to blow" the Malayans say "puput," New Zealanders "pupui," Australians "bobun," the Caffres "pupuza," Jews "paah," Germans "pusten" (from a table compiled by Wundt with reference to a book by Humboldt on the "kawi" language. Cf. Wundt, *Völkerpsychologie*, vol. I, p. 335).

12. For an exhaustive treatment of the argument, see S. W. Koelle, *Polyglotta africana*, London 1854.

13. That it is natural to express the concepts of duration and quantity by repeating the same sign several times is also made obvious by the fact that this technique is often used by deaf-mutes. For example, if repeated several times, the mimetic sign indicating money means a lot of money; the spiral-shaped sign meaning after (or the day after) if repeated means: after several days.

14. Numerous examples are to be found in A. F. Pott's essay *Reduplicazioni e germinazioni* (Duplications and germinations) and in the works we have already quoted by Müller and Gabelentz.

In certain languages duplications are used to form collective nouns. For example: in Malayan "pochon" = tree, "pochon-pochon" = wood; in Dakota "runa" = man, "runa-runa" = people. Similarly, in Chinese "zit" = day, "zit-zit" = every day; "si-si" = in all times; "gin-gin" = every man, etc. Sometimes reduplications (like the repetition of a gesture in mimetic language) serve to indicate something distant in time and space; this is at the basis of frequent repetitions in Greek and Latin verbal past tenses: "spopondi," "momordi," "cecidi," etc.

Not always, however, does the repetition of a syllable have onomatopoeic value as, for example, in the word *tetro* (Lat. "teter"). At times the seemingly obvious imitative value is contradicted by the etymology: for example, the Italian word *mammella* (Lat. "mamma") would seem to derive from the imitative sound "am-am" but instead derives from the root "mad" (Lat. "madeo," I'm damp); in such cases the onomatopoeic element superimposes itself upon the already existing conceptual element.

15. K. W. von Humboldt, *Sprachphilosophische Schriften*, ed. by Steinthal, Berlin 1884, p. 82.

16. W. Sievers, *Grundzüge der Phonetik*, Leipzig 1901, p. 217.

17. Grammont, *Traité de phonétique*, p. 128.

18. L. W. Osald, *Grammatik der T'ai oder siamesischen Sprache*, Leipzig 1881; H. G. C. von der Gabelentz, *Chinesische Grammatik*, Leipzig 1881, pp. 32ff.

According to Grammont, there are six different intonations in the language of the Cocincina. For example: (1) the syllable *me* (pronounced normally) signifies the tamarind-tree; (2) the syllable *mé* (pronounced with a high, dry, and short tone) means beach; (3) the syllable *mè* (in a lowered and slowly dwindling voice) means sesame; (4) the syllable *meh* (in a low tone similar to bleating) means mother; (5) the syllable *mé* (with an interrogative and surprised intonation as in the English "me!?") means to damage, to open a breach; (6) the syllable *me* (with a falling pronunciation) is equal to an exclamation of surprise.

But the same syllable may have at least seventeen different meanings, according to the tone.

19. T. Hahn, *Die Sprache der Rama*, Leipzig 1870, p. 23; H. Steinthal, *Mande-Neger-Sprachen*, Berlin 1867, p. 22.

20. G. Jaeger, *Über den Ursprung der menschlichen Sprache*, Berlin 1867, pp. 25ff.

21. In an experiment I conducted myself, the actor, who was hidden from my sight, succeeded in giving an almost perfect illusion of various voices and noises, but not in transmitting a concrete message. The most concrete scene he succeeded in conveying was that of a fight between a dog and cat, in which I could clearly distinguish when one of the two animals got the worst of it and the other triumphed.

3. Mimetic Language

Origins and Characteristics

1. P. Mantegazza, *Fisionomia e mimica* (Physiognomy and mimicry), Milan 1889, p. 105. In spite of the occasionally condescending attitude of this polymath personality, Mantegazza should be given the merit of having favored the diffusion of culture in this area as well, and of having been among the first scholars in Italy to dedicate himself to problems of mimicry.

2. Mantegazza, *Fisionomia e mimica*, p. 117.

3. In relation to this aspect see the characteristic designs of L. A. Rosa, *Espressione e mimica* (Expression and mimicry), Hoepli, Milan 1928.

4. Cf. R. Pellet, *Des premières perceptions du concret à la conception de l'abstrait*, Lyon 1938, p. 137.

5. P. Vuillemey, *La pensée et les signes autres que ceux de la langue*, Paris 1940, pp. 140–41.

6. Quintilian, *Institutiones oratoriae*, XI, 3, 87.

7. Abbot Sicard from Paris was one of the first to comment on this when he visited a London institute in 1815 together with his deaf-mute pupil Clerc and realized that the latter had no difficulty in understanding his English brothers. At the International Congress for deaf-mutes held in Paris in 1931, it was also observed that the deaf-mutes of fourteen different nations were able to talk for hours with no difficulty without using words. There were Spaniards, Swedes, Japanese, etc. (cf. Vuillemey, *La pensée et les signes*, p. 198).

8. Experiments were carried out at the Washington and Pennsylvania National Institutes between 1873 and 1888. A few Utah Indians famous for their mimetic ability were invited with a view to observing the reciprocal intelligibility of their mimicry. It was ascertained that the deaf-mutes understood all the details of a tale narrated in the mimicry of the Indians, but the latter did not always properly understand what was presented by the deaf-mutes who had been trained to use a number of systematically arranged conventional signs. Cf. G. Ferrari and Gaddi, *Manuale di pedagogia emendatrice ad uso degli allievi maestri dei sordomuti* (Handbook of pedagogy for student teachers of deaf-mutes), Milan 1938, pp. 1, 180.

Around 1920 Severin, the mime, expressed to the readers of "Comoedia" his wish of making pantomine a universal language for deaf-mutes, and in our day Sir Richard Paget has gone as far as proposing, as we will soon see, the invention of an international auxiliary language made of gestures.

Infant Language

1. Herodotus, II, 2. According to this legend, the first word to have been pronounced was "dekos." Consequently it was concluded that the Phrygian language, in which "dekos" means bread, is the original language of the human race.

2. O. Jespersen, *Origin of Linguistic Species*, in "Scientia," 1909, II, p. III.

3. Jespersen also neglected the mimetic element as the specific purpose of his research was to establish the influence of infant language on certain rapid changes in spoken languages. But generally the damage to studies by philosophers, linguists, and naturalists due to disregard for mimetic language is obvious.

4. Cf. the article cited in "Scientia," 1909. The two children of about five and a half years did not live far from Copenhagen. At the age of four they were admitted to a nursery school. When Jespersen saw them they already knew Danish quite well, but when alone they continued to speak in "their own" language. They often used a mute *h* that does not exist in Danish and often ended their words in *p*. The Danish word "sort" (black) became "lhop," Elisabet became "Lip," Charlotte "Lop,"

"maelhk" (milk) became "bep," "blomst" (flower) "bop," "lys" (light) "lhyl," "suker" (sugar) "lhalh," "kulde" (cold) "hlulh." To express "We will not go and look for food for the little rabbit," they would say: "Nina enaj una enaj halna mad enaj," where the negation ("enaj") is repeated several times as occurs in the Bantu languages and is frequent among deaf-mutes. To say "Mary, her brother's trousers are wet," they would say "Hos, ia, boy lhalh," that is, "Trousers, Mary, brother water," where the vocative "Mary" was probably emphasized by a calling gesture, and where the designation "water" for wet correspondends to usage in mimetic language.

According to a report by Ferrari and Gaddi (*Manuale di pedagogia*, p. 142), it seems that Hale and Hun in 1860 and 1868 respectively, spoke of other children who invented languages for their own use. The same authors quote the following paragraph from "Corriere della Sera," November 30, 1934, entitled *Una lingua nuova creata da due bambini svedesi* (A new language created by two Swedish children): "Stockholm, November 20. Two children who speak a language that nobody understands or ever taught them are under observation at the Municipal Hospital of Sunsvolt, in North Sweden. They are brothers of six and five years born in an out-of-the-way village in the North and who live in a completely isolated farm. The two children, to whose education their parents were only ever able to dedicate an extremely limited amount of time, were left to grow up by themselves. Having learned but very few words from their parents, they created a language of their own, coining words and expressions unlike those of any spoken tongue. Neither their parents nor anyone else are able to understand them any more. The case has attracted much interest in Sweden and has been taken up by the press drawing the attention of men of science, who have now decided to hospitalize the two otherwise normally developed children in order to place them under observation with the aim of discovering the key to their language" (in spite of the difference in date and country, I believe this is probably the very same case examined by Jespersen, reported second hand by a journalist with little respect for precision).

5. G. Mallery, *Sign Language Among North American Indians Compared with that Among Other Peoples and Deaf-Mutes,* Washington 1881.

Saint Augustine had already made a similar observation in his *Confessions,* in which he describes how he learned to speak as a child. He acknowledges that mimicry, that is, language spoken with the face, winks of the eyes, movements of the limbs, and voice accentuation which reveal the emotions of inner life, may be considered as the natural language of all peoples.

6. J. G. Herder, *Sämmtliche Werke,* Stuttgart and Tübingen 1827, p. 187. This observation is significant because, on the other hand, Herder believed (as was natural given the scarce ethnographic material he had at his disposal) that man would never have been able to reach through mimicry alone that state of reason that characterizes him: the "miraculous divine institution" of language was necessary.

7. Vico has the merit of having realized not only that this pre-logical character is proper to all primitive languages, but also that phonetic language was preceded by a mute language, that is, by mimicry.

8. Wundt, *Völkerpsychologie,* p. 275.

9. Cf. H. Gutzmann, in "Zeitschrift für pädagogische Psychologie," Munich 1899, I, p. 28.

10. Ferrari and Gaddi, *Manuale di pedagogia,* p. 60.

Mimicry among the Ancients

1. A. De Iorio, *La mimica degli antichi investigata nel gestire napoletano* (The mimicry of the ancients investigated in Neopolitan gesticulation), Naples 1832 (still today the best study on the subject); K. Sittl, *Die Gebarden der Griechen und Romer,* Leipzig 1890. A work rich in philological erudition, but which cannot compete with De Iorio's study

as far as the direct experience of popular gesticulation is concerned. Sittl, however, has the merit of having provided us, in the appendix to his book, with the critically revised text of the *Institutiones oratoriae* by Quintilian.

2. By contrast to usual mimetic vivacity, Tacitus describes the face of Tiberius as "vultus jussus," to reveal its intentional impassiveness.

3. Wundt, *Völkerpsychologie. Die Sprache*, Leipzig 1904, vol. I, 1, p. 147.

4. J. Goldziher, *Über Geberden [sic!] und Zeichensprache bei den Arabern*, in "*Zeitschrift für Völkerpsychologie und Sprachwissenschaft*," Berlin 1885, vol. XVI, n. 4, pp. 369–86; I. L. Portes, *Five Years in Damascus*, London 1870, pp. 75ff.

According to H. Petermann: for greetings and the expression of gratitude the Arabs move their right hand toward the ground so as to almost touch the dust, then they bring it to the breast, mouth, and forehead. The socially inferior person grasps the right hand of his superior, kisses it, and places it on his head as a sign of subordination. To say "yes" Arabs bow the head slightly (as though in sign of acquiescence), for denials they nod upwards clicking their tongue. To signify "nothing" they press the tip of the thumb-nail against the front teeth and make it click. To say that they have nothing to do with a certain matter they catch hold of the edge of their cloak and shake it, etc.

5. Cassiodorus, *Variae*, IV, 51.

6. A curious analogy with the correspondence between "dicere" and "digitus" is perhaps to be found in the Chinese ideogram meaning "to speak." This ideogram is composed of a sign meaning "ten" and therefore "fingers," and by extension "to gesticulate," and another ideogram meaning "mouth," so that the graphic etymon of "to speak" would be the same as "to gesticulate with the mouth" (cf. Diringer, *L'alfabeto nella storia della civiltà*, It. trans., p. 187).

The same association is probably that found in an Indian gesture: to signify the verb "to speak," gestures are made with the hand in front of the mouth (W. Tomkins, *Universal Indian Sign Language of the Plains Indians of North America*, San Diego 1936[7], p. 90).

7. In *Paolo e Virginia*, Saint-Pierre (who lived for some time in Ile-de-France, that is, on the island currently known as Mauritius in the Indian Ocean) describes a mimetic scene performed by the heroine and remarks that "pantomime is man's first language, a language known in all countries. It is so natural and expressive that the children of white men are quick in learning it from negroes."

8. D'Ovidio, translation of G. D. Whitney's book *La vita e lo sviluppo del linguaggio* (Original title: *Life and Growth of Language*, London, 1875), Milan 1876, p. 351 note.

9. "The practice of rites among primitive men may be considered as the mimetic expression of religious feeling," says Macchioro, *Zagreus*, Florence 1930, p. 214. Cf. also R. Allier, *Les non-civilisés et nous*, Paris 1927, p. 53.

Juridical ritualism, for which the gestures to be accomplished were prescribed in great detail, is closely related to religious ritualism. Many such ancient ritual gestures have been preserved through the procedures of Roman law (cf. P. Bonfante, *Istituzioni di diritto romano*, Milan 1926, p. 183).

Importance of Primitive Mimicry

1. Tciang-Tceng-Ming, *L'écriture chinoise et le geste humain*, Paris 1938, cited in van Ginneken, p. 99.

2. The signs studied in greater detail by the author are those discovered in the inscriptions of the Yin dynasty, which according to sinologists belong to the period extending from 1400 to 1100 B.C. That some of those signs are very ancient, or at least very primitive, clearly emerges, in our opinion, from the fact that in the inscriptions of the first Yin period graphic signs are not firmly established but are still in the process of formation. These writing systems do not have an already consecrated

tradition behind them so that each time someone writes he must help himself as best he can. We are, therefore, on the dividing line between free pictographic invention and writing through conventional signs.

3. Van Ginneken, in *Atti del III congresso internazionale di linguistica*, p. 102.

4. Jensen, *Geschichte der Schrift*, p. 30; Diringer, *L'alfabeto nella storia della civiltà*, p. 194.

5. A. Erman, *Die Hieroglyphen*, Berlin 1923. Regarding the cuneiform writing systems of the Sumerians we will recall the ideograms that refer to parts of the body (mouth, eyes, nose, feet, etc.). In mimetic language body parts are signified by pointing to them, and in the case in question by sketching a human figure and indicating the designated part with dashes (Diringer, *L'alfabeto nella storia della civiltà*, It. trans., p. 109).

6. Gestures and hieroglyphs are reproduced in Tomkins, *Sign Language*, p. 90. According to some authors, the gesture of crossing fingers and consequently the ideographic sign to signify barter derives from the custom of setting up markets at road crossings. In my opinion, however, it may derive from the crossing of the arms of two contracting parties ("With one hand I give you my merchandise and with the other I take yours"). Similar positions, encouraged by the friendly violence of brokers, may still be seen today in certain rural fairs, and correspond to analogous gestures contemplated by the archaic juridical ritual of the Romans.

7. Cf. W. J. Hofmann, *The Graphic Art of the Eskimos*, Rep. U.S. National Museum, Washington 1897. The Eskimo language also preserves syntactic structures proper to mimetic language.

8. The assertion that the system in twenties refers to the fingers of the hands and toes of the feet could seem rather rash, but various facts confirm this hypothesis. For example, the Indians indicate twenty mimetically by stretching out their two open hands in the direction of their feet, the Bacairi indicate twenty by saying "fingers hands feet" and the Eskimos "whole man." To express "seven" the Eskimos say "two toes of the second foot," and the Chibcha Muysca say "one of the foot" for eleven. The *vi* in the word "viginti" seems to indicate a collective noun so that it signifies "the two tens." The French "quatre-vingts," "quatre-vingts-dix" are also residues of a system based on twenties inherited from the Celts who, in their turn, had taken it from antecedent populations (L. Lévy-Bruhl, *Les fonctions mentales dans les sociétés inférieures*, Paris 1910; cf. Pott, *Die quinare und vigesimale Zahlmethode*).

9. For example, from the *Liber de loquela digitorum* of the venerable Bede.

10. In addition to the cited volumes by M. Müller and Pott, see: L. Frobenius, *Probleme der Kultur. Die Mathematik der Ozeanier*, Berlin 1901; K. von der Steinen, *Unter den Naturvölkern Zentralbrasiliens*, Berlin 1897, pp. 84ff.; W. I. MacGel, *Primitive Numbers*, in "Annual Report of the Bureau of Ethnology," Washington 1900, XIX; M. Schmidl, *Zahl und Zahlen in Afrika*, in "Mitteilungen der Anthropologischen Gesellschaft," Vienna, XLV, pp. 165ff.

Gestures in the Language of Ancient Egyptians

1. C. Abel, *Linguistic Essays*, London 1882. Our paper is based on the German edition, *Sprachwissenschaftliche Abbandlungen*, Leipzig 1885, chap. 8: *Über den Ursprung der Sprache*.

2. The Arabs called Copts those Egyptians who had adopted the Christian religion.

3. According to Diringer (see *L'alfabeto nella storia della civiltà*, It. trans., p. 194) the sound *shi*, for example, can have as many as 230 meanings. This number is subsequently reduced with the same syllable being pronounced in four musical tones, but it still remains very high, that is 54 for the syllable pronounced in the first tone, 40 for the second, 79 for the third, and 66 for the fourth.

4. Cf. J. Pichon, *Le Développement psychique de l'enfant*, p. 101.

The Syntactic Characteristics of Mimetic Language

1. Ferrari and Gaddi, *Manuale di pedagogia*, p. 28.

2. The following sentence was read in a class of deaf-mutes: "When the rich man Epulo found himself, after death, in the fires of hell, in vain he turned his prayers to poor Lazarus, asking him for a little water." On being invited to repeat this one of the students said: "Epulo rich dead, he fire hell burns. Prays Lazarus water. Nothing."

3. The younger deaf-mutes will use a single gesture to signify water, drink, glass, thirst; while the more expert will distinguish between the four concepts. For instance, to say "I'm thirsty" they will make the gesture of drinking and then pinch the skin of the throat with two fingers, subsequently they will use only the latter gesture, omitting that of drinking.

4. According to statistics, children generally use nouns before using verbs. For example, a normal two-year-old child, observed by Preyer, knew 489 words grouped as follows: 249 nouns, 119 verbs, 23 adjectives, 46 adverbs, 52 various little words. A little girl observed by Humphreys, who was also two years old, but above the average level of intelligence, knew 1121 words including 592 nouns, 283 verbs, 114 adjectives, 56 adverbs, and 76 various little words (cf. W. T. Preyer, *Die Seele des Kindes*, p. 449; M. W. Humphreys, in "Transactions of the American Philological Society," 1880). We may conclude that from a conceptual point of view it is easier to learn nouns than verbs, while in mimetic expression it is easier to signify action than a thing. For example, it is easier to represent the act of grinding a coffee-bean through gesture than to symbolize a coffee-bean.

5. Pellet, *Des premières perceptions*, p. 157.

6. The numerous philosophisms professed by the school of Croce also include the following: that every expression is so absolutely individual that it cannot be modified, nor translated, nor compared to others. Expressions which are similar to each other do not exist: each is identical only to itself. There is no such thing as an intuitive content that may be expressed in various different forms: content and form are an indissoluble unity. These propositions are true when we consider them from the point of view of aesthetic judgment (an *abstract* point of view, since purely aesthetic acts or facts do not exist), but false and capable of creating confusion when considered from the semiological point of view, which rightly postulates the separability of content and form. (We will return to the subject in the second part of this volume.)

7. Cf. Ginneken, in *Atti del III congresso internazionale di linguistica*, p. 140.

8. Cf. Ginneken, *op. cit.*, p. 139.

Syntactic Characteristics of Ancient and Primitive Languages

1. Müller, *Letture sopra la scienza del linguaggio*, It. trans., p. 53.

2. Jespersen, *Origin of Linguistic Species*, p. 111.

3. E. Pechul-Loesche, *Die Loango Expedition*, Stuttgart 1907, III, 2, pp. 91ff.

4. That children delight in forming new words and sometimes in listening to and fixing strange, haphazard sounds is made obvious not only by exceptional cases such as those examined by Jespersen but also by what each of us can easily observe in our own environment. I still remember a few words from a secret language I invented as a child with one of my friends: "clonta, che te clatta," "bimboc," "taclon," "nongimbelle". . . ; Ettore Cantoni re-evoked our exploits and the mysterious fairy-tale world of those distant years in his fine novel *Quasi una fantasia*, Treves, Milan 1926.

5. Mimetic movements of the face and mouth, accompanied by sounds are called vocal gestures ("Lautbilder," "Lautgebärden").

6. I. D. Westermann, *Grammatik der Ewe-Sprache*, pp. 83–84. Cited in Lévy-Bruhl,

Les fonctions mentales dans les sociétés inférieures. Cf. also his article published in *Festschrift für Meinhof, 1927.*

7. Junod, *Grammaire Ronga,* Lausanne 1897, pp. 196–97.

8. Mallery, *Sign Language,* I, p. 351.

9. F. Boas quotes a word that means "Do you think he really intends to concern himself with this?" And Thalbitzer another one which is thought to mean the following: "The fact that he is my younger brother meant too much to me to let myself refuse his request and be mean with him" (Cf. *Enciclopedia italiana,* the entry "Eschimesi" [Eskimos], paragraph "lingua" [language]). More than words in our sense they are probably lexical conglomerates with a function similar to our propositions.

10. Müller, *Letture sopra la scienza del linguaggio,* It. trans., I, p. 93.

11. Bühler, in *Atti del congresso internazionale di linguistica,* p. 107.

12. In many of these languages there is one word only for eye and to see, ear and to hear, tears and to cry, chair and to sit, etc. In many African, American and Malayan dialects, as in Tibetan, Siamese, Annamese, etc., cases are mainly indicated through the syntactic position of words (Wundt, *Völkerpsychologie,* I, 2, p. 87).

13. To give a few examples: in the Klamath language temporal prepositions are always locative as well. Time adverbs are all derived from space adverbs (Gatschet, *The Klamath Language,* pp. 433–34, in Lévy-Bruhl, *Les fonctions mentales dans les sociétés inférieures* p. 162). The same thing occurs in mimetic language in which "behind" or "back" is currently used for yesterday and before, and "in front" and "further on" for tomorrow and after. According to Humboldt the primitive Mexicans say "note-potzco" (from "teputz," back), that is, "back me," to say "behind me"; and "belly sky" ("rehuicatl itic") to say "inside the sky" or "in the sky." In the Mixtec language "back house" means "behind the house" and "belly house" means "inside the house" (Humboldt, *Sprachphilosophische Werke* p. 90). I myself have personally observed the gesture of pointing the index finger at one's own abdomen among certain deaf-mutes.

14. The dual and the plural are often signified by repeating the same sign one or more times in Sumerian, Egyptian, and Chinese ideograms also.

15. E. J. Eyre, *Journal of Expedition of Discovery into Central Australia,* II, pp. 392–93, quoted in Lévy-Bruhl, *Les fonctions mentales dans les sociétés inférieures,* p. 190.

16. In the language of the Ewes, studied by Westermann, there are as many as thirty-three words to describe the various modes of walking (peaceful, quick, jumpy, etc.), while a word meaning "to walk" in general is lacking. In Cushing's opinion also, the exceptional specialization of verbs that we are able to trace in all primitive languages derives from the influence exercised by mimetic language on the mentality of these people (*Manual Concepts,* in "American Anthropologist," V, in Lévy-Bruhl, *Les fonctions mentales dans les sociétés inférieures,* p. 180).

17. An exhaustive study could only be carried out by a specialized linguist in collaboration with a person who is familiar with the mode of expression of deaf-mutes. The collaboration of a physiologist to study Head's syntactic aphasia in which the sick present symptoms of agrammatism and speak a *petit-nègre* similar to that of primitive populations could also prove to be interesting. It would be a question of establishing whether brain lesions correspond to the manifestations of distant atavistic forms in this case also.

18. M. Müller, *Grundriss der Sprachwissenschaft,* IV, Vienna 1888, pp. 15f.

Mimicry in Primitive Man

1. Steinthal, too, who is not only a competent philologist, but also the best historian of doctrines on the origin of language, considered this idea absurd. Elsewhere, however, he acknowledged that phonetic and mimetic language must have been originally so closely connected as to constitute two integral parts of one and the same means of communication (H. Steinthal, *Der Ursprung der Sprache,* Berlin 1877, p. 334).

2. J. Chalmers, *Maipua and Namu Numerals*, in "Journal of the Anthropological Institute of Great Britain," (JAI), XXVII, p. 141.

3. Some peoples, for example, the Andamanese, only have names for the very first numbers but all the same they signify higher numbers through gestures (Lévy-Bruhl, *Les fonctions mentales dans les sociétés inférieures*, p. 213). The unattentive observer believed that these natives only knew the initial numbers; just as it could seem that the Hawaiians do not distinguish the color black from deep blue or dark green, or white from light yellow, brown, and red, given that they only have two expressions for the two color groups. On the contrary, the Hawaiians distinguish between these colors very well, but to designate them they intermingle words and gestures (cf. M. Müller, *Letture sopra la scienza del linguaggio*, It. trans., p. 350).

4. Lévy-Bruhl, *Les fonctions mentales dans les sociétés inférieures*, p. 182.

5. Ibid.

6. T. G. Tucker, *Introduction to the Natural History of Language*, London 1908, p. 463. According to A. H. Kingsley, certain West African dialects are so closely connected to gesture that they turn out to be incomprehensible in the dark (*Travels in West Africa*, London 1896, p. 149).

7. B. Spencer and F. J. Gillen, *The Native Tribes of Central Australia*, pp. 500–1, cited in Lévy-Bruhl, *Les fonctions mentales dans les sociétés inférieures*, p. 176; Spencer and Gillen, *The Northern Tribes of Central Australia*, pp. 525ff. Analogous observations were carried out among the Kutus of the Congo, the Sihnata of Madagascar, the Nandi of British Africa, the Kwakintl Indians of Columbia, etc. (cf. James George Frazer, *The Golden Bough* [It. trans. De Bosis, *Il ramo d'oro*, pp. 76f.]; A. C. Hollis, *The Nandi*, Oxford 1902, p. 72). The fact that mimetic language is used especially by women among these peoples and particularly in rituals seems to be proof of its antiquity, not only because, as Plato had already remarked in his *Cratylus*, women often use a more ancient language than men, but also because the use in religious rites of languages belonging to long extinguished civilizations is common among all peoples.

8. *On the Habits of the Aborigines in the District of Powel Creek Northern Territory of South Australia, by the Station Master Powel Creek, Telegraph Station*, in "JAI," XXIV, p. 178.

9. Wilhelmi, *Manners and Customs of the Natives of the Port Lincoln District*, cited by B. Smyth, *The Aborigines of Victoria*, I, p. 186. Mimetic language was observed in the Eastern and Western Islands of the Torres district. (*The Cambridge Expedition to the Torres Straits*, III, pp. 255–62; cf. "JAI," XIX, p. 380). It was also observed in German New Guinea (Hagen, *Unter den Papuas*, Wiesbaden 1899, pp. 211–12). The Masai in Africa possess a well-developed mimetic language as demonstrated by Fischer. (G. A. Fischer, *Bericht über die im Auftrage der geographischen Gesellschaft in Hamburg 1882–83 unternommene Reise*, Hamburg 1884). "A mimetic language seems to have spread throughout the whole of South America. The Indians of the various tribes do not understand each other's dialects and use gesture language as a *"lingua franca"* (Spix and Martius, *Travels in Brazil*, II, p. 252, cited in Lévy-Bruhl, *Les fonctions mentales dans les sociétés inférieures*, p. 178).

W. Roth has prepared a detailed dictionary of the mimetic language used throughout the whole of North Queensland (*Ethnological Studies among the North-West-Central Queensland Aborigines*, London 1897).

In addition to oral language, the Dieyerie tribes possess a rich gestural language so that a conversation may be carried out without pronouncing a single word.

10. Kohl, *Kitchi Gami, Wanderings round Lake Superior*, pp. 140–41, in Lévy-Bruhl, *Les fonctions mentales dans les sociétés inférieures*, p. 178.

11. M. Garrick, *A Collection of Gesture Signs and Signals of the North American Indians with Some Comparisons*, Smithsonian Institution, Bureau of Ethnology, Washington 1880; Garrick, *Sign Language among North American Indians Compared with that among Other Peoples and Deaf-Mutes*, Washington 1880; Garrick, *Pictographs of the North Amer-*

ican Indian's 4th Annual Report, Washington 1886; Garrick, *Picture Writing of the American Indian,* in "Bureau of American Ethnology," 10th Annual Report, Washington 1893; W. E. Roth, *Ethnological Studies Among the North-West-Central Queensland Aborigines,* London 1897; W. Tomkins, *Universal Indian Sign Language*; F. H. Cushing, *Zuni Breadstuff,* New York 1920.

Studies by Mallery are among the first as well as among the best in comparative mimicry. Not only did he collect and describe gestures used by the Indians, but he also compared them with those used by other peoples and with the pictographic writing systems of the Indians themselves. Tomkins gave us a dictionary of gestures used by the natives of America, and Roth of the gestures used in Australia. The studies by Cushing are valuable not only because he lived for a long period of time among the Zunis, but also because he had been initiated into their ceremonies; he entered their secret societies and, in short, endeavored as far as possible to lead the same life as these primitives and to feel their same emotions and instincts.

12. For example Humboldt, who asserts that the formation of concepts and thought is only possible through sound and voice which transform simple representations into objective realities (*Einleitung in die Kawi-Sprache,* p. LXVI).

13. Cushing, *Manual Concepts,* p. 291. The essay has been reprinted in his Zuni Breadstuff.

14. Roth also believes that the world view of primitive man is influenced by associations derived from the habit of expressing himself through gesture. His language is prevalently descriptive and gives particular importance to outlines, form, position, and movements, in short to those characteristics that can be expressed with gestures better than with words. Lévy-Bruhl, after having specified that the languages of primitive man give special emphasis to plastic and visual particulars, concludes: "Perhaps this need may be explained by observing that the same societies generally speak another language also, whose characteristics necessarily react upon the mentality of those who use it, upon their way of thinking and therefore of speaking. In these societies, in fact, use is made of mimetic language, at least in given circumstances, and where it has fallen into disuse, there are traces that testify to its existence in previous eras" (*Les fonctions mentales dans les sociétés inférieures,* p. 175).

15. Only when researchers finally decide to devote to the more important problems of comparative mimicry a small part of the intelligence and insight today dedicated to even the minutest problems of philology will it be possible to make a concrete estimate of how much of the *corpus gestorum* (vocabulary of gestures) is of recent formation and how much goes back to ancient times.

Mimetic Languages Created by Uneducated Deaf-Mutes

1. Some interesting pieces of information are to be found in the quoted volume *Völkerpsychologie,* by Wundt. Among modern writers *La pensée et les signes* by Vuillemey has the merit of being written by a man who lived in close contact with deaf-mutes, but his pseudo-scientific approach at times presents serious drawbacks. For instance, on speaking about man's age on the earth he bases himself on the legendary chronology proposed by the Bible.

2. Oral teaching which through lip reading and the help of touch and muscular sense trains deaf-mutes in the understanding and use of phonetic language, doubtlessly represents an important step forward with respect to the methods used in their time by Abbé de L'Eppé and by Sicard. Knowledge of a common language takes the deaf-mutes out of social isolation and enables them to learn how to read and write and, in certain cases, develop a higher cultural level.

To prohibit the use of mimetic language, obliging students to concentrate all their energy in one direction only, may perhaps make teaching easier and faster, but involves problems that are not currently taken into due consideration by modern didactic theories. We must not forget that for deaf-mutes oral language loses the directly expressive and suggestive force that it has for us thanks to its sound qualities. For deaf-mutes words with a harsh and loud sound or with a soft and faint sound do not exist, just as the infinite tonalities and inflections of the voice that give color and life to our discourse do not exist. On the contrary, for deaf-mutes phonetic language is no more than a rather abstract and artificial system of ideographic signs. Now, by forbidding them to express themselves naturally, we risk rendering their spirituality lifeless and accustoming them to conventional expressions that falsify the intimacy of their sentiments.

This problem is analogous to that often debated by teachers concerning whether use of the native dialect should be discouraged, not only at school but also in the family. In this case also the narrow-minded have always sided against the spontaneity of dialects in favor of literary language. In my opinion, the reasons in favor of spontaneous expression have even greater weight in the case of deaf-mutes, for with the diffusion of culture a literary language may become just as spontaneous as a dialect. On the other hand, that a phonetic language should ever become as spontaneous and plastic as mimetic language for deaf-mutes seems impossible.

3. In fact the good Abbot Sicard, who in his *Dictionnaire* classifies and gives an unnecessarily complex description of gestures used for teaching mimetic language to deaf-mutes, far too often acts like a blind man who wishes to teach painters how to draw (cf. Abbé Sicard, *Théorie des signes, ou Introduction à l'étude des langues: où le sens des mots, au lieu d'être défini, est mis en action. Ouvrage élémentaire, absolument indispensable pour l'enseignement des sourds-muets etc.*, Paris 1808).

4. Observations on the Psychology of Anthropoid Apes

Preliminary Observations

1. It is common knowledge that kissing among the Eskimos, in South East Asia, and in many islands of the Pacific, consists in the mutual contact and rubbing of noses. In addition to nose rubbing, the Chinese, Yakuts, and Laplanders also rub lips. It seems that the labial kiss was originally less widespread than the nasal kiss and was perhaps a peculiarity among Indo-Europeans and Semites.

Importance of Memory in the Spiritualization of Animal Life

1. For example, in time of famine and even after having realized through the smell of man's scent that the trap represents a mortal danger, the wolf draws near to it and moves away from it several times, until, unable to stand the hunger any longer, it throws itself on the meat, becoming a victim of the tormenting fantasy that had harassed him all that time (L. Bretegnier, *L'activité psychique des animaux*, Toulouse 1930, p. 268).

2. W. S. Hunter, *The Delayed Reaction in Animals and Children*, in "Behaviour Monography," 2, 1, 86 (cited in Buytendijk, *La psicologia degli animali* [Animal Psychology], It. trans., Sandron, Palermo 1930, p. 236).

3. Esteemed scholars testify to the fact that certain animals are capable of retaining memories even after several years. Bretegnier tells the story of one of his acquaintances who, travelling by horseback, crossed a certain bridge, turned into other roads and reached a hotel where he stayed for three days. Two years later, on arriving at the same bridge from another direction, he let the horse free as he was curious to see whether it would still remember the way. It took the right road without hesitation and reached the hotel.

During his lessons on comparative pathology, H. Boulej tells of a horse that, after having stayed in the galleries of a mine for ten years, was brought back into the light of day. After all that time, the impressions preserved in its memory permitted it to get its bearings and to reach the stable where it had lived ten years before (Bretegnier, *L'activité psychique des animaux*, p. 287).

It seems that memory of auditive perceptions and associations is also remarkable in horses. According to the observations of certain officers as reported by Bretegnier, the horses of their regiment often learned to distinguish between the different command sounds even before some of the recruits did.

As the psychic complexity of anthropoid apes is greater, their mnemonic capacity is probably superior and not inferior to that of dogs and horses, but this is not so easily verified through observation given the fewer occasions in which man and apes live together for any significant length of time.

4. H. Kluever, *Behaviour Mechanisms in Monkeys*, Chicago: University of Chicago Press, 1933.

5. O. L. Tinklepaugh, *Multiple Delayed Reaction with Chimpanzees and Monkeys*, in "Journal of Comparative Psychology," 1932, 13, pp. 207–43.

6. Various authors have commented upon the remarkable memory of monkeys. Brehm, for example, notes that they recognize and welcome their friends with manifestations of joy even after more than a year. Yerkes, who carried out experiments with a young gorilla during three subsequent winters, ascertained that it was gifted with a good memory and that it remembered situations it had already experienced even after a year (R. M. and A. W. Yerkes, *The Great Apes*, New Haven 1929).

Aesthetic Memory and Imitation

1. E. L. Thorndike, *The Mental Life of the Monkeys*, in "Psychological Monographies," 1901, 3, pp. 1–57.

2. A. J. Kinnaman, *Mental Life of Two Macacus Rhesus Monkeys in Captivity*, in "American Journal of Psychology," 1902, 13, pp. 98–148, 173–218, in Buytendijk, *La psicologia degli animali*, p. 240.

3. J. B. Wolfe, *Effectiveness of Token-rewards for Chimpanzees*, in "Comparative Psychology Monographies," 5, pp. 1–72.

4. In the art form described as objective or naive the imitative element is dominant and faithfulness to the real is greater than in romantic or lyrical art.

5. Cf. M. Tellier, *L'intelligence des singes inférieurs*, I: *La vision des formes et la généralisation*, in "Mémoires de la Société Scientifique de Liège," 1939, 19, pp. 1–76.

Imagination and Aesthetic Sense

1. Bretegnier, *L'activité psychique des animaux*, pp. 941–45.

2. Brehm, p. 663. Von Oertzen also observed a group of monkeys performing peculiar dances during which they moved their bodies similarly to certain women.

3. W. N. and L. A. Kellog, p. 81. Hachet-Souplet gave a piece of chalk and paperboards to some monkeys and observed that they delighted in drawing and doodling. According to the author some of the monkeys even managed to perceive some feature of the object they wished to reproduce. To represent a house or their cage they outlined what seemed like a barred window, and to portray the guardian, a shape in which the author thought he could make out an eye. The observation deserves further attention (cf. Hachet-Souplet, *De l'animal à l'enfant*, Paris 1913).

4. Brehm, p. 645.

5. However, the young monkey Joni also seemed to enjoy a joke played on itself. It had realized that when Mrs. Kohts, of whom it was very fond, entered the room with a book, this was a sign that she was to remain longer, which would make Joni happy, whereas when Mrs. Kohts entered without the book, Joni would anxiously follow all her movements fearing to see her leave. Sometimes Mrs. Kohts would play

a joke on Joni by hiding the book behind her back. Joni would then look sulky and agitated, but when at last Mrs. Kohts revealed the hidden book, the young monkey would display its appreciation of the joke through its joyful and noisy excitement.

6. Cited in Bretegnier, *L'activité psychique des animaux,* p. 246.

7. The experiment had been preceded by simpler ones. The experiments are reported by Bretegnier, *L'activité psychique des animaux,* pp. 336–38.

8. Brehm, p. 672.

Mimetic Expression and Phonetic Expression

1. A. H. Maslow, *The Role of Dominance in the Social and Sexual Behavior of Infra-human Primates,* in "Journal of Genetic Psychology," 1936, 48, pp. 261–77.

2. S. Zucherman, *The Social Life of Monkeys and Apes,* New York 1936.

3. Brehm, p. 669.

4. R. M. Yerkes and M. J. Tomlin, *Infant Relations in Chimpanzees,* in "Journal of Comparative Psychology," 1935, 20, pp. 321–48.

5. Brehm, pp. 630–37.

6. Ibid., pp. 643–44.

7. In Teuber's opinion this is how the kiss originated. In our opinion a sucking motion is the more probable origin.

8. W. Köhler, *Intelligenz-Prüfungen an Menschenaffen,* Berlin 1921.

9. Brehm, p. 669.

10. M. P. Crawford, *Cooperative Solution by Chimpanzees of a Problem Requiring Serial Responses to Color Hues,* in "Psychological Bulletin," 1939, 35, p. 705.

11. Bretegnier, *L'activité psychique des animaux* p. 345.

12. R. M. Yerkes and B. W. Learned, *Chimpanzee Intelligence and its Vocal Expression,* Baltimore 1925.

13. Yerkes and Learned, p. 179.

14. *Actes de la Société Linnéenne,* Bordeaux, 67, pp. 5–80. The author's assertion that the variety of sounds emitted by monkeys is far greater than in any other animal is not true. Birds and fowls at least should be excluded. Moreover, birds are far more skillful in imitating sounds than monkeys are. If we take a young bird out of its environment and raise it with birds of another species, it will usually imitate the sounds of that species which is not its own. Information and experiments are reported by J. A. Bierens de Haan, *Langue Humaine, langage animal,* in "Scientia," January 1934.

What follows is a list of the variety of sounds made by domestic fowls:

ROOSTER (1) cry of alarm ("cocò cocò") emitted in the presence of potentially dangerous animals; (2) cry of fear, similar to the so-called "cackle-cackle" of hens, produced after being chased for a while; (3) cry of anger, reproach, protest ("guuuu") when a hen takes flight or two hens fight. This is one of the rare cases in which the rooster reproaches the hen by pecking it; (4) a calling sound emitted by the rooster when it finds food (a very quick "chick-chick-chick"). The head is lowered while pecking at the food which, however, is allowed to fall from the beak to show the hens; (5) courtship call ("go-go-go-ggoo") produced as the rooster circles the hen with a lowered wing; (6) a varied and almost continuous sound, probably produced to keep the hens together as they shift from one place to another; (7) the so-called "cock-a-doodle-doo" to which the other roosters respond in their own way, and which is probably more a challenge to the other males than a calling sound for the hens, even if in the domestic context roosters very rarely move away from their own chicken-coop.

BROODING HEN (1) cry of alarm similar to the rooster's only shorter and less noisy; (2) threatening sound emitted to drive away any other fowls approaching the chickens ("co-o"); (3) a calling sound emitted on finding food (similar to the rooster's);

(4) a continuous clucking sound ("cluck-cluck-cluck") produced to keep the chicks together.

HENS (1) a chain of varied sounds, frequently repeated but less continuous than the rooster's. With respect to the male, the tone is different but the rhythm is similar; (2) cries of fear ("ga-ga-ga-ga-ga") usually produced while fleeing and fluttering; (3) cry of lamentation, dissatisfaction, and protest ("gaa-ga-ga-ga-gaa-ga-ga-gaa") emitted for example when a hen, on finding a good morsel of food, is chased away by the others. The same call is also characteristic of the brooding hen when it has finished sitting on its eggs; (4) the so-called "cackle-cackle" sound usually produced after having laid an egg, or at times as an expression of great fear.

CHICKS (1) the "cheep-cheep" of a chick as it calls for its lost mother-hen; (2) the short cheeping that expresses fear on being pecked; (3) the discursive "cheep-cheep" in a lower tone, when resting under the hen's wings.

I owe this list to my friend Giorgio Voghera from Trieste and take this opportunity to thank him and another friend, Sebastiano Timpanaro, for their numerous observations of great value to me in my work.

15. [In the past few years similar experiments have been carried out on the chimpanzee Washoe by Mr. and Mrs. Gardner from Nevada University. As emerges from their numerous publications, after a few years of patient experimentation the chimpanzee managed to learn more than thirty signs from the sign language of American deaf-mutes and used them intentionally to communicate with its instructors.]

Summing-Up and Concluding Remarks

1. Indications can sometimes be obtained from the anatomical conformation of prehistorical remains. For example, in the cranium found at Chapelle-aux-Saints, the site of convolutions in which the speech center is usually located is very limited; this should be interpreted as indicating that at the time when the caveman already knew how to construct utensils for himself, he did not yet have a phonetic language at his disposal.

2. Otto Witte attempted to establish the limits of the expressive capacity of mimetic language through appropriate experiments (*Untersuchungen über die Gebärdensparchen. Beiträge zur Psychologie der Sprache,* in "Zeitschrift fur Psychologie," 1930, 4-6, CXVI, pp. 225-308).

He tried to express a few propositions mimetically and then asked his observers whether they had understood what he was saying. For example, on wishing to express the proposition "I have two legs" he pointed to himself, then to his legs and held up two fingers. Two out of three observers understood wrongly. One gave the following interpretation: "Mr. W. wants to buy two shoes." Another: "Go for a walk and come to see me at two o'clock." It seems to me that such experiments are badly set up and unconvincing, for real live mimetic expressions do not arise in such an *ex abrupto* manner, but in well-defined situations. Let us suppose we see two men moving down the same road, one on horse-back and the other on foot. The first turns around and makes a gesture of impatience because of the slowness of his companion plodding along behind him, the other replies by winking at him, pointing to the horse's legs and displaying four fingers, then pointing to his own legs and displaying two fingers. In this case neither of the observers would have misunderstood. The truth is that even in phonetic language single expressions may prove to be imprecise and obscure when isolated from the context. Another disadvantage of such experiments is that the author begins with a proposition in his own language which he then tries to translate mimetically, and since the translation is not perfectly adequate (as is always the case), he wrongly deduces that mimetic expression is limited. We could accuse phonetic language of being deficient on the same basis for many mimetic expressions do not find an adequate translation in words. Moreover, Witte was not aware that abstract univocality is especially impossible in improvised languages, since the conventional element is not yet specified and fixed by use.

5. Transition from Mimetic to Phonetic Language

1. According to a study by J. Rae, published as an appendix to the volume *Human Speech* by R. A. S. Paget, primitive sounds generally derive from given gestures. Rae's study is interesting, but his mistake lies in having attributed universal and exclusive value to specific observations.

2. The same may be said of those semi-articulate, inspirate sounds produced by a sucking movement, which are observed in babies and in young children up to the age of two years. Some authors (e.g., van Ginneken) call these sounds "clicks."

3. It is common knowledge that the same natural sound may be rendered differently by the various human families because of physiological differences (and sometimes for completely accidental reasons). For example, in certain Indo-European languages the sneezing sound is rendered with the phoneme "pster!," in other languages of Germanic stock with "qsneus!," in the Baltic-Slavonic and Latin languages with "hapcchi!" and "acchi!," etc. These phonemes may then give rise to roots that have nothing in common with each other.

4. Language was one of the essential factors involved in that decisive leap, but not the only one. A number of other reasons and causes contributed: biological, anatomical, psychological, and environmental. The propensity to work, no doubt, was of fundamental importance: just as language was decisive for intellectual development (that is, for conscious finalized action), work was decisive for practical development. Language and work made greater sociability possible and in their turn were further developed by social life.

Herbivorous animals are generally more suited to social life. They are less ferocious and more timid. But man's ancestors had to combine the placidness of the herbivores, which was to make them fit for social life, and the wildness of the carnivores, which was to permit them to rule over the other animals: the conformation of the human jaw and teeth materially symbolizes the union of the two opposite tendencies.

The enormous importance, in the social organization of primitive peoples, of instinctive attachment to tradition and habit behind all daily actions (so that the individual is submerged by the collectivity) makes the life of those peoples resemble that of certain insects which form societies, such as ants, termites, and bees. In fact, the instinct for collective organization is strongest in man and in insects: that is, in animals that are even more distant from us than reptiles and fish. This is the reason why we almost have the impression that such an instinct was to remain latent within the biological substance itself only to accomplish the task for which it was destined after countless millennia: "tantae molis erat humanam condere gentem!"

6. Note on the Problem of Roots

1. Humboldt called roots that indicate substantial concepts objective roots and those that indicate relations subjective roots. In the same way Curtius and others distinguished between substantial or predicative roots and formal or indicative roots. As we have seen, an analogous distinction had already been made by Chinese grammarians, who called those words that designate substantial concepts full words, and those indicating grammatical relations empty words.

2. Cf. A. F. Pott, *Etymologische Forschungen*, Lemgo 1861,[2] II, 1, pp. 193ff.

3. These sounds come from a comic-strip by Walt Disney.

4. Wundt, *Völkerpsychologie. Die Sprache*, Leipzig 1904, p. 606.

5. Plato, on the other hand, distinguished even too clearly between the period of

roots or of the "foundation of language" and that of later evolution. He naturally limited the value of etymological research to the latter period. "And yet if anyone is, no matter why, ignorant of the correctness of the earliest names (τῶν πρότων ὀνομάτων), he cannot know about that of the later, since they can be explained only by means of the earliest, about which he is ignorant" (*Cratylus, 426*a, in *Plato*, vol. 4, with an Eng. trans. by H. N. Fowler, Cambridge. Harvard University Press, 1977).

6. Cf. W. Grube, *Die Sprachgeschichtliche Stellung des Chinesischen*, Leipzig 1881.

7. See on the subject K. Brugmann, *Grundriss der vergleichenden Grammatik der indogermanischen Sprachen*, Strassburg 1886; H. Paul, *Prinzipien der Sprachgeschichte*, Halle 1920.

BOOK ONE : Part Two

HISTORICAL SURVEY OF GLOTTOGONIC DOCTRINES FROM THE GREEKS TO THE PRESENT DAY

1. Antiquity and the Middle Ages

1. The first person to have underlined this distinction was called Archelaus, disciple of Anaxagoras; but Herodotus, on describing the differences in customs between the Greeks and the barbarians, so that what was well done for one of these peoples was evil for the other, had already concluded that Pindar was right when he said that convention reigns over every one of us (Herodotus, III, 38). Criticism is implicit in another passage also by Herodotus, which narrates the legend of Psammeticus, king of Pittus, who entrusted two newborn babies to a shepherd ordering the latter to keep the babies in isolation and then to report the first word they were ever to pronounce. According to this legend the first word pronounced was in the Phrygian language, with the result that all peoples consider their own language as the "natural" language of humanity (Herodotus, II, 2. Cf. *Frag. Hist., 1, 22, 23*).

2. Early man generally believed that knowledge of the "true name" confers a magic power over the thing itself, so that special importance is attributed to the occult knowledge of ritual words and formulae. For example, an Egyptian myth narrates the story of Iris who had the god Re in her power after having succeeded in discovering his *true name* which had been kept secret "so that no magician could acquire power over him" (cf. my *Teosofia orientale e filosofia*, p. 10).

3. Ammonius, *ad Arist. De interpret., 24*B, ed. Ald.

4. *Cratylus, 385*BD.

5. Diels, frag. 48. Cf. also *Procli comm. ad Parmen.*, ed. Stallbaum, p. 479.

6. Cf. C. Giussani, *La questione del linguaggio secondo Platone e secondo Epicuro*, (The problem of language according to Plato and Epicurus) in "Memorie di R. Ist. Lomb. di Scienze e Lettere," vol. XX, n. 11, p. 105. According to Cicero, Epicurus also believed that truth could be attained by analyzing words in order to discover the original element that reflected the very nature of things (*De finibus*, II, 2).

7. *De rerum nat.*, V, 1028–33.

8. Ibid., IV, 535; Diogene Laerzio, X, 53.

9. *Epistole ad Erodoto, 1375*. Cf. also *De rerum nat., 1061–70*.

10. Cf. A.-E. Chaignet, *Histoire de la psychologie des Grecs*, Paris 1890, vol. II, p. 348.

11. In the passage cited by Saint Augustine (*De dialectica, 6*), the idea of symbolic and figurative onomatopoeia is attributed to the Stoics.

12. It seems to me that the dialogue concludes on a note of reasoned eclecticism and not, as others thought, by leaving the problem undecided (cf. B. Croce, *Estetica* (Aesthetics), Bari 1950,[9] p. 189).

13. Proclus, *Commento al Cratilo*, (Comment on *Cratylus*), Liepzig 1908, p. 6.
14. The passage by Epicurus is reported by Diogenes Laertius, X, 75ff. Cf. "Bulletin de Correspondance Hellenique," 1897, pp. 391ff. (On the stone of Enoanda where Epicurean doctrines were discovered to be engraved). Cf. also W. Nestle, in "Berlinische Philosophische Wochenschrift," 1917, p. 1093; R. Philipson, *ibid., 1920*, p. 1030.
15. *De interpretatione*, II, 16ff. Cf. also IV, 4 and *De anima*, II, 8, in which Aristotle establishes a difference between the immediacy of animal cries and the conventionality of words.
16. *De interpretatione*, IV, 4.
17. *Metafisica*, XII, 8, 1074B.
18. Ammonius, *Schol. ad Arist., 103*B, 23.
19. Cf. Chaignet, *Histoire de la psychologie des Grecs*, p. 255.
20. *Cratylus, 422*E.
21. Ugo of San Vittore, Pietro Lombardo, Saint Bonaventura, and Saint Thomas Aquinas were all of the opinion that Adam had perfect knowledge of all things. Cf. P. Rota, *La filosofia del linguaggio nella Patristica e nella Scolastica* (Philosophy of language in Patristics and Scholasticism), Turin 1909, p. 185.
22. *De ord.*, II, chap. 12.
23. *Confessions*, I, chap. 8.
24. *De interpret.*, I, sect. 4.
25. *De vulgari eloquio*, I, 7: "Dicimus certam formam locutionis a Deo cum anima prima [scil. Adamo] concreatam fuisse: dico autem formam et quantum ad rerum vocabula, et quantum ad vocabulorum constructionem, et quantum ad constructionis prolationem."

2. Humanism and the Renaissance

1. Franc. Sanctii Brocensis, *Minerva seu de causis linguae latinae (1587)*. However, Scaliger's *De causis (1540)* does not contain anything worth noting for our own purposes.
2. Bk. I, chaps. 1–2.
3. Croce instead only says that according to Sánchez names are imposed upon things rationally, while interjections are excluded (*Estetica*, p. 230).
4. Bk. I, chap. 11. In the *Minerva* edition annotated by Perizonius, in a note at the beginning of chap. 14.
5. "La Grammaire est l'art de parler. Parler est expliquer ses pensées par des signes que les hommes ont inventés à ce dessein. On a trouvé que les plus commodes de ces signes étaient les sons et les voix. Mais parce que les sons passent, on a inventé d'autres signes pour les rendre durables" (preface). Chapter 1 begins as follows: "Les diverses sons dont on se sert pour parler, et qu'on appelle lettres, ont été trouvés d'une manière toute naturelle, et qu'il est utile de remarquer. Car, comme la bouche est l'organe qui les forme, on a vu qu'il y en avait de si simples, qu'ils n'avaient besoin que de sa seule ouverture pour se faire entendre et pour former une voix distincte, d'où vient qu'on les a appelés voyelles. Et on a aussi vu qu'il y en avait d'autres qui . . . ne pouvaient néanmoins faire un son parfait que . . . par leur union avec ces premiers sons, et à cause de cela on les appelle consonnes."
6. R. Simon, *Histoire critique de Vieux Testament*, Paris 1680. This author deals with the origin of language in chapters 14 and 15 of Book I.
7. *De dignitate et augmentis scientiarum*, Book VI, chap. 1.

3. The Eighteenth Century

1. In his essay, *L'interpretazione baconiana delle favole antiche* (Bacon's interpretation of ancient fables), Bocca, 1953, P. Rossi rightly asserts that the historical relation

between Bacon and Vico should be reexamined. Vico's concept of myth had also been anticipated to a certain extent in the *Advancement of Learning*. Though Vico was not familiar with this book, he may have found it mentioned in *De Sapientia veterum*.

2. "In order to discover the origins of writing, it was necessary to look into the origins of language" (*Opere* [Works], edited by F. Nicolini, Ricciardi, Naples 1953, p. 552). Like many other theses formulated by Vico, this one too had the singular fate of being fully appreciated in all its importance only after having been rediscovered through other authors. For my part, I must confess that after my early repeated readings of *Scienza Nuova* (New Science), distracted as I was by my predominant interest in problems relating to philosophy of history and aesthetics, I was not at all struck by this statement and I only remembered it under the influence of Saussure when studying the parallel between the origin of language and the origin of writing on my own account.

3. Vico, *Opere*, pp. 454, 458, 460, 535, 539, 542–43, 545.

4. Ibid., p. 533.

5. Ibid., p. 537.

6. Ibid., p. 563.

7. Ibid.

8. Ibid., p. 558.

9. Ibid., Degnita 50.

10. Ibid., p. 544.

11. Jespersen, *Die Sprache*.

12. J. Locke. *Essay Concerning Human Understanding* (Italian trans. by Pellizzi, *Saggio sull'intelligenza umana*, Bari, 1951), vol. II, Bk. 3.

13. Ibid., chaps. 1 and 2.

14. Ibid., chap. 4, pp. 44–51.

15. Leibniz, *Nouveaux essais*, Book 3, chap. 1.

16. Ibid., Book 3, chap. 2, pp. 1–4.

17. The idea that Chinese is an artificial language derives from the confusion between spoken Chinese and its ideographic writing system, which in fact has all the features of a spoken language.

In a letter of 1629 to his father Mersenne, Descartes expounded his project for the construction of an artificial and rational language. G. Dalgarno and Bishop J. Wilkins proposed another two projects in 1661 and 1734 respectively. These projects were based on the assumption that languages have purely rational characteristics and functions. In Wilkin's project, for example, "de" means element, "deb" its first sub-species, that is, fire, "debx" the first type of fire, that is, flame. From this example it is obvious that while the rationalists believed that languages of this kind should be just as stable and universal as algebraic formulae, in reality with the progress of experience words that were used initially would then become inadequate. In fact, for us today fire is certainly not a subspecies of the concept "element," nor is flame a logical subspecies of the concept "fire."

18. Condillac, *Essai sur l'origine des connaissances humaines*, Paris 1746, chap. 1, sec. 3; chap. 4, sec. 4.

19. De Brosses (birth, 1709, Dijon; death, 1777, Paris) was first president of parliament in Dijon. My reference is to the second edition of his *Traité de la formation méchanique des langues et des principes physiques de l'étymologie*, Paris an IX.

20. Court de Gébelin, *Monde primitif*, Paris 1773, 9 big quarto volumes. Subscribers to this volume not only include the names of the King of Sweden, the Prince of Orange, etc., but also De Brosses, Cousin, Diderot, D'Holbach, Mirabeau, Montesquieu, La Rochefoucauld, Turgot, etc.

21. Here are a few examples from his "universal dictionary of roots" of all languages: *a* or *ah* (which may become *ha, he, ai, aj, ei, ak, av, at, ek, he, kai, kei, wai,*

awi, we, vu, etc.) means possession, life, to be born, to give birth, family, joy, grass, world, tree, etc.

e (with its numerous modifications) means: existence, one, man, duration, place, color, nourishment, etc., as we see in the words "être," "esse," "est," in the German "bin," "bist," "ist," in the Greek word "ousia" (which pronounced "hose" became the French "chose"), etc.

The labials *p, m, b, f* signify things that are easy, dear, loved, infantile, as in "papà," "mammà," "bon-bon," "baiser," "poupée," "bien," "ami," "bouche," "boire," and in the Latin "bucca," "pulpa," "bibere," "potor," "manducare," "mentum," "mordeo," "puer," "pupillus," etc.

22. Rousseau, *Emile,* ed. Garnier, Book 1, pp. 45–46.

23. D. Diderot, *Lettre sur les sourds et les muets (à l'usage de ceux qui entendent et qui parlent),* Paris 1751.

24. J. B. Monboddo, *The Origin and Progress of Language,* Edinburgh 1774².

25. Other than considering the orangutan as similar to a human being, Buffon emphasizes the characteristics that distinguish it from our own species and particularly the fact that the orangutan's ability to learn certain movements and actions does not surpass that of a trained dog (*Storia naturale* [Natural History] It. trans., Livorno 1830, vol. XX, pp. 539ff).

26. Still today Monboddo is considered as one of our most important scholars and theorizers in the field of linguistics as emerges, for example, from the judgments expressed by Lefmann and Hans Arens. Cf. H. Arens, *Sprachwissenschaft,* Munich 1955.

4. The Nineteenth Century

1. D. Stewart, *Eléments de la philosophie de l'esprit humain,* French trans. by L. Peisn, Paris 1845.

2. *An account of the Life and Writings of the late Adam Smith,* in Smith's *Philosophical Essays,* London 1795.

3. T. Reid, *An Inquiry into the Human Mind, on the Principles of Common Sense,* Edinburgh 1846, chap. 4, sec. 2.

4. A. Smith, *Theory of the Moral Sentiments,* p. 29. English scholars working in this period show taste for exact observation and method in documentation to a degree unmatched by scholars of other countries. However they were often deceived into thinking that they could solve problems of logic and philosophy on the basis of psychological observations. The most obvious example of such a tendency is this book by Smith on moral sentiments. As a consequence of confusing naturalistic methods with philosophical methods, Smith, with all his scientific rigor, was led into believing that he could lay the foundations of morals uniquely upon the physiological reaction of the organism, and on this basis explain the sentiments of justice, rights, and duties. He did not realize that if the concepts of the economic sciences had been treated with a similar method, neither he, nor his immediate successors such as Ricardo and Malthus, would have been able to formulate laws of economics that were rational and rigorous.

5. A. C. Gregory, *Conspectus medicinae theorethicae,* Edinburgh 1782, sec. 345–48.

6. A report drawn up on the basis of Major Long's notes and published in 1823 by Edwin James.

7. In the *Sämtliche Werke* edited by Suphar, the *Essay* is reproduced in vol. V, pp. 3–147. I have placed Herder among the thinkers of the beginning of the nineteenth century whom he influenced so decisively.

8. J. P. Suessmilch, *Versuch eines Beweises, dass die erste Sprache ihren Ursprung nicht vom Menschen, sondern allein vom Schoepfer erhalten habe,* Berlin 1766.

The essay *Versuch einer Erklärung des Ursprunges der Sprache,* Riga 1772, by D. Tiedemann, appeared a few years later. This author also tends to privilege the theological thesis. Nonetheless Tiedemann acknowledges the probability that the first language ever used by human beings was a mimetic language.

9. *Ideen zur Philosophie der Geschichte der Menschheit*, in *Herder's Werke*, part II, Riga and Leipzig 1785.

10. M. Cesarotti, *Saggi sulla filosofia delle lingue e del gusto* (Essays on the philosophy of languages and of taste), Milan 1820. However, only a few pages of this book deal specifically with our problem.

11. A. Manzoni, *Opere inedite o rare* (Unpublished or rare works), Milan 1891–98, vols. IV and V.

12. J. M. Degerando, *Théorie des signes et de l'art de penser dans les rapports mutuels*, Paris 1880.

13. A *sui generis* science, from which we learn, among other things, that the Lord God, on having descended to see what was happening with the Tower of Babel, and afraid that the children of Adam would not stop in their intention of climbing to Heaven until they reached it, decided to stop them by confusing their languages (*Genesis 11:1–9*): "Et dixerunt [filii Adam] venite, faciamus nobis civitatem et turrim, cuius culmen pertingat ad caelum . . . Descendit autem Dominus ut videret civitatem et turrim . . . et dixit: 'Ecce, unus est populus et unum labium omnibus: coeperuntque hoc facere, nec desistent a cogitationibus suis, donec eas opere compleant. Venite igitur, descendamus et confundamus ibi linguam eorum.' "

14. Jaeger, *Über den Ursprung der menschlichen Sprache.*

15. H. Steinthal, *Der Ursprung der Sprache* (1st ed. 1851).

16. H. Steinthal, *Grammatik, Logik und Psychologie*, Berlin 1855.

17. As we have noted elsewhere, the movement of the head from right to left to signify refusal and negation is probably a residue of the movement used by children and young monkeys to refuse food that is offered to them.

18. *"Zeitschrift für Völkerpsychologie und Sprachwissenschaft," 1867–1868*, vol. V, n. 1, pp. 73ff.

19. Renan, *De l'origine du langage*, Paris 1864[4] (1st ed. 1848).

20. As is well known, there exist animal organisms that do not have eyes but have a black spot on their epidermis which, by absorbing the light, enables them to distinguish the light from the dark. In certain other organisms the black spot is located in a small cavity that protects it, in others a transparent membrane protects the cavity, in others still the membrane contains a liquid that acts as a lens, etc.

5. More Recent Theories

1. A. Schleicher, *Die Darwinsche Theorie und die Sprachwissenschaft*, Weimar 1873.

2. W. Wundt, *Völkerpsychologie*, vol. I and II; *Die Sprache*, Leipzig 1904.

3. Wundt, *Die Sprache*, Leipzig 1921[4], p. 342.

4. Vendryes, *Le langage.*

5. R. de la Grasserie, *De l'origine et de l'évolution première des racines des langues*, Paris 1895.

6. Callet, *Le mystère du langage*, Paris 1929.

7. O. Assirelli, *L'origine del linguaggio e il fallimento dei tentativi glottogonici* (The origin of language and the failure of glottogonic theories), 1951, n. 8.

8. H. Paul, *Prinzipien der Sprachgeschichte*, Halle 1937.

9. Paul maintains that the only scientific approach to the study of language is the historical, but he does not realize that, unlike sociology, history narrates individual facts: it neither describes constant types, nor searches for general rules. As proof of the historical character of linguistics Paul emphasizes the fact that all classifications used in this discipline must be based on historically ascertained material. However, by the same standard not only would psychology be considered as a "historical science," but so would botany and chemistry. As we have said elsewhere, whoever con-

fuses the psychological-naturalistic method with the historical is forced to declare the problem in question unsolvable because of the lack of documentation.

10. A. Pagliaro, *Il linguaggio e il problema delle origini* (Language and the problem of the origin) in *Responsabilità del sapere* (Responsibility of knowledge), Rome 1954.

11. A. Pagliaro, *Il segno vivente (Saggio sulla lingua e altri simboli)* (The living sign [Essay on language and other symbols]), Naples 1952.

12. A. Pagliaro, *Il segno e la funzione* (Sign and function), in *Idea*, Rome 1954.

13. G. Revész, *Origine et préhistoire du langage*, French trans., Paris 1950.

14. The author refers to the Italian word "chiamata" as the equivalent of "Zuruf," for our part we believe "richiamo" is more appropriate.

15. See his essay *Introduction à la psychologie musicale*, Bern 1946.

16. Cf. Bühler, *Arbeit und Rythmus.*

17. Vuillemey, *La pensée et les signes.*

6. Gradual Recognition among Modern Linguists of the Importance of Mimetic Expression

1. J. van Ginneken, *La réconstruction typologique des langues archaïques de l'humanité*, Amsterdam 1938. Cf. A. Meillet, *Linguistique historique et linguistique générale*, Paris 1921.

2. Cf. H. Gutzmann, *Die Sprachlaute der Kinder und der Naturvölker*, in "Westermanns Monatsschrift," 1896, pp. 358ff.

3. *Atti del congresso linguistico*, Rome 1936, p. 126. Cf. Negus, *The Mechanism of the Larynx.*

4. M. A. Ombredane, *Le langage de la gesticulation significative mimique et conventionnelle*, in the above mentioned volume (Paris 1933).

5. Tciang-Tceng-Ming, *L'écriture chinoise et le geste humain.* On the same subject see: Bruno Schindler, *Die Entwicklung der chinesischen Schrift aus ihren Grundelementen*, in "Ostasiatische Zeitschrift," 1914–15, III; B. Schindler, *Die Prinzipien der chinesischen Schriftbildung*, ibid., 1915–17, III; R. Stuebe, *Grundlinien zu einer Entwicklung der Schrift*, Munich 1906.

6. The Yins inscriptions, the remains of an ancient sacerdotal archive, were discovered in 1899 in a village of North Honan near the city of Myan-Yang, the capital of the Yins dynasty from 1400–1122 B.C.

7. F. Kainz, *Psychologie der Sprache*, Stuttgart 1941, pp. 268ff.

8. R. A. S. Paget, *Human Speech*, London 1930. An interesting study by Dr. J. Rae of Honolulu (taken from "The Polynesian," September and October 1862) is reprinted in the appendix. See also by Paget *L'évolution du langage.*

9. On the work carried out by van Ginneken see, for example, the criticism of Pagliaro and of Kainz in the works cited above.

A typical example of how certain authors still believe they can solve the problem of language origin thanks to sudden inspiration is offered to us by the publications of F. Bruni, *Un nuovo capitolo di fisiologia e di psicologia: L'origine del linguaggio* (A new chapter in physiology and psychology: the origin of language), in "Il Lavoro Neuropsichiatrico" (Neuropsychiatric work), 1949; *Alle vive sorgenti del linguaggio. Dalle voci della natura al pensiero* (At the living sources of language. From the voices of nature to thought), Rome 1951; *L'origine del linguaggio* (The origin of language), Rome 1953. Bruni believes that onomatopoeia played a fundamental role in the formation of language, but the imitative origin is rarely evident, so that many roots remain undecipherable, like a piece of writing in cipher without a key. It seems that the key is to be searched for in the numerous onomatopoeia of *percussion* and *breaking* which, through legitimate comparisons, would make it possible to recognize the natural origin of almost all words.

BOOK TWO:

ON THE NATURE AND ESSENCE OF LANGUAGE:
PRINCIPLES FOR A GENERAL LINGUISTICS

2. Formulation of the Problem

1. Pragmatists and Neopositivists have rightly emphasized the *principle of significance,* according to which all those propositions that cannot be verified through experiment, at least conceptually, are senseless. But, in their naive dogmatism, they did not realize that by speaking continuously about a world of events independent of thought, they contravene that very principle, for obviously a world that is not perceived or thought by anyone is not by definition experimentable.

2. Cf. Fano, *La filosofia del Croce,* p. 172.

3. Cf. Fano, *La filosofia del Croce,* pp. 171ff. to some pages of which I will now refer with due modifications).

4. Documentary Memory and Poetic Memory

1. It should be clear by now that when we speak of sensations, images, concepts, etc., we do not mean that pure feeling, pure intuition, or pure thought exist in themselves. Conscious activity always includes a sensitive, intuitive, conceptual, etc., component. For example, in addition to being a sensation, a bitter taste is always a representation and concept (in fact we could not talk about what we do not represent to ourselves and do not think), but when we say we like bitter coffee, our reference is to the sensation, abstracting from the aesthetic and conceptual element. Interrelation among the different aspects or phases of the cognitive act does not authorize that indistinct identification of all values which muddlers like so much.

2. Kant *Kritik der reinen Vernunft,* ed. Rosenkranz, p. 146.

3. "Quella materia ond'io son fatto scriba," says Dante, *Par.,* XXX, 27.

4. Croce no doubt was aware of these "antinomies of aesthetic judgment," but he did not refer them to the constitutive phases of synthesis. Consequently, the ascertainment of antithesis remains a kind of chance empirical observation, devoid of conceptual justification. In fact, we must remember that philosophical antinomies (those identified by Kant, like all others) always originate from one-sided emphasis upon one or the other of the dialectic stages in conceptual synthesis.

5. The importance of sensitivity in artistic creation has often been emphasized and particularly by the aesthetes of Romanticism. The importance of memory has been especially highlighted by the following authors: E. Bruecke, *Die Darstellung der Bewegung durch die bildenden Künste,* in "Deutsche Rundschau," XXVI, 1881; A. Riehl, *Das Problem der Form in der Dichtkunst,* in "Vierteljahresschrift f. Wiss. Phil.," 1897; E. Loewy, *Die Naturwiedergabe in der älteren griechischen Kunst,* Loescher, Rome, 1900; O. Fischer, *Über die Bedeutung der Erinnerung für die Poesie,* Fil. Congress of Bologna, 1911; L. Fuelep, *La memoria nella creazione artistica* (Memory in artistic creation), in "Bollettino della Biblioteca Filosofica di Firenze," Florence, February 1911.

Fuelep and Riehl tend to identify memory with intuitive activity.

5. Problems of Artistic Technique and of Language

1. We will return to this subject in chapter 19 where we will examine the linguistics of idealism.

6. Aesthetics and Semantics

1. As already stated, the term *semantics* is used (by analogy with the terms *ethics, logics, aesthetics*) to designate a "general theory of expressive signs."

2. We will thoroughly examine Croce's linguistics in chapter 19; here we will only point to one of the philosophisms most common to this approach: In Croce's opinion, it is not true that for anyone unfamiliar with the language, a literary work needs to be translated, while this is not necessary for a painting. In reality, translation is no more than a philological aid in the understanding of the artist's background, used at his starting point, and such aids are also necessary in the understanding of a painting. Croce here forgets that previous experience is formed of facts and not conventions, and that the conventional element is far more important in language than in painting or in music.

In *La filosofia del Croce (The Philosophy of Croce)*, I distinguished between the philological-semantic point of view and the aesthetic, but my subsequent studies convinced me that use of the semantic criterion in problems of linguistics is far more important than I realized at the time.

Among the Italian philosophers, the merit of having clearly distinguished between semantics and aesthetics goes to Guido Calogero (cf. his volume *Estetica, semantica, istorica* [Aesthetics, semantics, history], Turin 1947).

7. General Theory of Expressive Signs

1. F. de Saussure, *Cours de linguistique générale.*

2. With intentions very different from our own, Charles Morris proposed to do the same thing with his *Behaviorist Semiotics* which we will examine in chapter 18.

10. Characteristics of Linguistic Signs

1. Why do we say *scrittorello* and not *pittorello, figliastro* and not *padrasto*? Why *impudico* and *innocente* and not *impigro* and *infurbo*? *Illegibile* and not *illetto*? *Amorale* and *analfabeta* and not *amilitare* and *anartistico*? *Svendere* and not *scomperare, svogliato* and not *scompreso, disprezzare* and *disattento* and not *discredere* and *disallegro*? *Spirito-saggine* and *goffaggine* and not *rozzaggine* and *ignorantaggine*? *Socialistoide* and not *borghesoide*, etc.

2. In most cases these creations are anonymous, but not always. The term *"veli-volo,"* for example, was created by D'Annunzio and the term *"picchiatello"* was created by Tullo Grammantieri to signify someone who having been hit on the head as a child ends up a bit of a half-wit. (This expression was used for the first time in the film *E'arrivata la felicita, 1936*, to render the English "pixilated.") New signs created by speakers every day are at times refused by linguistic use and at other times they are adopted without rules of legitimacy.

11. Expressive Function of Verbal Musicality

1. The musicality of speech and chatter among the common people is the real object of poetic contemplation in some of Goldoni's plays (such as in *Baruffe chiozzotte*, admired by Wagner).

12. The Role of the Poetic Imagination in the Creation of Languages

1. Cf. Pagliaro, *Il segno vivente*, p. 119.

2. Cf. on the subject, chapter 19.

13. Antithesis between Semantic and Emotional Requirements in Language and Writing

1. "Yiddish" is medieval German ("Mittelhochdeutsch") mixed with Jewish and Slavonic lexical elements.

2. A more authentic example is the following: the word formed by the three letters *daleth, beth,* and *resh (dbr)* may be read as "davar," thing; "déver," plague; "dabbér," speak; and "dibbèr," he spoke.

3. Cf. Vendryes, *Le langage,* p. 378. There is no need to point out that the words just listed only serve to exemplify the procedure. It is a fact that cuneiform writing has, for example, seventeen signs to signify the syllable "tu."

4. It has been noted that in the word "oiseau"—where the soft "s" is usually indicated with a "z"—none of the letters correspond to the sound.

5. Nonetheless cases of false etymologies are not lacking.

6. It is strange that in such a rational spelling system there are still a few words with *cq* and one only with double *q (soqquadro),* and that there are alternative spellings for the plurals of words in *cia* and *gia (ciliege* and *ciliegie)* and for those in *io (vizii* and *vizi).*

7. Cf. H. G. C. von der Gabelentz, *Die Sprachwissenschaft,* ed. Tauchnitz, Leipzig 1891, pp. 138–42.
For Italian spelling see: G. Malagoli, *Ortoepia e ortografia italiana moderna* (Modern Italian Orthoepy and Orthography); P. G. Goidanich, *Sul perfezionamento dell'ortografia italiana* (On the perfecting of Italian orthography), Modena 1910; L. Gelmetti, *Riforma ortografica* (Orthographic reform), Milan 1886; L. Luciani, *Per la riforma ortografica* (For orthographic reform), Rome 1910.

8. See the following chapter.

9. How exciting such a simple matter as the rationalization of orthography can be emerges, for example, from the fact that Chancellor Bismarck decided to prohibit, with one of his decrees, the use of Puttkamer's rationalized orthography in official correspondence, even though it was later to prevail; on the contrary, President Theodore Roosevelt ordered the official acceptance of three hundred English words with rationalized spelling, but was subsequently forced to withdraw the order following violent protests.

10. Schelling, *Introduzione alla filosofia della mitologia* (Introduction to the philosophy of mythology), ed. Cotta, Stuttgart, p. 52.

14. Artificial Languages

1. The lexicon was prevalently Italian with Spanish and Arabic elements, verbs in the infinitive and grammar generally reduced to a minimum. Cf. *Dictionnaire de la langue franque ou petit mauresque,* Marseille 1830; E. Rossi, *La lingua franca in Barberia* (The *lingua franca* in Barberia), in "Rivista delle Colonie Italiane," 1926, pp. 143–51.

2. "Pidgin" is the corruption of "business" pronounced with a Chinese accent. Creole languages, which developed independently of each other in different parts of the world, follow similar grammatical procedures and (though fashioned artificially by the Europeans who used them, for example, in the commerce of slaves) have sometimes become the mother tongue of new generations. See G. Leland, *Pidgin-English "Sing-Songs" and "Stories,"* in *The China English Dialect, With a Vocabulary,* London 1900.

3. It will suffice to mention the names of Descartes, Leibniz, Peano, Poincaré, W. Churchill, H. Schuchardt, O. Jespersen, F. de Saussure, etc. The 1931 Linguistic Congress of Geneva examined the problem and expressed itself in favor of the institution of an auxiliary language. Important studies were published on the subject by the International Auxiliary Language Association set up in New York in 1924.

4. We will list the main ones: G. Dalgarno (1661), S. Wilkins (1668), Carpopho-rophilus (1734), Faignet de Villeneuve (1765), Delormel (1795), J. F. Sudre (1817), M. Gigli (1818), G. Matraia (1831), B. Sotos Ochando (1845), L de Rudelle (1858), S. de Mas (1863), Pirro (1868), G. Sertorio (1876), M. Schleyer (1879), G. Meriggi (1884), P. Steiner (1885), E. Courtonne (1885), Eichhorn (1886), American Philos. Society (1887), L. L. Zamenhof (1887), G. Henderson (1888), G. Bauer (1888), I. Braakman (1888), I. Lott (1889), A. Nicolas (1889), D. Rosa (1890), A. Liptay (1890), E. Heintgeler (1893), I. Guardiola (1893), E. Beerman (1895), Marchand (1898), L. Bollack (1899), F. Kur-schner (1900), W. Rosemberger (1902), H. Molenaar (1903), G. Peano (1903), B. Bijlev-elt (1907), R. Delagrasserie (1907), C. Spitzer (1907), F. de Saussure (1907), L. de Beaufront (1908), Ch. Lemaire (1908), R. Triola (1909), I. Weisbart (1909), E. de Wahl (1909), A. Seidel (1909), A. Michaux (1909), I. Barral (1910), M. Ferranti (1911), W. Rosemberger (1912), I. Weisbart (1912), S. E. Bond (1912), V. Cesichin (1913), G. I. Pinth (1914), V. Martellotta (1919), I. Rossello Ordines (1922), E. de Wahl (1922), S. Voirol (1922), W. M. Beatty (1922), A. Lavagnini (1923), F. Reidel (1923), Fibula (1925), A. Baumann (1925), S. Consoli (1925), O. Jespersen (1928), I. Iousten (1929), G. O. D'Harvé (1930), M. Wald (1930), S. Durant (1932), M. E. Amadas (1932), H. Heimer (1943), A. Martinet and I. P. Vinay (1945), L. Hogben (1947), etc.

5. I. M. Schleyer, *Volapük, die Weltsprache,* Sigmaringen 1880.

6. Among the first mentioned are the following: Th. Cart, C. Bourlet, H. Poincaré, L. Tolstoy, E. Beneš, Romain Roland, Pio X, E. Boirac, Maksim Gor'kij, A. Meillet, Upton Sinclair, W. Ramsay, L. Figl (President of the Austrian Ministers), W. Dress (President of the Dutch Ministers), V. Auriol (President of the French Republic), etc. International institutions include: the Society of Nations, the French Academy of the Sciences, Unesco, the Red Cross, the Geneva International Labor Office, the Paris Chamber of Commerce, the Rotary Club, etc.

7. A petition in 356 volumes of 2500 pages each signed by 895,432 people and by 492 organizations requesting that Esperanto be taught in schools and used as an international auxiliary language was presented to UNO and Unesco in 1950.

We do not know exactly how many people currently speak Esperanto, but ac-cording to official statistics 2,000 texts (grammars and dictionaries, etc.) were pub-lished in 50 national languages, and approximately 10 million copies were sold in all.

In 1950–51, 1267 evening courses were held in twenty-nine countries. Esperanto chairs and assistantships exist in thirty-one universities (Austria, England, Czechoslo-vakia, Germany, Hungary, Poland, Japan, Italy, Canada, Holland, and the United States).

The student of linguistic problems is not interested in whether Esperanto is spoken by hundreds of thousands or by millions of people as much as he is interested in the fact that some families use Esperanto as their everyday language and that children born into these families speak it from the very first years of life and consider it as their mother tongue.

8. D. Zamenhof himself translated Shakespeare's *Hamlet (1894),* Gogol's *The Gov-ernment Inspector (1907),* Molière's *Georges Dardin (1908),* Goethe's *Iphigenie auf Tauris (1908),* Schiller's *The Robbers (1908),* Andersen's *Fairy Tales* and the *Old Testament* (which appeared posthumously). Other scholars translated Homer, Virgil, Shake-speare, Dante, Byron, Racine, Victor Hugo, Turgenev, Tolstoy, Cervantes, Ibsen, Leibniz, Descartes, Kant, Mendeleyev, etc. Some works from central and eastern Europe were re-translated into Chinese and Japanese from translations in Esperanto.

9. Should some expert philologist decide to make a comparative study of artificial languages, useful results could ensue for a better understanding of important prob-lems, such as that concerning "linguistic value," that is, the criteria employed in judging the efficiency and beauty of a language. Such a study might also explain why all attempts at creating languages with rational methods have failed, even though they were projected by such men of genius as Descartes and Leibniz. Moreover, it would

be interesting to examine projects subsequent to Esperanto, such as *Ido, Noviol*, and *Occidental*, etc., in order to establish whether or not it is possible to make Esperanto more efficient, without wasting energy working in other directions. Precious materials for a study of this kind may be found in the publications of the International Auxiliary Language Association of New York.

10. The *act of will* fostered by the supporters of Esperanto consists of the unanimous decision made by the Education Ministers of major countries to fix one hour a week for the teaching of an auxiliary language during the last two years of primary school. In this way, all citizens in these countries would be able to correspond with each other within a few years.

15. Logic and Semantics (Thought and Word)

1. In 1817 J. F. Sudre elaborated the project (published in 1866) of an artificial language called *so-re-so*. All words are formed from musical notes (e.g., *la-fa-la-mi* means "geometry") and are either pronounced alphabetically or expressed in musical notes in writing or by singing them or playing them on a musical instrument.

Leaving aside the rather baroque idea of using a similar language for international communications, *so-re-so* remains a curious experiment that confirms the possibility of using instruments completely different from the usual for the development of a semantic system which is to function like a language.

2. Even more significant is the fact that the most intelligent Chinese deaf-mutes manage to learn their ideographic writing system and use it to follow complex scientific reasoning, without being familiar with the phonetic words of any language whatsoever. On the other hand, we cannot say that our own deaf-mutes (who are deprived of hearing from birth and are subsequently trained in the use of an oral language) use strictly phonetic signs (which would be impossible for them to perceive), on the contrary, they use signs based on visual, tactile, and muscular impressions. In other words, these signs do not have a phonetic character for the deaf-mute who pronounces them but they do take on such a character for anyone listening to them.

3. G. Harry, *Le miracle des hommes*, Larousse, Paris; H. Keller, *La storia della mia vita* (English original: *The Story of My Life*), It. trans., Florence 1907. Cf. Vendryes, *Le langage*, p. 12.

16. The "Improper" Identification of Semantics with Logic

1. In Hoffmann's opinion Parmenides' doctrine may be summed up as follows: "Words are false in so far as they give the impression of being identical to the things signified. Only what is may be the object of thought, only what is thinkable may be the content of 'real discourse': what is, what can be thought and what can be said are one and the same thing" (E. Hoffman, *Die Sprache und die archaische Logik*, 1925, p. 15).

2. Cf. Ammonius, *Ad Aristot. De interpret.*, *24*B, ed. Ald. as well as our own considerations on the subject in the appendix to the current volume.

3. "In clear contrast to Frege and Dedekind I consider signs themselves as the object of the theory of numbers. This is the solid philosophical position *[feste philosophische Einstellung]* which I consider indispensable for the foundation of pure mathematics and of science in general as well as of all scientific comprehension and communication: in the beginning was the sign" (Hilbert, *Neubegrundung der mathematik*, Hamburg 1922, p. 162).

4. C. S. Peirce, *Collected Papers*, *5.253–5.285, 5.420*. His "theory of signs" was outlined between 1868 and 1869 and reelaborated in 1905–1906.

5. For a more systematic treatment of these concepts see chap. 1 of *Filosofia del Croce*, pp. 40–43.

6. Calogero, *Estetica, semantica, istorica*, chap. 17, pp. 214ff; as well as *Logica, gnoseologia, ontologia* (Logic, epistemology, ontology), Turin 1948, chap. 3, pp. 25ff.

7. A noteworthy difference also consists in the fact that language analyzers of a Neopositivistic orientation have acknowledged that mathematics is a system of analytical judgments, in other words, a system of tautologies. Thus the criterion by which the truth of a mathematical proposition is judged is only that which is obtained by checking whether that truth can be deduced, by force of the principle of noncontradiction, from the accepted premises. On the contrary, Calogero who, unlike Hilbert or Russell for example, is not very familiar with mathematical procedures (just as the latter two do not have his competence in the moral disciplines) believes that mathematical truth is a "factual truth" equal to any other. A factual truth if we ascertain the geometrical properties of a triangle no more or no less than if we ascertain the biological properties of Koch's bacillus. This way of viewing things, which hardly corresponds to the scope and value of mathematics, put Calogero on the wrong track, inducing him to consider the principle of noncontradiction, upon which mathematical constructions are based, as a purely grammatical principle.

8. For a more lengthy discussion on the principle of contradiction and on the analytical character of mathematical judgments cf. *La filosofia del Croce*, part III, chap. 1, pp. 197 and 204.

17. The Conventional Character of Semantic Systems and of Logical Systems

1. Cf. B. Russell, *An Inquiry into Meaning and Truth*, New York 1940.

2. Leibniz discusses it in *Disputatio arithmetica de complexionibus* and in *Dissertatio de arte combinatoria* (both published in 1666). Cf. Guhrauer, *Leibnitz's Deutsche Schriften*, 1, pp. 377–81; B. Russell, *A Critical Exposition of the Philosophy of Leibniz*, Cambridge 1900; Couturat, *La logique de Leibniz d'après des documents inédits*, Paris 1901.

3. Tarski, *The Semantic Conception of Truth*, p. 75.

18. Charles W. Morris's "Behaviorist" Semiotics

1. We refer especially to Morris's *Signs, Language, and Behavior* (It. trans. by Silvio Ceccato: *Segni, linguaggio e comportamento*, Longanesi, Milan 1949); but also to *Logical Positivism, Pragmatism and Scientific Empiricism*, 1937; *The Concept of the Symbol*, 1927; and *Foundations of the Theory of Signs*, 1939. [On referring to the "science of signs" as conceived by Charles Morris, Fano uses the Italian equivalent of the term "semiotic" *("semeiotica")*. Morris most commonly used the term "semiotic," but also "semiotics," which is the term we have privileged throughout this translation. The latter, in fact, has become the term most widely used in the last two decades to designate studies related to the science of signs. In the present volume, page numbers refer to *Signs, Language and Behavior*, in *Writings on the General Theory of Signs*, The Hague and Paris: Mouton, 1971.—TRANS.]

2. There has been complex mutual influence between European Neopositivism and American pragmatism. For example, the "criterion of significance," which is one of the basic postulates of Neopositivism, had already been articulated in the *Treatise on Language* by the American thinker Albert Bryan Johnson in 1836. Furthermore, it is common knowledge that Peirce placed this criterion at the foundation of his own doctrine in his article "How to Make Our Ideas Clear," published in "Popular Science Monthly," January 1878. This principle was subsequently adopted by James and the other pragmatists (in Italy it was developed with serious scientific intention by Vailati and Calderoni, while Papini jokingly underlined those aspects of American pragmatism most suited to "épater les bourgeois"). According to the criterion of significance a proposition is devoid of sense if it cannot be verified in any of our concrete expe-

riences. Up to this point it fully corresponds to the Kantian principle that denies the possibility of knowing whatever transcends all possible experience. But given that all experimentable cognition causes predictions (e.g., if we know that a given vessel is made of glass we foresee that it will be more fragile than if it were made of metal) and that our behavior is based on these predictions, pragmatism has given rise to the behaviorist doctrine.

3. Concerning the value of philosophy and the place it should be assigned among other disciplines, our author's opinion is rather uncertain. Initially he unhesitatingly recognized that, just as fanciful and muddled alchemy was substituted for scientific chemistry, in the same way philosophy must now be substituted for semiotics, which is "the most complete expression of scientific empiricism and methodological rationalism." Subsequently, however, he acknowledges that philosophy has a function of its own consisting in the systematization of scientific thought.

4. Such elegant phrases abound in the book cited. For example, on p. 351: "una determinazione *osservativa* oggettiva" is not possible. On p. 374: "La pagina . . . sembra distinguere una *forma di assumere-il posto-di* che interviene prima dei simboli." On p. 375: "*un comportamento simbolico di origine socio-verbale.*" Ibid.: "Hull ed *i gestaltisti.*" On p. 377: "comportamento *segnico.*" On p. 58: "Un linguaggio e un sistema di famiglie di *comunsegni,*" etc.

5. C. W. Morris, *Signs, Language and Behavior.*

6. Such reliance on the common use of terms for enlightenment is not new among the neopositivists. I remember an author who, to define the ethical concept of "good," examined such propositions as "this is a good action," or "this is a good automobile," just as he could have analyzed the proposition "pasta is good," etc. Anyone can see what a fine ethical conception would have ensued from such an approach.

7. Morris, *Signs, Language and Behavior,* p. 84.

8. Ibid., p. 87.

9. Cf. F. Barone, *Il neo-positivismo logico* (Logical neo-positivism), ed. "Filosofia," Turin 1953, p. 319. This is an excellent and highly informative book, offering a clear exposition and intelligent evaluation of the principal Neopositivist doctrines. Barone's only error is that he sometimes takes too seriously the nonsense that abounds in the work of some of his authors.

10. Morris's exposition is even more complicated and confused than appears from our own account. Nonetheless, with a bit of patience, it is not difficult to understand what he means (even if it is not worth the effort).

11. In Morris's own words: "Suppose that S_1, S_2, S_3 are signals to the dog of food in three different places, so that the dog, when hungry, seeks food in the place signified by the stimulus presented to it. Now if a new stimulus, S_6, be combined always with two of these other stimuli (as in, say, S_1 S_6 S_2), and if the dog then, without preference, seeks food at one of the two places signified and at the other place if and only if food is not secured at the place first approached, then S would be a stimulus which has much in common with the exclusive 'or' of English ('at least one but not both'). If the dog could be further trained so that the signs which appear with S_6 may be appraisors and prescriptors as well as designators, then S_6 and the exclusive 'or' would be behaviorally identical. The introduction of the term 'formator' is intended solely to designate this and similar situations" (signs, p. 236).

12. In the *valuative* use the sign induces preference of one object rather than another, in the *incitive* use it induces certain kinds of behavior (to use Morris's words: "it incites response-sequences of some behavior family"). In the *systemic* use signs have the purpose of organizing behavior into a unitary system.

13. Reread, for example, such sentences as the following: "Let us now further suppose that D_1 and D_2 do not by themselves dispose the dog to seek food or water in one place rather than another; I_1D_1 when presented with I_2D_1 does not cause the

dog to go to one place rather than another; A and D_1 do not dispose the dog to turn in a circle; and so on for the other cases. Then to the degree that this is true, I, D, A, and P are signs with distinguishable kind of significata. Signs of the kind represented by I, D, A, and P are then respectively identifiors, designators, appraisors, and prescriptors" (*signs*, p. 145). A few pages further on, the two propositions "that is a fine deer" and "that deer is fine" are symbolized as follows: $X + (yz) = K$ and $(x + y)z = K$ (*Signs*, p. 153).

And on page 172: "A sign S will be said to be *used* with respect to a purpose y of an organism z if y is a goal of z and if z produces a sign which serves as means to the attainment of y." This is subsequently illustrated with the following example: If a person is seeking to earn money and writes a detective story to achieve that end, that story is to be considered as a "sign complex," because the author uses it as a way of achieving a given purpose. (The author could have just as easily said: If a father gives his son a spanking as a way of teaching him not to answer his mother rudely, those spankings are a "sign complex.")

The habit of cramming one's writings with pseudo-mathematical formulae is not a prerogative of our author. For example, Ducasse, in an article on Morris's doctrine, writes the following: "If we wish to define *sign of* as the function of the perceptibly observable behavior of a person, the definition will be this: S is a sign of D for an interpreter I to the extent that the presence of S together with the intentions of the P kind in I, and with the belief on the part of I that the circumstances are of the C kind, and again with the belief that the behavior of the B kind in such a circumstance backs up such intentions, causes I to behave in manner B, etc." ("Philosophy and Phenomenological Research," 3, 1942, pp. 43–52).

14. I will reproduce it for lovers of fun mathematics: $fx \cdot fy \geqq fx_1 \cdot fy_1 \cdot i$, where x and y should be the "independent variables" of the subject and of the object, that is, the "transcendentals of experience," x_1 and y_1 are the values that those variables assume in concrete experiences, and in the "transcendental dimension of individual experiences."

15. *Prolegomeni alla "Filosofia perenne"* (Prolegomena to "Perennial philosophy"), in "Giornale critico della Filosofia Italiana," December 1936.

16. Charles Morris taught at the Chicago Rice Institute, at Harvard University, at the New School for Social Research of Texas University [*sic*]. He is one of the promoters of the *International Encyclopedia of Unified Science* and vice president of the Institute for Unified Science.

Among the first Italian scholars to have judged Morris's work favorably, we should remember professors Filiasi Carcano, Geymonat, Preti, Somenzi, and Ceccato. Enzo Paci's position is more critical (see, *Filosofia e linguaggio* [Philosophy and language], Padua 1950).

An orientation similar to Morris's is adopted by the Centro di studi metodologici, in Turin, and the Centro Italiano di metodologia e analisi del linguaggio, in Milan.

In America, Morris is generally considered as one of the most important thinkers of our time. Nevertheless critical reservations have not been lacking, for example, those expressed by D. I. Bronstein, in "Phenomenological Research," 1947, 4, pp. 643–49; P. D. Wienpahl, *Are All Signs?*, in "Philosophical Review," 1949, 3, pp. 243–56; F. Smullyan, "The Journal of Symbolic Logic," 1947, 2, pp. 49–51; V. C. Aldrich, in "Journal of Philosophy," 1947, 12, pp. 324–29; G. Gentry, in "Journal of Philosophy," 1949, 12, pp. 318–24; L. O. Kattsoff, *What is Behavior?* in "Philosophy and Phenomenological Research," 1948, pp. 98–102; J. Wild, in "Philosophy and Phenomenological Research," 1947, 2, pp. 217–33; C. I. Ducasse, in "Philosophy and Phenomenological Research," 1942, pp. 43–52; M. Black, in "Philosophical Review," 1947, 3, pp. 258–72; A. F. Bentley, in the book by A. Bentley and J. Dewey, *Knowing and the Known*, Boston 1949; T. Storer, in "Philosophy of Science," 1948, 3, pp. 316–30; etc.

To form an idea of the extremely vast bibliography on Morris see Rossi-Landi's highly informative monograph, *Charles Morris*, Bocca 1953.

[Charles Morris (1901–1979) began his career as professor at Rice University. He then returned to the University of Chicago in 1931, where he had previously completed his doctoral dissertation under Mead in 1925. Later he served as visiting professor at the New School for Social Research, at the University of Texas, and at Harvard. He finished his teaching career at the University of Florida.—Trans.]

17. Carnap, *Logische Syntax der Sprache*, Vienna 1934.

18. Haskell B. Curry, *Outlines of a Formalist Philosophy of Mathematics*, Amsterdam 1951, p. 46.

19. The Linguistics of Abstract Idealism and of B. Croce

1. Herder, *Abhandlung über den Ursprung der Sprache*, Berlin 1789[2], pp. 60–65.

2. In a letter to Hamann of 1772 and in *Älteste Urkunde des Menschengeschlechtes*. In *Ideen sur Philosophie der Geschichte der Menschheit*, Herder indulges more and more in a mystical conception. Language, he says, is a miracle of divine institution, the greatest miracle of creation after the generation of living beings.

3. Humboldt, *Einleitung in die Kawi-Sprache*, reprinted in *Über die Verschiedenheit des menschlichen Sprachbaues*, pp. LV ff.

4. Humboldt, *Über die vergleichen Sprachstudien*, sec. 13.

5. Hamann too, who belonged to this circle of Romantic thinkers, maintained that language had not been invented by man. In his opinion, invention and intellect presuppose language and cannot be conceived without language, just as we cannot conceive of arithmetic without numbers.

6. Humboldt, *Abhandlung über den Ursprung der Sprache*, p. LXXVI.

7. Ibid., pp. XLVI and LXX.

8. Just how fruitful and advantageous for Germany's prestige had been the collaboration of those Jewish scholars who succeeded in combining the passionate idealism and intellectual skill of their own race with the scientific rigor of the German spirit is immediately obvious on skimming through the volumes of "Zeitschrift für Völkerpsychologie und Sprachwissenschaft," produced in the second half of the nineteenth century under the direction of Lazarus and Steinthal; the relevant articles and discussions reveal a cultural and spiritual level never to be attained again.

9. Abstract idealism aims at rejecting science in favor of philosophy, just as positivism, new and old, aims at rejecting philosophy in favor of science; in truth, not only are both disciplines legitimate in their own sphere and impossible to suppress, but both must concur in forming a single concrete scientific and philosophical conception of life.

10. Croce, *Estetica*, IX, p. 155. After *Estetica* Croce returned to the linguistic problem on several occasions. In particular in *Problemi di estetica* (Problems in aesthetics), Bari 1940[3], pp. 141–230; *Conversazioni critiche* (Critical conversations), series 1, pp. 87–113; *Ultimi saggi* (Final essays), Bari 1935; *Estetica in nuce* (Essential esthetics), etc.

Croce's views were further developed by: K. Vossler, *Positivismus und Idealismus in der Sprachwissenschaft*, Heidelberg 1904 and *Aufsatze zur Sprachphilosophie*, Munich 1925; Spitzer, *Stilstudien*, Munich 1928; Spitzer, *Stil- und Literaturstudien*, Marburg 1931; Bartoli, *Introduzione alla neolinguistica* (Introduction to neolinguistics), Geneva 1923; Bertoldi, *Questioni di metodo nella linguistica storica* (Questions of method in historical linguistics), Naples 1938, etc.

11. In *Filosofia del Croce*. See in particular the chapters on the contradiction of pure intuition, on the constitutive stages of aesthetic synthesis, and on the theory of pseudo-concepts.

12. For a detailed examination of empyrean-critical epistemology see the relative chapter in *La filosofia del Croce*.

13. So that hurried translators often make blunders; in the translation of *Quaranta giorni del Musa Dagh* (Die vierzig Tage des Musa Dagh, 1933) by Werfel (Mondadori) I found, for example, "Campi d'Olivi" (olive groves) for "Öhlfelder" (oil fields).

APPENDIX

The Problem of the Origin and Nature of Language in Plato's *Cratylus*

1. Confusion, Prolixity, and Bad Taste in Current Diction

1. *Cratylus* was written without doubt after *Euthydemus* and before *Parmenides* and *Theaetetus*. *Theaetetus* seems to have been written after 369 and *Cratylus* probably between 386 and 385.

2. For example, in 437A, Socrates explains the word ἐπιστήμη from ἐπί-ἵστησιν, because science stops (ἵστησιν) our soul on (ἐπί) things. This etymology is unfounded as are many others listed by Socrates, but it would seem that he accepts it, for it is not credible that he should have made fun of one of the concepts he treasured most. Far too often wise observations are indistinctly mixed with nonsense, as is the case, for example, with the correct observation that women—who lead a more withdrawn life than men—preserve the language of their fathers more tenaciously, so that their way of speaking can give us some indication of use in ancient speech (418B, C). The remark that it is not sufficient to look for the etymon of a word in another Greek word, but that—especially for the language spoken by the Greeks of Asia Minor—a Greek word may also derive from a barbarian word (409D, E) is also correct; but the tone with which this is said is certainly ironic and is repeated in 416A, while in 421C, D the same concept returns on a more serious note.

A rather humorous example of etymology, among many others, is offered by Selene (409B, C) which signifies: "it has always a new-and-old-gleam" from σέλας-ἀεί-νέον-ἕνον and therefore we ought to say Selaennoaéia—but this was shortened to Selanaia!

Extravagant etymologies are extremely common among ancient and medieval authors: Varro, Cicero, Saint Augustine, Saint Ambrose, etc. (in Saint Augustine: *Jovis* from *Jehova; Mercurius* from *medius currens; Proserpina* from *proserpendo*, etc. [*De civitate Dei*, VII, 14; VII, 20, etc.]).

Fortunaziano derives *verbum* from *verbero*, that is, from *verum bum*, which stands for *bombum* (sound) (*Dialectica*, ch. VI. Cf. K. von Prantl, *Geschichte der Logik*, p. 669). We find the same derivation in Saint Thomas: "unumquodque nomen illud praecipue significat a quo imponitur sed hoc nomen "verbum" imponitur a verberatione aeris vel a boatu, quasi verbum non sit aliud quam verum boans" (*Quaestiones disputatae, De veritate*, quaest. IV, 1).

3. Even a scholar like Wilamowitz who is gifted with a profound sense of psychological and historical intuition admires Plato's taste for joking and gesting as it is displayed in this dialogue, and which is held to be proof of a "joyous sense of superiority, reached by the philosopher in the maturity of his genius" (Wilamowitz-Moellendorf, *Platon*, Berlin 1920, vol. 1, p. 287). We invite the reader to consider the dialogue open-mindedly and judge whether this text, in the state it has reached us, can justify such admiration.

Manlio Buccellato, in one of his recent studies (*"La retorica" sofistica negli scritti di Platone, IV: Il "Cratilo" e l'interesse dottrinale della questione onomatologica*, in "Revista Critica di Storia della Filosofia," n. 1, 1953, pp. 14ff.), also admires this dialogue from a stylistic and conceptual point of view and maintains that it contains many of the best qualities characterizing classical Platonic dialogue. To the "fine details" present in *Cratylus* in relation to words, syllables, and letters, Buccellato opposes the details found in *Phaedo* in relation to hot and cold, fire and snow, the numbers two, one and a half, etc. We believe that the stylistic comparison with *Phaedo* is out of place: (1) because in *Phaedo* the "fine details," if this is how we wish to describe them, take up about one page out of a hundred, while in *Cratylus* they involve the whole central part of the work; (2) because in *Cratylus*, after initial etymological observations endowed with either doctrinal or satirical interest, the numerous observations that follow are no more than a series of pedantries and awkward remarks of no interest, nor were they of any interest in Plato's day; on the other hand, what in *Phaedo* might seem extravagant pedantries to the modern reader, were problems of great importance for Plato and the Greek mentality generally. For example, Socrates asks himself why once unit A is added to unit B, from 1 it becomes 2. " . . . for I cannot satisfy myself that, when one is added to one, either the one to which the addition is made or the one which is added becomes two, or that the two units added together make two by reason of the addition. I cannot understand how, when separated from the other, each of them was one and not two, and now, when they are brought together, the mere juxtaposition or meeting of them should be the cause of their becoming two" (*Phaedo*, 97A). To understand why Plato posed himself a similar problem, we must remember that he considers numerical determinations rationalistically as though they were objective qualities of bodies. When he says: unit A is one, he says it in the same sense as we would say: body A is heavy. Therefore the following problem arises: if body A, considered in itself, is heavy, and body B considered in itself there in the other room, is also heavy, how is it that put together, A and B are not heavier but lighter? The famous experiment in *Meno* is also founded on this lack of distinction between mathematical properties and perceptive qualities. For Plato the fact that an intelligent slave was able to rediscover a mathematical theorem solely through reason was just as astonishing as the possibility of deducing the flavor of a liqueur by merely looking at it.

4. Schaarschmidt, *Über die Unechtheit des Dialogs Kratylos*, in "Rheinisches Museum," XX, 1865.

5. Hermann and others believe that insertions have been introduced in chapter XLIII (437–438A), but many other passages have been manipulated just as much. See, for example, chapter XXXVII (426C): "Socrates: First, then, the letter rho seems to me to be an instrument expressing all motion. [We have not as yet said why motion has the name κίνησις; but it evidently should be ἴεσις, for in old times we did not employ eta, but epsilon. And the beginning is from κίειν, a foreign word equivalent to ἰέναι (go). So we should find that the ancient word corresponding to our modern form would be κίνησις; but now by the employment of the foreign word κίειν, change of epsilon to eta, and the insertion of nu it has become κίνησις, though it ought to be κιείνησις or εἶσις. And στάσις (rest) signifies the negation of motion, but is called στάσις for euphony.] Well, the letter rho, as I was saying, appeared to be a fine instrument expressive of motion to the name-giver who wished to imitate rapidity, and he often applies it to motion."

Not only the irrational interruption of an argument in order to stop by chance on a word and work on it with philological observations, but the whole style of the passage I have placed between square brackets, seems to have been manipulated by a grammarian of a later era.

The following interpolations are commonly acknowledged: 405C, 408B, 410B, 415D, 420A, 426D (beginning with ἡ δὲ στάσις) and many other shorter ones. The following passages are considered to be obscure and uncertain: 197D, 410E, 438A, 383B, 385A, 389E, 393D, 395C, 397D, 400B, C, 410E, 418D, 426D, 438A, 440D. Cf. Wilamowitz, *Platon*, vol. II, p. 344.

6. In his dialogues Plato himself often mentions single etymologies. See, for ex-

ample, *Protagoras, Phaedrus, Theaetetus, Republic, Sophist, The Laws, Gorgias, Phaedo,* etc. Approximately 140 etymologies are recalled in *Cratylus,* but little more than twenty are acceptable to modern philologists.

7. This state of affairs would seem to be confirmed not only by specific observations but also by stylistic considerations concerning the entire framework of the dialogue. In fact, it begins with a discussion on whether there are "true names and false names," the etymological part follows (391d–428d) and continues for several pages without any conceptual development, and once this disquisition is terminated, the question of the "true name and false name" is of course taken up again. That this argument should return after a brief parenthesis could have seemed natural but after such a long digression which causes the reader to lose sight of the previous chain of reasoning, it is an incomprehensible incongruity.

As we all know, interpolations of this kind may be perpetrated without the least intention of fraud, either because some of the commentaries, which at first stood out distinctly, are inadvertently incorporated into the text, or because the commentator's bad taste and philological insensitivity induce him to insert his own notes in the text from the very outset. Marchetti, for example, certainly did not intend to deceive anyone when he intercalated (no one knows why) a passage in praise of Gassendi in his translation of Lucretius.

2. The Essential Content of the Dialogue

1. A similar concept is also expounded by Plato in his seventh letter (342).

2. For example, (399E) ψυχή is derived from ἀναπνεῖν ἀναψῦχον (to blow cold air) and immediately after from φύσιν ὀχεῖ καὶ ἔχει (that carries and holds nature) which first became φυσέχη and then ψυχή (400B); and τέχνη from ἕξις νοῦ (habit of the mind), because "if you remove the tau and insert omicron between the chi and the nu and the nu and the eta we make ἐχονόη"(414C).

Socrates' warnings which treat ironically "that wisdom which fell upon him suddenly" are also repeated with excessive insistence (cf. 397D, 399A, 401E, 410E, 411A, 413A, 413C, 413D, 414C, 428D, etc.).

More than one of the etymologies in the dialogue recalls the famous derivation of the German "Fuchs" from the Greek ἀλώπηξ: "lopex," "pex," "fex," "fox," "fux"; "es ist ganz desselbe Wort!" This derivation is intended as a caricature but does not exclude the possibility that "alopex," "vulpis" and "Fuchs" may have the same root. As we know, a great difference in sound between two words will not suffice to exclude the possibility of a common root. For example, from the viewpoint of sound the English "steel" and the word "kila" are completely different and yet not only do they have a common root, but they are the same word "steel" which Hawaiians, speaking English, pronounce "kila." In fact, Hawaiians eliminate the *s* because they do not know how to pronounce two consonants together, they never end words in consonants and for this reason they add *a,* and they do not distinguish between *t* and *k.* This is further proof of the impossibility of distinguishing between legitimate and unfounded etymology by ear.

3. This passage repeats and confirms that which is said in 388C (that names must highlight the essential characters of things) and in 389B (that the artist must imitate the essence of things). It seems to contradict the Platonic theory according to which the artist gives us the copy of a copy thus increasing the distance between ourselves and the real essence of things. It should also be remembered that Aristotle never refers to *Cratylus* and was probably unfamiliar with it. Otherwise he would have probably dwelt a little upon this passage when he remarked, disagreeing with Plato, that art is not the imitation of mere exterior appearance, but rather of that which is essential in things. If the passage is authentic, then Plato would be admitting that Aristotle is right. However, we should remember that this was not a contradiction for Plato, who

was far from considering language as an artistic expression. Furthermore, just as he condemned art, he finishes up at the end of *Cratylus* by condemning language as well, as a means inadequate for the transcendent reality of ideas.

4. "I myself prefer the theory that names are, so far as is possible, like the things named; but really this attractive force of likeness is, as Hermogenes says, a poor thing, and we are compelled to employ in addition this commonplace expedient, convention, to establish the correctness of names" (435C).

5. In our opinion, the dialogue concludes on a note of reasoned eclecticism and not, as it seemed to others, by leaving the problem unresolved (cf. Croce, *Estetica*, p. 189). After having distinguished between the two possible different meanings of the terms "nomo" and "physei," Croce adds: "They were two different issues, which had been confusedly and ambiguously mixed, and they find a monument in Plato's obscure *Cratylus*, which seems to waver between different solutions."

4. Topicality and Importance of the Concepts Treated in the Dialogue

1. In chapter 19 I attempted to clarify the necessity of both components (natural and conventional) by examining those doctrines that, on rightly beginning with the concept of the unity of the spiritual act, subsequently deny all distinctions among signs, words, expressions, images, etc., and thus consider the problem solved. On the contrary, that this issue is topical is revealed by the widespread influence of the article by E. Benveniste entitled *Nature du signe linguistique*, published in *"Acta Linguistica,"* f. 1, 1939, in which Benveniste examines Saussure's thesis of the arbitrariness of the relation between significant and signifié. The discussion lasted for several years (1939–43) with contributions from: E. Benveniste, E. Lerch, E. Buyssens, A. Sechehaye, Ch. Bally, H. Frei, W. Borgeand, W. Brocker, I. Lohmann, etc.

2. Cf. Grimm, *De l'origine du langage*, pp. 34 and foll.; Ch. de Goieie, in *Atti del III Congresso internazionale di linguistica.*

3. Cf. *La filosofia del Croce*, pp. 128–45, 171–79, 284–87.

4. Ammonius, *ad Arist. De interpret.*, *24*B, ed. Ald.

5. Cf. my work on *Teosofia orientale e filosofia greca* (Oriental Theosophy and Greek Philosophy), Florence 1949, p. 10.

Works by Giorgio Fano

Books

1930 (ed. by G. Fano), E. Cantoni, *Vita a rovescio: Notizie sul pensiero di Ettore Cantoni,* Milan, Treves.

1935 (trans., intro., and notes by G. Fano), E. Kant, *Prolegomeni ad ogni futura metafisica* (extracts), Florence, Sansoni.

1937a *Il sistema dialettico dello spirito,* Rome, Servizi editoriali del GUF.

1937b (trans. by A. Monari, reduced by G. Fano), S. Hessen, *La pedagogia di John Dewey,* Rome.

1945 (trans. by R. Curiel, intro. by G. Fano), R. N. Coudenhove-Kalergi, *L'Europa si desta,* Rome.

1946a *La filosofia del Croce: saggi di critica e primi lineamenti di un sistema dialettico dello spirito,* Milan, Istituto Editoriale Italiano.

1946b (edit. by A. de Amicis and V. Marone), *Brevi conferenze e problemi di pedagogia,* Rome, Quintily (the following are the papers by G. Fano in this volume: "Il razionalismo e l'educazione," "L'empirismo e l'educazione," "L'educazione morale nella scuola elementare," "Insegnare dilettando," "L'idealismo e l'educazione," "L'Estetica di Croce e l'insegnamento della lingua").

1948 (ed. by G. Fano), E. Kant, *Prolegomena ad ogni futura metafisica,* Milan, Istituto Editoriale Italiano.

1949 *Teosofia orientale e filosofia greca,* Florence, La Nuova Italia.

1962 *Saggio sulle origini del linguaggio-Con una storia critica delle dottrine glottogoniche,* Turin, Einaudi.

1968 *Neopositivismo, analisi del linguaggio e cibernetica,* Turin, Einaudi.

1973 *Origini e natura del linguaggio,* Turin, Einaudi.

Articles

1911a "Discussione sull'estetica crociana," summarized in *Bollettino della Biblioteca filosofica di Firenze 111,* no. 19 (February): 411ff.

1911b "L'estetica nel sistema di Bebedetto Croce," in *L'Anima 1,* no. 12 (December): 355–80.

1913 "Recensione a Guido De Ruggiero, *La filosofia contemporanea,*" in *La Voce 5, 4* (September): 1153; 25 September, p. 1167.

1926 "Dell'universo ovvero di me stesso: saggio di una filosofia solipsistica," in *Rivista d'Italia 29,* vol. 11, nos. 7 and 8, pp. 917–42, 1107–32.

1928a "Una discussione indiana sull'idealismo," in *Rivista di Filosofia 19,* pp. 232–54 (now in *Teosofia orientale filosofia greca,* Appendix 1ᵃ, 1949).

1928b "La filosofia di Benedetto Croce: saggio di critica e primi lineamenti di un sistema dialettico dello spirito," in *Giornale critico della filosofia Italiana 9,* pp. 401–28; 10, 1929, pp. 1–40, 94–139 (now in *La filosofia del Croce,* 1946).

1931 "L'influenza dell'idealismo ebraico sulla religiosità mondiale," in *Rassegna mensile di Israel,* April.

1932 "La negazione della filosofia nell'idealismo attuale," in *Archivio di Filosofia Italiana 11,* no. 2, pp. 57–101.

1936 "Prolegomeni alla 'filosofia perenne': osservazioni sulla metafisica del prof. Orestano," in *Giornale Critico della Filosofia Italiana 17*, pp. 335–49.

1937 "La metafisica ontologica di P. Carabellese," in *Giornale Critico della Filosofia Italiana 18*, pp. 119–40.

1945a "Il movimento paneuropeo di Coudenhove-Kalergi," in *Mondo Europeo 1*, Oct.-Nov, pp. 97–106.

1945b "Democrazia e demagogia," in *La Nuova Europa, 4* November, p. 10.

1948a "A proposito di una nuova valutazione della filosofia crociana," in *Stoa 4*, Naples, p. 113.

1948b "A proposito di una nuova valutazione della filosofia crociana," in *Stoa 4*, Naples, p. 150.

1948c "Una messa a punto intorno alla dottrina di Kant," in *Stoa 4*, Naples, p. 152.

1948d "Togliatti e la filosofia nel numero 4–5 di *Rinascita,"* in *Stoa 4* Naples, p. 157.

1948e "Matematici e filosofi," in *Tecnica dell'insegnare*, monthly review of pedagogy and didactics, iii, n. 4, April, pp. 97–100.

1950a "Teosofia orientale e filosofia greca," in *Aevum 24*, p. 317.

1950b "Teosofia orientale e filosofia greca," in *Giornale di Metafisica 6*, pp. 667–68.

1953a "Religione come coscienza dell'universale," in *La Fiera Letteraria, 15* February.

1953b "Ciò che è vivo e ciò che è morto nella filosofia di Benedetto Croce," in the volume *Il problema della filosofia oggi, Atti del XVI Congresso nazionale di filosofia*, Bologna (19–22 March 1953), Rome-Milan, pp. 624–30.

1955a "Arte e linguaggio nel pensiero di Guido Calogero," in *La Fiera Letteraria, 13* March.

1955b "Il problema dell'origine e della natura del linguaggio nel Cratilo platonico," in *Giornale di Metafisica 10*, pp. 307–20 (now in *Origini e natura del linguaggio, 1973*).

1956a "Le aporie dello storicismo post-crociano," in *Il problema della conoscenza storica. Arte e linguaggio, Atti del XVII Congresso nazionale di filosofia*, Libreria Scientifica Editrice, Naples, vol. 2, pp. 80–82.

1956b "Origine e natura del linguaggio," in *Il problema della conoscenza storica. Arte e linguaggio*, vol. 2, pp. 250–52.

1956c "Origine del linguaggio," in *Umana 5*, nos. 5–6, pp. 7–8 (now in *Saggio dulle origini del linguaggio*, "Introduzione," 1962).

1957a "I momenti costitutivi della sintesi estetica," in *Atti del III Congresso Internazionale di Estetica* (Venice 3–5 Sept., 1956), Turin, pp. 247–50.

1957b "Verità e storia: un dibattito sul metodo della storia della filosofia," in *Giornale di Metafisica 12*, pp. 230–38.

1958 "Il mio idealismo," in the volume *La filosofia contemporanea in Italia: invito al dialogo*, Editrice Arethusa (Rome, Società Filosofica Romana), Asti, pp. 205–18.

1959a "La semeiotica behavioristica di C. Morris," in *Giornale di Metafisica 14*, pp. 475–82 (now in *Origini e natura del linguaggio, 1973*, chap. 18).

1959b "Indagine intorno all'origine e all'essenza del linguaggio," in *Il Ponte 15*, pp. 90–105, 217–88.

1959c "Recensione a F. Nicolini, Arte e storia nei *Promessi Sposi,"* in *Il Ponte 15*, pp. 722–23.

1959d "Recensione a Galileo Galilei, *Discorsi e dimostrazioni matematici intorno a due nuove scienze,"* ed. by A. Carugo and L. Geymonat, Turin, in *Il Ponte 15*, pp. 1629–30.

1959e "Indagine intorno all'origine del linguaggio," in *Il Pensiero critico*, new series 1, pp. 63–82 (now in *Saggio sulle origini del linguaggio, 1962*, chap. VI: "Nota sul problema delle radici").

1960 "Recensione a *Neopositivismo e unità della scienza* di AA.VV.," (Milan, 1958), in *Il Ponte 16*, pp. 255–56.

1961 "Il problema dell'origine del linguaggio nel pensiero moderno," in *Umana, 10*, no. 5–6, pp. 9–11 (now in *Saggio sulle origini del linguaggio,* "Introduzione," 1960).

1962a "Il problema dell'origine del linguaggio in Vico," in *Giornale di Metafisica 17,* pp. 489–500 (now in *Saggio sulle origini del linguaggio,* pt. 2, chap. 3: "Il Settecento. La linguistica di G. B. Vico," 1960).

1962b "Alessandro Manzoni e l'origine del linguaggio," in *Umana 11,* no. 11–12, pp. 6–7 (from *Saggio sulle origini del linguaggio,* pt. 2, chap. 4: "L'Ottocento. Manzoni").

1962c "Serietà scientifica e ciarlataneria nell'uso del simbolismo logico e dell'analisi del linguaggio," in the volume by various authors, *La filosofia di fronte alle scienze,* Adriatica, Bari, vol. 2, pp. 357–66.

1963a "L'Estetica crociana," in *Il Piccolo, 22* May.

1963b "Filosofia e fatalismo," in *Il Piccolo, 3* July.

1964a "Cibernetica e filosofia," in *Giornale Critico della Filosofia Italiana* XLIII, pp. 125–37 (now in *Neopositivismo, analisi del linguaggio e cibernetica,* chap. 6: "Cibernetica e filosofia," 1968).

1964b "La situazione anacronistica di P. Carabellese, ultimo dei grandi metafisici," in *Giornate di studi carabellesiani,* Selva, Genova, pp. 101–11.

1964c "Estetica e linguistica in Croce e dopo Croce," in *De Homine,* no. 11–12 (December): 129–39.

1973 "Minuta per una lettura a G. Voghera," in *Umana 22,* no. 5–8, pp. 16–18.

1978 "La consolazione degli afflitti," in *Il Piccolo,* Trieste, 20 September.

Brief Bibliography

The following are only some of the numerous and more significant publications on sign language and the language of animals, which appeared after the first edition of the present work.

Altmann, S. A., *Social Behavior of Anthropoid Primates: Analysis of Recent Concepts*, in E. L. Bliss (ed. by), *Root of Behavior*, Hoeber-Harper, New York 1962.

_____, *The Structure of Primate Social Communication*, in S. A. Altmann (ed. by), *Social Communication Among Primates*, University of Chicago Press, Chicago 1967.

Broadbent, D. E., *Human Perception and Animal Learning*, in W. H. Thorpe and O. L. Zangwill (ed. by), *Current Problems in Animal Behaviour*, Cambridge University Press, New York 1961.

Brun, T., *The International Dictionary of Sign Language; A Study of Human Behaviour*, Wolfe, London, 127 pp., ill.

Chomsky, N., *Aspect of the Theory of Syntax*, MIT Press, Cambridge 1965.

_____, *The General Properties of Language*, in F. L. Darley (ed. by), *Brain Mechanisms Underlying Speech and Language*, Grune & Stratton, New York 1967 (It. trans. in *L'analisi formale del linguaggio*, Boringhieri, Turin 1969).

Darley, F. L., *Brain Mechanisms Underlying Speech and Language*, New York 1967.

Gilbert, B., *How Animals Communicate*, It. trans. *Il linguaggio degli animali*, illustrated by C. Reneson ("Universo sconosciuto" 7), Sugar, Milan 1969, 190 pp., ill.

Greenberg, J. H. (ed. by), *Universals of Language*, MIT Press, Cambridge 1963.

_____, *Language Universals*, in T. A. Sebeok (ed. by), *Current Trends in Linguistics*, vol. III: *Theoretical Foundations*, Mouton, The Hague 1966.

Hayes, A. S., and M. C. Bateson (ed. by), *Approaches to Semiotics*, Mouton, The Hague 1964 (It. trans. by C. and A. Barghini, *Paralinguistica e cinesica*, Bompiani, Milan 1970).

Hockett, C. F., *The Problem of Universals in Language*, in J. H. Greenberg (ed. by), *Universals of Language*, MIT Press, Cambridge 1963, pp. 1–29.

Klopper, P. H., and Hailman, J. P., *An Introduction to Animal Behavior: Ethology's First Century*, Prentice-Hall, Englewood Cliffs 1967.

Koechlin, B., *Techniques corporelles et leur notation symbolique*, "Langages," 10, 1968, pp. 36–47.

Kristeva, J., *Le geste, pratique au communication?*, "Languages," 10, 1968, pp. 48–64; *Pratiques et langages gestuels*, "Langages," 10 June 1968; Didier, Paris; Larousse, Paris 1968, 149 pp.

Lenneberg, E. H., *Biological Foundations of Language*, Wiley, New York 1967.

Mayr, E., *Animal Species and Evolution*, Harvard University Press, Cambridge 1963 (It. trans. in *L'evoluzione delle specie animali*, Einaudi, Turin 1970).

Sebeok, T. A., *Communication Among Social Bees; Porpoises and Sonar; Man and Dolphin*, "Language," 39, 1963, pp. 448–66.

_____, Introduction to T. A. Sebeok (ed. by) *Portraits of Linguists: A Biographical Source Book for the History of Western Linguistics 1746–1963*, Indiana University Press, Bloomington 1966.

_____, *Animal Communication*, "International Social Science Journal," 19, 1967, pp. 88–95.

_____, *On Chemical Signs*, in *To Honor Roman Jakobson*, Mouton, The Hague 1967.

_____, *The Word "Zoosemiotics,"* in "American Speech," 42, 1967.

_____, (ed. by), *Animal Communication, Techniques of Study and Results of Research*, Indiana University Press, Bloomington and London 1968, XVIII–686 pp., ill., tab. Part I: Introduction by T. A. Sebeok, *Goals and Limitations of the Study of Animal Communication*, pp. 3–14. *Techniques of Study*. Includes: C. F. Hockett and S. A. Altmann, *A Note on Design Features*, pp. 61–72. Part III: *Some Mechanisms of Communication*. Includes: R. G. Busnel, *Acoustic Communication*, pp. 127–53. Part IV: *Communication in Selected Groups (Anthropods, Honey Bees, etc.) Implications and Applications;* Includes: A. A. Moles, *Perspectives for Communication Theory*, pp. 627–42 (It. trans. *Zoosemiotica*, Bompiani, Milan 1973).

Smith, W. J., *Message, Meaning and Context in Ethology*, "American Naturalist," 99, 1965, pp. 405–9.

_____, *Communication and Relations in the Genus* "Tyrannus," Publication of the Nuttall Ornithological Club, n. 6, Cambridge (Mass.) 1966.

For a more complete bibliography on animal communication we refer the reader to the excellent collection of studies proposed by T. A. Sebeok in *Animal Communication, Techniques of Study and Results of Research*, Indiana University Press, Bloomington and London 1968, ed. by T. A. Sebeok. Italian trans. *Zoosemiotica*, Bompiani, Milan 1973.

Index of Names

GIORGIO FANO (Trieste 1885–Siena 1963) was an Italian philosopher who worked mainly in the area of the philosophy of language and of science. Among his most important works are *La filosofia del Croce (1949)*, *Teosofia orientale e filosofia greca (1949)*, and *Neopositivismo, analisi del linguaggio e cibernetica,* published posthumously in 1968.

SUSAN PETRILLI works at the Institute of Philosophy of Language, Bari University. She is currently preparing her doctoral thesis on "Linguistic Theories and the Science of Signs." Among her publications is the volume *Significs, semiotica, significazione* (1988).